Murder,

Murder, in Fact

*Disillusionment and Death
in the American True Crime Novel*

Lana A. Whited

McFarland & Company, Inc., Publishers
Jefferson, North Carolina

This book has undergone peer review.

LIBRARY OF CONGRESS CATALOGUING-IN-PUBLICATION DATA

Names: Whited, Lana A., 1958– author.
Title: Murder, in fact : disillusionment and death in the American true
crime novel / Lana A. Whited.
Description: Jefferson, North Carolina : McFarland & Company, Inc.,
Publishers, 2021. | Includes bibliographical references and index.
Identifiers: LCCN 2020041821 | ISBN 9781476672243 (paperback : acid free paper) ∞
ISBN 9781476641003 (ebook)
Subjects: LCSH: American fiction—20th century—History and criticism. |
Naturalism in literature. | Homicide in literature.
Classification: LCC PS374.N29 W48 2020 | DDC 364.152/3—dc23
LC record available at https://lccn.loc.gov/2020041821

BRITISH LIBRARY CATALOGUING DATA ARE AVAILABLE

ISBN (print) 978-1-4766-7224-3
ISBN (ebook) 978-1-4766-4100-3

Front cover images © 2021 Shutterstock

Printed in the United States of America

*McFarland & Company, Inc., Publishers
Box 611, Jefferson, North Carolina 28640
www.mcfarlandpub.com*

Contents

"Violence is a part of America's culture. It is as American as cherry pie."—Jamil Abdullah Al-Amin (formerly known as H. Rap Brown), 27 July 1967

Al-Amin received a life sentence without the possibility of parole in March 2002 for the murder of a police officer.

"Listen to the story of anyone who has gone to prison, and see if he ever had a chance to go anywhere else."—Clarence Darrow, *The Story of My Life*

Acknowledgments

This is a book that has been a long time in coming. In fall 1984, I read *In Cold Blood* in a graduate course at the University of North Carolina at Greensboro. The course, Contemporary Prose Style, was taught by Chris Anderson, who became the first in a series of mentors for this project. After I decided to write a dissertation on fact-based homicide novels, Dr. Anderson left the university, and Dr. Keith Cushman became my second mentor, overseeing an advisory committee that also included Dr. Walter Beale, Dr. Charles Davis, and Dr. Randolph Bulgin. I am especially grateful to Dr. Cushman for introducing me to his cousin Calvin Trillin, whose collection of short articles *Killings* (1984) was published during my time at UNCG. My conversation with Mr. Trillin helped shape my sense of the relationship between homicide and American values, especially in small communities. (*Killings* is not discussed in this work only because it is not a novel.)

Elsa Nettels' course Realism and Naturalism in American Literature at the College of William and Mary, which I had taken in fall 1981, provided an important seedbed for the ideas that bloomed at UNCG. I received guidance and encouragement from several colleagues in a faculty writing workshop at Ferrum College (Ferrum, Virginia) in the early 1990s and from my sister-in-law Julia Grimes Hayes over the course of this project. Mary Papke included a version of Chapter Four in her very fine collection *Twisted from the Ordinary: Essays on American Literary Naturalism* (2003). I also appreciate the encouragement of John Easterly, a former editor with the Louisiana State University Press, who may have been the first person to suggest that I write this book, during our conversations at South Atlantic Modern Language Association conferences. I am grateful to Stuart Noel, president of the Truman Capote Literary Society, for his invitation to speak at SAMLA in 2017, an experience that energized me to complete this work. No one works in the tradition of American Naturalism completely outside the shadow of Donald Pizer, whose kind correspondence in the last months of this project was an encouragement. And I have greatly valued the counsel and patience of Gary Mitchem, my editor at McFarland.

All my scholarly endeavors were enabled by my parents, Paul and Joan Whited, who, from my childhood, fueled my love for literature with their enthusiastic support and obvious pride in my accomplishments, not to mention their investment in my lengthy education. I regret that neither lived to see this book's publication.

I would never accomplish any decent writing project at all without my professional and life partner, M. Katherine Grimes, who has also been my colleague at three institutions. I am fortunate that she is always willing to lend her keen intellect to improving my work. As this is my fourth book project, she has likely edited over half a million words on my behalf, mostly as a labor of love. I also treasure her complete devotion to our family. She has lived with this project as long as I have.

Preface

Taking a contemporary literary nonfiction course in the 1980s at the University of North Carolina at Greensboro, I visited a bookstore looking for a copy of Truman Capote's 1965 nonfiction bestseller *In Cold Blood*. After searching the Nonfiction and Crime sections, I was surprised when a clerk steered me to Fiction. As Capote's book is subtitled *A True Account of a Multiple Murder and Its Consequences*, I thought the bookstore had mis-shelved it. This was my introduction to the critical conundrum over where literary nonfiction exactly belongs, not only in bookstores but also in theory concerning nonfiction prose.

Homicide was a key theme in the American psyche during the 1960s, when Capote's book appeared. This stemmed largely from the notoriety generated by four sensational crime stories of that decade: the strangling deaths in Boston in 1962–64, the murder of eight student nurses in Chicago in July 1966, the mass shooting at the University of Texas less than one month later (the first mass campus murder in America), and nine murders committed by Charles Manson's followers at four locations in the summer of 1969. The preoccupation with true murder narratives was also fed by the assassinations of John Kennedy, Martin Luther King, Jr., and Robert Kennedy, as well the popular television and film adaptations based on books about many of these crimes. American casualties from the war in Vietnam ran on the nightly news as background to all this violence. The success of Alfred Hitchcock's *Psycho* also played a role, as the Hitchcock film was adapted from a book by Robert Bloch and loosely inspired by the crimes of the serial killer Ed Gein. In the decade that followed, several books based on real homicide cases drew the attention of both readers and film companies; these included Joseph Wambaugh's *The Onion Field* (1973; film version 1979), Vincent Bugliosi and Curt Gentry's *Helter Skelter* (1974; film version 1976), and Judith Rossner's *Looking for Mr. Goodbar* (1975, film version 1977), all based on fact.

Reviewers and literary scholars tended to view most of these books as examples of the sort of writing that Tom Wolfe called "the New Journalism"

1

in 1973, but as I studied Capote's narrative technique in *In Cold Blood*, I recognized a rhetorical intensity antithetical to objective reporting. How could Capote provoke my sympathy for Perry Smith, a man who killed four people in their own home? Why did the book seem a stronger argument against capital punishment than anything I had learned about the death penalty? Smith, whose whole life seems to have been a clinical case study in how being born into a dysfunctional family can warp a person's entire destiny, emerges as the book's protagonist. How does Capote orchestrate that? And how is this narrative advocacy for Smith consistent with the praise lavished on Capote for objectivity?

My first foray into literary scholarship as a graduate student had been an essay on Naturalism in Theodore Dreiser's *Sister Carrie* (1900). Based on that study and my own reading in Naturalism, I recognized the Naturalistic overtones of Capote's book. Then I examined other 20th-century American novels considered Naturalistic in whose plots homicide figured prominently, works such as Dreiser's *An American Tragedy* (1925), William Faulkner's *Light in August* (1932), and Richard Wright's *Native Son* (1940). I discovered that some of the most heralded novels in modern American literature were inspired by or based upon actual criminal cases that their authors not only knew about but in many cases actively studied. I soon recognized that the tradition of American literary Naturalism was the relevant critical lens for discussing these works, which, taken together, form a continuous tradition in American prose literature. It is possible to identify an archetype: a man, usually young, the pattern of whose life has been isolation from every possible community, ultimately kills a person or persons who represent the cause or source of his isolation, or the loss his isolation represents. A tension develops between the way the killer's society views him and the way he is handled by the novel's author, and the author attempts to persuade the reader to his (or infrequently her) view of his subject. The author mitigates the killer's culpability through deterministic means, presenting him as both victimizer and victim. Ultimately, the young man is condemned by the very society responsible for his isolation. The author takes a rhetorical stance outside this condemnation.

The first wave of American literary Naturalism crested just as the Great Depression began in the late 1920s, and a term first used in print in 1933 provides a useful context for understanding the marginalization of the archetypal figure featured in this discussion. In his 1931 book *The American Epic*, James Truslow Adams first used the phrase "the American dream," which Adams explained as "that dream of a land in which life should be better and richer and fuller for everyone, with opportunity for each according to ability or achievement" (qtd. in Clark). Failure in the pursuit of these ideals fueled perhaps every homicide discussed in this volume, and the victims whose deaths Capote narrates in *In Cold Blood* are almost that dream's epitome. Their home is located near the exact geographical center of the United States, and they represent Middle America: a prominent, well-respected farmer, his wife, and two of their four children, who are typical by every measure of their time and place. The Clutters are land-rich Methodist Republicans in a staunchly Republican era, with Dwight D. Eisenhower in the White House and wholesome family sitcoms on television. They are murdered in the middle of the night in their own home by intruders who represent the victims' antithesis in nearly every respect and who commit the crime for such a small amount of money that their actions seem ultimately pathetic. Capote's description of the killers' backgrounds evokes legendary defense attorney Clarence Darrow's suggestion, uttered in the course of defending Richard Loeb and Nathan Leopold in what some called "the Crime of the Century" in 1924: "Listen to the story of anyone who has gone to prison, and see if he ever had a chance to go anywhere else" (Linder; Darrow 341).

The rationale for this book is complex.

Novels based on homicide cases have been around since the inception of American literature. One of the first American novels, Charles Brockden Brown's *Wieland* (1798), revolves around killings that occurred in 1871 in Tomhannock, New York, and were known to Brown. (*Wieland* had a significant influence on subsequent Gothic writers, including Mary Shelley and Edgar Allan Poe.) But despite the pervasiveness of homicide as a plot element in American novels, not until the mid–20th century did scholars begin to formulate theory about novelistic treatments of violence. This begins in 1950 with W.M. Frohock's *The Novel of Violence in America*. Frohock discusses certain novels published between 1920 and 1950 in terms of two strains: "novels of destiny" and "novels of erosion" (22). The former, a term Frohock borrows from the French critic Jean Pouillon, is a work whose "hero finds himself in a predicament" that he can only escape by inflicting harm on someone else. In the course of escaping the predicament through violence, he also destroys himself (6). Nevertheless, the hero accepts that "violence is man's fate," and thus the novel has tragic meaning (7). Hemingway's *For Whom the Bell Tolls* (1940) and Faulkner's *Light in August* (1932) are cited as examples. In the "novel of erosion," however, the writer combines the elements of time and violence in a formula devoid of meaning, "in which ill luck took the place of fate" (21). Not surprisingly, these novels reflect increasingly dark mid-century philosophies, including existentialism. Frohock's case in point is James M. Cain's *The Postman Always Rings Twice*, a novel Frohock also discusses due to its influence on Albert Camus's *The Stranger* (13). Concerning the novels that form the subject of the present study, Frohock discusses only *Postman* and *Light in August*. (Considering the publication date, it is difficult to understand his omission of *Native Son*.)

As Frohock makes no attempt to define the term "novel of violence," that task is taken up 50 years later by Patrick W. Shaw in *The Modern American Novel of Violence* (2000). Shaw goes further than any author before him in crafting a definition: "a novel of violence has violence as its central narrative focus and as the conflict that energizes the plot" (6). Shaw also identifies the necessary characteristics for such a novel, including "a recognizable vocabulary of violence," primarily the generous incorporation into the text of verbs denoting harm (6). Shaw excludes from his discussion novels containing gratuitous violence, or that which serves no aesthetic purpose. His examples of novels containing violence whose purpose is primarily "to shock or nauseate the reader" are works by Stephen King and Anne Rice. (For some readers, his inclusion of a chapter devoted to Bret Easton Ellis's *American Psycho* might stretch his claim to exclude authors of gratuitous violence.) Shaw also excludes "hard-boiled" detective fiction in which, he argues, violence is used merely as part of a formula. Of works discussed in the present study, Shaw discusses *Light in August, The Postman Always Rings Twice*, and *In Cold Blood*.

However, despite the importance of Frohock's and Shaw's contributions to defining and characterizing the homicide novel in American literature, that subgenre would remain insufficiently explored without placing these novels in proper relation to two important tributaries in the stream of American literature: the tradition of American literary Naturalism that began in the 1890s and the phenomenon of the New Journalism that flourished in the 1960s. The American novel of homicide incorporates elements of both traditions.

Most scholars see Naturalism ending in American literature two to three decades earlier than the publication of *In Cold Blood*. Eminent critics such as Malcolm Cowley and Lionel Trilling were singing the movement's swan song in the 1930s and '40s, and in "Notes on the Decline of Naturalism" in 1942, Philip Rahv declared that Naturalism had died out because it had "lost its power to cope with the ever-growing element of the problematical in modern life" (589). Perhaps these men failed to notice instances of Naturalism after about 1940 because it manifested itself in a type of literature some considered too "low brow" for critical notice, or maybe the increasing interest in nonfiction prose style in the 1960s was a distraction. Whatever the reason, it is necessary to make the connection between the novels discussed in this study and the literary movement that Donald Pizer, the foremost scholar of American literary Naturalism, has called "one of the most persistent and vital strains in American fiction, perhaps the only modern literary form in America that has been both popular and significant" (*Twentieth* ix).

Thus, this study will survey novels forming the American fact-based homicide novel tradition, beginning with the first works of the American literary Naturalists in the 1890s. This tradition moves through the three waves of Naturalism identified by Pizer in *Twentieth-Century American Literary Naturalism*, but its examples will differ from Pizer's exemplars in the second and third waves. The examples discussed in this study constitute the application of the Naturalistic formula derived from Emile Zola by his true American disciple, Frank Norris. The discussion will begin with Norris's novel *McTeague* (1899) and Theodore Dreiser's *An American Tragedy* (1925), representing the first wave of Naturalism, which crests with the onset of Modernism. Second-wave Naturalism continues through the 1930s and '40s in well-known novels of those decades, including *Light in August* (1932), *The Postman Always Rings Twice* (1934), *Native Son* (1940), and *Compulsion* (1956). (As *Compulsion* is based on the Leopold-Loeb crime in Chicago in 1925, it belongs to the second wave, despite its publication early in what Pizer views as the third wave.)

But the fact-based homicide novel tradition also extends the lifespan of American literary Naturalism beyond the last two decades for which Pizer provides examples of Naturalistic novels. In fact, that tradition culminates about three decades after Naturalism is generally thought to have finally ended, in the publication of Truman's Capote's *In Cold Blood* (1965), a novel which skillfully blends the approaches of the master Naturalists with those of the New Journalists, traditions that are in some ways compatible and in others, irreconcilable.

The analysis will continue with examination of Naturalistic elements lingering in a quasi–Naturalistic and widely praised work, Norman Mailer's *The Executioner's Song* (1979); this discussion will help to clarify important distinctions between the New Journalism and the Naturalistic fact-based homicide novel. The Mailer discussion will be followed by examination of several other examples blending Naturalistic elements in differing proportions. And lest the reader conclude that Naturalism as a literary movement extends over two centuries only, this study will end with discussion of two 2006 works illustrating the lingering effects of Naturalism on two prominent contemporary writers thoroughly familiar with narratives of violence: Sebastian Junger's *A Death in Belmont* and John Grisham's *The Innocent Man*.

In *Twentieth-Century American Literary Naturalism* (1982), Donald Pizer writes, "some of the best fiction of the late 1940s and early 1950s has still to be described as a third significant phase of naturalism in America" (xii). It is a central purpose of this analysis to demonstrate that this third phase extended significantly beyond the 1950s and that it enjoys recognition as a permanent influence upon a certain type

of fact-based homicide narrative. I hope that the literary works examined herein—particularly those published after 1940—will help to illustrate the truth of Pizer's statement that the Naturalistic influence did
not dwindle in the early 20th century but has resurfaced again and
again because of Naturalism's particular response to the increasing
problem of violence in American life and the sociological implications of
that violence. That so many major writers have attempted their own narratives of the conflict between violence and stable domestic life is testament to
the fact-based homicide novel's centrality as a subgenre in American literature.

1) Naturalism is uniquely & particularly useful
for the thing responding to violence in Am.
life & making sociological implications from it.

2) A testament to _____'s centrality as
a subgenre in Am. lit. is that so
many people have written these books

1

The Critical Conundrum
Launched by *In Cold Blood*

"I truly don't believe anything like it exists in the history of
journalism."—Truman Capote (qtd. in Inge 50)

With the 1965 appearance of *In Cold Blood*, Truman Capote declared
the emergence of a new literary form—the nonfiction novel. Capote's narrative of the Clutters' murder and their slayers' pursuit was assembled from
material its author gathered using journalistic methods and shaped with
the narrative techniques of the novel. Shortly before his 1985 death, Capote
reiterated his claim for his novel's importance:

> I wanted to write what I called a nonfiction novel—a book that would read exactly like
> a novel except that every word of it would be absolutely true. I had written a book that
> was like that called *The Muses Are Heard*. It was a short book about Russia and every
> word of it was true and it read like a short novel, but I wanted to do it on a grand
> scale. I had two sort of dry runs with subjects that just turned out not to have enough
> material in them to do what I wanted to do and finally I settled on this obscure crime
> in this remote part of Kansas because I felt, if I followed this from beginning to end it
> would provide me with the material to really accomplish what was a technical feat. It
> was a literary experiment [qtd. in Grobel 116].

Asked by Lawrence Grobel, "So there's no doubt in your mind that you
achieved literary history with that book?" Capote replied, "Yes, I did. Just
look at the multitude of copycats" (116).

Initially serialized in *The New Yorker*, the novel was an immediate success. In *The New York Review of Books*, F.W. Dupee called it "the best documentary account of an American crime ever written" (3). George Garrett
said that it was "a frank bid for greatness" (3) and "a work of art, the work
of an artist" (12). And *Newsweek* described Capote's decision to write this
story as "one of the most inspired hunches in literary history" ("The Fabulist" 58). Almost immediately after the book's publication, Capote secured
a movie contract, and when the film was promoted in 1967, the author

appeared on the cover of *Life* along with Scott Wilson and Robert Blake, who played killers Dick Hickock and Perry Smith. He did the talk-show circuit and gave interviews to countless magazines. Asked years later to confirm a rumor that he made more than $3 million directly or indirectly from *In Cold Blood*, Capote replied, "I made more than that" (Grobel 207). He was, in the words of *Esquire* interviewer Barbara Long, "the Author of the Year" (124).

Despite the popular attention paid his book, Capote was disappointed in its critical reception; it received positive reviews but was not heralded as the literary feat that he believed it to be. When the Pulitzer Prize and National Book Award committees passed over *In Cold Blood*, Capote clearly felt cheated.[1] His biographer, Gerald Clarke, reports that a member of the National Book Award selection committee, Saul Maloff of *Newsweek*, had lobbied for awarding that prize to a "less commercial" book (398). Capote did win the 1966 Edgar Award for Best Fact Crime Novel given by the Mystery Writers of America in only the second year of the award's existence. Nevertheless, Clarke says that the author "felt like a war hero who has hobbled home, expecting a parade, only to discover that others, who have never even seen the enemy up close, have picked up all the medals" (398).

> Capote became particularly bitter two years later when one of the "copycats," Norman Mailer, won both the Pulitzer Prize and the National Book Award for *The Armies of the Night*, Mailer's account of his own participation in Vietnam War protests. Mailer subtitled his book "History as a Novel, the Novel as History," and Capote felt, according to Clarke, that he should have added "Variations on a Theme by Capote" (399). Thirteen years later, Mailer won the Pulitzer again for a book that resembled *In Cold Blood* even more closely: *The Executioner's Song* (1980), a narrative of the crimes of Gary Gilmore, whose death at the hands of a Utah firing squad was the first execution in the United States after the Supreme Court's 1977 reinstatement of capital punishment. Capote told Grobel that Mailer's book could not have been written without *In Cold Blood*. And the fact that Mailer never met Gary Gilmore, that he joined Lawrence Schiller's project as writer *after* Gilmore's execution, does seem to place him in the company of those who, in Capote's words, have "never seen the enemy up close" [Clarke 398].

Perhaps part of the reason for the mixed critical reception of Capote's "nonfiction novel" is that it raised so many questions. Some appeared strictly mundane, such as where to place it on bookstore and library shelves. But these cataloging questions reflected more complex critical disagreements about how much a nonfiction writer can fictionalize his or her material and still call it nonfiction. In addition, the book raised formal questions about what makes a narrative a novel in the first place. Attempts to answer these questions sparked a flurry of articles about nonfiction and the nonfiction novel in the 1970s and '80s in literary journals and papers at conferences of the literati. A glance at the *Annual Bibliography* of the Modern Language Association reveals a sudden sharp increase in interest in nonfiction—particularly the "nonfiction novel"—beginning in the late 1960s.

One fairly obvious context in which Capote's achievement was soon discussed is the New Journalism. With the publication of a 1973 anthology, Tom Wolfe began to use this phrase to describe the attempt "to write journalism that would … read like a novel"; Wolfe says that this attempt began in the early 1960s with journalists who coveted the novelist's status as "the reigning literary artist" (8). According to Wolfe, these journalists did not want to "quit the popular press and try to get into the big league" but merely to have "the privilege of dressing up like" novelists (*The New Journalism* 8–9). In other words, these writers wanted to use fictional techniques to shape material they gathered through traditional reporting, and they hoped to garner the critical acclaim typically reserved for novelists.

It should be noted that Wolfe *did not* coin the term "the new journalism" and claimed that he wasn't sure who did. He says that he borrowed it from a friend, Seymour Krim, who first heard it in the late '50s when Pete Hamill was looking for someone to do a story about fellow journalists including Jimmy Breslin and Gay Talese. Wolfe also admits that he does not like the term. He is suspicious of "new" anything—New Criticism, the New Deal, New Humanism, the New Frontier. He points out that the New Journalism "was no 'movement.' There were no manifestoes, clubs, salons, cliques, not even a saloon where the faithful gathered, since there was no faith and no creed" (*NJ* 23). Nevertheless, the term stuck and is generally credited to Wolfe. And the techniques of the writing stuck, too; in fact, Wolfe contends that "the new journalism" written to model the traditional novel eventually replaced the novel as "literature's main event" (*NJ* 9). But despite Wolfe's promotion of the popular label, the questions about form and method raised by Capote's "nonfiction novel" obviously remained unanswered nearly 15 years later, when *The Executioner's Song* won the Pulitzer Prize for *Fiction*, although the Pulitzer committee has recognized achievement in general nonfiction since 1962.

By the time of Capote's 1984 death, many other "nonfiction novels" had been written, the most notable of them by Mailer and Wolfe, as well as John Hersey, Michael Herr, and Joan Didion. By the early 1980s, some colleges and universities offered literary nonfiction courses, such as the one taught by Chris Anderson in UNC Greensboro's English graduate program in 1984. Perhaps the most common subject of the nonfiction writers who dominated this period is violence. Mailer examines his own involvement in Vietnam war protests in *The Armies of the Night*. Herr's *Dispatches* is an account of the author's experiences as a Vietnam war correspondent for *Esquire*. Didion's book *Salvador* is a description of the political, economic, and social conditions that the author observed in revolution-scarred El

Salvador during a 1982 visit. Anderson explains the nonfiction writers' pre-occupation with violence as a verbal attempt to explain a fundamentally nonverbal phenomenon. Violence, Anderson says, can be perceived as the breakdown or failure of language; a war, for example, represents the failure of the parties involved to resolve their differences through verbal negotiation (Lecture). Thus, writers such as Mailer and Didion attempt to bring order to human experience through communicating the "truth" of events. If traditional journalism satisfies "the public's right to know," "the new journalism" goes one step further in attempting to satisfy the public's need to *understand* (Anderson, Lecture).

Many of the nonfiction novels published in the '60s and '70s deal with a particular kind of violence—homicide. In addition to *In Cold Blood* and *The Executioner's Song*, the best examples of this genre in the 1960s are Hersey's *The Algiers Motel Incident*, the story of the shooting of three black men by police officers during the Detroit race riots of 1967, and Joseph Wambaugh's *The Onion Field*, an account based on the killing of a California police officer in 1963. By the late 1970s, the subgenre had become so popular that even Harper Lee was researching Alabama homicide cases she thought merited book-length treatment (Cep, "Harper"). Forty-five years after her famous research trip to Kansas with Capote in 1959, Lee was revealed by Casey Cep in a 2015 *New Yorker* article to have devoted time in the late 1970s to researching six related homicides in rural Alabama. The cases included the shooting death of the man suspected of committing the first five homicides, the Rev. Willie Maxwell. Lee so invested herself in researching cases associated with Maxwell that she lived for a time in a relative's motel in Alexander City, Alabama. Tom Radney, the attorney who represented Maxwell at his trial, gave Lee all his files, but the book Lee said she planned to call *The Reverend* never appeared (Madden-Lunsford 182–83). The Radney family never abandoned hope of seeing the book published, according to Cep, whose book *Furious Hours: Murder, Fraud, and the Last Trial of Harper Lee* explores the reasons Lee's planned true-crime book never materialized. When Lee's publisher announced in February 2015 that she would publish a new book, the Radneys assumed she had completed the manuscript about Maxwell's crimes. Until the publication of *Go Set a Watchman* after Lee's February 2016 death, her reputation was based entirely on *To Kill a Mockingbird*, the final draft of which she had submitted in the same year she accompanied Truman Capote to Kansas (Madden 109). Among the Truman Capote papers at the New York Public Library are approximately 150 pages that Lee typed and categorized (Cep, *Furious* 189). The historical record makes quite clear that Capote was powerfully indebted to his childhood friend, Lee, for the success of *In Cold Blood*, particularly for her careful records of specific details and her greater familiarity with the intricacies of criminal law (Cep, *Furious* 185, 189).[2]

Despite the fact that Lee's planned true-crime book never appeared, in the two decades following the publication of *In Cold Blood*, there was a proliferation of the sort of "copycats" Capote had mentioned to Lawrence Grobel. All of these books about high-profile murder cases are well known, and some are works of considerable literary reputation; in addition to *The Onion Field* (1973) and *The Executioner's Song* (1979), these include Gerald Frank's *The Boston Strangler* (1965), Vincent Bugliosi's *Helter Skelter* (1974), Judith Rossner's *Looking for Mr. Goodbar* (1975), and Joe McGinniss's *Fatal Vision* (1984). Two 2006 examples demonstrate that this sort of project still attracts writers of repute: Sebastian Junger's *A Death in Belmont* and John Grisham's only book-length work of nonfiction to date, *The Innocent Man*. These books have all been widely read, and all of them are still in print two decades into the 21st century.

Many other so-called "true-crime" books of the 1970s, '80s, and '90s seem aimed at satisfying a voracious public appetite for reading about sordid crimes. Some homicide cases led to multiple books, the implication being, presumably, that there is more than one version of any "true" story (or, perhaps, that fans of the genre will buy more than one account). This is particularly true of cases involving high-profile perpetrators who experienced long "careers" in the news cycle, such as the so-called Boston Strangler (whose identity is still disputed); Ted Bundy, the mass rapist and murderer of numerous women in the Pacific Northwest in the 1970s[3]; and David Berkowitz, the "Son of Sam" killer, who was responsible for eight separate shooting incidents in New York City in summer 1976. Some authors have made a career of writing predominately or exclusively "true-crime" novels. A prominent example is Ann Rule, a former Seattle policewoman whose web site says she is "regarded by many as the foremost true-crime writer in America, and the author responsible for the genre as it exists today" ("Ann Rule Bio"). Rule published 36 books, the best-known of which is *The Stranger Beside Me* (1981), about Ted Bundy, who worked with Rule answering phones at a Seattle suicide hotline. She died in 2015.

But the alliance of true crime with the New Journalism also fails to account entirely for what Truman Capote had achieved in 1965 because the sort of true-crime writing for which Rule claims responsibility bears little resemblance in theme or approach to *In Cold Blood*. Rule used the methodology of the journalist in researching homicide and sexual assault and wrote with realistic detail about criminal cases. Rule's narratives tend to focus on three aspects of criminal cases: the victims, the investigators, and the perpetrators ("Ann Rule Bio"). The crime narratives in the vein of *In Cold Blood* focus predominately on perpetrators, minimize attention to victims, and reflect a very specific authorial and rhetorical stance with regard to the issue of culpability and the larger social meaning of the crimes. In order to fully account for the literary tradition of which *In Cold Blood* is the epitome, it is necessary to return to the turn of the 20th century and to American literary Naturalism.

A central tenet of Naturalism and its philosophical corollary, determinism, is the displacement of culpability beyond any individual and onto the social environment that produced him (or, very infrequently, her). This culpability is explored by authors in complex terms, dispersing it across multiple contributing factors or determinants. For the characters in a Naturalistic work, the environment affords few choices. In Stephen Crane's *Maggie: A Girl of the Streets* (1893), a young girl grows up in a tenement building on the lower East side of New York City in an Irish-American family. Her abusive and alcoholic parents leave the parenting responsibility for Maggie's two younger brothers largely to her, and the death of one brother as a toddler underscores the harshness of the environment. In the first scene of *Maggie*, small children are throwing rocks at each other in a literary representation of Charles Darwin's principle of "survival of the fittest." As she approaches adulthood, choices for Maggie appear to range between working hard in poor conditions for low wages and finding a man who can support her and raise her to respectability. When both of these avenues fail and Maggie is rebuffed by a minister who obviously cares more about his own respectability than her well being, Crane suggests that only prostitution is left as an option, and although it is not entirely clear that the "girl of the painted cohorts of the city" wandering around the lower East side in a late chapter is the protagonist, the book's subtitle, "A Girl of the Streets," strengthens the correspondence. Whether Maggie has turned to prostitution or is still exploring it as an option, whether her mother is wailing accurately or inaccurately for her daughter's lost reputation in the closing scene, it is abundantly clear that Maggie's choices have narrowed to the disgusting and the despicable. Whether she drowns herself in the river or is drowned by the repulsive man following her just before her death ultimately matters little; her death signifies that she is out of choices.

Crane's narrative sympathy in this account is focused on Maggie, whose victimization is purest among these characters. In his inscription to Hamlin Garland in the first edition, Crane wrote that Maggie's story "tries to show that environment is a tremendous thing in the world and frequently shapes lives regardless. If one proves that theory, one makes room in Heaven for all sorts of souls (notably an occasional street girl) who are not confidently expected to be there by many excellent people" (Crane, *Maggie*). Crane's sympathetic presentation of Maggie illustrates a central, perhaps paradoxical characteristic of Naturalistic writing: authors present their characters as having little chance against the biological, economic, environmental, and social forces prevailing upon them, and these forces and their effects are depicted in Realistic terms (i.e., following the tenets of Realism); however, the authorial stance of the Naturalistic author toward these characters reflects the lingering influence of Romanticism, with authors demonstrating enormous sympathy toward, and even identification with, their struggling protagonists. In the Preface to *Lyrical Ballads* (1800 edition), William Wordsworth argues that the common man is a more valid subject for poetry than the heroes celebrated in works from previous literary periods. In "Michael" and "We Are Seven," Wordworth illustrates his sympathy for characters from ordinary life, who, he felt, illustrate "the primary laws of our nature."

Perhaps no writer has a bigger heart for his or her characters than the Naturalist. Think of Thomas Hardy, with Tess Durbeyfield. Think of George Eliot, with Hetty Sorrel. This remnant of Romanticism in American Naturalistic writing has been explored at length by Donald Pizer.

This hallmark of Naturalistic writing is abundantly clear in *In Cold Blood*. The book's overture is a brief section that sweeps from the vast plains of western Kansas into the Clutter home; it ends with Capote's lament for "four shotgun blasts that, all told, ended six human lives" (15). Tony Tanner has said of *In Cold Blood* that "Capote worked on the valid assumption that a fact is simply a moment in an ongoing sequence, that it ramifies in all directions, and that to appreciate the full import of any incident you must see as much of the sequence and as many of the ramifications as possible" (345). In the novel, he is essentially describing the "ramifications" of those "four shotgun blasts" on a much wider range of people than Herbert, Bonnie, Nancy, and Kenyon Clutter. Capote's intent in *In Cold Blood* is to show that all of the principals in the story were victims. The Clutters, obviously, were victims of Dick Hickock and Perry Smith (and, in a larger sense, of fate). Close family friends such as Bobby Rupp (Nancy's boyfriend) and Susan Kidwell (Nancy's friend) also had their lives altered by the murders. Kansas Bureau of Investigation Agent Alvin Dewey and the other law enforcement officers and their families were victims of a long, loathsome case. And the author found himself at the mercy of the legal system, as the trial and appeals extended the book's completion over an agonizing five years. Capote's biographer, Gerald Clarke, has said that Capote never recovered from the trauma involved in writing the book (397). Capote told Clarke, "No one will ever know what *In Cold Blood* took out of me. It scraped me right down to the marrow of my bones. It nearly killed me. I think, in a way, it *did* kill me. Before I began it, I was a stable person, comparatively speaking. Afterward, something happened to me" (qtd. in Clarke 398).

Ultimately, Capote sees even Richard Hickock and Perry Smith as victims (Smith to a greater extent than Hickock): Dick Hickock was a victim
of an automobile accident, of his own lack of conscience and, eventually,
of the justice system. Perry Smith, too, was a victim of the justice system,
but he was also the victim of a lonely, unhappy childhood, like Truman
Capote; like Nancy Clutter, he was a thwarted artist who, had not circumstances intervened, might have traded life's unpleasantries for art, as Nancy
Clutter's friend Susan Kidwell had done in the end of *In Cold Blood*, and as
Capote himself did. Capote's characterization of Perry Smith is so skillful
that "critics have generally agreed that Smith is the protagonist of the book
and that one of Capote's central aims is indicated by the intended irony
of the title: it is Smith rather than the Clutter family who is killed 'in cold
blood'" (Heyne, "Toward" 481–82; readers may be more comfortable with
"in addition to," instead of "rather than").

Capote's primary strategy is mediating a reader's contempt for Perry
Smith by describing the kind of society that produced him, from the abuse
and neglect Smith suffered at the hands of his own parents to the attitudes toward him of average people in an average middle–America town
like Holcomb, Kansas. Capote obviously feels that human beings are at the
mercy of forces beyond their control, and this philosophical undercurrent
aligns him with the Naturalistic writers who preceded him by several decades but whose influence persists in his monumental book. This and many
other books about homicide, fictional and nonfictional, raise repeatedly the
question of whether chance is an operative force in our lives or whether
our acts are determined, at least to some extent, by forces we do not control. The role of chance is often underscored in novels about homicide by
symbolism; cats, representing fate (the concept of nine lives), frequently
cross people's paths, and characters win lotteries and play cards. A reader's answer to Darrow's question about how much control a person like
Perry Smith exercises over his own life is, of course, directly proportional
to the amount of sympathy the reader can be brought to feel for him. By
invoking impressions of Leopold and Loeb as children themselves, Darrow
convinced a judge to spare their lives.

Of course, Darrow's clients were from two of the wealthiest families in
Chicago, families that could afford top-notch legal representation. Loeb's
father was a successful lawyer and a vice president with Sears & Roebuck,
while Leopold's father was a financier who was both a Great Lakes ship-
ping magnate and founder of a paper mill. Both families probably appeared
to others to be living the American dream in an affluent neighborhood,
dwelling in ostentatious homes complete with household staff. Leopold and
Loeb claimed they kidnapped and murdered 14-year-old Bobby Franks, a
neighbor, out of curiosity about whether they could get away with murder.

College graduates by the ages of 18 and 19 respectively, they were enamored of philosopher Frederich Nietzsche's concept of the *Übermensch,* or Superman, and fancied themselves capable of outsmarting the legal authorities. Their crimes were a sort of intellectual experiment, and they escaped execution only because of their social class, their ages, and the rhetorical skill of their lawyer. The dilettantish nature of their motive was central to the case's being dubbed "the Crime of the Century."

The outcome of the Leopold-Loeb case may appear to stand in sharp relief against the lot of convicted murderers like Perry Smith and Dick Hickock. After all, recalling Clarence Darrow's conviction that such a person "[n]ever had a chance to go anywhere" but prison, one might protest that Darrow's clients had advantages that might have allowed them to go anywhere they wished. But it is arguable that these two cases are cut from opposite ends of the same thematic cloth. That cloth might well have been spun in the great textile mills that emerged with the technology of the Industrial Revolution, the period that gave birth to the American dream ideology (myth, some would say). But the ideology to which James Truslow Adams assigned a name was well in evidence in the late 19th century, including in American literature, and most notably in the stories of Horatio Alger. The son of a Unitarian minister, Alger wrote formulaic stories for young readers featuring young men born in poverty who "pulled themselves up by their own bootstraps," or raised themselves to success and respectability through hard work, persistence, and good character. In Alger's fiction, juvenile protagonists could "rise from humble backgrounds to lives of respectable middle-class security and comfort through hard work, determination, courage, and honesty" ("Horatio"). Beginning as paper or shoeshine boys, Alger's characters improved their socioeconomic standing incrementally, their social momentum reflecting what philosopher Ralph Waldo Emerson called "Self-Reliance." The achievement of Alger's protagonists was commendable for both what they achieved and the way they achieved it. Alger wrote over one hundred books, and his influence was widespread.

As early as 1881, Kate Gannet Wells, a Boston philanthropist, identified "Americanism" as "the fixed conviction that one man is the equivalent of another in capacity, and that his failure to prove it by results is the consequence of circumstances beyond his control" (Clark). Of course, one of the predominant "circumstances beyond his control" of the Industrial Age was the futility of competing with machines in the new marketplace. This fact warped the American dream in two directions. At the bottom of the social ladder, fewer and fewer young men could hope for the achievements of Horatio Alger's characters merely by relying on themselves, and the more machines transformed the economy, the truer this became. Industry rapidly became hierarchical. The majority of workers took home a minimal wage earned through long hours of physical labor, often in dangerous or difficult conditions such as those described in the meat-packing industry by Upton Sinclair in his 1906 novel *The Jungle*. As the gap in American incomes, living conditions, and social status widened, the "American dream" was increasingly out of these workers' reach.

And although living conditions were pleasanter higher up the socioeconomic ladder, fewer and fewer young men could hope to imitate Horatio Alger's characters merely by relying on themselves, for the very same reason: the emergence of machines that needed to be operated by workers. The emergence of this new working class expanded the socioeconomic ladder at the bottom, with the establishment of slums in large cities. The influx of immigrants at the turn of the 20th century caused growth in the working class to outpace growth of the entrepreneurial class. In short, for every titan of industry putting dollars into his bank account or reinvesting them, there were thousands of workers turning wheels and pulling levers. Furthermore, as these titans amassed wealth from building railroads, steel mills, and the other technologies transforming the economic and physical landscape, they were also aided in their drive toward riches and status by monopolies and other forms of corruption. Increasingly, the wealthiest Americans were economically, socially, and often physically far removed from the people whose labor built their vast, ostentatious mansions such as the Vanderbilt family's Biltmore Estate in Asheville, North Carolina. But although they accumulated wealth at a rate that might previously have been inconceivable, the titans of "the Gilded Age," as Mark Twain called it, were no more living the American dream than were the majority of their employees, because they amassed fortunes largely due to the capital available to them to invest in the first place, and they benefited from the transformative nature of the technologies in which they invested, as well as the physical labor of others. They did not "pull themselves up by their own bootstraps"; they capitalized on advantages with which they were, for the most part, born. If the "Americanism" described by Kate Gannet Wells requires all people to be "equal in capacity," in the era of industrialization, it fails before it begins.

Research by Peter Lindert and Jeffrey Williamson for *Unequal Gains: American Growth and Inequality Since 1700* (2016) accounts for the shift in equality in the socioeconomic sphere. Lindert and Williamson write, "on the eve of the American Revolution[,] incomes in the 13 colonies that formed the United States were more equal than in virtually 'any other place on the planet'" (qtd. in "As You Were"). Before the American Revolution, living standards for the American colonists were superior to those in England, according to Lindert and Williamson, but that advantage was lost three times in the 150 years that followed: during the Revolution, during the Civil War, and during the Great Depression. The first "great wave" of rising income inequality occurred between 1774 and 1860,[4] the authors say. According to a special report on the economy published in *The Economist* in 2012, "Before the industrial revolution, wealth gaps between countries were modest: income per person in the world's ten richest countries was only six times higher than in the ten poorest.... [But] the industrial revolution widened the gaps both between countries and within them" ("As You Were"). By the end of the 19th century, socioeconomic stratification was well established in the United States.

The last part of Kate Gannet Wells' definition of "Americanism" is especially relevant to stories concerning homicide: that the American's "failure to prove [his equivalency of capacity] by results is the consequence of circumstances beyond his control" (qtd. in Clark). In literature, this philosophy concerning circumstances beyond characters' control is expressed in Naturalism, a movement entirely compatible with social Darwinism. This logical extension of Wells' definition would stipulate that because life can be capricious, certain individuals will be impacted by negative forces which they do not control, and consequently their offspring will *not* be equivalent in capacity with the offspring of other individuals impacted by more positive forces. Such a dichotomy could worsen with subsequent generations.

Contrasting the members of the Clutter family with their killers illustrates this principle. The murder of the Clutter family came to Truman Capote's attention in the first place because Herb Clutter had achieved such prominence for his contributions to agriculture, both regionally and nationally, that his obituary was published in the *New York Times*. After earning his bachelor's degree in agriculture at Kansas State University (then College), Clutter rose to prominence through hard work and a series of good investments. He served as county agent before founding both the Kansas Wheat Growers Association and the National Association of Wheat Growers. Eventually, he was appointed by President Dwight Eisenhower to the Federal Farm Credit Board. By the time of his death, he had been involved in about 20 civic organizations, according to Rachel Keely Turner, who profiled members of the Clutter family in 2016 for the *High Plains/ Midwest AG Journal*. Turner writes that Mr. Clutter was a leader in the project to put a stained-glass window in the family's Methodist Church, a window that was dedicated, after the murders, to the Clutter family. She quotes a younger farmer who describes him as a mentor in reverent terms. Another person she interviewed ascribes the success of a local newspaper to Clutter's having promoted it, also recalling that his modesty made him reluctant to be photographed. As a result of her extensive research, Turner writes, "Herb Clutter was a man who thoroughly earned the recognition he receives to this day." Although Capote is sometimes derided by those who knew the Clutters for his limited attention to their characterizations, even he makes clear that Nancy and Kenyon Clutter were following in their father's civic-minded footsteps. For example, Capote mentions Nancy's 4-H activities and her mentoring role with younger girls; on the last day of her life, he depicts her teaching a protégé to bake pies. Turner terms the Clutter family "decent, hardworking people who deserve to be remembered [as] a family steadfast in community, agriculture, faith and goodwill." From all accounts, even the family's behavior in the face of death was civilized and compliant. It seems entirely possible that such a horrible act was so fundamentally antithetical to their natures that they truly believed they would be left bound and gagged but alive.

This family and the lives of its members could hardly provide a sharper contrast with that of their killer, Perry Smith, whose entire upbringing and development to the point of the murders is marked with dysfunction. Born to a Native American mother and an Anglo-American father, Perry grew up conscious that many regarded him as a "half breed," a term considerably more derisive and animalistic than most other terms commonly used to refer to mixed-race status. He spent his early years traveling on the rodeo circuit with his parents, who were performers. When their alcoholism fueled their inattention to him and his father ran off to Alaska on a get-rich-quick scheme, Perry was sent to a Catholic orphanage. There, his abusive treatment by the nuns include shaming him for bed-wetting and administering painful ointments to his penis; this abuse shaped his sense of the uselessness of conventional religion and his status as outsider to yet another social institution, the Church. By the time he ended up in prison and met Dick Hickock, we might ask, like Clarence Darrow, "if he ever had a chance to go anywhere else" (341).

The story narrated by Capote in *In Cold Blood* is orchestrated to emphasize the confrontation between opposing values in American life. On the one hand, the reader sees the Clutter family on their idyllic farm, solid and settled in the heartland of America, and according to Rachel Keely Turner, the "cornerstone" of their community. Up to the point of his death, Herbert Clutter has proved himself the equivalent of any other American man in capability, and his circumstances have proved to be entirely within his control. Like the protagonist of Horatio Alger's stories, Herbert Clutter is the shaper of his own destiny. On the other hand, the Clutters' killers are depicted frequently moving in a car, crisscrossing the landscape in a series of pathetic attempts to find the "score" (Hickock's term) that will buy them a temporary benefit such as dinner and a hotel room. Life has presented Hickock with more favorable circumstances than Smith, as, by all accounts, Hickock's family seems typical for its time and place. But even Dick has been the victim of brain damage suffered in a car accident which, according to the mental health experts who testified at his trial, likely set him on his criminal course, altering his life irreparably. If a novelist put these characters and events into a work of fiction, an editor or critic might say their symbolism was *too* obvious, almost to the point of being allegorical.

From its emergence in American fiction in the 1890s, Naturalism took as its mission accounting for the caprices of the world, helping readers to comprehend how a girl like Maggie ends up on the unforgiving streets of the Bowery tenements in the 1890s and how a girl like Nancy Clutter ends up dead in her bucolic farmhouse in the 1950s.

A woman subjected to Maggie's circumstances generally loses respectability and, when she also loses her self-respect, sometimes her life. But a man under the same circumstances has a different response—at least in literature. A male protagonist subjected to the same determinants as Maggie will generally build up frustration to the point of drastic action, often violence perpetrated against another person. Beginning with Frank Norris's novel *McTeague* (1899) and continuing through Theodore Dreiser's retelling of the case of Chester Gillette in *An American Tragedy* (1925) and for several decades beyond, fiction writers established a subgenre featuring a young male protagonist so convinced of his entrapment by his life circumstances that he thrusts his frustration outward, usually victimizing a young woman. Although we think of the Naturalistic period in American literature as eventually giving way to a more experimental, symbolistic mode in the 1930s and 1940s, novels exploring the criminal behavior of human beings acting out "drama[s] of determinism" continued to be written through those decades: William Faulkner's *Light in August* (1932), James M. Cain's *The Postman Always Rings Twice* (1934), Richard Wright's *Native Son* (1940), and Meyer Levin's *Compulsion* (1956) are prominent examples. Although generally categorized as fictional, these novels were all based on actual cases, and, to varying degrees, journalistic techniques were instrumental in the creation of the narratives. Characters such as Clyde Griffith, McTeague, Joe Christmas, and Bigger Thomas are the quasi-fictional prototypes for Perry Smith. Their stories may not be entirely factual, but thematically, they are entirely true. And the use of journalist techniques to create vérité in their accounts results in narratives impossible for readers to dismiss as purely works of fiction.

In 1951, poet Langston Hughes published his poem "Harlem," therein asking his famous question about what happens to unfilled dreams. Hughes suggests several alternatives, most associated with sickness or depression, before suggesting, with the emphasis of italics, that perhaps the dream *explodes.*

In posing these alternatives, Hughes certainly had foremost in mind African Americans' struggle for equality, which must have seemed to him to be progressing at a snail's pace, despite the fact that his poem appeared over 75 years after slavery officially ended. Almost all the outcomes that Hughes suggests for his unfulfilled dream are gradual and incremental. The idea of explosion, however, is powerful and instantaneous. Perhaps no other author has described better than Hughes the theme of novels published in the United States between 1890 and the mid-twentieth century that revolve around a central act of homicide perpetrated by a protagonist who views himself as an outsider to every American ideal and whose trajectory is toward the point where he can no longer tolerate his ostracism. Hughes's explosion echoes in the gunshots central to the plot of these works.

A clear progression of this theme—the explosions created by outsiders to the American dream—can be demonstrated from the novels of the first American Naturalists to the "nonfiction novel" of Truman Capote by tracing the development in certain novels, beginning at about 1890, of three factors: (1) the notion of philosophical determinism (the central preoccupation of the Naturalists), represented in these novels in the question of whether man is free to pursue success as defined by the conventional indicators of his culture and by his own desires and aims; (2) the research and writing techniques of the journalist and the verisimilitude and emphasis on factuality these techniques bring to the narratives; and (3) Thomas De Quincey's contention in "On the Knocking at the Gate in 'Macbeth'" that the "poet" writing about murder "must throw the interest on the murderer" (733). Viewed from these perspectives, any true assessment of true-crime narratives depicting the implosion of the American dream must trace the headwaters of this subgenre in the tradition of American literary Naturalism. These narratives occupy a place within the main stream of American literature through the 20th century in works generally labeled as novels, and in the 1960s, the New Journalism enters that stream, introducing the notion of the nonfiction novel as the emphasis on factuality increases. If, as Capote famously claimed, nothing quite like *In Cold Blood* had existed in American journalism, his book did have close relatives among a select group of American Naturalistic novels featuring central acts of homicide. *In Cold Blood* represents the confluence of the Naturalistic tradition with the New Journalism; after it, the emphasis on factuality introduced in the New Journalism re-routes the narrative stream. By 1980, when Mailer wins the Pulitzer Prize, this re-routing is evident, and while Mailer's book may have Naturalistic overtones, it is primarily what the New Journalists termed *reportage*, not a Naturalistic novel. Following Mailer, authors vary in the balance of their attention to factuality, the question of determinism or agency, and the location of narrative focus. But the "true-crime" novel following the Naturalistic prescription never completely disappears; in fact, its most faithful practitioner after Capote will come early in the 21st century.

2

The Evolution of American
Literary Naturalism

"[N]aturalism is not a school, as it is not embodied in the
genius of one man … in naturalism there [are] neither inno-
vators nor leaders; there are simply workmen, some more
skillful than others."—Emile Zola, *Le roman experimental*

To a student of Naturalism, Emile Zola's declaration in 1880 that "Naturalism is not a school … as it is not embodied in the genius of one man"
("Novel" 285) seems as ludicrous as Charles Darwin's announcing in 1859
that evolution theory was the product of a committee. Reference guides
to literature routinely acknowledge the Frenchman as the father of literary Naturalism and the author of "the most influential statement ever made
of the theory" (Holman 302). Certainly the work of such writers as Stephen Crane, Frank Norris, Jack London, and Theodore Dreiser suggests
that, at least in the United States, Naturalism might be viewed accurately
as a "school." But it is also true that Naturalism does not depend for its life
on the "genius" of Emile Zola; in fact, it might be more accurate to say that
Zola was Naturalism's midwife rather than its mother. And the prevalence
of American Naturalistic works in the 1890s and early 1900s is, finally, a testament not to the influence of these writers on each other but to the impact
of certain scientific and philosophical theories on them all.

In its most basic sense, American literary Naturalism is an application of the principle of scientific and philosophical determinism to literature, generally demonstrated in the novel but also in shorter fiction such
as Stephen Crane's *Maggie: A Girl of the Streets* (1893) and "The Open Boat"
(1898). The Naturalist period in literature began in France in the early 1870s
and was taken up in the United States in the early 1890s by practitioners
such as Crane. It influenced Russian and English fiction as well. Determinism, at least as it has been applied to literature, has many facets, attributable to the rather large number of influential scientists and philosophers

working in the second half of the 19th century. The two most important of these were Charles Darwin and Herbert Spencer, from whose work Naturalism acquired overtones of biological determinism and two crucial metaphors: the notions of the world as a "lawless jungle" and of life as a competitive struggle which only the "fittest" survive.

If the Naturalistic writers may be accurately referred to as "workmen," then much of their raw material must be attributed to Darwin, whose *On the Origin of Species by Means of Natural Selection*, the first thoroughgoing statement of the principles of evolution and natural selection, appeared in 1859. In *Free Will and Determinism in American Literature*, Perry Westbrook declares Darwin "the strongest single influence on literary Naturalism from its beginning down to the present" (100). Donald Pizer, the most prolific and best-known critic on the subject of American literary Naturalism, devotes two chapters in his book *Realism and Naturalism in Nineteenth-Century American Literature* to a discussion of how evolution theory is reflected in late 19th-century literary criticism. Darwin's work is so significant that it alone would almost certainly have prompted the Naturalistic response in literature, even without any of the other influential theorists.

Darwin's theory of natural selection resulted from a notion put into his head by an experience in the Galapagos Islands in 1832, while he was serving as naturalist[1] aboard the HMS *Beagle*. Darwin noticed that the native giant tortoises varied from individual to individual in details such as shell contour: those who lived on islands where vegetation was not within easy reach had developed carapaces with notched, domed fronts which permitted them to stretch their necks and reach food, while those who lived where grasses were within easy reach had smooth-fronted shells. The British vice-governor told Darwin that natives could even tell which islands tortoises had grown up on from such distinguishing characteristics. The Galapagos trip led Darwin to the conclusion that "species were not fixed for ever. Perhaps one could [even] change into another [over thousands of years]" (Attenborough 13). For nearly 27 years, Darwin continued to gather evidence to support his theory that some members of a species are genetically predisposed to develop characteristics (such as longer necks or differently shaped shells) which render them more successful in their environments, and therefore more likely to survive, than members of the same species without those characteristics. Thus, over generations of the same species, the characteristics fostering survival will be "selected" and those that do not will be abandoned. Darwin wrote,

> Variations, however slight and from whatever cause proceeding, if they be in any degree profitable to the individuals of a species, in their infinitely complex relations to other organic beings and to their physical conditions of life, will tend to the preservation of such individuals, and will generally be inherited by the offspring. The offspring,

also, will thus have a better chance of surviving, for, of the many individuals of any species which are periodically born, but a small number can survive. I have called this principle, by which each slight variation, if useful, is preserved, by the term Natural Selection, in order to mark its relation to man's power of selection [385].

Darwin argues that natural selection is "truer" than man-made selection because man tends to be self-serving, whereas nature selects in the best interest of the species. In breeding animals, for example, man "does not allow the most vigorous males to struggle for the females" (388); instead, he selects the male whose characteristics appear the most desirable or beneficial to him. Ultimately, Darwin says, "Nature's productions ... plainly bear the stamp of far higher workmanship" (388).

By far the most revolutionary of Darwin's ideas, particularly for nonscientists, was his theory that *homo sapiens* constituted just another branch on the evolutionary tree (but not a superior one). Darwin wrote that all life forms have so much in common, particularly in terms of reproductive processes, that "it does not seem incredible that, from some low and intermediate form, both animals and plants may have been developed; and, if we admit this, we must likewise admit that all the organic beings which have ever lived on this earth may be descended from some one primordial form..." (389). In a world where human beings had occupied a distinctive position—as superior creatures who are, according to many religions, specially fitted by a divine creator with spiritual capacity which distinguishes them from all other organisms—the idea that man and other creatures might be descended from a "low and intermediate" ancestor was not universally well received. Darwin concluded that the variations among different species and among members of the same species resulted not from the ordination of a divine creator but from "the struggle for life" (385). His premise led the Naturalistic writers to portray human behavior more in the context of the animal than the spiritual nature, attributing characters' motivation to such factors as genetics and environment more than to factors such as education and religious training. This conception of humans as part of a larger animal continuum, illustrated in Zola's novel title *La Bête Humaine* (the human beast), contrasts sharply with the notion of man as made in the image of God, and the influence of natural science on behavior shows up in the Naturalistic writers' interest in violence. When Victorian poet Alfred, Lord Tennyson wrote of "nature red in tooth and claw," he was thinking of the so-called "lower" animals, as opposed to "Man ... / Who trusted God was love indeed / And love Creation's final law" (Canto 56).

But the Naturalists recognize the violent nature of the human species, and the personification of violent animals in their fiction is another means of stressing this continuum. This principle is illustrated nowhere better among the first-wave American Naturalists than in the work of Jack

London. The numerous dogs, wolves, and other animals in London's fiction are the most familiar example. In *The Call of the Wild*, Buck is a docile pet, but once returned to the wilderness, he quickly learns "the law of life" and becomes a survivor, his triumphs in fights with other dogs demonstrating his superior nature. Ultimately, Buck abandons human civilization altogether, becoming the ghost dog of the wilderness, a creature of myth. In *White Fang*, the metamorphosis occurs in reverse: White Fang, trained in savage practices, response to Weedon Scott's kindness and becomes a virtual pet (although at the end of the novel he is still capable of protecting the family). Mitchell theorizes that London used dogs as central characters because readers were less likely to think of dogs as exercising conscious choice, and therefore "the consequences of heredity, temperament, and innate capacity were more easily isolated" (540–41). Thus, London could illustrate Darwinian principles more clearly in his canine characters, as dogs are still a class of animal with individuals in both wild and tame states. In these novels, London examines the concept of domestication, suggesting that domesticity or civilization is no more than a veneer for any animal's baser instincts.

The Naturalists' interest in man's animalistic and instinctive tendencies is also reinforced in their use of imagery and symbolism. Westbrook points out that "the love of animal similes" characterizes all the Naturalists (144). An episode often cited as the epitome of the Naturalistic influence is the scene in Chapter One of Dreiser's novel *The Financier* when young Frank Cowperwood is mesmerized by the life-and-death struggle of a lobster and a squid in a store-front aquarium. The episode, Dreiser says, was "a tragedy which stayed with [Cowperwood] all his life and cleared things up considerably intellectually" [3]. It clarifies for young Cowperwood the Darwinian nature of existence:

> The incident ... answered in a rough way that riddle which has been annoying him so much in the past: "How is life organized?" Things lived on each other—that was it. Lobsters lived on squids and other things. What lived on lobsters? Men, of course! Sure, that was it! And what lived on men? he asked himself. Was it other men? [5].

One of the strongest theories connecting human behavior with that of other species is the notion of "survival of the fittest," borrowed by Darwin from the philosophy of Englishman Herbert Spencer. In *On the Origin of Species*, Darwin wrote that Spencer's phrase "survival of the fittest" was "more accurate" than the term "natural selection" in describing the process of preserving characteristics that had proven genetically advantageous (385). Herbert Spencer had discussed evolution in print at least four years before Darwin's first public discussion of the theory. Darwin and naturalist Alfred Russel Wallace, who had been conducting independent research in Brazil remarkably similar to Darwin's, presented papers on evolution before an English scientific society in 1858, and Darwin subsequently published *On the Origin of Species* in 1859. But Spencer had used the terms "struggle for existence" and "survival of the fittest" in an essay called "The Theory of Population" and had discussed the principle of evolution in "The Development Hypothesis" as early as 1852. (So perhaps the theory of evolution *is*, after all, the product of a committee.)

As an evolution theorist, Herbert Spencer is both more and less important than Charles Darwin. He is less important than Darwin primarily because he did not have the evidence on which to base his theories, and Darwin, from his travels and studies, did. Spencer was not a scientist; in fact, he was not even formally educated. As involved as he was in the evolution mania of his time, Spencer did not read *On the Origin of Species* upon its 1859 publication or, apparently, at any time later (Durant 269). He was not much of a reader at all and freely admitted that he was "a bad observer of humanity in the concrete, being too much given to wandering into the abstract" (*Autobiography* 461). In general, he liked to articulate theories and leave others to their examination and verification; he worked deductively, while Darwin worked inductively, and the inductive method makes for sounder science.

But as an influence on late 19th-century literature, Spencer is more important than Darwin, largely because he conceived the theory as operating on a much larger scale than the strictly biological. In 1858, while collecting and revising his earlier essays for publication, Spencer realized, according to historian Will Durant, that "the theory of evolution might be applied in every science as well as in biology; that it could explain not only species and genera but planets and strata, social and political history, [and] moral and esthetic conceptions" (272–73). He subsequently undertook an attempt at synthesizing evolution theory with every discipline of human knowledge. The codification of that attempt, *Synthetic Philosophy*, occupied 10 volumes and took nearly 40 years. Along the way, he founded the modern science of sociology, a discipline whose perspectives are integral to Naturalism.

Spencer's prominence in late 19th-century philosophy stems from the comprehensiveness and clarity of his ideas. Will Durant has called him "the clearest expositor of complex subjects that modern history can show; he wrote of difficult problems in terms so lucid that for a generation all the world was interested in philosophy" (271). A good example is his definition of evolution: in *First Principles*, Spencer identifies evolution as the process whereby "matter passes from an indefinite, incoherent homogeneity to a definite, coherent heterogeneity" (367). Just as America was named for Amerigo Vespucci because Vespucci made a map showing territories whose

discovery was claimed by others, Spencer came to be regarded as the leading philosopher of his age because he was able to clarify and synthesize the
ideas of important naturalists and scientists working at the time (Durant
268). In Durant's words, Spencer "summed up his age as no man had ever
summed up any age since Dante" (299).

The natural science of Darwin and the philosophy of Spencer were the
strongest influences on literary Naturalism, but certainly not the only ones.
From Spencer and Isaac Newton's work in physics, the concept of determinism acquired mechanical implications. Philosopher and historian
Hippolyte Taine theorized that hereditary, environmental, and historical
factors could account for the artistic products not only of an individual
but also of an entire culture, thus turning determinism in a decidedly literary direction. Philosopher Arthur Schopenhauer pronounced the notion
of free will an illusion, concluding that the human will is subject to the
unconscious forces of the natural world, while, closer to the turn of the century, Sigmund Freud suggested that man's will is driven by his own subcon-
scious. Karl Marx and Friedrich Engels' work contributed questions about
economic inevitabilities that influenced the naturalists' preoccupation
with socioeconomic status. The work of all these men formed the scientific, philosophical, historical, psychological, and economic underpinnings
of American literary Naturalism; each writer worked by his own recipe, but
the ingredients varied little.

In 1880, Emile Zola attempted to graft the dominant scientific and
philosophical ideas of his age onto the writing of fiction; he published *Le
roman éxpérimental,* widely regarded as "the most influential statement
ever made of the theory of Naturalism" (Holman 302). Zola claimed that
he could substitute "novelist" for "scientist" in Claude Bernard's "Introduction à l'Étude de la Médecine Éxpérimentale" and thus produce a theory of the novelist's method. Like the scientist, Zola says, the novelist puts
an experimental subject (a character) into a situation in which certain
forces are brought to bear upon him or her and then observes the effects
of those forces; Zola called this process "provoked observation" ("Novel"
271). For Zola, the forces in question are beyond the control of the subject;
the forces, in other words, *determine* the subject's behavior. He wrote that
"determinism dominates everything; ... there is an absolute determinism
for all human phenomena" ("Novel" 277). Finally, he defined "the experimental novelist" as

> one who accepts proven facts, who points out in man and in society the mechanism
> of the phenomena over which science is mistress, and who does not interpose his per-
> sonal sentiments, except in the phenomena whose determinism is not yet settled, and
> who tries to test, as much as he can, this personal sentiment ... by observation and
> experiment ["Novel" 288–89].

Zola's earliest attempt to put that method into practice is his novel *Thérèse Raquin* (1867), which covers the entire life of its titular character, including an arranged marriage to her hypochondriac cousin, Camille; Thérèse's affair and subsequent marriage with Camille's friend, Laurent; Thérèse and Laurent's murder of Camille in a boating incident; their subsequent feelings of guilt and loss of passion; their caretaking of Camille's mother, Madame Raquin, who is paralyzed by a series of strokes but increasingly aware of Thérèse's and Laurent's guilt; and their eventual joint suicide in Madame Raquin's presence. Zola wrote that his aim was "to study temperaments and not characters" (Preface). Zola's principle series, *Les Rougon-Macquart*, comprises 20 volumes written between 1871 and 1893; it is subtitled the "natural and social history of a family under the second Empire." His interest in the scientific method led him to insist on the accuracy of what Tom Wolfe would later call "status details," adding a documentary-like quality to such works as *Germinal*, a novel about the French mining community, which Zola researched through first-hand experience. The Frenchman's fundamental notion was that the Naturalist "strives to be objective, even documentary, in his presentation of material" (Ellmann 304). Thus, the roots of the emphasis on factuality that intensified with the New Journalism are part and parcel of Naturalism.

As with the American Naturalists of the first wave, Zola's emphasis on realistic detail came partially from his early work as a journalist. According to F.W.J. Hemmings in "Zola's Apprenticeship to Journalism," the Frenchman spent approximately the first 16 years of his writing career (1864–1881) working on fiction while also publishing a weekly column in one newspaper and two columns weekly in another. Over that time, Zola wrote for at least eight newspapers in all; quite phenomenally, during that same period, he wrote 14 of his 31 novels, including *Thérèse Raquin* in 1867 and *L'Assomoir* in 1877, as well as some theoretical works, including *Le roman Expérimental* in 1880 (343, 340). Early on, the journalism consisted mainly of reviews, and he made very clear that his motivation was to earn money and make his name known. Looking back on this work, Zola viewed it as commercial and was resentful of the time it took from writing fiction. He also felt that he was writing for a mostly unsophisticated audience and that journalism restricted him from the expansion of ideas (342). For the last five or six years of his career as a journalist, he turned primarily to political writing, which he considered more valuable, but even then, his work "needed to conform with the line favored by the editor and management" (Hemmings 342).

But there were benefits for Zola from his apprenticeship in journalism besides the fact that it fed him, whether he recognized them or not. His biographer Hemmings notes that writing opinion suited Zola's temperament, and journalism generally "taught him versatility in the handling of materials" (343). It is clear that Zola himself knew he had gained discipline from this apprenticeship; in middle age, when he had achieved some affluence, he was proud of this work and enthusiastically recommended journalism as a training-ground in a speech to younger writers on the day of his retirement from it:

> Throw yourself into the press at the loss of your body [i.e., completely], as one throws one's self into the water to learn to swim. It is the only manly school at this hour; it is there that one rubs shoulders with men and burnishes [i.e., improves] himself; it is still there, from the special point of view of the trade, that one can forge his style on the terrible anvil of the article on a day-to-day basis [qtd. Hemmings 343].[2]

Not the least of the benefits of journalism was that writing reviews brought Zola familiarity with the work of a great many other writers, which may have increased his sense of formulating literary and aesthetic theory that applied more broadly than to his own work. His sense of his own presence at the headwaters of a literary stream is clear; he wrote that "it [is] necessary, above all things else, to inspire [young writers] with the scientific spirit, and to initiate them into the ideas and the tendencies of modern science" ("Novel" 284–85). He called his prescription "Naturalism" and viewed it as "not a personal fantasy, but ... the intellectual movement of the century" ("Novel" 285).

When he began his career as a full-time writer of fiction, Zola tended to draw his "material" from the working and lower classes. In the series *Les Rougon-Macquart*, he attempted to present a panoramic view of working-class life in 19th-century France. The 20 volumes of the series documented the lives of various members of that culture: washerwomen and tavern keepers (*L'Assommoir*, 1877), miners (*Germinal*, 1885), farmers (*La Terre*, 1887), merchants (*La Ventre de Paris*, 1873), and soldiers (*La Débacle*, 1892), among others. Zola described his purpose in *L'Assommoir* as "to depict the inevitable downfall of a working-class family in the polluted atmosphere of our urban areas" (21). In his preliminary notes for *Germinal*, he described the problem he sought to address:

> I must start with all the woes and fatalities which weigh down on the miners.... The miner must be shown crushed, starving, a victim of ignorance, suffering with his children in a hell on earth...; he is simply overwhelmed by the social situation as it exists.... The worker is the victim of the facts of existence—capital, competition, industrial crime [qtd. in Tancock 5–6].

An important influence on Naturalism's tendency to focus on the working and lower classes—and on Zola—was the work of Edmond and Jules de Goncourt, who, in the preface to their novel *Germinie Lacerteaux*

(1864), wrote that the Naturalistic writer "sees the novel as a clinic specializing in the diseased conditions of the lower classes" (qtd. in Ellmann and Feidelson 231). They considered many of their works as much social documents as literature.

The brothers de Goncourt also had a rhetorical agenda: they wanted not only to describe accurately the lives of the lower classes but also to arouse sympathy for them. They viewed *Germinie Lacerteux* and *Soeur Philomene* as experiments intended to show whether "the tears that are shed in low life have the same power to cause tears to flow as the tears shed in high life" (qtd. in Ellmann and Feidelson 270). The purpose of the novel in general, they felt, was

> to disclose misery and suffering which it is not well for the fortunate people of Paris to forget, and to show to people of fashion what the Sisters of Charity have the courage to see for themselves, what the queens of old compelled their children to touch with their eyes in the hospitals: the visible, palpitating human suffering that teaches charity; to confirm the novel in the practice of that religion which the last century called by the vast and far-reaching name, *Humanity* [qtd. in Ellmann and Feidelson 270, emphasis theirs].

A fourth Frenchman to exercise a powerful influence on Naturalistic principles (and on Theodore Dreiser in particular) was Honoré de Balzac. Balzac's 91 work series *La comédie humaine* (1827–1847) proposed to examine late 17th- and early 18th-century French life from several perspectives, one of which was analytical (*Études analytiques*). Balzac thought of the works in the *Comédie humaine* series as studies, and social improvement was very much a part of his program. His interest in the effect of environmental forces on the individual established a foundation for the fuller treatment of that effect by subsequent writers, French and otherwise.

The Naturalism of Zola and his contemporaries quickly spread. The Anglo-Irish novelist George Moore became interested in the work of Zola, Balzac, and the brothers de Goncourt when, as a young man, he studied painting in Paris. When he returned to England in the early 1880s, he embarked on an attempt to transplant the English novel from a Victorian to a Naturalistic universe. His novel *A Mummer's Wife* (1885) is often called the first Naturalistic work in English. Two of the most prominent late 19th-century English novelists, Thomas Hardy and George Eliot, were also sympathetic to the Naturalistic mindset; Hardy's *Tess of the d'Urbervilles* (1891), with its ill-fated protagonist, is perhaps the best example of Naturalism in the English novel.

But the contagion of Naturalism moved farther westward, across the Atlantic, ultimately having a widespread influence on four late 19th-century American writers: Stephen Crane, Jack London, Frank Norris, and Theodore Dreiser. Crane's novella *Maggie: A Girl of the Streets* (privately issued 1893; published 1896), the story of a girl driven to prostitution and, eventually, death, by social and economic forces that oppress her, is generally considered the first expression of Naturalism in American literature. London's explorations of man's struggle to conquer the forces of the natural world include *The Call of the Wild* (1903), *The Sea-Wolf* (1904), and *White Fang* (1906).

Norris's *McTeague: A Story of San Francisco* (1899) and Dreiser's *An American Tragedy* (1925)—considered to be among their authors' best novels—both feature a central homicide. *McTeague* is the story of one man's inability to cope with the forces of capitalism. McTeague is a dentist through training rather than education and a big lummox of a man ("his mind was as his body, heavy slow to act, sluggish" [2]); he marries and eventually murders a woman whose inability to spend her lottery winnings ruins them both. The Erich von Stroheim film based on the novel is appropriately entitled *Greed*.

Dreiser's novel *An American Tragedy* (1925) tells the story of Clyde Griffiths, a young man from the lower social stratum whose desire for wealth and status propels him uncontrollably toward death—his girlfriend's and his own. The struggles of Griffiths and of Dreiser's earlier characters Caroline Meeber and George Hurstwood (*Sister Carrie*, 1900) effectively illustrate that "survival of the fittest" applies to humans as well as other species.

Because the United States was founded on the notion of individual liberties and freedom from the control of exterior forces, some critics have tended to see Naturalism as "foreign to American values and interests" (Pizer, *Nineteenth* 41). But the scientific and philosophical developments of the late 19th century are actually quite compatible with the social and economic changes taking place in the United States at the turn of the century. In *History of English Literature*, Hippolyte Taine identified three factors that "shape" the artist: "his race, with its inherited characteristics; the milieu in which he lives; and the moment of history when he appears" (qtd. Ellmann and Feidelson 230). It is worth noting that two of Taine's three factors— milieu and moment—are environmental, and even race and one's sense of racial identity are profoundly shaped by culture and beyond one's control.

The environment in which the early American Naturalists worked was characterized by flux and extremes. Change and expansion dominated: as large metropolitan areas became commercial centers, hundreds of thousands of Americans and immigrants hurried to them in search of economic improvement. When they arrived, they found the streets lit by electric lamps and populated by automobiles. They could eat food grown halfway across the country and shipped in on refrigerated boxcars via the transcontinental railroad, and if they missed the folks back home, they could send a telegram or use one of the 1,356,000 telephones available by the turn of the century (McMichael, "Age" 2). Economic growth was phenomenal. Having become more powerful during the Civil War, the federal government instituted a draft, issued national paper currency, and levied an income tax. It also encouraged capitalistic enterprises, and by 1900, the national income had quadrupled, and there were more than four thousand American millionaires (McMichael, "Age" 4). Industrialization had indeed revolutionized the United States.

But Mark Twain's appellation for the period—"the Gilded Age"—is a reminder that the opulence of the new millionaires was a façade propped up by the toil of countless Americans who were not nearly as affluent as the "captains of industry" whose empires workers were building with their own sweat. For every Vanderbilt, Rockefeller, or Carnegie, there were thousands of Caroline Meebers and Roberta Aldens hard at work in his industries, and thousands of young men like Clyde Griffiths eager to shine his shoes.[3] Between 1870 and 1890, the U.S. population doubled, but while the nation enjoyed prosperity, the people prospered disproportionately. The four thousand millionaires constituted only about six one-thousandths (.006) of one percent of the total population (about 70 million). Despite the Horatio Alger stereotype popular in the late 19th century, many Americans made the urban migration only to discover stiff competition for the most mundane jobs, which were increasingly being phased out by machines. For those who did not see their place in a more mechanical world, the outlook was bleak: in this increasingly industrialized world, poet Edwin Arlington Robinson's miller commits suicide, prompted by his awareness that "there are no millers anymore" ("The Mill" l. 5).

The population of large metropolitan areas became increasingly stratified; families like that of Clyde Griffiths' uncle or Clyde's object of desire, Sondra Finchley, might have seemed a different species from the Johnson family of Crane's *Maggie: A Girl of the Streets*, Irish Catholic immigrants in in the Bowery slums of New York City. The socioeconomic circumstances that Crane describes in *Maggie* and in his Bowery sketches existed in every large city; panhandling and prostitution rose even as the stock market surged, and large-scale urban poverty became a reality. Not surprisingly, the age of American social reform also began. The Salvation Army established a base in the United States in 1880, and Jane Addams established Hull House in Chicago in 1889 to help the city's impoverished residents.

In "Naturalism and the Languages of Determinism," Lee Clark Mitchell claims that during the Industrial Revolution, American society "displayed practices fully at odds with its republican ideals" (526–27). Indeed, it is easy to see how the nation's late 19th-century socioeconomic complexion could be more aptly described by Spencerian principles of natural selection than by Jeffersonian ideals. In *Free Will and Determinism in American Literature*, Perry Westbrook explains the American fascination with scientific theories based on struggle and dominance:

> The vogue of Spencer was immense, especially in America. This nation was then not yet beyond the frontier stage. Huge fortunes were to be had and were struggled for in a multitude of areas from politics to the production of oil, and political and economic freedoms were highly touted national institutions. This nation delightedly accepted a philosophy that saw competition as fundamental to social progress. Individualism was the password of the times [104–5].

For the "captains of industry," evolutionary theory was a great moral convenience; if capitalism exploited those on the lowest rungs of the socioeconomic ladder, Darwinian science permitted entrepreneurs to rationalize that their dominance was in the interest of society. The "selection" process had favored them, and the species as a whole would profit. Andrew Carnegie wrote in *The Gospel of Wealth* that the competition principle "is sometimes hard for the individual, [but] it is best for the race, because it insures survival of the fittest" (qtd. in Mitchell 528). "Survival of the fittest" became, for many, a religion; Westbrook observes, "To the financier who ruthlessly beat down all competitors in his own rise to the top, Darwin had more comforting words to say than did Jesus" (116).

Of course, these so-called "captains of industry" were an elite niche of late 19th-century American society, generally not the niche that attracted the Naturalistic writers of that age. While the American Realists Henry James, Edith Wharton, and William Dean Howells were writing about the middle and upper-middle classes, the American Naturalists increasingly turned their attention to those who were all too often excluded from the American dream, despite the fact that their labor in many cases fueled it. Applying the scientific approach advocated by Zola to the lives of characters who often found themselves on the losing end in Darwinian struggles, the Naturalists turned American literature in a new and sometimes disturbing direction.

3

First-Wave Naturalism
and the Homicide Novel,
1899–1925

> "Environment is a tremendous thing in the world and fre-
> quently shapes lives regardless. If one proves that theory,
> one makes room in Heaven for all sorts of souls (notably an
> occasional street girl) who are not confidently expected to
> be there by many excellent people."—Stephen Crane, note
> in Hamlin Garland's copy of *Maggie: A Girl of the Streets*

The American Naturalistic writers were all young men during "the
Gilded Age," which scholars say began around 1870 (Samuel). When Zola
published *Le roman experimental* in 1880, Frank Norris was 10 years old,
Theodore Dreiser and Stephen Crane were both nine, and Jack London
was only four. Biographically, these four men seem to have little in common. Crane was an Easterner, born in New Jersey; Dreiser, born in Indiana, was a Midwesterner; and London and Norris were both Westerners,
though Norris was born in Chicago. The economic separation was larger
than the geographic: Dreiser and London were born to families so poor
that the boys were probably lucky to have survived childhood, while Norris, whose father was a resourceful businessman (a jeweler), was raised in
an atmosphere of affluence and culture. Crane, whose father was a Methodist minister, grew up in a family with social standing but little money.

Norris was the most traditional student of the group, studying art in
Paris as a teenager, creative writing at Harvard, and literature (particularly
French) at the University of California. Dreiser, who had completed only
one year of high school, went to Indiana University through the generosity
of a benefactor but left after one extremely average year because he was
too anxious about not being accepted by girls and fraternities. Crane, a
bright enough boy to go from first to third grade in about six weeks, was
unsuccessful—due to lack of motivation, not ability—at a series of private

schools. For one year, he attended Syracuse University, where he seems to have majored in girls, fraternities, and baseball. And London, who dropped out of grammar school at 14 to support his family after his adoptive father was injured and who wanted to go to college probably more than the other three future writers combined, entered the University of California as a non-traditional student at 19 but had to quit at the end of one semester, again to support his family.

All four men were well acquainted with the prevailing scientific and philosophical thought of the time, having largely educated themselves through reading. But their primary influences where Naturalism is concerned were very different. Dreiser was most profoundly influenced by Spencer; his biographer, W.A. Swanberg, says that Dreiser "never entirely outlived [the] dismay" he experienced in the face of Spencer's theories (61). Dreiser himself said, "[Reading Spencer's *First Principles*] nearly killed me … took every shred of belief away from me; showed me that I was a chemical atom in a whirl of unknown forces" (qtd. in Swanberg 60). His most important literary influence was Honoré de Balzac, whose novels Dreiser began to read as a young newspaperman in St. Louis on an editor's recommendation. Early in his reporting career, Dreiser learned "that he could hastily fake a harmless 'human interest' story, which was what his editors wanted, and could spend the valuable hours of the day in the public library, going through Balzac and Darwin" (Shapiro vi). He found in Balzac's novels "social implications that echoed his own fumbling observations" (Swanberg 56).

Norris was influenced primarily by Zola, whose work he studied at the University of California, where he was remembered by classmates "as often carrying copies of French editions of Zola's novels and always willing to give a passionate defense of that leading Naturalist" (Collins x). Norris would later give his wife one of his novels inscribed "from the boy Zola" (Frohock 12). Norris was more heavily indebted to Zola than was any other American Naturalist, and is thus generally considered to be "the link between our local Naturalism and one of the great exponents of the French variety" (Frohock 9). Norris was also affected by Romantic influences, predominantly Kipling and the medieval romancers whom he read as a student in Paris (where he was busy imitating them). Norris's peculiar blend of two leading 19th-century literary movements—Romanticism and Naturalism—is an underdeveloped vein in Norris scholarship.

Perhaps because of his own impoverished background, London was taken by the ideas of Darwin and Spencer; as Charles Child Walcutt has suggested, London saw the "struggle for existence" as a powerful factor in his own life. The poverty of his first two decades also drew London to the economic theories of Karl Marx, and several critics have suggested that

London's success in overcoming the poverty of his youth must have seemed to him a confirmation not only of Spencer's notion of "survival of the fittest" but also of Friedrich Nietzsche's theory of the Superman (Walcutt 5–6).

Crane claimed that he read nothing (Mitchell 525), a statement that is almost certainly an exaggeration, as Crane's work bears the definite stamp of late 19th-century science and philosophy. Nevertheless, he remains the most individual of the four, in his thought as in his art. Edwin Cady has noted that, surrounded by the turn-of-the-century conglomeration of ideas, Crane was "more fluid than any scheme could show...; [he] was fated to be a Seeker after the secret of his own vision" (79).

Confronted with these differences, a reader might begin to feel that the four writers' historical synchronicity was their only common denominator, an observation that Lee Clark Mitchell has described:

> Unlike their counterparts abroad ... [the American Naturalists] lacked any sense of common purpose that might have made them a self-conscious "school." Few of them knew each other's work[;] none persevered in the mode throughout his career, and those who theorized, did so badly. On first glance, in fact, the American [N]aturalists seem to have had little more in common than their historical context [525].

But the tendency to see these writers as linked primarily by the chance of having been born in the same decade, or even by the philosophy that their epoch so conveniently illustrated, is a drastic oversimplification, one that denies Naturalistic fiction any aesthetic or formal dimensions and ultimately reduces it to little more than literature written during roughly the same historical period.

Despite their disparate backgrounds, the Naturalistic writers created works similar in three important aspects: journalistic, formal, and philosophical. The journalistic element represents a borrowing from and enhancing upon the Realistic tradition's insistence on accuracy of detail and verisimilitude; in the Naturalistic novel, this accuracy borders on the documentary and is more often than not the result of thorough research. The formal similarity concerns the protagonist of the novel. The Naturalistic novelist selects for his Zolaesque "experiment" a subject who is common or average. This represents a departure from the Realistic tradition, wherein protagonists may be "common," such as Huck Finn, but are more likely middle or upper-middle class, for example, Isabel Archer, Silas Lapham, or Daisy Miller. Characters in Realistic fiction may also change their socioeconomic status (as Silas Lapham does), a change rarer in Naturalistic fiction; Dreiser's title character Carrie's rise to some status and comfort in *Sister Carrie* is atypical for the mode. Finally, Naturalism is also permeated by the deterministic philosophy that is sometimes mistaken as its sole defining characteristic. This is a second movement away from the Realistic tradition, as Realistic characters generally have control over their actions and destinies. Daisy Miller, for example, has control over her decision to flaunt the social codes of Europe in acts such as walking in the streets at night with young men below her station; Isabel Archer is bound by her affection for Pansy but not by any forces beyond her control in her decision to return to Gilbert Osmond, and Silas Lapham makes a conscious choice in his refusal to sell his business to an English syndicate.

These three aspects—a journalistic insistence on accuracy, the protagonist of lower social standing, and the deterministic outlook—will continue to be present in works of the "second round" of writers influenced by Naturalism (see Chapter 4). Particularly as they are demonstrated in Norris's *McTeague* and Dreiser's *An American Tragedy*, they constitute the base of the branch along which the contemporary nonfiction homicide novel later grew.

Most of the American Naturalistic writers either began as journalists or had extensive experience as reporters and editors. Mitchell writes, "Contributing as well to the emergence of Naturalism was the curious vocational fact that neither before nor since have so many American authors been journalists first" (528–29).

Crane worked about five years in the 1890s as a freelance journalist in New York City (largely for the New York *Herald*), during which time he wrote many sketches of Bowery and slum life. For those sketches, he studied the habits and attitudes of New York's downtrodden. As it was the Nelly Bly era of American journalism, Crane on one occasion actually impersonated a wino for 24 hours to understand how the prosperous residents of the city interacted with the less fortunate; the result of that 24-hour experience was the sketch "An Experiment in Misery." Crane's observations of the Bowery and its residents also figured prominently in *Maggie* as well as *George's Mother*. In addition, his journalistic experience included reporting from the American Southwest and Cuba (most notably the experience that inspired his short story "The Open Boat"). Even though he had no previous war experience, after the publication of *The Red Badge of Courage*, he was sent to Greece to cover its 1897 war with Turkey and to Mexico to cover the Spanish-American War in 1898 for Joseph Pulitzer's newspapers. Crane, whose brother Townley managed a New Jersey news bureau, got an early start in journalism, writing his first news releases at 16, and continued in it on and off throughout his short life.

Early in his career, Dreiser worked as a journalist at the St. Louis *Globe-Democrat* and *Republic*, the Chicago *Daily Globe* (for which he covered the 1892 Democratic national convention), the Pittsburgh *Dispatch*, and the New York *World* and *Daily News*. His experience as a reporter included all the basic "beats"—meetings, fires, courts, accidents, social gatherings, etc. After the 1900 publication of *Sister Carrie*, Dreiser worked as an editor at several publications, including some of the so-called "ladies'" magazines. He worked continuously in journalism until about 1911, when the publication of *Jennie Gerhardt* sufficiently established him as a fiction writer that he did not need additional income. Even after that, he worked sporadically as a reporter and editor, including a stint as a founding editor of *The American Spectator* and a continued close association with reporter, editor, and linguist H.L. Mencken (of the *Baltimore Sun*), whom Dreiser considered his mentor. Donald Pizer has estimated that the "full record of Dreiser's newspaper stories would make a work exceeding 2,300 pages" (*Nineteenth* 151).

London's forays into newspaper writing took the form of what would now be called feature writing. He wrote sketches based on his own adventures and travels, including a serialized account in the Hearst newspapers of his 1894 journey on foot from Oakland to Washington, D.C., with about two thousand out-of-work men to protest unemployment. The book that resulted from that serialization, *The Road*, has been called "the first major work on tramping in American literature" (Sinclair 20). Like Crane, London had experience as a war correspondent; in 1904, he accepted an offer from the Hearst organization to report the conflict developing in Korea between Russia and Japan, and he had offers from three other news agencies as well (Sinclair 102); he covered the Mexican Revolution for *Collier's* magazine in 1911. London shared Crane's interest in slum life, and, like Crane, he also used the immersive fact-gathering methods associated with Nelly Bly, occasionally working in disguise. In 1902, in England on his way to South Africa to cover the Boer War for the Associated Press, the writer learned that the war had ended and turned his attention instead to the London slums. In addition to countless interviews and guided tours with slum residents, he spent two nights in a Whitechapel workhouse and stood in line for breakfast at the Salvation Army, where he was indignant to have to endure a lengthy sermon before being fed (Sinclair 88); his research in the city led to *The People of the Abyss*, which London later said was "the book he loved the most" because "no other book had taken so much of his young heart and tears" (Sinclair 89). London was the only one of the four major Naturalistic figures with experience in sportswriting. He covered numerous prizefights, usually for the Hearst newspapers, and his accounts often turned into books such as *The Game* and *The Abysmal Brute*. Sinclair notes that London "made prizefighting the subject of his best journalism" and that subsequent writers including Ernest Hemingway and Norman Mailer are indebted to his pioneering in the macho tradition (248). Prize fighting is a particularly apt metaphor for "survival of the fittest."

Norris began contributing to various campus publications as a student at the University of California and, at about the same time, began writing for several San Francisco newspapers and magazines, including *The Wave*, a magazine with which he had a long association, publishing about 120 pieces (Kwiat 109n). He wrote travel sketches from South Africa in 1895–96 for the San Francisco *Chronicle* and covered the Boer War for *Collier's* and the Spanish-American War for *McClure's*. Later, as an editorial reader at the Doubleday publishing house, he called to the attention of his superiors the manuscript of Dreiser's novel *Sister Carrie*. It is also interesting to note that some of Norris's characters are young journalists: Strelitz, in the short story "His Sister," and Condy, the largely autobiographical hero of *Blix*.

The boom of the 1890s did not exclude the American news industry. Although a handful of newspapers were already well established (including the New York *Evening Post*, founded in 1801, and *Times*, founded in 1851), the 1880s and '90s saw a growth in the newspaper business that has never been equaled. According to Shelley Fisher Fishkin's *From Fact to Fiction*, a study of how journalistic experience influenced the work of Whitman, Twain, Dreiser, Hemingway, and Dos Passos, the number of daily newspapers in the United States was six times greater in 1900 than it had been in the 1860s. Fishkin calls the last two decades of the 19th century "the Age of the Reporter" and accounts for "reporters' growing sense of their own importance" by several factors: increased individual recognition via use of by-lines, better salaries, and a significantly improved market due to improved literacy and general population growth (87).

The 1890s also saw the emergence of the great news agencies: the Associated Press (AP) and United Press (UP), both founded in 1892, and the International News Service (INS), founded in 1906 by William Randolph Hearst (which merged with UP in 1958 to become United Press International). The establishment of these international news organizations, combined with the international circulation of the *New York Times* (a late 19th-century development), drastically improved the job market and travel opportunities for American writers. The emergence of numerous "little magazines" such as *The Wave* had a similar effect.

As Joseph Kwiat has pointed out in "The Newspaper Experience: Crane, Norris, and Dreiser," one of the prime benefits of reporting for the Naturalists was its training in "the ability to see ... [and] to observe" (101). The observer's perspective is intrinsic to Naturalism as Zola conceived it; following Claude Bernard's guidelines for experimental science, Zola believes that the novelist should set up his literary "experiment" and then

> disappear, or rather transform himself instantly into an observer, and it is not until after he has ascertained the absolute results of the experiment, like that of an ordinary observation, that his mind comes back to reasoning, comparing, and judging whether

the experimental hypothesis is verified or invalidated by these same results [Bernard qtd. in Ellmann 273].

Of course, a writer drawing material entirely from the imagination cannot logically participate in such an experiment; the writer cannot be said merely to "observe" what happens to characters when he or she is the primary force in determining their actions. But when authors transplant characters from their real experience—when Crane, for example, "borrows" Maggie and the trappings of her environment from his observation in the New York Bowery—and their fortunes are based on what the writer has actually observed in the lives of people like them, then Zola's task for the writer is feasible.

Zola's criticism of Romantic literature was harsh. He believed that when writers imposed their "personal authority" on literature, reading became a process of "taking little recreations in the world of lies." Instead of their own imaginations or other literary sources, writers should draw material from the world around them, "recogniz[ing] no authority but that of facts" (qtd. in Ellmann 285–86). He wrote, "The experimental method alone can bring the novel out of the atmosphere of lies and errors in which it is plunged. All my literary life has been controlled by this conviction" (qtd. in Ellmann 284).

The Naturalists' experience as reporters made this credo of "no authority but the facts" possible. Just as Zola spent hours learning the vocabulary and idiom of the working-class French miners, laundresses, prostitutes, and others for novels such as *Germinal* (1885) and *l'Assommoir* (1877), Crane, Dreiser, Norris, and London spent countless hours in the laboratory of the streets, watching experiments that they had not set into motion and documenting the "results." Because the newspapers employing these men were located in large, urban areas, many of the most important works of the first American Naturalistic time period are city novels and novellas: *Maggie* (1893, set in New York), *Sister Carrie* (1900, Chicago), *An American Tragedy* (1925, Kansas City, Chicago, and "Lycurgus," New York), and *McTeague* (1899, subtitled "A Story of San Francisco"). London, who in his gold-mining, seal-hunting, and tramping expeditions was reporting from a different front, is a notable exception.

The journalistic experience of the Naturalists also accounts for the copiousness of detail for which their works have been repeatedly praised. The journalist's eye, by habit, notices virtually everything in its view and has more opportunity for viewing than the eye of the more secluded writer. Zola's description of the washhouse in *l'Assommoir* is nearly photographic:

The washhouse was about half way up the street, just where the road began to go uphill. A flat-roofed building was surmounted by three enormous tanks, big grey

galvanized cylinders heavily studded with rivets, while behind them rose the dry-
ing-room, which formed a lofty second storey [sic], enclosed on all sides by nar-
row-slatted shutters through which the air could blow, and you could see washing
drying on lines of brass wire. To the right of the tanks the narrow exhaust pipe of the
engine coughed out jets of white steam with a harsh, regular beat [33].

Dreiser's description of Clyde Griffiths' first impression of the Green-Da-
vidson Hotel in Kansas City in *An American Tragedy* is similarly detailed;
a reader can only surmise that it reflects Dreiser's own wonder at the ambi-
ance of big-city finery:

[A]fter hours, instead of going directly home, he walked north to the corner of 14th
and Baltimore, where stood this great hotel, and looked at it. There, at midnight even,
before each of the three principal entrances—one facing each of three streets—was a
doorman in a long maroon coat with many buttons and a high-rimmed and long-
visored maroon cap. And inside, behind looped and fluted French silk curtains, were
the still blazing lights, the à la carte dining room and the American grille in the basement near one corner still open. And about them were many taxis and cars. And there
was music always—from somewhere [36].

Irving Howe has written that Dreiser's books are "crowded with exact
observation" (817). Many of the Naturalistic writers were so faithful to the
geography of the cities they wrote about that a reader with a fairly accurate,
contemporaneous map of certain neighborhoods and districts could have
traced characters' routes. The Norton Critical Edition of *Maggie* comes complete with a three-page map of lower Manhattan in the 1890s labeled "New
York City Locales Mentioned in *Maggie*" (62–64). One is reminded of the
meticulousness with which another author influenced by Naturalism, Dostoevsky, detailed Raskolnikov's movements through St. Petersburg in *Crime
and Punishment*. Although the fairly common critical view of Naturalism as
merely an extension or exaggeration of Realism is a risky oversimplification,
it is true in the sense that the Naturalists carried to new degrees the Realists' insistence on verisimilitude; if the Realists sought to paint scenes which
approximated reality, the Naturalists sought to reproduce photographic like-
nesses, a tendency which came from their experience as reporters.

Another benefit of the news boom was that it provided writers with a
steady supply of potential material. When Jack London was accused in 1906
of plagiarizing in one of his Alaska tales, he defended himself by claiming
that both he and the writers he was alleged to have copied had drawn on
the same newspaper sources. London argued that because "his style transformed journalism into literature," there was no substantive plagiarism
(Sinclair 132). News was in wider circulation than ever before, and London
and his peers scoured newspapers and magazines for interesting tidbits and
kept files and journals for later use.

In fact, just such a method inspired two of the most significant novels of Naturalism's first wave, *McTeague* and *An American Tragedy*. Norris's novel was "suggested by [October 1893 San Francisco *Examiner*] newspaper accounts of a particularly squalid murder in a poor section of San Francisco" (Frohock, *Norris* 10). Collins notes that while Norris was a University of California student, he had begun "to record details of life in the poorer section of San Francisco" (x). Already thoroughly familiar with the city as a long-time resident, Norris did not need further research to aid in his description of life in a working-class neighborhood there. He did visit the mining regions of the Sierras when he was working on the last section of the novel, in an attempt to narrate accurately McTeague's flight through those geographic areas after Trina's murder.

The murder that "suggested" *McTeague* to Norris actually took place in a kindergarten, as does McTeague's murder of Trina in the novel's climax (Pizer, *Nineteenth* 13); in fact, the address of the kindergarten in *McTeague* is the same as that of the actual kindergarten that Norris's mother founded and supported (Pizer, "Genesis" 296). Norris's use of specific San Francisco locales, particularly the commercial district of Polk Street, is heavily documented, and his use of that milieu is the subject of at least two dissertations. The Norton Critical Edition of *McTeague* includes two of the original San Francisco *Examiner* articles and three articles about the textual background of the novel.

For *An American Tragedy*, Dreiser was heavily indebted to both research and primary sources. It is a matter of established record that Dreiser modeled Roberta Alden's death on Chester Gillette's 1905 murder of Grace Brown, who at the time was six months pregnant with Gillette's child. Dreiser had been following murder cases since 1891 and keeping clippings, with the idea of writing a book. When Dreiser was a young reporter for the St. Louis *Globe-Democrat*, he was assigned to write about a 1900 case in which a young man had poisoned his girlfriend with candy. This was the first of many cases to illustrate a pattern that intrigued Dreiser: "a young man … murders his pregnant sweetheart because he has met a richer and more beautiful woman in the meantime" (Lehan 143). In other words, the young man had felt the allure of the American dream. For the poisoning case, Dreiser wrote seven chapters of a novel before abandoning the project (Schechter). Lehan and Swanberg document over a dozen similar crimes occurring between 1891 and 1907 with which Dreiser was familiar, some of which he had reported himself (Lehan 143; Swanberg 253). This pattern interested Dreiser, illustrating how young men could be led to transgressions less by innate moral principles or propensity toward violence and more by a combination of sexual desire and social ambition, a motivation which the novelist saw as "a recurrent and bloody indictment of the nation's false standards" (Swanberg 253).

In the early 1920s, when Dreiser was writing *An American Tragedy*, he took several steps to assure the novel's accuracy. As Donald Pizer has stressed, Dreiser drew extensively on *the New York World* accounts of the case (*Nineteenth* 52)—so extensively that John F. Castle, who devoted his dissertation to tracing Dreiser's sources, makes clear that the novelist could not have defended himself against a plagiarism charge. Among Castle's conclusions are the observations that about 190 pages of Dreiser's 814-page novel "closely parallel the original materials" and that about 220 pages "appear to be direct extensions or expansions of facts or allegations which appear in the documents." More damaging is his contention that Dreiser "either carelessly or purposely transferred to *An American Tragedy* about two thousand words verbatim" (qtd. in Algeo 41). The issue of whether Dreiser also used the actual court transcripts from Chester Gillette's trial is unresolved. Philip Gerber maintains that he did (79), but Ann Algeo, drawing heavily on the work of others (such as Castle) who have traced Dreiser's sources, says there is no record of a response to Dreiser's request for access to the transcript (13). If he did not see it, this impediment would certainly account for his heavy reliance on newspaper accounts.

Whether or not he saw the official court record, though, Dreiser did attempt to put himself in Chester Gillette's shoes. In June 1923, he and his wife Helen toured the area around Cortland, New York, where Chester Gillette and Grace Brown had lived. They inspected the factories and tree-lined avenues of Cortland, drove to see the rural farm where Brown had grown up, visited the lodge where Gillette had sequestered himself after the murder, talked with a boat attendant who showed him where Brown's body had been found, and rowed a boat to the middle of Big Moose Lake, to the approximate spot where the murder had occurred (Swanberg 277; Gerber 79–80). Describing the visit in her memoirs, Helen Dreiser remembered feeling concern that her husband was so caught up in the experience that he might even attempt to re-enact the crime (*My Life* 85). Two years later, writing the section about Clyde's imprisonment and execution, Dreiser, through the intervention of H.L. Mencken, visited the Auburn penitentiary, where Chester Gillette had been put to death 19 years earlier.

Another important source for Dreiser was the collection of letters from Grace Brown to Gillette, and these became the models for Roberta's written pleadings with Clyde (Salzman viii). In Dreiser's novel, some of Brown's letters are reprinted unmodified except for name changes (Algeo 26), a fact which lends credence to the notion that Dreiser suffered little guilt about borrowing others' words. This borrowing is substantiated by Ann Algeo in *The Courtroom as Forum: Homicide Trials by Dreiser, Wright, Capote, and Mailer* (1996), as well as by Donald Pizer in the Modern Critical Interpretations edition of *An American Tragedy*. For example, the letter written to Clyde by Roberta in Chapter 45 and containing the threat of exposing him if he does not contact her by the deadline she specifies is identical in substance and very similar in wording to a letter written by Grace Brown to Chester Gillette in the summer of 1906.[1] During Clyde's trial, District Attorney Orville Mason reads aloud excerpts from Roberta's letters in order to convince the jury of Roberta's expectation that Clyde planned to marry her. These excerpts are the last evidence presented by Mason, who cries while reading them. Pizer writes that Dreiser "mixed verbatim quotations, loose paraphrase, and new material—yet maintained the emotional texture of alternating pleading and recrimination, and hope and fear, of the original letters" ("An American Tragedy" 66–67).

A more original area of Dreiser's work involves his description of Clyde's motivation. The section in which the defendant describes Roberta's drowning is Dreiser's imagining of events based on primary sources, as "no information about what happened in the boat appeared in the evidence presented at trial in the Gillette case" (Lingeman 245). To shape his understanding of Clyde's motivation, Dreiser, living in Manhattan while drafting the novel, visited two prominent New York psychiatrists to discuss homicide from a psychological standpoint. In late 1923 and early 1924, when he was writing about the trial, he consulted two attorney friends who shared his office building about legal authenticity. This example illustrates a portion of homicide narratives where the imagination of the author often must step in, as, in most cases, reassembling the sequence of events that constitute the murder act itself is difficult, even for modern forensic experts.

Perhaps the strongest example of "the power of the press" in *An American Tragedy* is the fact that the idea for Roberta's "accidental" drowning occurs to Clyde when he reads about a similar case in the newspaper. Clyde's attention was drawn ("Because of his great interest in canoeing," Dreiser writes) to the front page of the *Albany Times-Union*, bearing the headline, "ACCIDENTAL DOUBLE TRAGEDY AT PASS LAKE—UPTURNED CANOE AND FLOATING HATS REVEAL PROBABLE LOSS OF TWO LIVES AT RESORT NEAR PITTSFIELD—UNIDENTIFIED BODY OF GIRL RECOVERED—THAT OF COMPANION STILL MISSING" (*An American Tragedy*, 438). In his slow-witted way, Clyde realizes a few pages later that "if only such an accident could occur to him and Roberta," then he could have the "glorious future" he covets (440). It seems perfectly apt that a novel inspired by newspaper accounts of actual crimes should feature as its central incident a crime suggested to its perpetrator by a newspaper article. Appropriately, when Clyde's mother cannot afford to travel East for his sentencing, she gets a Denver newspaper to hire her to cover the event.

A major contribution of late 19th-century journalists was their documentation and detailed exploration of urban poverty. One notable example is *How the Other Half Lives*, published by Danish immigrant Jacob Riis, a photojournalist for the *New York Tribune* and *Evening Sun*. In 1892, Riis followed up with *The Children of the Poor*. Riis, whose work was later praised by President Theodore Roosevelt, was probably the first American writer to treat urban poverty in a book-length study. The slum captured the imagination of many American thinkers and writers in the 1890s, partially because it was a new concept in the United States. W.E.B. DuBois, who would go on to found the National Association for the Advancement of Colored People (NAACP) in 1910, studied the living conditions of black residents of Philadelphia's Seventh Ward. After more than five thousand field interviews, in 1898 DuBois published *The Philadelphia Negro*, "the first study of the effect of urban life on blacks" (Divine et al. 560). Interestingly, many of DuBois's observations were strikingly Naturalistic; his conclusion about the causes of crime (a particular interest) was that it "stemmed not from inborn degeneracy but from the environment in which blacks lived. Change the environment, and people would change, too" (Divine et al. 560).

The Naturalistic writers saw in the increasing stratification of American society an effective illustration of Darwinian and Spencerian principles. Consequently, they drew their protagonists disproportionately from the lower echelons. It does not seem an exaggeration to say that in many Naturalistic works, the higher class, respectable people are merely the ones who have regular jobs. A central part of Pizer's definition of Naturalism in *Realism and Naturalism in Nineteenth-Century American Literature* is the contention that "the [N]aturalist populates his novel primarily from the lower middle class or the lower class. His characters are the poor, the uneducated, the unsophisticated" (10–11). Examples are not hard to supply: Maggie Johnson (and her whole family and community), Caroline Meeber, Clyde Griffiths, McTeague (who is not even given a first name), Henry Fleming, Wolf Larsen.

With the novella *Maggie: A Girl of the Streets*, which the author published at his own expense in 1893 after commercial firms rejected it as too coarse, Stephen Crane opened a new social milieu to American writers. Perry Westbrook has called *Maggie* "the first self-consciously naturalistic piece of extended fiction in American literature" (132–33). Crane dealt perhaps more frankly than any American writer before him with alcoholism, abuse within a family, premarital sex, and prostitution; the degradation of the Johnson family prompts one neighbor to ask Maggie's brother Jimmy, "eh, Gawd, child, what is it dis time? Is yer fader beatin' yer mudder, or yer mudder beatin' yer fader?" (10). It is little wonder that many editors and some critics considered the work offensive to public sensibilities.

Largely because of Crane's dealing with these issues, *Maggie* is considered by more than a few critics to be "the novel which first clearly differentiated the American from the English novel tradition" (Magill 54).

An American Tragedy and *McTeague* comprise the genesis of the homicide novel subgenre in American Naturalistic literature, and both feature protagonists who fit the Naturalistic socioeconomic prescription. McTeague's father was a miner who was "for thirteen days of each fortnight ... a steady, hard-working shift-boss" but who became on his day off "an irresponsible animal, a beast, a brute, crazy with alcohol" (2). McTeague's mother, her imagination fired by a traveling "charlatan" who passed through the mine camp, chose dentistry as her son's career and left him a little money upon her death to begin setting up his "Parlors." So he becomes a dentist, by training (apprenticeship) rather than by education. He establishes a practice in a San Francisco shop where he works as a pseudo-dentist (without training) and where "his only pleasures ... [were] to eat, to smoke, to sleep, and to play upon his concertina," for which he knows six tunes (1).

The extent of McTeague's ambition is "to have projecting from that corner window a huge gilded tooth, a molar with enormous prongs, something gorgeous and attractive" (3).

He inhabits a world of small shops and practitioners: bars, butchers, drug stores, restaurants, barber shops, stationers' stores, etc. Polk Street is lively but tedious and monotonous; in fact, the opening paragraph of the novel presents McTeague as a creature of *habit*: "It was Sunday, and, according to his custom on that day," he has lunch at a cheap restaurant and picks up his filled beer pitcher on the way home at a neighboring saloon.

Despite his wife's good fortune in winning a $5,000 lottery jackpot, McTeague's socioeconomic situation never really changes—another characteristic of the Naturalistic protagonist. Trina is so miserly that she will not buy butter for the bread, though she doesn't know why she is saving. The author attributes her parsimony to genetics:

> A good deal of peasant blood still ran undiluted in her veins, and she had all the instinct of a hardy and penurious mountain race—the instinct which saves without any thought, without idea of consequence—saving for the sake of saving, hoarding without knowing why [99].

Trina is like a squirrel, storing up nuts with a vague notion of needing them someday. When her family requests $50 to save them from financial disaster, she wonders why they can't be "a little more economical"; upon her mother's second appeal, she convinces McTeague that they might send the family $25 together and even then withholds her $12.50, reminding herself that her family is asking for a sum which represents two months' interest

(183–84). "It's mine! It's mine! It's mine!" she thunders repeatedly, "her teeth clicking like the snap of a closing purse" (152). Her stinginess draws her further inside herself and away from her husband, whose resentment and frustration eventually drive him to murder her in the cloakroom of a kindergarten where she works as a cleaning lady for minimal pay that she would not even need if she could administer her lottery winnings sensibly.

Clyde Griffiths' case also illustrates the failure of the Naturalistic protagonist to significantly improve his or her social standing, even when favorable opportunities present themselves. Born to a family of street evangelists with a father known as "old Praise-the-Lord Griffiths," Clyde learned early that his family had not received an ample share of "the Lord's blessings":

> the family was always "hard up," never very well clothed, and deprived of many comforts and pleasures which seemed common enough to others. And his father and mother were constantly proclaiming the love and mercy and care of God for him and for all. Plainly there was something wrong somewhere [9].

Although Clyde does not suffer the physically abusive atmosphere of *Maggie*, Dreiser's novel is even more explicit about sexual matters, including abortion. (Dreiser is generally the most sexually explicit of the first-wave American Naturalists.) After his girlfriend Roberta Alden becomes pregnant, Clyde procures several medicines thought to be abortifacients, none of which works. In an earlier episode, Clyde's mother helps his unmarried sister Esta through her pregnancy and lover's abandonment, all without the moralistic father's knowledge. Not surprisingly, Dreiser's frankness about sexual matters in *An American Tragedy* earned him a major censorship trial (in Boston). One of the novel's courtroom defenders was Clarence Darrow, who would later figure prominently in the Leopold-Loeb case in Chicago, the basis for Meyer Levin's novel *Compulsion*. Pizer has said that one of the most modern aspects of the Naturalistic novel is its rejection of "the 'great lie' of nineteenth-century fiction—the convention that insofar as literary art is concerned relations between the sexes consist either of high romantic love or the minor rituals of middle-class courtship and marriage" (*Twentieth* 5). Dreiser certainly rejects this "lie."

Like *McTeague*, Griffiths does not seem to be able to improve his position significantly even when presented with the opportunity to do so. Although he progresses, over the duration of the novel from his job as a bellhop in a large hotel to a supervisory position in his uncle's factory, he is clearly operating in a culture to which he is an outsider. His situation illustrates the isolation often suffered by the person who tries to change social class, suggesting the impossibility of social mobility. Although Clyde's uncle is good enough to invite the young man to Lycurgus and to employ him, the uncle's attitude is largely charitable, not that of a mentor taking on a protégé. Clyde is "quite good looking and well-mannered too," and he looks remarkably like Samuel Griffiths' son Gilbert, so the elder Griffiths is moved to "do a little something for him—give him a chance to show what he could do, at least" (156–57). However, sensing Gilbert's fear of displacement, the father is quick to add that the family need not treat Clyde as a social equal:

> he wouldn't be coming [to Lycurgus] with any notion that he was to be placed on an equal footing with any of us. That would be silly. Later on, if he proves that he is really worth wile [sic], able to take care of himself, knows his place and keeps it, and any of you wanted to show him any little attention, well, then it will be time enough to see, but not before then [158–59].

As his Griffiths relatives make up their minds not to include Clyde in their "set," Clyde is also strictly forbidden (by his cousin Gilbert) from fraternizing with the young women who work at the factory. Thus Clyde's dilemma: the Lycurgus Griffiths expect him to conduct himself as a member of their class (so as not to embarrass the family) but deny him the privileges associated with that status and, simultaneously, frown on his associating too closely with the workers, particularly women. This leaves Clyde with an extremely limited social circle.

Another aspect of Clyde's dilemma is the fact that other people seem as confused as he about his status. While Gilbert is conducting him through the factory on his initial tour, Clyde encounters a worker named Whiggam, a man who has made slight advances toward authority and who impresses Clyde with his ability to adjust his behavior toward other employees depending on their position relative to his own. Whiggam is respectful almost to the point of genuflection with Gilbert, the heir apparent, but somewhat condescending toward the workers who lack his seniority. As Clyde and Whiggam move farther from the administrative offices into the bowels of the factory, Clyde notes that his companion gradually raises his eyes and addresses people more "directly" and "authoritatively" (186). Whiggam has clearly acclimated to the corporate evolutionary chain.

Clyde, on the other hand, never masters the concept of status-appropriate behavior, largely because he and others are confused about his status. After his initial visit to the factory, having encountered the evidence of his uncle's wealth and position, Clyde feels both fortunate and unfortunate. Leaving the factory, he "congratulated himself on being connected with this great company," while at the same time feeling slighted that his uncle did not receive him in person. Whiggam's behavior is a balancing act which Clyde never learns to achieve, largely because the younger man is confused as to where he begins: workers like Whiggam, aware that Clyde is a Griffiths, address him as "Mr. Griffiths," even when he is working on the lowest rung of the company ladder, in a veritable sweatshop where collar material is steamed and shrunk. But the members of the Griffiths family treat him like nobody, waiting months after his arrival before inviting him to their house, and then only for a brief introduction, not for any real social activity.

When Clyde does finally begin to receive social invitations, the sender's motives are not genuine. Sondra Finchley takes an interest in him because he looks like Gilbert, and she sees a way to make other young men jealous. Later, as Clyde shows up at more and more parties with Sondra because she develops affection for him, inviting him begins to be "the thing to do." And even when Clyde is on the verge of being accepted in the Griffiths' circle and they are forced to begin inviting him themselves, the problem of Roberta's pregnancy threatens his hopes of social improvement. In fact, thanks to Dreiser's counterpointing of the Roberta plot and the Sondra plot, when Clyde is arrested, he is simultaneously as close to being somebody and as close to being nobody as he has ever been in his life. He effectively illustrates Donald Pizer's contention that Naturalistic novels are generally "about people who seem to be going nowhere" (*Nineteenth* 40); in Clyde's case, he is "going nowhere" because he is taking steps forward and backward at the same time. Dreiser's working title for the novel, *Mirage*, reflects this lack of real movement.

Perry Westbrook has noted that because Naturalism shares with Realism the aim of verisimilitude and because most people fall within the realm of "the dull general average," the common protagonist is consistent with the Naturalists' goals; "since mediocrity is the lot of most mankind," Westbrook declares, "the naturalist must concern himself with mediocrity" (143). Crane's *The Red Badge of Courage*, Westbrook notes, is about not a heroic officer but "the common private soldier" (143); "The Open Boat" is about characters so typical that, except for one (Billie, the oiler), they do not even have individual names (and Billie has a very common one). Crane's choice for Maggie's family of the second or third most popular surname in the United States—Johnson—is not coincidental. Similarly, *McTeague* and *An American Tragedy* focus on characters who, except for a single sensational act, might never have been distinguishable from anybody else in their milieu.

The third central aspect of Naturalism—and the one most frequently used in isolation to define it—is the presence of a deterministic philosophy. Basically, determinism is the belief that a person's actions are caused or determined by something other than his or her will. Those factors might be biological, psychological, sociological, or historical. Perry Westbrook offers a more formal definition; he says that determinism is the doctrine that all occurrences in the universe are governed by inexorable laws of cause and effect. Since human activities, whether of the body or the mind, are subject to these same laws as part of the universal order, *determinism* is more narrowly used to denote absence of freedom in our volitions and choices [ix].

It is central to determinism that these forces influencing human fortunes are outside a person's control. According to philosopher James Downey, determinism does not preclude the possibility of limited control over one's volitions and actions, but that control is very minimal and may be an illusion.

Determinism is so central a part of the Naturalistic formula that, as Westbrook has suggested, the terms *determinism* and *Naturalism* are almost synonymous (133). While this is something of an overstatement, the deterministic aspect of the Naturalistic novel is more integral to its identity than the influence of journalism or the social class of the protagonist. Mitchell offers a "negative test" for the Naturalistic novel: "any sure evidence of effective choice, of free will or autonomous action, makes a novel something other than Naturalistic" (530). Between the publication of *Maggie* in 1893 and that of *An American Tragedy* in 1925, this question of agency alone can often be used to distinguish works in the vein of American Realism from those of American Naturalism.

This adherence to determinism is also part of the legacy of Emile Zola, who wrote, "Determinism dominates everything.... [T]here is an absolute determinism for all human phenomena" (qtd. in Ellmann 277). Zola believed that identifying determinants should be the goal of modern science:

> The end of all experimental method, the boundary of all scientific research, consists in finding the relations which unite a phenomenon of any kind to its nearest cause, or, in other words, in determining the conditions necessary for the manifestation of this phenomenon. Experimental science has no necessity to worry itself about the "why" of things; it simply explains the "how" [qtd. in Ellmann 271–72].

The Naturalistic novelist, to use Zola's analogy, places a character in a situation and brings certain environmental and genetic forces to act on him or her. The narrative thus becomes the explanation of what consequences would inevitably follow, given these forces and the factor of chance that generally does not favor the Naturalistic protagonist.

In *Maggie*, Crane demonstrates the natural result of a young girl's growing up in an atmosphere of alcohol, abuse, and parental neglect with two brothers who are even more susceptible to the effects of that environment than she: despite her attempts to protect her brothers and to create a more stable environment for herself (which the possibility of a relationship with Pete suggests), she becomes a prostitute and, eventually, throws herself into the river or is thrown, depending on the reader's interpretation of the story's conclusion. Crane wrote in Hamlin Garland's first copy of *Maggie* that the novella "tries to show that environment is a tremendous thing in the world and frequently shapes lives regardless" (Katz 1).

The forces acting on Clyde Griffiths are both genetic and environmental. Although Dreiser drew heavily on sources for Books II and III of *An American Tragedy*, Book I is the product of his imagination (and, one might argue, his experience as a seeker of the good life and the son of religious zealots). Dreiser attempts in Book I to account for how a young man like Griffiths could end up on death row by manufacturing a past to go with the present of young men like Chester Gillette. Clyde's genetic legacy is described very early:

> Asa Griffiths, the father, was one of those poorly integrated and correlated organisms, the product of an environment and a religious theory, but with no guiding or mental insight of his own, yet sensitive and therefore highly emotional and without any practical sense whatsoever.... [H]is wife was of a firmer texture but with scarcely any truer or more practical insight into anything [13–14].

And Dreiser is quick to note that this information is not important "save as it affected their boy" (14). As Pizer points out, Clyde has also inherited a religious temperament from his parents, although he rejects their particular beliefs. He "still worships as zealously as they—only he worships the worldly rather than the unworldly" (54–55). Pizer says that although Clyde still has the enthusiasm of his parents' belief, he also, unfortunately, has their naiveté (54–55). Additionally, Clyde shares his parents' lack of "practical insight." How different his fate might have been had he given some attention to avoiding pregnancy or told the truth about Roberta's death.

The environment in which Clyde finds himself and his urge to live like the people in the big houses on Wykeagy Avenue are the primary forces in his undoing. He is virtually overcome by economic forces: born with almost nothing, he sees in Sondra the opportunity to have everything. In fact, he has imagined a totally impractical "happily ever after" in which he marries Sondra and becomes an heir to the Finchley fortune; she is the personification, for him, of the American dream. Economic determinism is also apparent in Clyde's trial, as Sondra is able to keep her name out of the proceedings because her family has money. A secondary problem is Clyde's lack of patience or discernment: he wonders, for example, why he ever got involved with Roberta: "Just because of a few lonely evenings! Oh, why, why couldn't he have waited and then this other world would have opened up to him just the same. If only he could have waited!" (428). Of course, every reader knows that the answer to "Oh, why, why couldn't he have waited" is another biological drive—sex. Philip Gerber has commented that Dreiser's "detailing" of the pressures that affect Clyde prevents the novel from being "just another 'fictionalized' account of a sordid crime'" (82).

The central incident of *An American Tragedy*—the death of Roberta—is determined by a combination of all these factors and by chance. Although Clyde has thought and thought about killing Roberta in some sort of staged "accident" and clearly realizes the advantages of her death to himself, Roberta's plunge into the lake and the camera's and boat's striking her when they do happen are pure bad luck: she simply loses her balance in a shaky boat. Her death results from Clyde's vulnerability to the forces preying on him throughout the novel, represented by the "little voice" that speaks to him while Roberta is in the water. But chance plays a larger role than in this episode alone. In the form of an automobile accident, it drives Clyde from Kansas City to Chicago, where by chance he meets his uncle Samuel. That Roberta becomes pregnant involves more bad luck, and Clyde just happens to read the newspaper article about the murder which prompts his boat trip with Roberta.

That Dreiser did not believe in free will is abundantly documented. His subscription to Darwinian and Spencerian principles did not leave much room for the possibility that man fully determines the consequences of his own actions. When, toward the end of Dreiser's novel *Jennie Gerhardt*, Lester Kane tells Jennie, "all of us are more or less pawns. We're moved about like chessmen by circumstances over which we have no control" (401), he is speaking for Theodore Dreiser.

The determinants acting on McTeague are almost purely biological. Because of the impact of Darwin and Spencer, the American Naturalists tended to see man as "subject to the same laws as the rest of the organic and inorganic universe" (Pizer, *Nineteenth* 115). As Zola put it, "Science proves that the existing conditions of all phenomena are the same in living beings as in inanimate.... A like determinism will govern the stones of the roadway and the brain of man" (qtd. in Ellmann and Feidelson 276–77). The notion that the same biological and environmental determinants affect man and all other matter caused the Naturalists to see humans in more animalistic terms; that is to say, the writers tended to focus on man as subject to the same instincts and drives as organisms which in the traditional vitalistic scheme were thought of as "lower."

Norris's characterization of McTeague consistently places him somewhere between the human and the animal. Included in the initial description is the detail that McTeague's jaw is "salient, like that of the carnivora," that both his body and his mind are "heavy, slow to act, sluggish," and that "he suggested the draught horse, immensely strong, stupid, docile, obedient" (2–3). His movements are described as "bull-like" (3); answering Marcus, he "wags" his head (10); Marcus calls him a "lazy duck" (7); he sits gazing at Trina's pulled tooth in his palm with what Norris describes as "some strange elephantine sentiment" (20).

Early in the novel, when he is alone with Trina, who is anesthetized, McTeague begins to struggle consciously with his animal instincts:

> There in that cheap and shabby "Dental Parlor" a dreaded struggle began. It was the old battle, old as the world, wide as the world—the sudden panther leap of the animal, lips drawn, fangs aflash, hideous, monstrous, not to be resisted, and the simultaneous arousing of the other man, the better self that cries, "Down, down," without knowing why; that grips the monster; that fights to strangle it, to thrust it down and back [22].

With "the fury of a young bull in the heat of high summer," McTeague kissed Trina sloppily on the mouth, dissipating his lust somewhat, but Norris is quick to point out that the "dormant" beast, once aroused, will not be tamed: "From now on he would feel its presence continually; would feel it tugging at its chain, watching its opportunity" (23). Poor confused McTeague is left to wonder "Why he could not always love [Trina] purely, cleanly.... What was this perverse, vicious thing that lived within him, knitted to his flesh?" (23).

The "perverse, vicious thing" grows harder to ignore as Trina becomes more and more selfish. In the weeks before the murder, McTeague is like "a caged brute"; when he is drunk, he takes pleasure "in abusing and hurting [Trina]" (223). At one point, he even gnaws her fingers. He walks the streets, attempting "to fight the wolf away" (267). After the murder, McTeague becomes a pursued animal, possessing even a sort of "sixth sense" or "animal cunning" about his pursuers which often rouses him from sleep and drives him into the night (285). Searching for the mining region of his youth, he returns "[s]traight as a homing pigeon, and following a blind and unreasoned instinct" (281). His flight into Death Valley "through a primeval river bed" is virtually an evolutionary regression. Westbrook has called McTeague "a walking—or lumbering—embodiment of every atavistic trait a Darwinian could think up" (134–35). This characterization of man as beast is the strongest link in the literary evolution between Norris and Zola.

In *An American Tragedy*, after Clyde realizes that Roberta's death would free him from his entanglement, he suffers nightmares about being chased by "a savage black dog that was trying to bite him," then being lost in a jungle filled with snakes and other "menacing" reptiles, and finally having his path blocked by a gigantic "horned and savage animal" (442). On the day of Roberta's death, the strange cry of the "weird, unearthly" bird, sitting on its dead branch, sharpens Clyde's anxiety; he does not know whether the bird's cry is "a warning—a protest—a condemnation?" (490).

The use of animal imagery to reinforce the notion of humans as animals with a veneer of civilization is pervasive in *McTeague*. A central symbol is McTeague's little canary, whose cage represents McTeague's own entrapment by the forces—largely biological—which act on him; the canary is the only thing McTeague takes with him during his flight, and the final image in the novel is that of "the half-dead canary chittering feebly in its little gilt prison" (324). The canary is also part of McTeague's undoing, as a deputy pursuing him notes, "It isn't hard to follow a man who carries a bird cage with him wherever he goes" (286).

Besides the canary, one of McTeague's oldest possessions is a stone pug dog. McTeague's friend/adversary Marcus Schouler assists at an animal hospital and frequently appears with a dog on the end of a leash (yet another symbol of lack of freedom). The activity of the Polk Street butcher shop and its employees is frequently noted. When Trina takes up wood carving, she specializes in Noah's ark animals. Every time the cleaning woman, Maria, is asked her name, she inexplicably replies, "Maria—Miranda—Macapa. Had a flying squirrel an' let him go" (15). The reader collecting animal images can open *McTeague* to nearly any page; for example, on page 218, selected randomly, McTeague twice tells Trina that she'd "rather live in a rat hole" than give him a nickel. On page 183, also selected randomly, Trina and McTeague discuss Marcus's departure to work on a cattle ranch.

Animal imagery is central to both of the murders in the novel—Trina's and the earlier murder of Maria. After Trina finds Maria propped up with her throat cut ear to ear, she stumbles out into the street to encounter two images invoking slaughter: "a butcher's boy … getting into his two-wheeled cart" and "a peddler of wild game … coming down the street, a brace of ducks in his hand" (231). Before Trina's murder, McTeague walks the San Francisco streets, struggling "to fight the wolf away" (267). Trina's murder is witnessed by the kindergarten cat, and her body is found by two five-year-olds, one of whom is a butcher's daughter and declares that the cloakroom "'Tsmells like my pa's shop" (276).

The Naturalists' determinism resulted in a rhetorical orientation that placed them outside the social norm in several ways. First, they tended to reject traditional religion. In a world where events are determined by biological and environmental forces and by chance, God is vulnerable to displacement, which accounts for the protests against evolution that have persisted since the theory was originally articulated. Dreiser, for example, said that his faith was "blown to bits" by his reading of natural science (Swanberg 60). Kaplan has noted that "the vulnerability of the religious imagination" is a common theme in Naturalism. There is no better example than *An American Tragedy*, wherein Clyde as a young boy rejects the God his parents worship because he can't believe that a merciful God would let believers suffer as the Griffiths family does. Pizer has said, "The major characteristic of the form of the naturalistic novel is that it no longer reflects

… certainty about the value of experience but rather expresses a profound doubt or perplexity about what happens in the course of time" (*Nineteenth* 34). Such doubt is a direct consequence of the shift away from the belief that "God's in his heaven; all's right with the world."

The Naturalists also exhibited a previously unprecedented interest in criminals and criminal behavior, especially violent crime. Their writing about crime reflects a tendency to downplay or diffuse its moral implications and to emphasize instead the biological and sociological circumstances that can lead to criminal behavior. This resulted largely from their view that man's behavior is determined by deep-seated biological drives and impulses and their awareness that the capacity for violence is one of the closest links between man and the other animals. In "Vitalism and Redemptive Violence," Harold Kaplan calls this "[p]rimordial violence, 'the red animal,' [which] releases the most elemental and unsocialized passions and instincts" (96).

The crime beat was an aspect of daily life for many reporters in the 1890s, and Dreiser, in *A Book About Myself*, recalls getting together with other reporters to talk about particularly sensational crimes. This was a fairly common habit among urban reporters, and some turned their interest in the macabre into a more elaborate social opportunity: Fishkin describes a club formed in 1889 by reporters in the Chicago area called "the Whitechapel Club" after the lower-class area in London where Jack the Ripper had preyed on prostitutes in the late 1880s. Members met in a room "decorated … with a coffin-shaped table, murder weapons, and human skulls" (91). According to a 2016 feature about the club in *Chicago* magazine, "Jack the Ripper himself was named (absentee) president," and the walls of the club's chambers were adorned with weapons used in actual crimes, often obtained through law enforcement officials (Abramovich). The décor included artifacts from other violent incidents, including the Battle of Little Big Horn and the Chicago fire of 1871, as well as photographs such as those depicting the beheading of a group of Chinese pirates, before and after (Abramovich). The superintendent of a local asylum donated a collection of skulls, refitted with gas lighting contraptions that caused the eye sockets to glow. For refreshments, says Rebekah Abramovich, "goblets were fashioned from the skulls of local prostitutes—a special cup reserved for guests consisted of a skull lined entirely in silver, originally belonging to Waterford Jane, a well known figure of the local red-light district." Only two members of any given profession could belong to the Whitechapel club at the same time, although the membership of reporters was unlimited (perhaps because they had the most gruesome stories). A popular ritual for members involved sifting their fingers through the cremains of Morris Alan Collins, a Texas suicide club member who donated his body to the society;

society members conducted a ceremonial cremation that sounds a little like a Ku Klux Klan rally on the outskirts of the city. Though technically a secret society, the club was recognized by the state of Illinois, and future presidents Theodore Roosevelt and William McKinley were both guests. The same environment that generated interest in violent crime and criminals among educated professionals created a market for Naturalistic novels depicting homicide and other violent crimes.

Developments in criminology in the late 19th century also helped to create that market. In *McTeague*, Norris was heavily influenced by the work of criminologist Cesare Lombroso and consequently focused on the scientific, rather than the moral, causes of McTeague's behavior. Lombroso's book *L'Uomo delinquente* (*The Criminal Man*, 1876) is generally regarded as the first study in criminal anthropology. The book was translated into French in 1887, and although an English translation did not appear until 1911, Pizer documents that Lombroso's ideas were in circulation in the United States by the late 1880s (*Norris*, 189, n57) and acknowledges Norris's awareness of and debt to Lombroso's work, particularly for Norris's "depiction of man as beast" ("Frank"). In 1899, he published a second book, *Le Crime, Causes et Remèdes* (*Crime, Causes and Remedies*). Reflecting Darwin's influence, Lombroso viewed crime from an evolutionary perspective, believing that some individuals had "throwback" genetic traits predisposing them to criminal behavior and viewing these individuals as less evolved than those who lacked the traits. Lombroso identified certain "atavisms" that he declared present in those who commit criminal acts and varying for different crimes ("Cesare"). The criminal, he concluded, is "an atavistic being who produces in his person the ferocious instincts of primitive humanity and the inferior animals" (Simon).

Among those who studied crime, Lombroso's ideas were immediately contested, particularly his endorsement of anthropometry, the notion that criminals had physical defects that were readily apparent, even measurable. For example, he sought to categorize prison inmates based on measurements such as the lengths of their skulls. Unfortunately, some attempted to use this pseudoscience to explain racial and ethnic differences before more sophisticated techniques such as genetics emerged. As Matt Simon writes, "Lombroso took Darwin's recently published theory of evolution and added a horrifying twist that would reverberate for decades," particularly in "the towering whirlwind of racism that accompanied his hypothesis." Ultimately, anthropometry proved to be more useful to historical anthropologists studying human evolution than to sociologists.

Despite the eventual perception of Lombroso's work as "fantastically wrong," his theories were immediately applied to fiction by Emile Zola, whose novel *La Bête Humaine* was subsequently critiqued by Lombroso from a sociological perspective (Simon). When Frank Norris read in the San Francisco papers of the Collins murder which inspired *McTeague*, he immediately recognized its illustration of themes he was encountering in Zola's novels. Lombroso's work presumed that criminal traits were "atavisms" or throwbacks to previous evolutionary stages. Pizer writes that in Norris's characterization of McTeague, the novelist "adheres closely" to Lombroso's view that criminals bear the "stigmata" of "atavistic regression" ("Frank"). Thus, McTeague acquires primitive dimensions, and the reader comes to feel that his criminality is the result of biological inheritance and his economic circumstances rather than of sheer immorality.

This view of the criminal as to some extent victimized by his own biology contributed to perhaps the most controversial aspect of Naturalistic fiction: the writer's attempt to mitigate the subject's culpability by inviting the reader to understand and even sympathize with him. A traditional philosophical position holds that the concept of morality exists only so far as men are free to choose their behavior; both Thomas Aquinas and Aristotle, for example, believed that "any meaningful concept of moral responsibility must be based on the assumption that a choice between good and evil actions is possible; and such choice can exist only where the will is free" (Westbrook 1). Thus, in a world governed by biological and environmental forces, such a choice is not feasible, and the concept of moral culpability is moot. As Westbrook points out, this is a revision of Calvinistic determinism, as, in a Calvinistic universe, we deserve punishment for our sins, regardless of why we commit them (7).

McTeague and *An American Tragedy* mark the real commencement of the murderer-as-victim tradition in American literature. Both McTeague and Griffiths are the victims of biological and economic forces beyond their control; ultimately, neither man can overcome what his biology and environment have made of him. When, *in An American Tragedy*, the attorney Jephson describes the circumstances of the murder as a "case of being bewitched, by my poor boy—by beauty, love, wealth, by things that we sometimes think we want very, very much, and cannot ever have" (681), he could be speaking of either novel and for either author. He is describing the elusive American dream.

As much as Norris's novel deals with the central issues of the later nonfiction homicide novels, it is Dreiser who really cast the mold, particularly where creating sympathy for the protagonist is concerned. Dreiser's comprehensive examination of the circumstances that propel Clyde to want Roberta dead and then to allow her to drown is his primary means of arousing sympathy for him. In the weeks before Roberta's death, Dreiser portrays Clyde agonizing over merely entertaining such a notion, and the death scene itself does no serious damage to the reader's perception of Clyde; it is, as Gerber has pointed out, "neatly balanced between guilt and innocence" (86). It is Roberta, in fact, who sets the small boat into motion; noticing a strange expression on Clyde's face, she stands, unsteady in the rocking boat, reaches for his hand, and when he flings his arm forward ("not even then with intention to do anything other than free himself of her," the novelist writes), he strikes her in the face with the camera he has been holding by its strap, and, standing, capsizes the boat, which strikes Roberta again on the head (*An American Tragedy* 492–93). Roberta is stunned, Dreiser writes, by "the blow [Clyde] had so accidentally and all but unconsciously administered" (493). From that point, Clyde's culpability is inaction, not action: he simply does nothing, and Roberta, who cannot swim, drowns. Like Hurstwood's feelings in the safe-locking scene in *Sister Carrie*, Clyde's motives are sufficiently ambiguous that premeditation is not apparent. He suffers from what Perry Smith will later call "blood bubbles"—lack of resolve. During the trial, Dreiser adds to the sympathy for Clyde by referring to him in fictionalized newspaper accounts as "young Griffiths" and the "boy slayer," although he is 22 (620–22). He is so hapless a criminal that 127 witnesses testify against him (648). And despite all this, the circumstances of Roberta's death are such that, had Clyde been honest from the start of the investigation against him, he could likely have been convicted of a lesser homicide charge, especially if an attorney of Clarence Darrow's talent had defended him. It is easy to see how the great defense attorney's own statement of pure determinism would apply to Clyde Griffiths: "We are all poor, blind creatures bound hand and foot by the invisible chains of heredity and environment, doing pretty much what we have to do in a barbarous and cruel world. That's about all there is to any court case" (qtd. in Farrell). Darrow's great skill was, in the words of biographer John Farrell, to make the case about the defendant, not the crime.

Dreiser's novel establishes another theme which, though absent from Norris, is highly significant in subsequent novels based on real murder cases: the issue of capital punishment. Another of Dreiser's means of maintaining sympathy for Clyde in Book Three is emphasizing that his punishment is too harsh. Questions about the death penalty are raised in nearly every work in the homicide novel tradition, and in most it is opposed, partly because the Naturalistic novelists endorse a view that determinism mitigates a person's legal responsibility for his actions. The anti-capital punishment stance is as strong in *An American Tragedy* as in any subsequent work in the subgenre. Dreiser's concern with how young men like Chester Gillette ended up on trial for murder led him to create Book One of the novel, a section which H.L. Mencken, a staunch defender of the death penalty, thought "a great mistake" (Gerber 82). Chapter 29 of *An American Tragedy* is an extended description of "the death house," which Dreiser calls "one of those crass erections and maintenances of human insensitiveness and stupidity principally for which no one primarily was really responsible" (*An American Tragedy* 758). He describes the activity and effect of the death chamber in equally condemnatory tones:

> without anything worthy of the name of thinking on any one's part—there had been gathered and was now being enforced all that could possibly be imagined in the way of unnecessary and really unauthorized cruelty or stupid and destructive torture. And to the end that a man, once condemned by a jury, would be compelled to suffer not alone the death for which his sentence called, but a thousand before that [759].

Clyde endures long days spent contemplating the death house and the men around him who also have appointments with it. He constantly reminds himself that "there [is] a door. It [leads] to that chair. *That chair*" (758, emphasis Dreiser's). Clyde agonizes through the executions of each man to go before him. The effect on him of one such execution, that of Pasquale Cutrone, is described in extended fashion; during the entire procession and subsequent dimming of the prison lights, Clyde is "literally shivering with fear and horror" (771). He attempts to console himself with the knowledge that "this whole business of the death penalty was all wrong. The warden thought so.... He was working to have it abolished" (773).

Perhaps the most unpopular of the Naturalists' themes was the notion that society itself must share the blame for the crimes of men like McTeague and Clyde Griffiths. As Westbrook has said, *An American Tragedy* encourages the reader to question the concept of "individual responsibility in all murders, at least those perpetrated by amateur criminals" (149). This was not a role which society particularly wanted questioned. Not surprisingly, the censorship trials involving both *Sister Carrie* and *An American Tragedy* were based to a large extent on Dreiser's sympathetic treatment of both protagonists despite their transgressive behavior. If, as Ellmann and Feidelson say, the Realists were motivated by "aesthetic conscience," the obligation to depict life objectively or to be a "secretary to society," the Naturalists were motivated by social conscience and the Zola-inspired obligation to examine society under a microscope and to determine how it acted upon its constituents. Their portrayal is uniformly of man as a creature placed at a considerable disadvantage by biological and social factors who merits some sympathy as a result of his (or her) struggle against those forces.

Even after the publication of his *magnum opus*, Dreiser continued to be drawn to stories of young men like Chester Gillette. In October 1934, for example, he was present in the Luzerne County Courthouse in Wilkes-Barre, Pennsylvania, to cover the trial of Bobby Edwards for the *New York Post*. According to newspaper accounts, he was one of about 50 reporters present (Taylor). The 21-year-old Edwards was convicted of and eventually executed for the murder of 27-year-old Freda McKechnie, whose body was pulled from a nearby lake the morning after she went for a late swim with Edwards. The local coroner discovered two interesting facts: Miss McKechnie "had not drowned. She had died from a savage blow to the back of her head with a blunt instrument" (Taylor), and she was four months pregnant, by all accounts with Edwards' child. Edwards' motives fit the archetype: he had fallen in love with a more attractive, more accomplished woman from a middle-class family, a college graduate, music teacher, and performer, Margaret Crain. He wanted to marry Miss Crain; Miss McKechnie was an impediment, and the social milieu of 1934 Wilkes-Barre offered few escape routes, none without consequences. For Dreiser, the Edwards case was *An American Tragedy* all over again, differing only in minor details; despite their being no evidence that Edwards knew of the novel or the Gillette case, the novelist even wondered if his book had inspired the later crime (Taylor). Dreiser was drawn to both cases because he perceived the development of an American archetype, one characterized by Philip Gerber:

> Abstracted, the murders followed lines that might be predicted with near-scientific exactness, and their significance tallied rather well with Dreiser's own notions of an American society that had become materialist to the core, glittering with blandishments for the young and encouraging them to pursue "the dream of success" at all cost ["Society" 77].

"Such a crime," Dreiser wrote, "seemed to spring from the fact that almost every young person was possessed of an ingrowing ambition to be somebody financially and socially" (Taylor). By the time of Bobby Edwards' trial, Dreiser was 63 years old, and the sheer number of similar cases that he had observed over the course of his newspaper career caused him to doubt the concept of individual responsibility and to distribute the guilt for such an offense instead over a society that, in his mind, had come to resemble a Darwinian jungle.

In all such cases, Dreiser naturally sympathizes with social underdogs, as he was in many ways an underdog himself. Mitchell has pointed out that Dreiser was "the first major American novelist raised on the wrong side of the tracks ... the first Catholic, the first to hear a foreign language at home, the first whose family was impoverished and disreputable" (542). He was Clyde Griffiths' brother, just as, according to Ellen Moers' famous suggestion, he was "in every sense, the brother of Sister Carrie" (567). Donald Pizer has observed that this sympathy for the underdog, for the "poor" and "impotent" "mark[s] the entire range of [Dreiser's] fiction—and his life" (*Nineteenth* 152), but it really marks much more than that: it applies equally to all the Naturalistic writers, who held firm in their conviction that all human beings have inherent worth. Gerber says that this notion that "a reader, loathing Clyde's motives and his methods, can still understand and sympathize with the boy in his predicament" is "the great point" of *An American Tragedy* (85). And Crane wrote to Hamlin Garland in the *Maggie* inscription that if one accepts the theory of environmental influences, "one makes room in Heaven for all sorts of souls (notably an occasional street girl) who are not confidently expected to be there by many excellent people" (*Portable* 1).

Despite the pessimism often associated with Naturalism, the Naturalists also felt that society was improvable, a belief consistent with their more optimistic perception of evolution as progressing in a positive direction. At the conclusion of *An American Tragedy*, Dreiser points the way to the society in which young men like Clyde Griffiths will not want so much that they kill to get it: Clyde's nephew Russell is allowed by his grandmother to run to the corner for an ice cream cone. Mrs. Griffiths realizes that she "must be kind to him, more liberal with him, not restrain him too much ... for [Clyde's] sake" (814).

Zola insisted that the difference between determinism and fatalism was that determinism "considered the human condition to be alterable and improvable" (Ellmann and Feidelson 232), whereas fatalism did not. The role of literature in the Naturalistic scheme was to help facilitate this alteration, one which Dreiser, Norris, Crane, and London felt particularly necessary in light of America's late 19th-century growing pains. As Michael Millgate explains in *American Social Fiction*,

> American writers have repeatedly been worried, confused, or angered ... by the irreconcilability of American ideals and American experience, and one result of this sense of the gulf between the way things should be and the way things are, has been a readiness to regard the novel as a political instrument [196].

Perhaps no other period in American literature has elicited as much misunderstanding and negative criticism as the first wave of American literary Naturalism. Dreiser has been roundly criticized for his cumbersome, often awkward style,[2] and Norris, for his tendency toward melodrama. All of the Naturalists (with the possible exception of Crane) have been viewed by some critics as overly dogmatic, compromising their art in the service of their sermons. Their works have drawn fire from critics whose objections are quite obviously political, who do not share the writers' emotional attachment to lower-class figures, or who are troubled by the fact that nearly all the Naturalists flirted with Socialism or, in the case of Dreiser (the only one of the four to live long enough) with Communism. They have traditionally been viewed as somewhat pedestrian, largely because, for the most part, they were not intellectuals, not well educated (with the notable exception of Frank Norris), and sometimes inconsistent in their thinking. For example, their detractors like to point out that the concept of social reform is not consistent with a purely deterministic orientation.

A significant misunderstanding of American literary Naturalism is that its practitioners were in unanimous agreement with some aesthetic and philosophical prescription for the novel. Although many of the same winds blew upon the four early Naturalists, those winds tended to blow them in different directions, so that Crane's work takes on more impressionistic overtones; London's, more biological; and Dreiser's and Norris's, more economic and social. Neither is the period characterized by one particular kind of novel, as Pizer has pointed out. The writers produced quest novels, about protagonists such as Carrie and Henry Fleming who search for self-fulfillment; works in which individuals such as Maggie and McTeague are overwhelmed by socioeconomic forces; and novels about characters such as Clyde Griffiths who are failed by society (*Twentieth* 151–52).

Pizer's comment that Naturalism "has been one of the most persistent and vital strains in American fiction" (*Twentieth*, ix) is borne out by the Naturalists' contribution: the adaptation to fiction of the most revolutionary scientific and philosophical ideas with which any age has been presented. If their achievement is less magnificent than some critics would have hoped, perhaps that is due not only to their personal and artistic limitations but also to the enormity of their task. Regardless of the mixed critical estimation of their work, they cast a long and important shadow on 20th-century American literature.

4

Second-Wave Naturalism
and the Homicide Novel,
1930–1960

"After the Depression, with the entry of a new generation
into literature, we can observe another thematic change in
realistic American fiction. By and large, the plebian classes,
the lower class, and special groups of the American population were not centrally treated in American fiction before
the end of the Twenties. But suddenly we can observe the
change. It is mirrored in the racial backgrounds of writers,
in the themes, in the subjects, and in the conditions of life
which are treated. The orphan asylum, the streets of the city,
poolrooms, lower-class homes and family life, the backward
sections of America, such as parts of Georgia or the decaying
sections of New England, hobo life—all this is introduced
into the American novel…. A bottom-dog literature, in the
social sense, began to develop."—James T. Farrell, *Literature
and Morality*

Many critics and literary historians believe that after the 1925 publication of *An American Tragedy*, Naturalism went into remission. In "Naturalism and the Languages of Determinism," Lee Clark Mitchell writes that the
"particular constellation of influences at work on writers now thought of
as Naturalists disappeared with World War I," concluding that "the movement was … short-lived" (545). Richard Martin says that by the 1920s or
'30s, "literary naturalism of the sort practiced by London, Norris, and Dreiser … seemed to be played out" (210). As Pizer notes in *Twentieth-Century
American Literary Naturalism*, by the 1940s, critics as eminent as Malcolm
Cowley, Lionel Trilling, and Philip Rahv were heralding Naturalism's death
(85). In "Notes on the Decline of Naturalism" (1942), Rahv declared that
Naturalism had fallen into a state of "utter debility" and "lost its power to
cope with the ever-growing element of the problematical in modern life"

(589). In the early '40s, in essays later collected as *The Liberal Imagination* (1950), Trilling outlines what he sees as the causes of Naturalism's decline, and Cowley's "A Natural History of American Literary Naturalism," which appeared in 1947, reads like an obituary for the movement.

Evidence to support Naturalism's reported demise was not difficult to compile. In 1925, Jack London had been dead for nine years, Frank Norris for 23, and Stephen Crane for 25. Over the remaining 20 years of his long life, Dreiser published no more novels; the two remaining, *The Bulwark* and *The Stoic*, were published posthumously in 1946 and 1947, respectively. He wrote short stories, several collections of vignettes and of socio-political propaganda, and three or four autobiographical works, including *Newspaper Days*. By the late '30s, people were often surprised to learn that Dreiser was still alive.

Dreiser himself had reason to doubt the longevity of his achievement. Confident that *An American Tragedy* would win the 1926 Pulitzer Prize, the author was dismayed and somewhat surprised when Sinclair Lewis won instead, and declined, for *Arrowsmith*. When he and Lewis were finalists for the 1930 Nobel Prize, a recognition he had coveted since 1911, Dreiser sent an emissary to Europe to wage a publicity campaign on his behalf. American newspapers predicted that Dreiser would be chosen, but the Swedish Academy selected Lewis by a vote of two to one. Dreiser was, according to his biographer Swanberg, "bitterly disappointed" (368), and not just because the prize carried a cash award of over $46,000. Certainly Dreiser, realizing at 59 that his best work was behind him, yearned for the validation that being the first American writer named a Nobel laureate would have brought. His failure to win—especially on the heels of *An American Tragedy*'s publication—cemented his life-long perception of himself as an outsider. The whole episode was, in Swanberg's words, "a deep and lasting" wound (368). The selection of Lewis also implied to some that Realism had never been displaced as the dominant mode in American letters.

But the swan songs for Naturalism were premature. Most critics have tended to see the publication of *An American Tragedy* as the end merely of the first phase of American Naturalism, which might accurately be regarded as the major phase but is certainly not the only one.

Some critics have tended to see more than one stage in the early period itself. For example, in *The American Novel and Its Tradition* (1957), Richard Chase argues that Frank Norris was really the "father" of American Naturalism because of his familiarity with Zola and his conviction that Naturalism had distinctly Romantic elements, a conviction (and practice) which, according to Chase, established continuity with the Romantic tradition. Chase argues, for example, that "Norris's romance-novels succeeded in reclaiming for American fiction an imaginative profundity [present in the novels of Hawthorne and Melville] that the age of Howells was leaving out" (203). In Chase's view, Dreiser's work was a second stage; Chase groups Dreiser with other writers, including William Faulkner, who adapted the approaches of the early Naturalists to their own work (204). Robert Spiller and his colleagues in *Literary History of the United States* (1948) corroborate Chase's view, maintaining that upon the publication of *Jennie Gerhardt* in 1911 and the republication of *Sister Carrie* in 1912, Naturalism entered a second, more mature, phase and that the earlier phase had been "experimental" (1037).

Until the 1982 publication of Donald *Pizer's Twentieth-Century American Literary Naturalism*, there was no book-length study of American Naturalism focusing on the 20th century alone; the majority of full-length critical works have always tended to cover the period between *Maggie* and *An American Tragedy* (Pizer, *Twentieth* 156, n1 to "Preface"). Pizer sees two clearly distinct Naturalistic periods after the 1920s. The first, the 1930s, involves the novels, often called "proletarian" for their examination of working-class lives, of John Steinbeck, James T. Farrell, and John Dos Passos. When Pizer examines the tendency, begun with *An American Tragedy*, to focus on how man is limited by socioeconomic circumstances, his primary illustrations are as follows: Farrell's Studs Lonigan trilogy—*Young Lonigan* (1932), *The Young Manhood of Studs Lonigan* (1934), and *Judgment Day* (1935)—together comprising a life-long examination of an Irish-American in a depressed urban environment; Steinbeck's *The Grapes of Wrath* (1939), the story of the migratory Joad family's attempt to survive the Great Depression; and Dos Passos' *U.S.A.*, a collection of three novels (*The 42nd Parallel*, 1930; *1919*, 1932; and *The Big Money*, 1936), which "have as their protagonist the social background of the nation, and as their major theme the vitiation and degradation of character in a decaying civilization based on commercialism and exploitation" (Hart 209). Dos Passos' trilogy also uses several nonfiction, media-inspired techniques: a "Newsreel" comprised of "contemporary headlines, advertisements, popular songs, and newspaper articles" intended to establish atmosphere (Hart 209) and interwoven biographies of famous Americans. Farrell uses a technique similar to the "Newsreel" in the first Studs Lonigan book. Clearly, the Naturalistic writers of the 1930s were still borrowing from journalism.

Pizer points out that the Naturalism of this era "had its roots in the social conditions of the decade and in the intellectual and literary currents of the previous decade" (*Twentieth* 13). The social conditions were, of course, those of the Great Depression. The literary influences were the increasingly psychological approaches of writers such as James Joyce; Farrell, for example, makes extensive use of stream-of-consciousness in *Young Lonigan*, and Dos Passos and Steinbeck are both indebted to the epic tradition of which Joyce's *Ulysses* was the most successful recent example. The intellectual forces that operated upon the 1930s Naturalists were not Darwin and Spencer but Marx and Freud, in the work of whom the writers discovered their theme: "that life [specifically, economic conditions and biological drive] placed tragic limitations on individual freedom, growth, and happiness" (Pizer, *Twentieth* 13). The psychological and deterministic approaches found synthesis in Freud, who wrote in *A General Introduction to Psychoanalysis* (1920) that "there is within [man] a deeply rooted belief in psychic freedom and choice [which] is quite unscientific … and must give ground before the claims of a determinism which governs even mental life" (qtd. in Westbrook 112). Both Pizer and Tasker Witham have noted that Farrell, Dos Passos, and Steinbeck continued to imply the necessity for (and possibility of) social reform that Dreiser had advocated (Pizer, *Twentieth* 16; Witham 275); Pizer describes "the basic cast of the naturalistic novel of the 1930s" as "the diagnosis of an illness and the suggestion of a remedy" (*Twentieth* 16).

The post–World War II Naturalists of the late '40s and early '50s were less sure that improvement was possible. More heavily influenced by nihilism and existentialism, the writers of what Pizer sees as the third American Naturalistic period had new reasons to question man's ability to control his own destiny: the Holocaust, the atomic bomb, the Korean conflict, and McCarthyism. Pizer describes the impact on the writers of the 1940s and '50s of a world that seemed increasingly bent on mass destruction and denial of individual liberty:

> these events of the war years and post-war period offered massive evidence of the impotence of the informed will when confronted by the atavistic destructiveness of human nature and the vast, uncontrollable power of the social and political institution of modern life. The distinctive note of the age was not the hope implicit in tragedy but the chaos present in the struggle for survival and power [*Twentieth* 86].

In this environment, Pizer maintains, freedom "is not categorically denied but is rather submitted to a close scrutiny of its nature and efficacy in a world consisting largely of conditions which limit and qualify it" (*Twentieth* 88).

In discussing the Naturalism of the 1940s and '50s, Pizer focuses on three novels: *The Naked and the Dead* (1948) by Norman Mailer, *Lie Down in Darkness* (1951) by William Styron, and *The Adventures of Augie Marsh* (1953) by Saul Bellow. Pizer says that the early novels of Mailer, Styron, and Bellow exemplify "the third major expression of the American attempt to explore at moments of national stress through highly structured dramatizations of particular social moments the problem of man's belief in his freedom in an increasingly restrictive world" (*Twentieth* 89). Like Crane in *The Red Badge of Courage*, Mailer uses war (in this case, the Pacific theater of

World War II) as a metaphor for man's struggle to find meaning in his life, exploring American social stratification through its manifestation within the microcosm of one army platoon (for a more thorough discussion of Mailer's mature Naturalism, see Chapter 6).

Criticism of *Lie Down in Darkness* has focused primarily on Styron's tendency to echo Faulknerian themes of family disintegration and the loss of potential in the younger generation to mental incapacity or suicide. Pizer observes that "oddly neglected as a major approach … is its character as a naturalistic novel, and in particular as a novel in which the metaphor of a troubled journey through life is used to explore the naturalistic question of our responsibility for our fates" (*Twentieth* 116). Although the Loftises in their middle-class comfort do not fit the Naturalistic socioeconomic prescription, they act as though conditioned by social and psychological forces. Also significant, says Pizer, is Styron's tone of "naturalistic tragic compassion" (*Twentieth* 132).

Bellow's picaresquely entitled novel *The Adventures of Augie March* follows the search for self-fulfillment of the title character, a young Jewish man from Chicago. Pizer maintains that

> *Augie March* is about the "rough forces" of experience, about all that compels and conditions and shapes man, particularly the shaping power of other human wills. It is also about the darkness in nature, the nature of decay and death rather than of eternal renewal. And it is also about the human effort to maintain hope despite these realities, the hope which musters as much grace and wit as is possible in the face of the permanent and insoluble enigma of man's condition. *Augie March*, in short, for all its comic vibrancy, picaresque swiftness of movement, and larky prose is also a naturalistic novel of ideas [*Twentieth* 134].

Certainly all three of these novels illustrate Pizer's comment that the Naturalistic novels of the late '40s and early '50s increasingly focused on the failure of institutions and groups, the necessity of searching for meaning on an individual level, and the difficulty of finding any (*Twentieth* 87), all themes that reflect the encroachment of Modernism. Neither the army of *The Naked and the Dead* nor the Loftis family of *Lie Down in Darkness* could be considered a well-functioning unit. Augie March's family, like the Loftis family, is disintegrating: his mother is unable to support the family; one brother is mentally retarded; another brother marries for money, and Augie's grandmother dies. In at least two of these novels, the reader leaves the characters in a pretty bleak state: the surviving platoon members in Mailer's novel return from a dangerous mountain patrol to find that their efforts have had no bearing on the outcome of the battle for the island, and the Loftis family, having buried Peyton without finding a way to heal their emotional and psychological wounds, leaves the station on a train heading into darkness. Witham echoes Pizer's observation of the philosophical difference between the second round of Naturalists and the third (and his delineation of those separate periods) in his comment that in *An American Tragedy* and the proletarian novels of Steinbeck, Farrell, and Dos Passos, the Naturalistic writer "suggested a hope that the lot of man might be improved through ... control of his physical and social environment," whereas "[the Naturalistic novels] of the forties and fifties either painted a dark picture in which human happiness was largely a matter of chance ... or [those novels] sought for hope in specifically human values" (265). The continued optimism and humor of Augie March might be an example of those values.

During the 1930s, '40s, and '50s, another formulation of literary Naturalism continued to appear in American novels: the protagonist who, through a combination of biological and environmental factors, was driven to homicide. This formulation has not previously received critical attention as a subgenre of Naturalism. Four important examples exist, two from the second Naturalistic period and two from the third. Those from the earlier, more optimistic period are William Faulkner's *Light in August* (1932) and James M. Cain's *The Postman Always Rings Twice* (1934). The works from the later, darker 1940s and '50s are Richard Wright's *Native Son* (1940) and Meyer Levin's *Compulsion* (1955). All four novels focus on a protagonist who commits murder, and all four have some basis in fact. All four writers explore the question of how much free will the protagonist exercises, and, in every case, it is not much. Some variation exists from novel to novel: for example, *Compulsion* follows the facts of an actual case far more closely than the other three, and in *Postman* the deterministic element often seems to be pure chance, whereas in the other three the determinism is a complex of social, psychological, and historical circumstances. *Light in August* and *Native Son* are works very much within the literary mainstream, while *Postman* has had a more commercial reputation, and *Compulsion* is now somewhat obscure. But variation from author to author and work to work has always characterized Naturalism, in the United States and elsewhere. The point is that the literary influence of Norris and Dreiser continued to be present in significant examples during the 40 years between *An American Tragedy* (1925) and the resurgence of the archetype in 1965 in *In Cold Blood*.

Calvin in Mississippi: William Faulkner's Light in August

Upon *Light in August*'s publication in 1932, William Faulkner was acquiring a reputation as the author of violent novels. The rape and murder that are central incidents in *Sanctuary*, published the previous year, had caused a prejudice among readers that led some to condemn Faulkner as objectionable without even reading his books (Brickell 571). Upon *Sanctuary*'s publication, Henry Seidel Canby announced that Faulkner had joined the "cruel school" of fiction and become "a prime example of American sadism" (109). Certainly Faulkner's next novel, featuring the brutal murder of a white spinster by a man rumored to have black blood, a man who is himself later killed and castrated by a vigilante, did nothing to mitigate the "cruel school" image. Indeed, Michael Millgate says that reviews of *Light in August* indicate "the extent to which the violence and ... sensationalism of *Sanctuary* had come to dominate [critics'] sense of Faulkner as a novelist" (*New* 13).

Light in August is saturated with violent acts; reviewer Evan Shipman observed that the novel contains as much violence as an Elizabethan blood tragedy (300). The brutal, grotesque deaths of Joanna Burden and Joe Christmas constitute the violence of the novel's foreground—the 10 days that comprise the narrative present, from Lena Grove's arrival in Jefferson to her departure. These two acts are set against a background of other deaths, mostly violent, all in the past: Doc Hines (Joe's grandfather) murdered Joe's father and subsequently allowed his daughter Milly (Joe's mother) to die in childbirth; Colonel Sartoris killed Joanna Burden's grandfather and half-brother over a question of voting rights for African Americans; Gail Hightower's Confederate grandfather was shot raiding a chicken house; and Hightower's wife, driven to promiscuity and self-annihilation by her husband's withdrawal into the past, killed herself. Every major character except Lena Grove has a violent death somewhere in the family album, in a novel written by a man whose great-grandfather was himself both killer and victim: William Clark Falkner (1825–1889) killed at least two men during heated arguments, apparently in self-defense (Blotner 16–17) and was later murdered by a business associate (Blotner 47–48).

Like the subjects of the earlier Naturalistic homicide novels, the murder which is the central act of *Light in August* was not a product of Faulkner's imagination but derived from an actual homicide just outside Oxford on September 8, 1908. Nelse Patton, a black "trusty" from the county jail in Oxford, went to the home of Mrs. Mattie McMillan on an errand from Mrs. McMillan's husband, an inmate. When Mrs. McMillan apparently spurned his advances, Patton slit her throat with a razor. Arrested after a mob pursuit, Patton was killed the same night by a group of local men who broke into his cell. The men castrated Patton and hung his naked body from a tree in the public square. Details of the pursuit were readily available to 10-year-old Billy Falkner: 15-year-old John Cullen, the son of a Lafayette

County sheriff's deputy and brother of Faulkner's friend Hal Cullen, was involved in the pursuit and claimed to have fired squirrel shot through Patton after intercepting him in a thicket. John Cullen was also present later at the jail. Nelse Patton's crime is detailed in two standard Faulkner sources: Joseph Blotner's definitive *Faulkner: A Biography* (113–14) and *Old Times in the Faulkner Country*, a collaboration of John Cullen and Floyd C. Watkins. The Cullen-Watkins book contains a whole chapter about the Nelse Patton Affair, including selections of original newspaper articles about the case (89–98).

A second crime offered by Blotner as a potential source was the 1919 murder, again just outside Oxford, of a black woman by her husband, Leonard Burt. Burt was apprehended four months later and was shot to death in an escape attempt en route from the Oxford jail to the courthouse. Although Joe Christmas's crime ultimately resembles Nelse Patton's more closely than it resembles Burt's, Blotner points out two important details of the Burt case: first, Burt's wife's body was badly mutilated, reminding one of Joanna Burden, with her head so nearly severed that it faces a direction different from the rest of her body, and second, leaving the house, Burt had set a fire in an attempt to hide the murder (762–63).

Despite these two models, however, Faulkner did not focus *Light in August* on the murderer, Joe Christmas, right away. He insisted that the novel began in his imagination with "Lena Grove, the idea of the young girl with nothing, pregnant, determined to find her sweetheart" (Gwynn and Blotner 74) and that, at the outset, he knew "no more about it than a young woman, pregnant, walking along a strange country road" (qtd. in Blotner 703). But even if the image of Lena did cause the novel to crystallize in Faulkner's mind, she was not the first of the major characters to occur to Faulkner. Millgate maintains that University of Texas manuscripts confirm the primacy of the material about Gail Hightower (6–7), and, according to Blotner's account, Faulkner had been initially working on a novel to be called *Dark House* and had written and discarded two preliminary pages featuring Hightower. Blotner further demonstrates that the minister was a revision of an even earlier character, Dr. Gavin Blount, in a story called "Rose of Lebanon," which was rejected by *Scribner's* about a week before Faulkner began writing *Light in August* (700–1). Joe Christmas came along later than both Hightower and Lena, as Regina K. Fadiman confirms in her detailed textual study *Faulkner's Light in August: A Description and Interpretation of the Revisions* (33–34). But Christmas soon came to dominate the story in Faulkner's mind, as Blotner attests:

> As Faulkner worked his way further into the novel, Joe Christmas had taken an increasingly powerful hold upon his imagination. Lena Grove was still an important figure, but ... she had not remained both the generative figure and the central one. She

was [now] integrated into the Christmas plot … she served more and more as counterpoint for the obsessed and doomed Christmas [761].

Fadiman's conclusion that Faulkner added "late" the long flashback section which comprises the story of Joe's youth (chapters six through nine,
pages 111 to 206) indicates the writer's increasing concentration on his murderer (33–34). It was a creative act motivated by the same impulse that
led Dreiser, in inventing Book I of *An American Tragedy*, to give Clyde a
past which led up to the present Dreiser already knew from his nonfiction
models.

Drawing on the Patton and Burt cases, Faulkner supplied an original
motive for Joe Christmas's murder of Joanna Burden, and in doing so, he
created a drama of major deterministic proportions. Like Norris and Dreiser, Faulkner was interested in the circumstances that led his protagonist
to murder; in the case of *Light in August*, those factors are largely religious
and racial. Christmas is the victim of a society characterized by an absolutist Calvinism, illustrated in the novel by his grandfather, his "adoptive"
father Simon McEachern, and Joanna Burden and her ancestors. One great
virtue of the Calvinist system is simplicity, as it employs basic dichoto-
mies: good and evil, elect and damned, and heaven and hell. The Calvinist's
world is thus ordered and predictable, but it does not allow for gradations
of human behavior. The legacy of Calvinism for Christmas is that it causes
him to need to polarize experience and to agonize over anyone or anything
that does not fit neatly into a category.

Joe Christmas has also incorporated Calvinism's insistence on the
sober, dispassionate life. He cannot find pleasure in food, sex, or human
companionship, largely because of a formative experience at the orphanage where his grandfather left him. Five-year-old Joe has sneaked into the
dietitian's room to eat her sweet toothpaste when she returns with a doctor
and begins having sex. Concealed behind a curtain and increasingly upset
by his predicament and the "pinkwomansmell" of the dietitian's clothes,
the boy gulps down toothpaste until he vomits, at which point the dietitian
flings back the curtain and hurls at young Joe the double epithet "you little
nigger bastard!" (114). As a consequence of this unfortunate juxtaposition
of events, Joe develops a distaste for food, women, and sex which prevents
him from enjoying any of the three for the rest of his life. One might say
that his attitude toward and his appetite for food, women and sex are *determined* by the orphanage experience.

Finally, Joe is shaped by the Old Testament theology of Calvinism,
which holds that a person controls what happens to him: if he is obedient,
he is rewarded; if he is disobedient, he is punished. The utter predictabil-
ity of this system explains why Christmas stays with McEachern, whom he
hates, for 13 years; it is, as Robert Gibb has said, "an awfully easy code to

live by" (335): at least Joe always knows what to expect, and McEachern's fundamentalist attitude gives order to the boy's life. Only when McEachern becomes unpredictable, losing control of himself over Joe's liaison with Bobbie Allen, does Christmas finally leave.

Joe's negative attitude toward women is also colored by the fact that, from his perspective, they do not toe the Calvinist line as rigidly as men. After the orphanage episode, for example, Joe expects to be punished; when the dietitian gives him a silver dollar instead of a whipping, he is confused and loses more respect for her, because she has broken the rules he understands (116–17). Three years later, when Joe's refusal to learn his catechism has earned him a day of fasting imposed by McEachern, the boy is similarly confused—even outraged—when Mrs. McEachern brings him a tray of food; he throws the tray into the corner and, an hour later, eats from the floor like a dog, on his hands and knees, the posture he feels he deserves (144–46). Until Hightower's attempt to save him by inventing an alibi late in the novel, any mercy extended to Joe Christmas is always extended by women. That mercy, a New Testament concept, is foreign to Calvinistic doctrine. Thus, Joe is like Flannery O'Connor's Misfit in "A Good Man Is Hard to Find," for whom Jesus's teaching that God is merciful to sinners has "thrown everything off balance" (O'Connor 1957).

The social circumstances acting upon Faulkner's protagonist have an effect similar to the polarizing effect of Calvinism. In the orphanage at the age of five, Christmas is introduced to the possibility of his biraciality when his grandfather (the orphanage janitor) encourages the naive children to call Christmas "Nigger! Nigger!" and subsequently asks the five-year-old to consider why God made him "a nigger" (361–62). Confused by Hines' questions, Joe innocently asks a black gardener, "How come you are a nigger?" and draws a scathing and scarring response:

> "Who told you I am a nigger, you little white trash bastard?" and he says, "I aint a nigger," and the nigger says, "You are worse than that. You don't know what you are. And more than that, you wont never know. You'll live and you'll die and you wont never know," and he says "God aint no nigger," and the nigger says, "I reckon you ought to know what God is, because dont nobody but God know what you is" [363].

The frightening notion that no one but God knows who he is haunts Joe for the rest of his life. The question of Joe's racial heritage remains unanswered and unanswerable, as both his parents are dead. His grandfather has presumed that the child is black because, in Hines' dichotomized Calvinistic thinking, black is associated with evil and the child, as a bastard, must be evil (354). Once raised in Hines' consciousness, the possibility of Joe's blackness becomes a fact. Interestingly, a similar assumption characterized much early scholarship about the novel, as Millgate attests, with a surprising number of critics referring to Christmas as black or mulatto (*New* 18–19).

Not knowing his racial heritage devastates Joe Christmas. His tragedy, like Oedipus's, is a tragedy of identity (except that in *Light in August*, it is lack of knowledge rather than knowledge which destroys). When Joanna Burden asks him how he knows that one of his parents had black blood, Christmas, after a silence, responds, "I dont [sic] know it…. If I'm not, damned if I haven't wasted a lot of time" (240–41). Alexander Welsh says Christmas lacks what psychologist Erik Erickson's called "somebodyness" (124); indeed, in a culture polarized as black and white, the protagonist's ambiguous status leaves him feeling very much a nobody, a pariah, as Cleanth Brooks has argued ("Community"). Faulkner said that "the tragic, central idea of [Joe's] story is that he didn't know what he was, and there was no way possible in life for him to find out" (Blotner 762). Joe's murder of Joanna Burden is an attempt to exercise control, to forge an identity. Burden represents the forces that have haunted Christmas throughout his life: she is female; she encourages him to pray, just as McEachern had; and she insists, for the sake of what Blotner calls her "Negrophiliac" purposes, on seeing him as black, so that she can educate and "improve" him. Thus, by her murder, he seeks to kill the nobody she reminds him that he is. Like Richard Wright's Bigger Thomas, Christmas fills some hole in his psyche through the murder of the white Negro sympathizer, and thereby gains dimension (at least from his own point of view): he escapes into the natural world, of which he, unlike Lena Grove, has never been a part. After a few days there, he is no longer hungry, and feels "peaceful … cool, quiet" (316). He goes to meet his death at the appointed time, and, when Percy Grimm is pursuing him, Christmas does not fire his loaded pistol.

Ironically, the identity he achieves is a tragic one—the community perceives him as the black murderer of a white woman—and, in finally achieving a sense of somebody-ness, Christmas seals his own doom. He thinks he has free will, that he acts of his own volition and has finally reinstated the Calvinist balance (by committing the act which will bring the punishment), but Faulkner makes clear that he does not; instead, Joe's acts are determined by the religious and social conditioning he has experienced. Blotner says that "Faulkner presented Christmas in his maturity as thinking he acted out of something like free will, though his history made it clear that he had largely been shaped by his environment" (763–64).

The deterministic scope of *Light in August* extends beyond the protagonist to include every other major character, as scores of critics have confirmed. Perry Westbrook contends that "not one of [the characters in the novel] is a free agent in the sense of having the ability to break out of the fated groove of his will" (180). The factors that have determined the grooves of characters' wills are, in Faulkner's work, predominantly historical. As Frohock puts it, "out of [the] past come the obsessions and anxiety states of the characters which stand in the place of motives, determining their conduct" (*Violence* 154).

As Ilse Dusoir Lind and Edward Volpe have discussed extensively, Joanna Burden is, like Christmas, a victim of her Calvinistic past. Into her life has fallen the "shadow" of her family's attempt to help black Americans, an attempt which claimed the life of Joanna's grandfather and half brother Calvin, who were murdered, her father says, "not by one white man but by the curse which God put on a whole race before your grandfather or your brother or me or you were even thought of" (239). As a young woman, Joanna asks her father how she can "escape, get away from under the shadow," but he makes clear that there is no escape, and Joanna dies in her attempt "to raise the *shadow* with [her]" (240). In fact, the word *shadow* occurs four times in the paragraph in which Joe kills Joanna.

The minister Gail Hightower is also the product of his past and the victim of dichotomized perceptions: he cannot reconcile his grandfather's ignominious death in a chicken coop with his otherwise idealized portrait of that relative. Faulkner writes that the minister "grew to manhood among phantoms, and side by side with a ghost" (449). Hightower also suffered the misfortune of having been born to middle-aged parents not suited for parenting, an incommunicative father and bedridden mother, to whom he was not close. Volpe says Hightower is "not responsible for the conditions which make him afraid of life. He is a victim of the character and circumstances of his parents" (158).

Even Lena Grove is tainted by the Calvinism around her; for example, she believes that her reunion with Lucas Burch, the father of the child she is carrying, is foreordained. She tells Martha Armstid, "a family ought to be all together when a chap comes. Specially the first one. I reckon the Lord will see to that" (18). The early Naturalists (Dreiser in particular) would also have recognized the biological determinism of Lena's pregnancy. But Lena Grove is also the only character is *Light in August* who shapes her own destiny to any significant extent. Her actions in the novel's present are determined by the past, but the significant past actions were her own, not those of her forebearers: because she had sex with Lucas Burch and became pregnant, she must now inevitably seek him. It might be argued that Lena's course in the novel is determined at least as much by her *offspring* as by her ancestors.

Westbrook says that just as "the orthodox Christian ascribes the perverted will of man to the sin in the Garden of Eden, Faulkner relates the sorry plight of his doomed characters to family histories of violence and crime" (179)—and, one might add, illicit sex. *Light in August* is an extended dramatization of the past living in the present, a reminder that, as Gavin Stevens tells his nephew Chick in *Intruder in the Dust*, "[y]esterday won't be over until tomorrow and tomorrow began ten thousand years ago" (194).

Just as he is interested in the past, Faulkner is also interested in *tomorrow*, especially in how today's victim becomes tomorrow's victimizer. The presentation of the victimizer as not only formerly but simultaneously a victim is perhaps the most remarkable aspect of *Light in August* and one which was clearly important to Faulkner. Asked by a University of Virginia student why he would impose Christ symbolism on "such a sort of bad man as Joe Christmas," Faulkner replied that "man is the victim of himself, or his fellows, or his own nature, or his environment" (qtd. in Welsh 125) and that Christmas seemed to him "tragic" rather than "bad" (Gwynn and Blotner 118). Blotner notes that Faulkner's "anguished sympathy for his victim is clear throughout the novel" (763). Every other victimizer in the novel is also accorded victim status. By virtue of his blinding Calvinism, Doc Hines is, in Volpe's words, "[l]ike all the pursuers in the novel ... in reality, the pursued" (162). McEachern suffers from the same ailment. The victim Hightower in turn victimizes his wife. Joanna Burden, overshadowed by the "burden" of the family's philanthropic commitment, victimizes Joe Christmas in not examining the attitudes her ancestors have associated with blackness.

Even Christmas's ultimate victimizer Percy Grimm is presented as a victim of his own history and culture; the tragedy of his life is that he was prevented by age from seizing the identity he wanted as a soldier in the First World War (a tragedy he blames on his parents) and thereby demonstrating his manhood; Grimm is "saved" by the National Guard's establishment and, donning that uniform, becomes, in his mind, a symbol of an America that includes white supremacy (425–26). In Faulkner's scheme, Grimm is entirely shaped by the timing of his birth and the beliefs of his sociopolitical niche. Volpe explains the cycle which makes the victim a victimizer:

> Grimm is a volitionless victim of a racist concept. The fear and guilt of his society, which initially produced the concept, are reinforced by his act [of castrating Christmas], and the concept will be imposed, during childhood, upon the heirs of the executioners and make these victims, in their turn, executioners [173].

Hightower's final vision of Christmas's and Grimm's faces blending into each other drives home Faulkner's point (466).

Several critics have been quick to point out that Faulkner's novel cannot accurately be viewed as Naturalistic because the forces acting on his characters are not scientific and biological forces. In *The Myth of Southern History*, for example, F. Garvin Davenport, Jr., holds that Faulkner's determinant is "the force of history and not the force of glands and hostile

universes" (118). And in *Free Will and Determinism* in American Literature, Westbrook says that the characters' "bondage will not seem so great
as that presented in a strictly [N]aturalistic novel where the characters are
the playthings of environment and biochemistry"; ultimately, he concludes,
Faulkner's determinism "squares more closely with Calvinism than with
[N]aturalism" (178).

While Westbrook is right that Faulkner's determinism is more Calvinistic than Naturalistic, two responses to his and Davenport's contentions are necessary. First, Davenport's contention that biological forces do
not influence the characters is an overstatement, if not an outright mis-
characterization. Obviously, the factor of Joe's biological identity weighs
heavily in his predicament. Also, Faulkner is very much interested in the
clash between Joe Christmas's human and more primitive tendencies, as
the toothpaste scene makes clear: "Even at five, [Joe] knew that he must
not take more than [a single mouthful]. Perhaps it was the animal warning him that more would make him sick; perhaps the human being warning him that if he took more than that, she would miss it"; despite these
warnings, the boy continues to eat "worms" of paste, until he vomits (113–
14). The orphanage itself is described as "enclosed by a ten-foot steel-and-
wire fence like a penitentiary or a zoo" populated by children who chatter
"sparrowlike" (111). And certainly Faulkner is interested in the animalistic
dimensions of Joanna Burden's newly awakened sexuality; often, arriving
for a sexual rendezvous, Joe actually "hunts" Joanna:

> sometimes he would have to seek her about the dark house until he found her, hidden,
> in closets, in empty rooms, waiting, panting, her eyes in the dark glowing like the eyes
> of cats. Now and then she appointed trysts beneath certain shrubs about the grounds,
> where he would find her naked, or with her clothing half torn to ribbon upon her, in
> the wild throes of nymphomania.... She would be wild then, in the close, breathing
> halfdark without walls, with her wild hair, each strand of which would seem to come
> alive like octopus tentacles, and her wild hands and her breathing: Negro! Negro!
> Negro! [245].

Clearly, Joanna Burden wants sexual gratification at least as much as she
wants Joe Christmas's social advancement. And, as noted previously, Lena
Grove's course in the novel is largely dictated by her response to her pregnancy. As Blotner notes, in both *Light in August* and *Sanctuary*, Faulkner
is interested in "the psychopathology of sex" (761). This interest is Naturalism, not Calvinism.

A second response to Davenport's and Westbrook's contentions that
Faulkner's determinants are not strictly biological or Darwinistic would be
that Naturalism has never concerned itself purely with biological causes.
Rather, it has concerned itself, following a Darwinian model, with the environment of man; that environment might present biological determinants,

but it might just as easily present economic or social ones. Even in the work of the early Naturalists who emphasized the biological determinants most heavily—Zola and Norris—the economic and social determinants are always present. Faulkner's recurring use of "the Player" who moves Percy Grimm and Joe Christmas around like chess pieces (an analogy also present in Dreiser's *Jennie Gerhardt*) during the pursuit sequence late in the novel makes clear that the novelist saw man as characterized by an essential lack of freedom. His determinism may begin with different causes, but it ends with the same (often violent) result.

The indictment of society characteristic of Naturalism is also present in *Light in August*. Irving Howe observes that in "Percy Grimm, the small-town boy who has absorbed sadism from the very air, Faulkner gives form to his pained awareness that a society of inequality can lead only to abuse of status and arbitrary violence" (126). Richard Church calls the novel "a great book" which "burns throughout with a fierce indignation against cruelty, stupidity, and prejudice" (qtd. in Millgate, *New* 16). Millgate notes that the "social sweep" of *Light in August* has often earned Faulkner comparison with Charles Dickens ("Novel" 48) and theorizes that British reviewers of the novel were more positive than American ones (who sometimes found the various plots disconnected) because non–Americans "did not ... confront so directly the bleakness of the novel's social and political implications" (*New* 17). Several critics, foremost among them Cleanth Brooks, Olga Vickery, and André Bleikasten, have explored the phenomenon of isolation in the novel, noting the social disruption that can result when an individual's values clash with those of society. Brooks points out that nearly all the characters in the novel "are outcasts ... pariahs, defiant exiles, withdrawn quietists, or simply strangers" ("Pariah" 55). All of them are fundamentally disconnected from the American dream. Thus, as Dreiser portrays a young man who is destroyed by his attempt to conform to his society's values, Faulkner illustrates case histories of those who deviate from the community. Both writers illustrate how the sheer force of society can crush the individual. And although it is deeply grounded in the Southern experience, dealing with what Millgate calls "the South as a conditioning environment" (*Social* 205), the novel has also achieved universality, having been "widely regarded as a fable of the modern predicament" (Millgate, *New* 5) and examining what Volpe terms "the crippling clutch of abstract concepts upon the mind and soul of the human being ... the effect of any absolutist view that makes the human being its servant and victim" (173).

Asked by a local reporter why he didn't seem very "excited" about winning the Nobel prize for literature, William Faulkner replied, "Well, ... they gave it to Sinclair Lewis and Old China Hand [Pearl] Buck, and they passed over Theodore Dreiser and Sherwood Anderson" (Blotner 1342). He later called his award "a recognition of all the writers of [his] time—Dos Passos, Hemingway, Dreiser, and Anderson" (Blotner 1351). In that statement, Faulkner aligns himself with American writers who were continuing the tradition of Naturalism. His subscription to a deterministic philosophy, his employment of characters from what Cleanth Brooks calls "the ranks of the plain fold" (*Yoknopatwpha* 47), and his insistence that the culture he inhabited was seriously flawed all justify his own place in that tradition as well as Donald Pizer's comment that "the Faulkner of the 1930s can be plausibly viewed as a Southern exponent of several major naturalistic qualities" (*Twentieth* 86).

Naturalism Can Be Stylish: The Postman Always Rings Twice

Until recently, literary critics have treated James M. Cain primarily as a writer of novels characterized by their immense popularity, including successful translation to motion pictures, and by their somewhat explicit (for the 1930s and '40s) sex and violence. This critical tendency is substantiated by both David Madden and Paul Skenazy, authors of the only two full-length critical works on Cain (Madden's in 1970, seven years before Cain's death; Skenazy's in 1989). Skenazy verifies that Cain had traditionally been "treated more often as a cultural phenomenon than as a writer of substance" (ix). For example, W.M. Frohock claims that "nothing [Cain] ever wrote was completely outside the category of trash" (13).

To a large extent, Cain suffered from a stereotype—the notion that a writer's popular success signaled the absence of real literary merit in his work. The basis of this stereotype is apparently the elitist notion that a novel of artistic merit would not be popular with the general reading public. Three of Cain's novels, *The Postman Always Rings Twice, Mildred Pierce*, and *Serenade*, each sold over two million hardcover copies (Madden 121). *Postman*, whose phenomenal success in 1934 catapulted Cain to international status almost overnight, has undergone numerous printings over the years in at least 18 languages (Hoopes 248) and remains, according to Madden, "one of America's all-time best-sellers" (121).

The degree to which the motion picture industry has embraced Cain's work has also tainted his reputation as a serious writer. Although he was not particularly successful himself as a screenwriter, he enjoyed a long association with Hollywood, including a failed attempt in the 1940s to change the handling of writers' copyrights. At least 18 films have been based on his novels and stories. *Postman* alone has spawned six or seven films, including four in Europe, and one of the two American adaptations was produced by a major studio as recently as 1981 (Skenazy 195–96). In addition, the novel has been adapted for the stage, both dramatic and operatic. These circumstances have made it difficult for critics to get past the notion of Cain's novels as, in Edmund Wilson's words, "simply the preliminary design for a movie" (qtd. in Skenazy 137).

The amount of violence and sex in Cain's works has also damaged his reputation, as it has led some critics to view him as a soft pornographer. Madden says that "reviewers often attack Cain as though he were running for public office and would certainly misguide the multitude if elected" (122). Several of Cain's novels contain murders, including, in both *Postman* and *Double Indemnity*, the premeditated murder of a man by his wife and her lover for their own gain. The scene in *Postman* when, immediately after their murder of Nick Papadakis, his wife Cora and Frank Chambers have sex on the ground outside the wrecked car containing Nick's body, with Chambers (the narrator) declaring, "I had to have her, if I hung for it" (46), illustrates the juxtaposition of sexual and violent content in some of Cain's works that troubled some readers. Although fairly mild by modern film and literature standards, *Postman* was not adapted for the screen until the mid–1940s, after the success of the milder *Double Indemnity*.

The critics' assignment of Cain to the "tough guy" school of writing and, thereby, to the company of writers such as Raymond Chandler and Dashiell Hammett, in its labeling of him as a genre writer, has also tended to reduce him in stature. Of course, Cain does have much in common with these writers, particularly the gritty realism of his characters and landscapes. But Cain's placement in the "tough guys" camp has largely had the same effect as perceptions of him as commercial or exploitive: it has tended to limit critical consideration of his work.

Most of the criticism about Cain over the past 60 years (excepting reviews) falls neatly into two categories: discussions of film adaptation of his books and analyses of those works as examples of the '30s' "tough guy" school. Almost entirely ignored is the presence of Naturalistic elements in Cain's work—*Postman* in particular. Several writers have mentioned these elements in relation to *Postman*, but only in passing. For example, in "Coming to Terms with the Murderer," John Dale acknowledges the Naturalistic influence on *McTeague* and *An American Tragedy* (as novels of violence preceding Cain); however, Dale declares the novelist's approach to Frank Chambers' characterization to be "incompatible" with the "mechanism" of "building engagement with the protagonist by narratological strategies." Instead, Dale writes, "writers like James M. Cain [and Faulkner and Hemingway] witnessed the advent of protagonists who demonstrate their autonomy from the kind of narratorial analysis and explication practised by Norris and Dreiser."

No critic has heretofore developed a full-scale argument of the influence of Naturalism on *Postman*, whose publication marks a kind of transition in homicide novels from the classic explicit Naturalism of Norris and Dreiser to Truman Capote's more implicit, detached style.

To suggest that Frank Chambers merely "drifts into murder when his lover Cora suggests he help her get rid of her husband" is like claiming that Clyde Griffiths "drifts into murder" to solve the problem of Roberta Alden's pregnancy. For both men, their conception of murder as a solution reflects the extent to which the choices of each are limited by circumstances. Could Chambers have left the Papadakis place and drifted on down the highway? Not if his and Cora's animalistic appetites for each other are to be taken seriously. The strongest Naturalistic element about *Postman* is the degree to which the events of the novel are outside Frank and Cora's control. To begin with, the drivers of the hay truck on which Chambers has hitched a ride happen to discover and evict him just down the road from Nick and Cora Papadakis's restaurant and "auto court" (motel). From that point (at the end of line one), Cain takes the reader on the roller coaster ride which is Frank and Cora's fortune. Their first attempt to murder Nick effectively illustrates the fragility of their situation. The lovers plan that Cora will hit Nick over the head while he bathes, hold him underwater until he drowns, and then escape out the bathroom window and down a ladder (so that the locked bathroom door will corroborate their contention that Nick had an accidental fall). Frank, watching from below, will blow the car horn if anyone drives by or pulls in.

But their scheme begins to go awry when, waiting for Cora to appear at the window, Frank notices a cat and is frightened by what he views as an omen: "A cat was the last thing I wanted to see then … it wasn't anything but a cat, but I didn't want it around that stepladder" (19). Frank is so vexed by his superstition that he doesn't notice the policeman pull in. Just as Cora strikes Nick, the cat steps off the ladder and onto the fuse box, causing a fuse to blow and the power to go off. Ironically, Frank and Cora (and Nick temporarily) are saved—just when Frank thinks they will be caught—by this feline embodiment of luck. The image of Frank standing beside the policeman watching the cat and expecting Cora to appear any moment in the bathroom window to announce that Nick is dead comes to be an appropriate symbol for the degree to which he and Cora fail to control their fortunes.

The up-and-down pattern continues, just as unpredictably. After Nick's murder, just when it looks as though the prosecution has frightened Chambers into turning state's witness, Frank's shyster lawyer (whose name, Katz, echoes the luck motif) smooth-talks Nick's insurance company out of cooperating with the prosecution (arguing that Frank, if granted immunity, will file a whopping lawsuit against Cora for his own injuries). Frank is taken to Katz's office expecting to learn when Cora will be hanged and finds instead that she has not only been freed but also awarded $10,000 from Nick's insurance policy. Much later, after Frank and Cora have re-established their trust (breached by his willingness to testify against her), married, and declared their commitment to each other and the child Cora is carrying, Cora is killed instantly when Frank slams into a culvert wall while attempting to pass a truck.

Throughout the novel, Frank and Cora may seem the passive victims of circumstances over which they have no control. Although they think of themselves as "up on a mountain" (85) after Nick's murder, they later realize that the murder bound them inextricably and determined their fate: Frank says, "We're chained to each other, Cora. We thought we were on top of a mountain. That wasn't it. It's on top of us, and that's where it's been ever since that night" (108). The final irony of the novel, that Frank, thinking he has escaped punishment for Nick's murder, must suffer execution for the accident which killed Cora, also reinforces the inescapability of fate.

The tone of inevitability in the novel is reinforced by the tempo, what Tom Wolfe has called its "momentum" or "acceleration" (v). Frank and Cora meet on page four, have sex for the first time on page 11, begin planning Nick's murder on page 14, attempt it for the first time on page 18, and accomplish it on page 43. As Skenazy says, by page 46 (of the paperback), "the lovers' wish has come true" (22). The novel begins in motion, as Frank is thrown from the hay truck, and never slows down. This pace underscores the sense of an inevitability which they neither control nor perceive. That Cain intended the out-of-control theme as central is obvious from his introduction to the novel *The Butterfly* in 1947, in which he describes the basic Pandora's box plot he generally favored. He calls the notion of Pandora's box

> a conceit that pleases me, somehow, and often helps in my thinking. I think my stories have some quality of the opening of a forbidden box, and that it is this, rather than violence, sex, or any of the things usually cited by way of explanation, that gives them the drive so often noted. Their appeal is first to the mind, and the reader is carried along … by his own realization that the characters cannot have this particular wish and survive [Madden 61].

Cain's title for the novel also reflects his own perception of Frank Chambers' entrapment. After Alfred Knopf asked Cain to replace the original title, *Bar-B-Q*, Cain happened to be talking with the playwright Vincent Lawrence about the anxiety of waiting for his first novel to be accepted. Lawrence described his own experience of waiting for news of his first play's fate, which was to come via mail. When he could no longer stand watching for the mail carrier, he told Cain, he would go out into the backyard, knowing that he would recognize the postman's ring: there was "no fooling about that ring. The son of a bitch always rang twice, so you'd know it was the postman" (qtd. in Hoopes 237–38). Lawrence's comments reminded Cain of the Irish tradition "that the postman must ring twice, and in olden times, knock twice" (Hoopes 238). When he announced that his new title would be *The Postman Always Rings Twice*, Lawrence observed that "he sure did ring twice for Chambers, didn't he?" and Cain responded "[t]hat's the idea" (Hoopes 237).

But the determinism of *Postman* is more complicated than simple luck. Without his powerful, animalistic, sexual attraction to Cora, Frank would never have been standing under a window waiting for her to kill Nick. Frohock has said that Chambers' "response to stimuli [is] automatic and completely physical," noting a scene when Frank vomits because he cannot have sex with Cora (19). Frank is rough and forceful with Cora, once drawing blood from a bite on her lip; she has solicited his behavior with the plea, "Bite me! Bite me!" (11). After Nick's murder, Frank socks Cora in the eye to make her look injured, and this stimulates them both:

> I hauled off and hit her in the eye as hard as I could. She went down. She was right down there at my feet, her eyes shining, her breasts trembling, drawn up in tight points, and pointing right up at me. She was down there, and the breath was roaring in the back of my throat like I was some kind of animal, and my tongue was all swelled up in my mouth, and blood pounding in it....
>
> Next thing I knew, I was down there with her, and we were staring in each other's eyes, and locked in each other's arms, and straining to get closer. Hell could have opened for me then, and it wouldn't have made any difference [46].

Joyce Carol Oates says that Frank and Cora behave "as if the world extends no farther than the radius of one's desire" (111). Skenazy reinforces the connection between Frank and Cora's sexual nature and the inevitability of their destruction in his comment that the two are "entrapped by their circumstances and longings" and "destroyed by the fulfillment of their passion, the limits of their lives, and the horrible demands of fate" (27, 29). And David Fine argues that although the lovers "beat a murder rap ... [they] are unable to escape each other" (28).

Frank is destroyed, essentially, by his own appetites and impulses. That he is a creature of appetites is verified by his constant mention, in a novel with minimal extraneous detail, of what he eats. In an opening chapter less than 750 words long, Frank catalogs his first meal at Nick and Cora's, a breakfast consisting of "orange juice, corn flakes, fried eggs and bacon, enchilada, flapjacks, and coffee" (4). In fact, Frank's relationship with Cora is equated throughout with consumption. They make their sexual overtures in Cora's kitchen. During their first sexual encounter, Frank bites her lip like a starving man suddenly given food. The food motif is as central to this novel as it is to *Light in August*, although the offering of food stimulates Chambers but repulses Joe Christmas. Madden comments that "*Postman* is characteristic of many Cain novels in its depiction of sex as enhanced vividly and palpably by the elements of violence, food, [and] drunkenness" (77). Skenazy says that Frank and Cora engage in "a kind of consumerism of each others' bodies," a "cannibalism [which] is a caricature of their culture's materialist hungers" (31). The initial title, *Bar-B-Q*, suggests that Cain saw a connection between the food motif and the novel's themes.

Postman is also characteristic of many Naturalistic novels in that Cain uses animal imagery to reflect the beast-like tendencies of the characters. Frank finds Cora in the kitchen the morning after their first sexual encounter "snarling like a cougar" and giving off a particular "smell," like an animal in heat (13). Starting out on the car trip which will culminate in Nick's murder, the trio are delayed by a customer who "raised rabbits at Encino," for whom they stage an elaborate argument, as a part of their alibi, about who is too drunk to drive (40). Singing in the back of the death car, Nick is "pleased as a gorilla that [had] seen his face in the mirror" (43). One of Cain's favorite family excursion destinations upon first moving to Los Angeles was the Goebels Lion Farm (Hoopes 225); thus, it is not surprising that the dominant animal symbol in *Postman* is the cat. When Cora asks if she looks like "a little white bird" in the uniform Nick makes her wear, Frank replies that she reminds him of a "hellcat," a metaphor she transfers immediately to her desire to be rid of Nick (15). After Frank bashes in his skull with a wrench, Nick crumples, "curled … like a cat on a sofa," in the back seat of the car (43).

The ladder-climbing cat who foils the first murder attempt is echoed later by the jungle cats of Madge Allen, the woman with whom Frank goes to Mexico while Cora returns to Iowa for her mother's death. Allen raises jaguars and pumas for film work and novelty performers and later gives Cora a puma kitten (proving to Frank that the two women have met). For some reason, the kitten is dragged into the courtroom during Frank's trial for Cora's death. Allen and Chambers's discussion of the difference between "outlaw" or "jungle" pumas, who become "lunatics" when they are bred in captivity, and more domestic cats (95) obviously parallels the tension between Frank's brutishness and wanderlust and Cora's much more civilized ambitions (having an outdoor dining area with colorful awnings and a beer garden, for example). Skenazy observes that the range of cats in *Postman* "suggest[s] the characters' need to choose between the 'road' world with its wildness, abandon, and animality, and the entrepreneurial and domestic life" (28). It is not surprising that one of the titles Cain suggested when Knopf rejected *Bar-B-Q* was *Black Puma* (Hoopes 237).

Besides the animal symbolism and imagery, the atmosphere of *Postman* is also, recognizably, that of the Naturalistic novel. Tom Reck might just as easily be describing Crane's *Maggie* when he comments that the main characters are "Anglo-Saxon whites descended from traditions of economic, educational and moral poverty" who lead "a life of misery, drunkenness, adultery, violence, of economic and emotional woe" (381). Despite the differences between urban New York and rural California, the garbage piles on which Jimmy Johnson conducts his "warfare" in the opening pages of *Maggie* were not foreign to Cain—at least not according to Raymond Chandler, who vividly describes Cain's fascination with life's dirtier aspects:

> James Cain—faugh! Everything he touches smells like a billy goat.... Such people are the offal of literature.... Hemingway with his eternal sleeping bags got to be pretty damn tiresome, but at least Hemingway sees it all, not just the flies on the garbage can [qtd. in Skenazy 169].

Madden corroborates that several critics have felt that Cain "worked a literary lode bordering a trash heap" (123). The commonness of Nick and Cora's place is stressed in Chambers' initial description of it: "a roadside sandwich joint, like a million others in California" (3). These characters live a gritty, tarnished existence. Both Frank and Cora work in an atmosphere of grease—his automotive, hers culinary—and Nick is repulsive to Cora because he "is greasy and he stinks" (16).

Of course, Nick is the exception to Reck's description of these characters as Anglo-Saxon whites, and Frank's constant reference to him as "the Greek" calls attention to his ethnicity. In the 1946 film adaptation starring Lana Turner and John Garfield, Nick's last name is changed to Smith, and the erasing of Nick's immigrant identity dilutes one of the novel's significant themes—the pursuit of the American dream. The scale and tawdriness of Nick's dream of being a successful American businessman are aptly reflected by the new neon sign Frank talks him into buying: a red, white, and blue monstrosity bearing the words, "Twin Oaks Tavern, and Eat and Bar-B-Q, and Sanitary Rest Rooms, and N. Papadakis, Prop.... It also had a Greek flag and American flag, and hands shaking hands, and Satisfaction Guaranteed" (10, 12). Cora's was the Hollywood version of the American dream, fueled by her victory in an Iowa high school beauty contest, but it died when she realized, during her first screen test, that she came across as "a Cheap Des Moines trollop, that had as much chance in pictures as a monkey has" (12).

Frank Chambers is a creature of impulses and drives rather than of dreams. His desires draw him to Cora and also to the open road. Fine has pointed out the appropriateness of the automobile as a symbol for Chambers, who lives in the present, always going or dreaming of going. He shows up in Cain's novel as a hitchhiker on a turnip truck, claiming to have been a vagabond for his first 24 years and listing the cities he has visited (57). Although he has compiled a record of petty crimes, "he has escaped the system by presenting a moving target" (Shaw 37). He commits Nick's murder in the back seat of Nick's automobile, and kills Cora (and their unborn child) when he crashes the car into a culvert, the act for which he receives a death sentence. Frank's restlessness makes him an apt precursor of Perry Smith and Dick Hickock, who spend weeks on the road, crisscrossing the United States and eluding police.

Despite his physical wanderlust, however, Chambers shows little evidence of desiring social mobility. Skenazy says that Chambers "has no ambitions because he has never thought that he might achieve anything" (24). While *Postman* lacks the social indictment of *An American Tragedy* and *McTeague*, Cain does, nevertheless, convey a realistic sense of social inequity during tough times; this is clearly the same culture as that of Steinbeck's novels. Skenazy writes that Cain

> taps into the frustrated ambition, suppressed anger, and unsatisfied yearnings of masses of struggling people during the Depression years, confronted not only by a hopeless future, but forced to recognize the comparative success and prosperity of others (Katz, Sackett, and the other lawyers, businessmen, and politicians of Cain's novels).
>
> The America of *Postman* has failed in its promises of opportunity and fulfillment [23].

These characters' awareness of the gulf between "the American dream" and their reality is apparent during the murder scene, when Cora tells Nick that she wants to detour along the isolated, precarious Malibu road so that she can see "where the movie stars live" (41). It is instructive to recall that James Truslow Adams first used the phrase "American dream" in print three years before *Postman*'s publication.

Cain's style, characterized by economy and objectivity, prevents him from commenting directly on Frank's plight, but his remarks about the novel clarify his sympathy. In his correspondence with Alfred Knopf, Cain wrote, "Superficially, this is a murder story, but basically it is a romantic love story, and if this love story doesn't move, everything goes to pieces" (qtd. in Hoopes 236). His insistence on viewing *Postman* as a love story stemmed from a conversation with Lawrence in which the playwright pointed out that Dreiser had failed with his play *The Hand of the Potter* because "it made a plea for a degenerate without ever getting you interested in that degenerate" (Hoopes 232). Lawrence said that with any story, "you had to make the reader or audience *care* about the people, which inevitably led into a love story" and that "[o]ne of the lovers had to be a losing lover"; otherwise, "[w]hat makes [the reader] want to give a damn about him?"

(Hoopes 232). Although much of the early positive response to *Postman* focused on its style, writers also noted their sympathy for Frank Chambers. Joyce Carol Oates writes that "between Frank Chambers and Meursault [of Camus' *The Stranger*] one believes ultimately in Frank: he is as probable as the roadside sandwich joint we have all seen ... [a]ggressor but really victim" (113). Camus was forthright about his debt to Cain, acknowledging that he got the idea for the writing-from-death-row flashback structure of *The Stranger* from *Postman*. Of Cain's skill in orchestrating the "transference of sympathy" to Frank and Cora from their victim, Nick, Patrick Shaw argues the novelist has "kidnapped [readers] emotionally," contravening "our own sacred social codes" in our eagerness for Frank and Cora to get away with murder (42).

A final aspect which *Postman* shares with the Naturalistic homicide novel is that Cain's narrative was inspired by fact. Cain described to his biographer, Roy Hoopes, how he got the idea for the novel from a gas station he regularly patronized during his drives in the California countryside:

> Always this bosomy-looking thing comes out—commonplace, but sexy, the kind you have ideas about. We always talked while she filled up my tank. One day I read in the paper where a woman who runs a filling station knocks off her husband. Can it be this bosomy thing? I go by and sure enough, the place is closed. I inquire. Yes, she's the one—this appetizing but utterly commonplace woman [225].

Cain also claimed that the Ruth Snyder/Judd Gray case in New York, a high-profile murder trial which, according to Hoopes, "dominated" newspapers in 1927, served as an important source (232). Discussing his plans for the novel with Lawrence, Cain learned of an interesting twist in the Snyder/Gray case: after the lovers had killed Snyder's husband, Snyder had sent Gray off on a train to Syracuse with a bottle of arsenic-laced wine, which, fortunately, he did not open for fear that he would call attention to himself (Hoopes 232–33). Cain realized that the true tension in the story he wanted to tell lay not in the murder but in its aftermath, that, as he told Lawrence, "no two people can share this terrible secret and live on the same earth. They turn against each other, as Judd and Ruth did" (qtd. in Hoopes 233). Thus, Cain conceived the tense scenes in which Frank and Cora ask themselves, "if he (or she) could kill Nick, what's to stop him (or her) from killing me?" They learn, as Sartre wrote in *No Exit*, that "hell is—other people!"

Like the earlier Naturalists, Cain was a journalist by training and loyalty. Despite his success in fiction, he insisted throughout his life that he be described in *Who's Who* as "a newspaper man" (qtd. in Hoopes 199). He worked for the *Baltimore American* and *Sun*, *The American Mercury*, and the *New York World*. He even spent a nine-month stint as the 26th "Jesus" (managing editor of *The New Yorker*) before he left in frustration over the magazine's eccentricities and his difficulties with *New York* co-founder and editor-in-chief Harold Ross. Cain was probably happiest when writing editorials, and he was good at it, as the collection *60 Years of Journalism by James M. Cain*, edited by Hoopes, makes clear. The meticulousness of detail which journalism demands carries over to his fiction. He researched with an insurance agent in California the complicated scheme whereby an insurance company decides not to cooperate in Cora's and Frank's trials; the agent assured him that the scenario was not only plausible but precedented and sent Cain a copy of the California Motor Vehicle Act in which he had highlighted information "that'll make [your book] better" (Hoopes 234).

Cain claimed not to have read the major writers of his time because of a "disinterest [sic] in fiction" (Madden 113). His close friends, with the exception of Lawrence, were journalists. And yet, his novels are clearly a product of the same culture as those of the 1930s proletarian novelists. Frohock calls *Postman* "the ultimate exploitation of the climate of sensibility which also produced the best novels of Faulkner, Hemingway, Wolfe, Steinbeck, Farrell, and Dos Passos" (22) and notes that the novel "followed the lines of an early novel of Zola's called *Thérèse Raquin*" (16). Madden points out that the novel involves its protagonist in "tangles" similar to those in which Clyde Griffiths struggles (164). In his well-known essay "The Boys in the Back Room," Edmund Wilson also notes the similarity between *Postman* and *An American Tragedy*. Wilson says that Cain, like Dreiser,

> is particularly ingenious in tracing from their first beginnings the tangles that gradually tighten around the necks of the people involved in those bizarre and brutal crimes that figure in the American papers; and is capable even of tackling ... the larger tangles of social interest from which these deadly little knots derive [21].

Wilson also notes that *Tragedy* is the greater novel because Cain's involves plot turns that may seem to some readers like gimmicks. Skenazy compares the characters Cain created in the '30s to those of Faulkner, Fitzgerald, and Hemingway in their "suspicion of the grave pronouncements and reigning ideals of American civilization" (7); he also says that *Postman*, *Mildred Pierce*, and *Double Indemnity* "provide as revealing a rebuke to the Chamber of Commerce image of [California] as Steinbeck's *The Grapes of Wrath* and Nathanial West's *The Day of the Locust*" (ix). These fiction writers to whom Cain is compared by such critics are usually Naturalists or writers whose work felt the Naturalistic influence in the 1930s.

The Naturalistic element of Cain's fiction has not been ignored by the movement's historians. In a discussion of the "undying vitality" of Naturalism in the 1930s and '40s, Frederick J. Hoffman mentions "the contribution made by James Cain to the surface picture of American violence" (186). Stoddard Martin argues that the authors who are the focus of his book *California Writers* (1983)—London, Steinbeck, Hammett, Cain, and Chandler—"were all firmly based in the Naturalistic mode which Frank Norris had pioneered in before them" (7). In his specific discussion of *Postman*, Martin holds that it reveals "a Naturalistic distinctness," and that Frank Chambers has a "beach bum mentality" in that "his only intimation of divine power comes not from the law or justice or love even so much as from the waves" (156).

But if *Postman* shares much of the Naturalistic agenda, it also represents an important step in the homicide novel's transition toward the New Journalism. The aspect of Cain's work that received highest praise from critics—his style—is generally recognized as the weakest aspect of the work of the early Naturalists, Dreiser and Norris in particular. In this respect, particularly in his linguistic economy, his closest parallel among the early Naturalists is Crane, who had the most facility with language.

Cain's primary stylistic achievement was the efficiency of his prose, which definitely reflects a journalistic influence. He accomplished this economy primarily by pushing the action forward and resisting the urge to comment on it. This restraint distinguishes him from McTeague and Dreiser as a chronicler of what Jim Dale calls "the transgressive protagonist." In *Postman*, of course, he achieves this restraint through a first-person narrator who is not introspective. Although he was initially uncomfortable with David Madden's term "pure novel," Cain decided after extended correspondence with Madden that this was, in fact, what he wrote. He told Madden that his understanding of the term was a novel "whose point is developed from the narrative itself, rather than from some commentary on the social scene or morality of the characters, or economic or political aesthetic preachment." His goal, he said, was "to let the fable deliver its own 1, 2, & 3" (qtd. in Hoopes 516). Chapter 6 of Madden's book *Cain and the Pure Novel* makes clear that the restraint Cain described was what the critic had in mind and also that any philosophy emerging from a Cain novel is disseminated by characters, their actions, or symbols, and not through authorial commentary.

Another important aspect of Cain's detachment is increased reliance on dialogue to propel the narrative, a characteristic he shares with Hemingway. He eliminated what he called "saysing" (says-ing), authorial explanation surrounding dialogue to indicate who is speaking and how, insisting that "if Jake is to warn Harold, 'an ominous glint appearing in his eyes,' it would be a great deal smoother and more entertaining to the reader … to slip … the right subtle amount of ominous glint in the speech" (qtd. in Hoopes 234). Thus, Cain's prose shares the dramatic style of Hemingway, containing long passages of dialogue through which the reader moves quickly without narrative interruption. His linguistic refinement is his strong link with the "New" journalists of the 1960s. In the homicide novel tradition, it establishes him as the immediate stylistic progenitor of Truman Capote.

Murder on the South Side: Richard Wright's Native Son

Placing *Native Son* in the tradition of the homicide novel requires little more than a bibliography, one which reveals much that is expected and a few surprises. Among the 31 reviews of the novel collected in *Richard Wright: The Critical Reception* (ed. Reilly), 11 critics compare *Native Son* to *An American Tragedy*, 10 to *The Grapes of Wrath*, and eight to *Crime and Punishment*. At least two doctoral dissertations trace the impact on Wright of Naturalists earlier than and contemporaneous to him: in "Richard Wright's Use of His Reading of Fiction," Susan McBride describes Wright's interest in Dreiser, Farrell, and Hemingway, and in "The Influences of Stephen Crane, Theodore Dreiser, and James T. Farrell [on Wright]," Alvin Starr traces the influence of those writers. Tony Magistrale's "From St. Petersburg to Chicago: Wright's *Crime and Punishment*" describes parallels between *Native Son* and Dostoevsky's best-known novel. Michael Francis Lynch, in "Richard Wright, Ralph Ellison, and Dostoevsky: The Choice of Individual Freedom and Dignity," examines the concept of free will in the work of those writers, and Horst-Jurgen Gerigk, in "Culpabilité et liberté: Dostoevskij, Dreiser et Richard Wright," discusses the interrelatedness of freedom and guilt, especially in *Crime and Punishment*, *An American Tragedy*, and *Native Son*.

The strong critical alignment of Wright's novel with Steinbeck's work, particularly with *The Grapes of Wrath*, might seem more disproportionate today than it would have in 1940. Because of the stature which the passage of time has accorded other writers working in the 1930s (Faulkner and Hemingway, for example), Steinbeck's importance to his contemporaries can be underestimated. If the proletarian or protest novel was the dominant mode of the decade, then certainly *The Grapes of Wrath* must be considered among its foremost manifestations. Hakutani argues that *Native Son*, *Grapes*, and *Of Mice and Men* are informed by the same concept of sacrifice as *Native Son*, that "Bigger sacrifices himself to gain a new vision of moral and social justice" just as George "sacrifices" Lenny and Tom Joad "sacrifices" his family ("*Native* Son" 224). In *The New Republic*, Malcolm Cowley called *Native Son* "the most impressive American novel I have read since *The Grapes of Wrath*" (which had won the previous year's Pulitzer Prize,

67), and Lewis Gannett called Wright's novel "*The Grapes of Wrath* of 1940" (42).

In his introduction to *Images of the Negro in American Literature* (1966), Seymour Gross calls *Native Son* "the culmination of the protest tradition … and its finest example" (18). Although one might quibble over the superlative, it is logical, as Gross maintains, that the "proletarian ideology" of the '30s' writers would eventually find fodder in "the image of the Negro, [as] he was clearly the most dislocated and deprived figure on the American economic landscape" (16). In *The American Dream: A Cultural History* (2012), Lawrence R. Samuel explains that the aspirations associated with the dream in the early decades of the 20th century had a trickle-down effect for African Americans, whose buy-in with the dream was essential to its survival. Particularly in the early 1960s, the African American community was divided over the rate of progress on Civil Rights, with some gravitating toward the Black Muslim movement and the notion of a separate state. In this climate, in 1962, the Rev. James J. Reeb of Washington, D.C., claimed, "It is absolutely certain that this dream cannot be saved unless the Negro continues to believe in its value" (qtd. in Samuel). Samuel and Jim Cullen, author of *The American Dream: A Short Idea That Shaped a Nation* (2003), both contend that the centrality of the dream metaphor in the rhetoric of Dr. Martin Luther King, Jr., helped to ensure the concept's permanence in American mythology. In his most famous speech, that given at the March on Washington in August 1963, King declared his own dream "deeply rooted in the American dream," and he mentioned the American dream specifically in at least half a dozen other speeches, including on the last day of his life (qtd. in Samuel). In viewing *Native Son* as a mature expression of the protest novel, Seymour Gross recognizes Wright's contribution to the American dream's continuity through the 1940s and '50s, until King's ascendancy.

A surprising aspect of *Native Son*'s early reviews is the scarcity of comparisons with Faulkner and specifically with *Light in August*. Several later studies, some book-length, discuss the two authors in the same context, although it is not always directly relevant to the current study. For example, In *Drawing the Line: The Father Reimagined in Faulkner, Wright, O'Connor, and Morrison* (2013), Doreen Fowler explains the father's distinctive role, to "support the construction of a social identity by mediating between cultural oppositions" ("*Drawing*"). Perhaps the most thorough treatment of *Native Son* and *Light in August* in 20th-century literary criticism comes in Walter Taylor's "How to Visit the Black South without Visiting Blacks," wherein Taylor argues that Wright's and Faulkner's novels might be perceived as the same problem in two different manifestations: "Nine years before Wright showed what his transplanted South had done to Bigger,"

Taylor maintains, "Faulkner ... visit[ed] a South that sounded remarkably like the one Wright had escaped" (66). Indeed, Joe Christmas and Bigger Thomas enact the same prototypical crime in two different geographies that constitute the same Naturalistic landscape: a young black man isolated from every measure of "somebodyness" commits homicide against a victim who is in almost every sense "somebody" and his demographic opposite: female, white, affluent, educated. Yoshinobu Hakutani points out that Bigger, like Joe Christmas, achieves identity through the act of murder and that Wright, like both Faulkner and Steinbeck, tends to be highly symbolic ("*Native Son*" 219, 221). Faulkner scholar Noel Polk, accepting the Richard Wright Literary Excellence Award in 2006, declared Wright and Faulkner to be "two near contemporaries whose views…were more alike than we may have thought."

A reasonable supposition concerning the absence of references to *Light in August* in early criticism of *Native Son* is that Wright was not really under Faulkner's influence at the time. Because the reading program upon which Wright embarked in the late 1920s was based almost exclusively on the writers mentioned in H.L. Mencken's essays, Wright tended to read the writers Mencken admired and encouraged—the earlier Naturalists and European and Russian novelists whom Wright mentions in *Black Boy* (268–74). For example, the influence of Dostoevsky has been thoroughly demonstrated by Tony Magistrale in his excellent article "From St. Petersburg to Chicago: Wright's *Crime and Punishment*" (1986). Wright did not add Faulkner to his reading list until the mid-'30s (Gayle 77). As Wright was working on *Native Son* as early as 1935 (Kinnamon 4), one might plausibly argue that whatever similarities exist between *Light in August* and *Native Son* resulted more from their authors' responding to the same social environment than from the demonstrated influence of Faulkner on Wright.

Faulkner's awareness of Wright's achievement is much clearer; he said that Bigger Thomas's story moved him "powerfully" and that "the man who wrote *Native Son* is potentially an artist" (qtd. in Blotner 1190). His congratulatory letter to Wright implies that he recognized their common Naturalistic purpose: "I think you will agree that the good lasting stuff comes out of one individual's imagination and sensitivity to and comprehension of the suffering of Everyman, Anyman" (qtd. in Blotner 1190–91). Five years later, Faulkner also sent Wright a note praising *Black Boy*, although he expressed a continuing preference for *Native Son* (Gayle 176).

In his own accounts of his literary influences, Wright aligned himself firmly with the Naturalists. In his autobiographical work *Black Boy*, Wright describes using a white friend's library card and a forged note to borrow books from a Memphis library. He lists the many literary acquaintances he made through the library card, authors whose names he often did not even know how to pronounce. At least a third of the authors on his library list were Naturalists or writers whose works demonstrate a strong Naturalistic influence: Sherwood Anderson, Fyodor Dostoevsky, George Moore, Leo Tolstoy, Thomas Hardy, Stephen Crane, Emile Zola, Frank Norris, Henrik Ibsen, Honore de Balzac, Ivan Turgenev, Theodore Dreiser (272). He was drawn to Dreiser in particular:

> I read Dreiser's *Jennie Gerhardt* and *Sister Carrie* and they revived in me a vivid sense of my mother's suffering; I was overwhelmed. I grew silent, wondering about the life around me. It would have been impossible for me to have told anyone what I derived from these novels, for it was nothing less than a sense of life itself. All my life had shaped me for the realism, the naturalism of the modern novel, and I could not read enough of them [274].

Hakutani points out in "Richard Wright and American Naturalism" that while Wright treats the terms *Realism* and *Naturalism* rather synonymously here, it is clearly the idea of suffering, a concept at the heart of the Naturalistic orientation, that he is drawn to (217), just as Faulkner suspected.

Although Wright acknowledged the effect upon him of Dreiser's earlier novels, *An American Tragedy* has spawned the bulk of the comparisons between the two men. In the *New York Times Book Review*, Peter Monro Jack hailed Wright's novel as "the Negro 'American Tragedy'" (53) and Clifton Fadiman, reviewing *Native Son* for *The New Yorker*, declared that the novel "does for the Negro what Theodore Dreiser in *An American Tragedy* did a decade and a half ago for the bewildered, inarticulate American white" (48). Fadiman said the two novels are alike "in theme, in technique, in their almost paralyzing effect on the reader, and in the large, brooding humanity ... that informs them both" (48–49). Edward Skillin, Jr., commented in his review of *Native Son* that Wright succeeds "in making environment the principal villain in this new American Tragedy" (62). Irving Howe discusses Max's final speech to the jury as "a device apparently borrowed from Dreiser" (9). John P. McWilliams, Jr., discusses the long trial sections in both *An American Tragedy* and *Native Son* in "Innocent Criminal or Criminal Innocence: The Trial in American Fiction." More recently, Ann Algeo has explored how the trials in Dreiser's and Wright's novels as well as those in *In Cold Blood* and *The Executioner's Song* reflect the societies in which the crimes occurred. Barbara Foley takes a predominantly rhetorical approach in "The Politics of Poetics: Ideology and Narrative Form in *An American Tragedy* and *Native Son*." Blyden Jackson says that Wright shares not only Dreiser's vision but also his major flaw: "[Wright] was ... another Dreiser with an elevated mission and a hopelessly flatulent prose style" (445), a shared weakness also mentioned in relation to the earlier novelist by Richard Lehan in *Dreiser and the Hostile Critics*. And Harold

Bloom says that Bigger Thomas "can be apprehended only as we apprehend Dreiser's Clyde and Carrie, which is under the sign of suffering…. There is something maternal in Wright's stance towards Bigger, even as there [is] in Dreiser's towards Clyde or Carrie" (*Bigger* 1). Bloom declares Wright "[a] legitimate son of Theodore Dreiser" (*Bigger* 3). And Blyden Jackson has written that Wright

> cut his writer's teeth on naturalism, and much of the reason that most black writers for more than twenty years seemed decidedly more akin to Frank Norris than to Henry James may be discovered in the simple circumstance that Wright was similarly so akin [447–48].

Wright's description of his methodology for *Native Son* places him squarely in the Naturalistic tradition. Like Zola, he viewed his narrative as a sort of sociological experiment with Bigger as subject; his comments in "How 'Bigger' Was Born" about the approach he planned to take could (except for Bigger's name) have been lifted directly from the pages of "Le roman expérimental":

> [W]hy should I not try to work out on paper the problem of what will happen to Bigger? Why should I not, like a scientist in a laboratory, use my imagination and invent test-tube situations, place Bigger in them, and, following the guidance of my own hopes and fears, what I had learned and remembered, work out in fictional form an emotional statement and resolution of this problem? [523].

Just how familiar Wright was with the work of the French Naturalists is unclear; he mentions Zola in *Black Boy*, but he is recalling a list of names from Mencken's *Book of Prefaces*, some of which, at the time, he didn't even know how to pronounce (272). Susan McBride does not discuss Wright's familiarity with Zola in her dissertation, *Richard Wright's Use of His Reading of Fiction* (Pennsylvania, 1975), nor does Alvin Starn in *The Influences of Stephen Crane, Theodore Dreiser, and James T. Farrell [on Richard Wright]* (Kent State, 1974). Robert James Butler, in "Wright's *Native Son* and Two Novels by Zola," points out striking similarities between the American work and Zola's *Thérèse Raquin* and *La Bête Humaine*. Houston Baker has also noted this connection in *Long Black Song*. Whatever Wright's familiarity with Zola's work, he obviously endorsed the Frenchman's aims, employing them in his own fiction. In fact, if he was *not* familiar with "Le roman expérimental," his comments in "How 'Bigger' Was Born" are all the more remarkable.

Foremost among Wright's goals for *Native Son* as he describes them in "How 'Bigger' Was Born" was the necessity of making his protagonist authentic. He was tempted, he says, to create in Bigger "a symbolic figure of American life, a figure who would hold within him the prophecy of our future" (523). But he felt cautious concerning the responses of both black and white readers. Idealizing Bigger might result in black readers' finding the character artificial, while depicting Bigger honestly might cause professional and middle-class black readers to feel "ashamed of Bigger and what he meant" (525). He describes a sort of "mental censor" or hesitation about depicting Bigger's anger, ignorance, and instability honestly without alienating or angering white readers (523). If Bigger seemed too ruthless and too angry at white Americans as the cause of his limited choices, he could reinforce white readers' stereotypes and fears (523–24). In the end, Wright says, he decided he must write Bigger honestly as he saw him, in order to ensure the integrity of his narrative and his own immunity from the fear that controls his protagonist:

> The more I thought of it, the more I became convinced that if I did not write Bigger as I thought and felt him, if I did not try to make him a living personality and at the same time a symbol of all the larger things I felt and saw in him, I'd be reacting as Bigger himself reacted: that is, I'd be acting out of *fear* if I let what I thought whites would say constrict and paralyze me [524].

Initially, as his model for Bigger, Wright had in mind not one person but several; Bigger's birth, he said, had its genesis in his childhood, and there were several models, to whom he assigns numbers in his essay. One of these models, Bigger no. 5, who challenged a segregated streetcar conductor in the Jim Crow South of Wright's boyhood, was actually called "Bigger Thomas" by onlookers ("How" 509). What the models all had in common was a spirit of defiance; the "Bigger Thomases," Wright says, "were the only Negroes I know of who consistently violated the Jim Crow laws of the South and got away with it, at least for a sweet brief spell. Eventually, the whites who restricted their lives made them pay a terrible price" (509–10). Wright also attributed Bigger's "authenticity" to his own work at the South Side Boys' Club in Chicago, whose purpose was not only to "reclaim" black boys from "the dives and alleys" but also to protect "the valuable white property which adjoined the Black Belt," property some feared the boys might otherwise damage or steal (530). The Boys' Club's distractions basically consisted of ping pong and checkers, and Wright was so horrified at the notion that recreation could cure social ills that he quit (530), but his experience there lends authenticity to his narrative.

For nearly three years, Wright worked toward creating a composite of the Biggers he had known in Mississippi and Chicago. Then, in May 1938, almost in endorsement of Bigger's verisimilitude, Wright found the character he was shaping fully formed in the Chicago papers. Robert Nixon and Earl Hicks, both young, illiterate black men, were charged with the rape and murder of a white woman, Florence Johnson, whose head has been smashed, apparently with a brick, the same weapon with which Bigger would murder his girlfriend, Bessie. Very early, the case focused on Nixon, who, under duress, confessed to several other crimes with which he was apparently not connected; this prefigures Bigger's being grilled by authorities about other crimes in Chicago and in Los Angeles. Whether Nixon was guilty of Johnson's murder is not clear; Wright's discussion in "How 'Bigger' Was Born" suggests that he thought Nixon a symbol of the hysteria which threatened all young black men (532). In fact, in "How 'Bigger' Was Born," he writes, "scarcely was *Native Son* off the press before Supreme Court Justice Hugo L. Black gave the nation a long and vivid account of the American police methods of handling Negro boys" (532).[1]

Wright, living in Brooklyn at the time of Nixon's arrest, sent two airmail special delivery letters to his friend Margaret Walker (later Margaret Walker Alexander) in Chicago requesting that she send him clippings about the case. Walker later recalled that she sent enough clippings for Wright to cover the floor of his nine-by-12-foot bedroom and that "he was using them in the same way Dreiser had done in [*An*] *American Tragedy*. He would spread them all out and read them over and over again and then take off from there in his own imagination" (Alexander 60). Of particular significance in the press accounts was the "openly racist" Chicago *Tribune*'s description of Robert Nixon in an article headlined "Brick Slayer Likened to Jungle Beast":

> [C]ivilization has left Nixon practically untouched. His hunched shoulders and long, sinewy arms that dangle almost to his knees; his outthrust head and catlike tread all suggest the animal.... He is very black—almost pure Negro. His physical characteristics suggest an earlier link in the species [qtd. in Kinnamon 5].

The *Tribune* reporter, Charles Leavelle, went on to compare Nixon to the ape murderer of Edgar Allan Poe's "The Murders in the Rue Morgue" (Kinnamon 5). Leavelle's "Brick Slayer" story and many others like it are reprinted, some verbatim, in *Native Son* (the excerpt above appears with minor changes on page 260). Wright acknowledges in "How 'Bigger' Was Born" that "[m]any of the newspaper items and some of the incidents in *Native Son* are but fictionalized versions of the Robert Nixon case and rewrites of news stories from the *Chicago Tribune*" (532).

Wright's autobiographical *Black Boy* suggests a second source that he might have had in mind as a model for Bigger's accidental killing of Mary Dalton. When Wright was nine, he and his mother and siblings lived with his Aunt Maggie, who was regularly visited late at night by a mysterious "uncle." Soon young Richard was told that white people were looking for the man and that, if asked, he should say that uncle wasn't there. The older women refused to tell him more. Finally, Aunt Maggie and uncle leave in the middle of the night, for reasons clarified in a conversation the boy overheard:

"[Y]ou've done something terrible," Aunt Maggie said. "or you wouldn't be running like this."

"The house is on fire," 'uncle' said. "and when they see it, they'll know who did it."

"Did you set the house afire?" my mother asked.

"There was nothing else to do," 'uncle' said impatiently. "I took the money. I had hit her. She was unconscious. If they found her, she'd tell. I'd be lost. So I set the fire."

"But she'll burn up," Aunt Maggie said….

"What could I do?" 'uncle' asked. "I had to do it. I couldn't just leave her there and let somebody find her. They'd know somebody hit her. But if she burns, nobody'll ever know" [76–77].

For a reader familiar with *Native Son*, Aunt Maggie's fussing with her trunk brings to mind Bigger's concealment of Mary Dalton's body in her own half-packed trunk (*Native Son*, 87). Wright must have recalled the rationalization of "uncle" that "if she burns, nobody'll ever know" when writing Bigger's realization, "[h]e would *burn* her! That was the safest thing of all to do" (89).

Like his Naturalistic predecessors Dreiser, Norris, and Crane, Wright also took pains to assure the authenticity of his locale. In November 1938, he traveled to Chicago with a typed list of goals, all aimed at matching his novel to the city terrain. His agenda, now contained in the Wright Archives at Yale, is reprinted by Kinnamon; it includes selecting sites for many landmarks, most notably the Dalton home, an "empty house for Bigger's murder of Bessie," and Bigger's home; tracing Bigger's flight through the 43rd to 39th blocks of Indiana Avenue; obtaining copies of official documents from the Nixon case, such as the indictments and the inquest verdict; and visiting the Cook County jail, the courtroom where Robert Nixon had been tried, the death house at the Statesville penitentiary, and, if possible, Nixon himself, who awaited execution.

Two additional items on Wright's list reveal his interest in another Chicago homicide: he planned to check local libraries for accounts of the Leopold-Loeb case and to find the homes of Nathan Leopold, Richard Loeb, and Bobby Franks (Kinnamon 28). In July 1924, Leopold and Loeb had been convicted of murdering 14-year-old Franks, their motive ostensibly intellectual, colored by their study of Nietzsche—to see if they could get away with it. The fact that Franks was not a stranger to them and that Leopold and Loeb were both heirs to corporate fortunes made the crime all the more sensational. Wright's curiosity about the Leopold-Loeb material confirms both his inclination toward factual accuracy and his awareness that he was working in a tradition.

Although the Nixon case helped Wright with what Hakutani has called "documentary detail characteristic of naturalistic style" ("*Native Son*" 222), Wright's own experience in the racial climate of the South made the plot almost intuitive. He wrote, "Never for a second was I in doubt as to what kind of social reality or dramatic situation I'd put Bigger in, what kind of test-tube life I'd set up to evoke his deepest reactions. Life had made the plot over and over again, to the extent that I knew it by heart" ("How" 532). The pervasiveness of the scenario he planned to describe caused Wright to feel an inevitability about Bigger's fate which permeates the novel. He began writing, Wright said, and "the plot fell out" ("How" 532). The story of Bigger's crime and punishment was so well established in its author's mind that he wrote the 576-page first draft in four months ("Bigger" 535).

The rat scene which opens *Native Son* symbolizes and encapsulates the entire deterministic struggle described in the novel (and was actually written later than the main narrative). Wright intended to establish immediately "the motif of the entire scheme of the book, that would sound, in varied form, the note that was to be resounded throughout its length" ("How" 534). Clearly, that note is entrapment and violence. The rat, trapped in the Thomas's flat with its escape hole covered and Bigger and Buddy in conspiracy against it, does not have a chance. Guided purely by instinct, it can only stand on its back legs and utter a shriek that Wright characterizes as "furious" (*Native Son* 3). Undaunted by the rat's helplessness, the Thomas family perceives it as an aggressor; Bigger's mother, for example, is convinced that the rat has the volition to sneak in while they sleep and cut their throats. The point, of course, is that the Thomas family are to the rat as white society will be to Bigger when he becomes the prey. Just as the rat grabs instinctively at Bigger's pants leg in panic, so Bigger, bewildered by a society that perceives him as vermin, will kill Mary and then Bessie in acts of desperation. Robert Butler says in "The Function of Violence in Richard Wright's *Native Son*" that "society does to [Bigger] precisely what he did to Mary and Bessie … it kills him, partly out of fear and partly out of hatred" (19). His assault on the rat and the empathy with which Wright describes the rat foreshadow all the subsequent victimization.

Bigger Thomas is trapped within the narrow range of possibilities that a predominantly white power structure allowed young, illiterate black men in the 1930s. He goes to work for the Dalton family because he has no choice—otherwise, his family's "relief" will be cut off (12). He places the pillow over Mary Dalton's face because he does not see another alternative to being caught in her room by her parents—and as Wright testifies in "How 'Bigger' Was Born," young black men had been convicted of rape and hanged on much weaker evidence. Bigger's actions throughout the death scene are instinctual, like the rat's, motivated entirely by fear. Her mother is in the room? Thank goodness Mrs. Dalton is blind. Is Mary beginning to mumble? Cover her face with a pillow. It does not occur to him that Mary could suffocate, and he is surprised when he realizes that she has (84–86). Cutting off Mary's head and putting her corpse into the basement furnace is a loathsome task for Bigger, but again, he sees no other option. As soon as he realizes Mary is dead, he begins to think of himself as prey:

> The reality of the room fell from him; the vast city of white people that sprawled outside took its place. She was dead and he had killed her. He was a murderer, a Negro murderer, a black murderer. He had killed a white woman. He had to get away.... In the darkness his fear made live in him an element which he reckoned with as "them." He had to construct a case for "them" [86–87].

Recalling Roberta Alden's drowning in *An American Tragedy*, Joseph T. Skerrett, Jr., calls Mary Dalton's death "Dreiserian, determined by Bigger's social conditioning and the terrible pressure of the moment" (134).

Again, in his rape and murder of Bessie, Bigger is presented as acting on impulse and instinct. When Bessie begs him not to rape her, "he paid her no heed. The loud demand of the tensity of his own body was a voice that drowned out hers." He feels as if he were "on some vast turning wheel that made him want to turn faster and faster ... conscious of nothing now but of her and what he wanted" (219). He tells himself that "[h]e had to now. Imperiously driven, he rode roughshod over her whimpering protests, feeling acutely sorry for her as he galloped a frenzied horse down a steep hill in the face of a resisting wind" which "became so strong that it lifted him high in the dark air, turning him, twisting him, hurling him" (219–20). Before Bessie's murder, he again realizes his entrapment: "What about Bessie? He could not take her with him and he could not leave her behind." And the fact which seals her doom—that he has confessed to her—Bigger also blames on her: "It would have been much better if he had not said anything to Bessie about the murder. Well, it was her own fault. She had bothered him so much that he had had to tell her" (220). Even his choice of a weapon is presented in deterministic terms: his gun would make noise and draw attention, so "[h]e would have to use a brick" (221). Still, Bigger struggles until he convinces himself that he is in a corner; three times in the next two paragraphs, he reminds himself that "[h]e could not take her and he could not leave her." The third time, he adds the decisive rationalization: "It was his life against hers" (221–22). Wright's comment that Bigger is "a hot and whirling vortex of undisciplined and unchannelized impulses" is borne out in these pages ("How," 520).

The deterministic aspect of the novel has been uniformly recognized by critics. For example, Harold Bloom has commented on the novel's "rhetorical pathos of terror" which "seems to overdetermine all of [Bigger's] actions" (*Bigger* xv). In "Richard Wright and *Native Son*: Not Guilty," Dorothy S. Redden argues that while Bigger may feel that he makes choices, his choices are determined by the culture of which he is a product and that "accountable" might be a better word for him than "guilty" (80–81). In his essay comparing *Native Son* and *Crime and Punishment*, Tony Magistrale maintains that a central difference between Raskolnikov and Bigger Thomas is that Bigger lacks control over his fate, while Raskolnikov does not. Skerrett says that Bigger is "[t]rapped by the economics of the Depression and the resultant intensification of racial prejudice and discrimination" (129). James Baldwin has called the novel "the story of an unremarkable youth in battle with the force of circumstance," adding that, in Bigger's case, "the force of circumstance is not poverty merely but color, a circumstance which cannot be overcome" ("Thousands" 240).

A common position in *Native Son* criticism is that through Mary Dalton's death, Bigger breaks out of his deterministic lock-step and ceases to apprehend the world merely intuitively. Hakutani articulates the argument in his comment that "in rebelling [Bigger] leaps from determinism to freedom," that he "triumphs" over the society that produced him by disregarding the "rules" ("*Native* Son" 220, 223). Bloom calls this the novel's "Dostoevskian aspect, in which murder is the mode of creativity" (xv). The argument largely stems from Bigger's insistence in the novel's conclusion that Mary's death prodded his awakening: "What I killed for must've been good!… When a man kills, it's for something…. I didn't know I was really alive in this world until I felt things hard enough to kill for 'em" (392). Bigger undeniably undergoes a transformation by virtue of Mary's death, thereafter demonstrating a broader awareness of events in the world around him (such as revolutions in China and the U.S.S.R.) and a greater capacity for introspection (as his conversations with his attorney Max demonstrate); in this respect, the comparisons with Raskolnikov are valid. But it is a stretch to imply that Bigger becomes a free agent. After Mary's death, Bigger himself clearly views his choices as dictated by that event, including his killing of Bessie. He is also still at the mercy of society, as the newspaper articles and jeering crowds make clear. In a literal sense, Bigger at the end of the novel is more trapped than ever—in a cage, with no way out, save the electric chair. He may feel more "alive," but he is certainly not more free.

A final dimension of Bigger's entrapment is his isolation. "Half the time," Bigger says, "I feel like I'm on the outside of the world peeping in through a knothole in the fence" (23). In "How 'Bigger' Was Born," Wright said that a significant experience in his preparation for *Native Son* was reading in a magazine about Gorky and Lenin, in exile, touring London, with Lenin pointing out the landmarks: "'Here is *their* Big Ben.' There is *their* Westminster Abbey.' 'There is *their* library'" (517, emphasis Wright's). This clarified for Wright what he came to call "the Bigger Thomas reaction"— the notion that everything in the world is "theirs," not ours (518). And while Bigger may participate in "their" world only with "their" permission (as when Mary and Jan invite him along on their outing), they may poke their noses into his world whenever they choose.

Wright locates Bigger's isolation as not on the external periphery of any particular identity or group (such as "the outside of the world") but generally between one and another, as if he is isolated *between* binaries. The most obvious of these binaries is race, as he is a young black man in a world dominated by whites. Mrs. Dalton's blindness is a metaphor suggesting her incapacity (and perhaps the incapacity of most American white people in the late 1930s) even to fully perceive Bigger and his life. Just as she cannot see him in her daughter's darkened bedroom, he does not exist for her except as someone her family might employ. (And because of Bigger's criminal record, their benevolence in hiring him brings them satisfaction.) Their family name is also ironic; "Daltonism" is another term for color blindness, but the Daltons do not practice colorblindness where relationships between the races is concerned. His real estate career exists on a scaffolding that leaves families like Bigger's in substandard housing, and her charitable work comes with expectations, just as her advice to Bigger does. They can donate to the concept of education for African Americans because that is an abstraction; however, they do not consider whether Bigger himself might want to be educated. Throughout the novel, Wright uses the metaphor of sight and blindness made famous by Ralph Ellison in *Invisible Man* to convey the nobodyness of being black in late 1930s America. And when Bigger is among members of his own race, his nobodyness is not so painfully apparent to him.

Bigger is also torn between his identity as an American, a "native son," and the ideologies of the nascent black nationalist movement, between integration in American society and segregation in an African state. Like all Americans, Wright says, Bigger believes in the value of the Constitution, believes that the Bill of Rights is "a good legal and humane principle to safeguard our civil liberties, that every man and woman should have the opportunity to realize himself, to seek his own individual fate and goal, his own peculiar and untranslatable destiny" ("How" 527–28). Bigger knows these things, Wright says, not consciously but "intuitively" ("How" 528). In other words, Bigger has incorporated principles that sound very much like what James Truslow Adams, writing less than 10 years before *Native Son*'s publication, called "the American dream." And yet is he quite consciously aware that he lives in a society where few African Americans can capitalize on the opportunities that are readily available to white citizens.

In "How 'Bigger' Was Born," Richard Wright ultimately indicts society for his young protagonist's social exclusion and its consequences. Wright points to two specific factors that caused Bigger to "revolt":

First, through some quirk of circumstance, he had become estranged from the religion
and the folk culture of his race. Second, he was trying to react to and answer the call of the
dominant civilization whose glitter came to him through newspapers, magazines, radios,
movies, and the mere imposing sight and sound of daily American life ["How" 27].

In the first respect, being separated from his culture and belief system, he is
Joe Christmas; in the second, his isolation from "the dominant civilization,"
he is Clyde Griffiths. Wright says, "What makes Bigger's social consciousness most complex was the fact that he was hovering unwanted between
two worlds—between powerful America and his own stunted place in
life—and I took upon myself the task of trying to make the reader feel this
No Man's Land" ("How" 527). Like Clyde Griffiths, he drifts between where
he came from and a place he can never get to, a destination for which his
culture has nevertheless taught him to aspire. James Baldwin called him "a
monster created by the American republic" (240).

Perhaps the most remarkable aspect of *Native Son* is Wright's avoidance of reductive stereotyping, so that the characters avoid pure victim or
villain status. Not a single black woman is presented as wholly good, and
the Daltons, the embodiments of the white establishment, are, at worst,
"blind" to the real desperation of young men like Bigger. In a novel very
much about the oppression of black Americans by white Americans, the
most redeeming character is a white man, Max, who, in his impassioned
plea for Bigger's life, puts society itself on trial. Wright said that in *Native
Son*, he wanted to write a novel which readers "would have to face … without the consolation of tears" (37), i.e., without oversimplified emotional
reactions. Harold Bloom recommends precisely the kind of novel which
Wright wanted to avoid in his argument that the novelist should not
have had Bigger kill Bessie because that murder "calls in doubt the novel's apparent outcry against social injustice" (*Bigger* 2). The implication—
that Wright's message would be more effective if Bigger were clearly "more
sinned against than sinning"—fails to take into account that Bessie's murder is intended to *intensify*, not mitigate, Bigger's status as a victim. Like
generations of black men before him, he enacts his revenge on a racist society by lashing out at the only person whom it is within his power to victim-
ize—the black woman. The irony is that society will punish Bigger for the
death that was accidental, Mary Dalton's, and not for the one that was premeditated, largely because of this racist ideology. Bigger shares this irony of
intentionality and accident with *Postman*'s Frank Chambers.

As Irving Howe has argued, Wright's real achievement is the novel's double-barreled approach to racial problems in the United States; it
forced white Americans "to recognize [themselves] as the oppressor" while
also forcing black Americans "to recognize the cost of [their] submission"
("Black" 7). Wright made clear, Baldwin says, that "the oppressed and the

oppressor are bound together within the same society" ("Protest" 5)—
that the victimizer's abuse of the victim will ultimately have consequences.
Irving Howe has said that "[t]he day *Native Son* appeared, American culture was changed forever" because the novel "[a]ssaulted the most cherished of American vanities: the hope that the accumulated injustice of the
past would bring with it no lasting penalties" ("Black" 7). We want to think
that Bigger Thomas is a monster, an alien; we must realize, Wright reminds
us, that he is a native son.

How the Other Half (of Chicago) Lives: Meyer Levin's Compulsion

When Meyer Levin's biographer Steven J. Rubin wrote that Levin left
behind the writing of social novels after the 1940 publication of *Citizens*,
Rubin must have been forgetting Levin's 1956 novel *Compulsion*, a book
based on the Leopold-Loeb murder case of 1924. *Compulsion* is a literary
oddity: a novel that borrows the outline, details, and some of the actual
reporting (from Levin's own articles) of a real murder case but fictionalizes
the names of the participants and employs alternating first- and third-person points of view. It is also unusual in that Levin was revisiting material
from a crime he had covered in 1924 as a young Chicago reporter, but he
waited 20 years to write a book that was assured of strong sales due to the
notoriety of the case.[2] Although the book does not fit neatly into the Naturalistic homicide novel tradition, it does fulfill most of the major require-
ments. And while it may appear to reflect a very different Chicago from
that depicted in *Native Son*, the two novels actually bear many similarities.

As Rubin's comment indicates, Levin in the 1930s was working in the
proletarian novel tradition. Both *The New Bridge* (1933) and *Citizens* (1938)
are informed with the same concern central to the works of Steinbeck, Farrell, and Dos Passos: that an increasingly capitalistic system was eroding
the country's values. *The Old Bunch* (1937), more a social than a political
novel, nevertheless explores the preservation of values within a community.
All three novels are "collectivist" works, in which, as Rubin says, "concern
for the individual is subordinate to concern for the group as an entity" (36).
The community in question in *The New Bridge* consists of the residents of
Joe Joracek's apartment building as they struggle to prevent the eviction
of Joe, who is unemployed but intrinsic to the building itself, as he was a
member of the crew that constructed it. As in Wright's novel *Lawd Today*,
the action of *The New Bridge* is restricted to one day in Joe's life—that of
his threatened eviction. *The Old Bunch* treats the second-generation Jewish community of Chicago's West Side, an area where Levin himself grew

up. The novel is a kind of collage of voices, those of young Jewish boys and girls growing into an awareness of what it means to be Jewish in America. In Levin's epic attempt to use multiple perspectives "to encompass an entire social system," *The Old Bunch* resembles Dos Passos' *U.S.A.*, says Rubin, He also argues at length that the novel has a distinctly Naturalistic orientation, based largely on the meticulousness of Levin's cultural details and the focus on individuals who are "overwhelmed by the forces of environment and the grinding weight of a capitalistic economy" (38).

Before *Compulsion*, Levin also made two attempts at writing novels which were virtually "documentary" (Rubin 87). *Reporter* (1929), based on Levin's experience on the *Chicago Daily News* in the mid–1920s, was aesthetically undistinguished but significant (especially as predecessor to *Compulsion*) because of Levin's aim, which he described in his autobiography as concerning

> the relationship of printed news—the appearance of things—to the reality of events. This was not so much a search for the "news behind the news" as a wish to somehow render the fluidity of experience that became lost in the arid little paragraphs of newspaper stories. It seemed to me that if I could put down precisely what happened, down to the most trivial of events, I would inevitably capture reality [*In Search* 28].

Levin wanted to achieve what David Madden, in *Proletarian Writers of the Thirties*, calls "higher journalism," reporting that transcended the factual accounts of daily newspapers to get at a higher truth. Levin's fidelity to the truth of his own experience is perhaps best indicated by the fact that *Reporter* was withdrawn a few months after publication, after a local newspaperwoman recognized herself clearly enough to threaten a libel suit ("Levin" 282).

Levin's second attempt at the documentary mode was *Citizens*, an account of the Memorial Day 1937 confrontation between members of a local steelworkers' union and the Chicago police. Ten workers were killed in the melee; they are represented in Levin's novel in biographies interrupting the narrative, functioning much like the biographies in Dos Passos's *U.S.A.* Levin's research for *Citizens* reminds one of Zola's research for some of the Rougon-Macquart novels, especially *Germinal*. Levin spent months studying the workers in the mill environment, dining with them at a local boarding house, attending union meetings, and interviewing workers. His goal for the book was not so much to achieve an accurate narrative of the "Memorial Day Massacre" itself but "to understand the meaning of the workers' lives, their relationship to the economic system, and their role in the class struggle … taking place in America" (Rubin 54). Thus, Levin aimed to write what might now be called explanatory journalism or feature writing.

In the mid–1940s, Levin was discouraged by uneven reviews of his earlier novels and was pressing a lawsuit over the rights to a dramatic version of *The Diary of Anne Frank*, which he felt, apparently with good reason, had been appropriated from him by playwrights who went on to win every major theatrical award. Levin eventually won $15,000 and agreed to give up his appropriation claims (Mitgang). After his publisher reminded him that his Chicago experiences had always produced his best work, Levin decided to return to his newspaper days of the 1920s (85).

The story of Nathan Leopold and Richard Loeb's "crime of the century" had stayed with Levin, partially because of his identification with the two murderers. Like Levin, Leopold and Loeb were Jewish (as was the victim, Bobby Franks); the murderers were Levin's age and, like him, had been roughly his contemporaries as students at the University of Chicago.[3] Levin wrote in his autobiography that he understood Leopold and Loeb's feeling of "being strangers to our parents and our past, unsure of our place in society" (*In Search* 21). Rubin says that Levin identified with the teenage murderers' "alienation from their parents, their pathological intellectual curiosities, and their obsessive need for experience" (85). He clearly wanted to cultivate in readers his own understanding of the killers' motives; in his foreword, he defends himself against anticipated public opposition to exhuming the Leopold-Loeb material, explaining, "I write of it in the hope of applying to it the increase of understanding of such crimes that has come, during these years [since 1924], and in the hope of drawing from it some further increase in our comprehension of human behavior" (ix).

One of the strongest ties between Levin and the earlier Naturalists is the importance of journalism as a training ground for his novels. He followed a noteworthy succession of writers, most notably Theodore Dreiser, through the doors of the *Chicago Daily News*. Clearly, he saw his position there as a means to a career, not a career in itself; he wrote in his autobiography that in the 1920s "[o]ne's development as a writer required an apprenticeship on the *News* ... one didn't apply for a newspaper job in order to become a journalist. At least, not on the *Chicago Daily News*. One applied in order to become an author" (17–18). Levin's remark prefigures Tom Wolfe's contention in *The New Journalism* that reporters in the early 1960s were biding their time in reporting jobs, awaiting their novels—"literature's main event." In the case of *Compulsion*, Levin's involvement in the Chicago newsroom proved fortuitous: *Daily News* reporters had provided an important clue when they matched a ransom note from the Leopold-Loeb case to documents typed on Nathan Leopold's typewriter by friends who had borrowed it. The reporters subsequently won a Pulitzer Prize for reporting (Rubin 85), and Levin had near-proprietary access to this material.

Despite Levin's providing the fictional names "Judd" (Leopold) and "Artie" (Loeb) for the characters, he apparently adheres quite closely to the facts of the actual case. The accuracy of *Compulsion* is aided by Levin's use of many of his own original news stories. He interviewed the families and friends of Leopold, Loeb, and Franks, and, although Richard Loeb had been killed in prison in the 1930s, Levin received the full cooperation of Nathan Leopold (Rubin 87–88). The proceedings of Loeb and Leopold's trial closely follow the court records, and fictional attorney Jonathan Wilk's speech is reproduced verbatim from its author, Clarence Darrow (ix). By the time Leopold was released from prison in 1958 and gave Levin's book a repeat reading, he said he had difficulty distinguishing fact from fiction himself ("Fiction").

However, Levin makes no pretense to the sort of accuracy Capote would claim less than 10 years later in the preface to *In Cold Blood*. Levin admits in his foreword that

> [s]ome scenes are … total interpolations, and some of [the] personages have no correspondence to persons in the case in question….
>
> Though the action is taken from reality, it must be recognized that thoughts and emotions described in the characters come from within the author, as he imagines them to belong to the personages in the case he has chosen [ix].

It is frequently at the points where Levin departs from journalistic accuracy that he infuses Naturalism into his narrative. For example, early in Book I, the body of "Paulie Kessler" (Franks) is found stuffed in a drainage pipe in an outlying marsh by a laborer whose identity is not developed in the original newspaper accounts. In *Compulsion*, however, this character is Peter Wrotzlaw, a steel worker who has fortuitously veered off his usual path to work to run an errand. Wrotzlaw notices a foot sticking out of the pipe and realizes, according to Levin, on an entirely instinctual level, that something is wrong: "It was even said to be providential that Wrotzlaw has once lived on a farm, for in a submerged way his nature sense knew something strange was there, neither animal nor fish" (22). Because of his ability to detect the unnatural, Wrotzlaw is also able to find a stocking and the glasses that will eventually help to convict the killers. Levin's characterization of the steel worker as a person who interacts instinctually with the world is clearly Naturalistic; Wrotzlaw might be McTeague on the way to work. (Note that Levin suggests a Polish ethnicity for the laborer in the choice of his name.)

Levin's treatment of the two main characters, Judd Steiner (Leopold) and Artie Straus (Loeb), is not strictly Naturalistic. The author is clearly interested in the "why" of the case, as his comments in the novel's foreword confirm. Rubin says that "an understanding of the deviant personalities of the two intellectual criminals themselves" is "essential" to Levin's purpose (89). But if the causes of Judd and Artie's crime can be called deterministic in any sense, it is the more psychological determinism of Sigmund Freud—concerned with the workings of the mind—rather than that of Zola and Norris. It is also, to some extent, the more sociological determinism of Dreiser.

The Leopold-Loeb case was "one of the earliest cases in which a psychoanalytical study of the defendants had been attempted" (Rubin 86), and its employment in that case owed largely to the affluence of the Leopold and Loeb families (Richard Loeb's father, for example, was a vice president with Sears). According to Douglas O. Linder, the defense hoped that Sigmund Freud himself could testify, but the famous psychoanalyst was too ill to travel. The psychoanalytical nature of the defense is replicated in Levin's novel. The two boys, the narrator/reporter says, "would virtually be taken apart, to see what made them tick" (307). Two psychiatrists, reportedly getting $1000 a day, interview first family members, then Judd and Artie themselves. Then a third, a man of real professional prominence who studied in Europe and knew Jung and Freud, arrives to synthesize the results. The philosophy of these men is essentially deterministic: they feel that "[t]he entire aim of psychiatry was to unravel the causes of behavior. And if all behavior had a cause, where was guilt?" (342).

The experts' conclusion is that neither boy is in control of his actions, yet neither is insane. The specialists trace the "deviance" of both boys to negative experiences with nannies. Judd's, called Trudy, was "illiterate … animalistic, indulgent, teaching him to gratify every selfish desire, walking around slovenly and half naked, even taking him into her bed and initiating him as a child to perversions as well as to normal acts" (330). Trudy and Judd speak entirely in German, and he thinks of her as a "moron" (325). Artie's governess, Miss Newsome, is as conservative as Judd's is permissive; she strenuously encourages his intellectual and moral development— so strenuously that he quickly develops mechanisms of evading her, like lying and stealing (330–31). Miss Newsome is particularly "prudish" about sexual matters, and when she refuses to answer nine-year-old Artie's questions about his new brother's birth, he is left confused and resentful (331). The result is that both young men have grown up with the habit of deviating from prescribed norms and without an adequate sense of what is morally and sexually acceptable.

The Straus and Steiner family situations are basically the same: both boys are raised in an atmosphere of parental detachment and affluence. (The house where Nathan Leopold grew up is about a block from the Chicago home owned by the Obama family today.) A family friend says that Artie's father is "a man entirely occupied with his affairs. On festive occasions he would put in an appearance, at Artie's birthday parties" (310). Mrs.

Straus characterizes her husband as "not a demonstrative man" (312). When young Artie wants to talk to someone about his brother's birth, he reminds himself that "you never ask your father" (331). Mrs. Straus prides herself on being "a new woman, a leader," with "advanced knowledge of child care," but it is clear from her cultural involvements and her leadership of "all sorts of committees for settlement work with children" that she has put the welfare of other children before that of her own (310). During the crucial period of Artie's childhood—the arrival of his brother—he perceives that his mother is too preoccupied with "her adorable new baby that everyone adores" to talk to him (331). To compensate Artie for their detachment, the Strauses strive to make their home a center of teenage social activity: "young people were always welcomed ... and everybody was always going in and out, on the grounds, using the tennis court" (310). What they do not realize is that they are just putting more people between them and their son. The degree of the Strauses' separation from their son is indicated by the mother's attempt to explain to psychiatrists why the family never sought help for Artie when he exhibited symptoms of abnormality: the family "simply hoped [he] would grow out of it, as boys do" (313).

It is revealing that, during the psychiatric interviews, Judd Steiner never mentions his father. Judah Steiner, Sr., is a person of little consequence to his son, as Judd is preoccupied with the memory of his mother, whose inherited kidney disease worsened after Judd's birth and eventually caused her death. (Nathan Leopold's mother died of complications of kidney disease in 1921.) His idealization of his mother is clarified in his answer to the psychiatrist's question, "How did you think of your mother?": "I used to picture her as the Madonna. I still do" (321). Fueled largely by Mrs. Steiner's absence, Judah Steiner indulges his son; for example, after Judd is caught without a fishing license and has his expensive equipment confiscated, his father simply buys him more (314). Judah Steiner's actions are motivated by his belief that "nothing should stand in the way" of a boy as gifted as his son, an attitude which is, unfortunately, conveyed to the boy. And in both families, the nanny, who might be expected to relieve the child's suffering, compounds it.

Each boy also suffers from the suspicion that his family might have been better off without him. Because his mother's nephritis worsened after his birth, Judd blames himself for her death. Even when a psychiatrist reminds him that her condition was inherited, he insists, "I contributed to her death.... I often wish I had never been born" (323). Further isolated from his parents by the birth of his brother, Artie tortures himself with a disturbing possibility: "Mumsie and Popsie are having the baby really because they want someone else, not you. Nobody wants you" (331).

Finally, both Judd and Artie suffer from a superiority/inferiority paradox. Their considerable affluence has led them to feel an overdeveloped sense of entitlement. Their remarkable intelligence also contributes to this problem; like his model Loeb, Artie was the youngest student ever to enter the University of Chicago, and Judd's intelligence, the psychiatrists learn, exceeds the Stanford-Binet scale's ability to measure it. Thus, when the boys encounter the Nietzschean Superman in philosophy class, they convince themselves that the German philosopher was writing about them. Indeed, it is not difficult to see how Nietzsche's elitist arguments would have appealed to two young, rich, brilliant boys who had always been told they were exceptional. Despite the obvious difference in socioeconomic class, there is much in *Compulsion* to remind one of Dostoevsky's Raskolnikov plotting his murder of the pawnbroker and rationalizing it based on his sense of himself as an *Übermensch* or Superman.

The boys' preoccupation with Nietzschean philosophy might seem to obscure a Naturalistic reading of their actions, but it is important to remember that, despite Nietzsche's harsh criticism of evolution theory, the Superman concept is entirely consistent with Darwinism. The Superman can be viewed as the inevitable victor in the selection process, who survives because of his superiority. The dimensions of that superiority, as spelled out by Will Durant in *The Story of Philosophy*, are

> that in this battle we call life, what we need is not goodness but strength, not humility but pride, not altruism but resolute intelligence; that equality and democracy are against the grain of selection and survival; that not masses but geniuses are the goal of evolution; that not "justice" but power is the arbiter of all differences and all destinies [301–2].

Subscribing to this philosophy of natural power, Judd and Artie convince themselves that committing the "perfect crime"—determining the destiny of another human being and exerting their intelligence and perceived power over the police—would verify their belief that they *are* Supermen.

A final aspect of Nietzsche's philosophy appeals to Judd and Artie: his insistence that "[t]he man who does not wish to be merely one of the mass" should "have a purpose for which [he] will do almost anything *except betray a friend*," a loyalty which Nietzsche called "the final patent of nobility" (320–21, emphasis Nietzsche's). After compiling their profiles of the killers individually, the psychiatrists conclude that "a good deal can be made out of how these two distorted personalities conjoined, and how each functioned in their union" (329–30). Truman Capote called the fatal combination of Perry Smith and Dick Hickock a *folie à deux* (a French term meaning "madness of two"), and the same concept can certainly be applied to Straus and Steiner. Judd says that when he is near Artie, he feels "alive"; he characterizes his relationship with his accomplice as "blind hero worship" (328).

Artie is more casual about his feelings for Judd but clearly needs the rein-
forcement of Judd's adoration; this fits the pattern of the *folie à deux*, as one
partner generally appears more overtly needy, while the needs of the other
are more subdued. Indeed, there is every implication that Artie kills Paulie Kessler at least partially to impress his friend. In true Nietzschean form,
the moment when Judd realizes that Artie has betrayed him to the police
is far worse for Judd than the murder itself (252), and this is also true in
Capote's book, when the men are traveling separately with authorities from
Las Vegas to Garden City and Perry begins to suspect that Dick has implicated him. Asked to explain his motive for participating in the murder of
Bobby Franks, Nathan Leopold could only describe his loyalty to Richard
Loeb: "My motive, so far as I can be said to have had one, was to please
Dick. Just that—incredible as it sounds. I thought so much of the guy that
I was willing to do anything—even commit murder—if he wanted it bad
enough. And he wanted to do this—very badly indeed" (Leopold). Most
people who have researched the Leopold-Loeb case agree that the relationship between the two young men included sexual intimacy, a theory bolstered by a letter found in Nathan Leopold's bedroom during the murder
investigation. The PBS-produced *American Experience* documentary on
the case suggests that Leopold had a "master/slave fantasy" in which he
played the role of slave, and Loeb's insecurities were assuaged by Leopold's
behavior as his acolyte. The theory is that Leopold wanted sex, and Loeb
complied to secure Leopold's cooperation in the crimes that excited Loeb
("Perfect Crime"). If the partnership was driven to some extent by sexual
compulsion, that only increases its Naturalistic dimensions.

In Levin's account, the intellectual stimulation of the crime is a powerful motive for both Artie and Judd, and they view it almost as a scientist might view an experiment. Leopold has been famously quoted in his
remark to a *Chicago Tribune* reporter (Levin?) that the murder "was just
an experiment. It is as easy for us to justify as an entomologist in impal-
ing a beetle on a pin" (Leopold). Before Artie and Judd have even been
arraigned, family members and attorneys discuss their awareness that the
appropriate plea may be insanity, but their attorney, Wilks, ultimately does
not enter this plea because it would send the trial to a jury, which would
mean a certain death sentence. At the time of the Leopold-Loeb sentencing hearing, attorney Clarence Darrow sent men out into the streets of
Chicago to gauge public sentiment about the outcome. Sixty percent
favored hanging ("Perfect Crime"). With a plea of guilty, on the other
hand, the punishment would be set by a judge, and judges are characteristically less vindictive than juries (280). Motivated by the same fear that Judd
and Artie may be insane and that they will have to say so in court, the
psychiatrists hired by the boys' families agonize over whether to proceed

with their examinations. Levin characterizes their dilemma like a medical procedure:

> Storrs and Allwin [the psychiatrists] stood as a pair of surgeons might stand in an operating room, staring into an incision that disclosed not only a known cancer, but a number of other dreadful growths. To cut out all of them would mean sure death. Would it not be best then to close the incision quickly? [335–36].

A final word concerning the novel's determinism must be said about the closing argument of defense attorney Jonathan Wilk, the Clarence Darrow stand-in. The speech, reprinted verbatim from court records of the Leopold-Loeb trial (Rubin 91) took two days (four court sessions) to deliver, and Levin's description of it via the novel's narrator can be described as nothing short of laudatory. The narrator calls it the most eagerly anticipated speech "in all courtroom history" (424), and historians and journalists have documented that close to 2,000 people sought to enter the Chicago courtroom in order to hear it ("Perfect Crime"). At its conclusion, after Wilk quotes famous lines about *The Book of Love* by the Persian poet Omar Khayyám (just as Darrow did), the narrator offers this commentary: "We did not dare speak to each other, for our words might deride sentiment. We rather made the comments professional. A great plea. His greatest. A valedictory. It could suit any case and no case at all. It was a plea for every human life" (Levin 454).

Wilk's speech is rooted in two basic principles: that crime is a disease, and that whether it is caused by heredity or environment (or both), the individual can do nothing to prevent contracting it. Put simply, the attorney asserts that the deterministic factors are so strong that his clients could not assert free will. In the course of the speech, Wilk refers repeatedly to his clients as "these two unfortunate boys" who killed Paulie Kessler "because somewhere in the infinite processes that go to the making up of the boy or the man something slipped" (431). His belief that Straus and Steiner are victims of forces beyond their control is verified by his conviction that "any mother might be the mother of Artie Straus, of Judd Steiner" (432) with a son who "must tread the same road in blind childhood that these poor boys have trod" (454). Some legal experts maintain that the Leopold-Loeb trial marked a transition in criminal prosecution by introducing the notion of mental disease as a mitigating factor in the consideration of administering justice ("Perfect Crime"). Douglas O. Linder of the University of Missouri–Kansas City Law School writes of Darrow's closing argument, "Never before or since the Leopold and Loeb trial has the deterministic universe ... been so clearly made the basis of a criminal defense."

For the something that "slipped" in Judd Steiner and Artie Straus, Wilk indicts (albeit apologetically) heredity, the parents of each boy, and even the University of Chicago, which taught them Nietzsche, for not keeping "a closer watch, if possible, upon the individual" (447). But the central thrust of Wilk's appeal is toward "society," which he blames for its blood-thirstiness, as evidenced in other crimes, in zealous public support for World War I, and, most of all, in its clamoring for the executions of his clients. His indictment of the justice system makes quite clear that, to him, the criminals are victims, too:

> Crime has a cause as certainly as disease, and the way to rationally treat any abnormal condition is to remove the cause.
>
> If a doctor were called on to treat typhoid fever he would probably try to find out what kind of water the patient drank, and clean out the well so that no one else could get typhoid from the same source. But if a lawyer were called on to treat a typhoid patient he would give him thirty days in jail, and then he would think that nobody else would ever dare to drink the impure water [448–49].

Wilk finally suggests that a death sentence for Artie and Judd would become, in itself, a determinant, a brand which would stigmatize the Straus and Steiner families for generations to come (452). As Jim Craig and others have demonstrated, the notoriety generated by the real crime had a catastrophic effect on Leopold's father and brothers, who left their family home partially to avoid the spotlight; although Nathan Leopold, Sr., remarried, he died five years after his son's sentencing due to complications of surgery to treat "something similar to gallstones" (Craig, "Nathan"). Within a space of eight years, Michael and Samuel Leopold lost both their mother and father and saw their brother sent to prison for a horrific crime. Albert Loeb died of complications of heart disease less than two months after his son's sentencing, but Richard Loeb's family remained supportive of him. His oldest brother, Allan, eight years Richard's senior, represented the family in the courtroom each day and subsequently visited his brother in prison. Their mother, Anna Bohnen Loeb, also visited regularly and believed that Richard reformed as he matured ("Loebs"). As Anna Loeb lived until 1950, she and Richard's three brothers also endured his violent death in prison in 1936. Richard's youngest brother, Thomas, is said to have been the most profoundly affected among the Loeb brothers by the notoriety thrust upon his family, his bitterness likely contributing to three divorces and a problem with alcoholism ("Loebs"). Thomas "was closest to Richard before the crime and struggled throughout his life to overcome the tragedy" ("Loebs"). In addition, some of the Loeb relatives legally changed their surname. Just as Leopold and Loeb's actions were influenced by a combination of genetic and environmental influences, their families' lives after Bobby Franks' death were largely *determined* by the actions of the two sons.

The concluding section of *Compulsion* confirms Rubin's contention that Levin's theme is the question of free will versus determinism (91); the complexity of this theme is illustrated by two stories. The first is about a meeting between the reporter/narrator and Willie Weiss, a prominent Chicago psychologist who had been Judd and Artie's classmate and friend; Weiss explains Judd's "compulsion" to participate in Paulie Kessler's death as a need to destroy himself, to return to the womb (signified by the burial place, which Judd seemed to him to have chosen in the form of a cistern filled with water). The point of Levin's including this story is the author's desire to suggest that Judd's actions are not completely of his own volition and not purely motivated by his strong attachment to Artie but compelled by his own psychosexual needs.

The second story concerns the narrator's World War II experience in Germany, on a platoon with another soldier whom he prevents from raping a girl, recalling Jonathan Wilk's warning that the point of the Straus/Steiner case should be to prevent future violence. For the narrator, the clarifying of Judd's "compulsion" raises the question of free will: "If something like this [explanation] were valid," he considers, "then we were hopelessly driven, in the grasp of such dreadful forces" (490). The second story seems intended to answer the narrator's question, for in preventing the rape, he feels that he has exercised autonomy. Yet it is equally apparent that his behavior is influenced by the great speech of Wilk, and the speech's effect on the young man seems to bear out the attorney's conviction that with proper influences, young people can function more successfully than did Artie Straus and Judd Steiner. Thus, while Levin deals with the same question asked by the Naturalists, his answer is ultimately more ambiguous: the individual can, if he is strong and decent enough, exercise free will, but that strength and decency are difficult to achieve, given our environment. The final ambivalence of Levin's position is articulated in his foreword: "I do not wholly follow the aphorism that to understand all is to forgive all. But surely we all believe in healing, more than in punishment" (x).

Levin's fictionalization of his material makes his book, in some ways, difficult to classify. In his use of fictional names, he follows in the tradition of the Naturalists, who, even when they were writing about actual cases, never used murderers' real names. Rubin explains that Levin wanted the license that fictional identities would allow him: "By not using the names of those involved in the case, Levin allowed himself the freedom to transcend actual events in order to discover inner feelings and to speculate as to motivations" (89). Thus, Levin sought to achieve truth, a higher value than fact. But he also had a more practical reason: he hoped to avoid a lawsuit over appropriation. When Leopold was paroled in 1958, the lawsuit came anyway, and Levin prevailed. Only the previous year (1957), he had reached a settlement with Otto Frank involving Levin's stage adaptation of *The Diary of Anne Frank*, and attempts to adapt *Compulsion* for the stage and screen would bring more legal entanglements. For example, the cast of a Broadway production, which included Dean Stockwell and Roddy McDowell, was admonished always to use the character names Judd and Artie, never Nathan and Richard, when discussing the play with anyone (Zambrana 29). A detailed account of *Compulsion*'s adaptations may be found in Maria L. Zambrana's master's thesis, "'Compulsion': The Fictionalization of the Leopold-Loeb Case and the Struggle for Creative Control of 'The Crime of the Century'" (Northern Michigan University, 2015).

Levin's most important structural technique, the alternating of a third-person omniscient point of view and a first-person point of view (that of Levin's fictional counterpart, reporter Sid Silver) is a formalistic deviation from the Naturalistic tradition. Through Silver, Levin allows the reader to see simultaneously the killers and the case being assembled against them. In Book I, he often achieves irony through this effect, as when Judd and Artie are waiting for the ransom to be dropped off, when the police have already informed the Kessler family that Paulie's body has been found. Even more significantly, Levin makes clear the novel's theme through the involvement of Silver. Because the point of view in the third-person sections is so much more detached than in Silver's, it is difficult to imagine how the author could achieve the same commentary on the killers' motivations and on the question of determinism without his reporter/stand-in. If the real virtue of the Straus/Steiner case is its potential to make society more humane, then certainly Sid Silver is a tangible argument for that. In a sense, Levin has taken two threads which have always existed in the Naturalistic novel—the narration of the story and the narrator's need to comment on the story—and separated them.

Compulsion, with its dual narrative perspective, is actually the closest work in the Naturalistic homicide novel tradition to the nonfiction novel as it would be practiced a decade later by Tom Wolfe and Norman Mailer. As illustrated in Wolfe's *The Electric Kool-Aid Acid Test* and Mailer's *The Armies of the Night* (both 1968), the writer dramatizes himself with a stand-in as a participant in the action; Hunter S. Thompson calls this technique "gonzo journalism." Levin's need to see himself as a central figure in the case is obvious from his romanticizing of Sid Silver's involvement and this authorial stance anticipates gonzo journalism. When Silver goes to the mortuary to see the body, he immediately establishes his importance. He says, "It was even said afterward that but for my going out there just then, the murderers might never have been caught" (21), then immediately effaces himself: "it has always bothered me that I received a kind of notoriety, a kind of advantage out of the case. Obviously what I did that morning was only an errand" (21). And Levin sets up a framework for his novel—with basis in fact—of Silver's having been asked by the Illinois parole board to interview

Judd Steiner because "better than anyone else still alive, [his editors] said, [he] knew the story" (495). In 1954, before beginning his own manuscript, Levin had approached Leopold in prison about assisting him with an autobiography. In Levin's version of events, he created for himself the role of Most Knowledgeable Survivor.

As in other works of gonzo journalism, the participation of the author in the story is intrinsic to its theme: *Compulsion* is as much the story of the Straus/Steiner case's importance to Sid Silver and, by extension, to Meyer Levin as it is a narrative about the crime. In that sense, it cannot claim to represent reality—only a particular individual's experience of it. Silver says in his pseudo-preface, "there is no finite reality; our idea of actuality always has to come through someone, and this is the reality through me" (4). The most persuasive critics of literary nonfiction—John Hollowell, Ronald Weber, John Hellman, Chris Anderson—have all argued against what Mas'ud Zavarzadeh calls "zero-degree interpretation," the possibility of reporting anything with absolute objectivity (Anderson, *Style* 2). In its anticipation of the practices of the New Journalists, Levin's Leopold/Loeb novel seems quite contemporary.

Compulsion has been compared, by the few scholars who have written about it, to other books in the homicide novel tradition, most notably *An American Tragedy* (because every book in this tradition is compared to *An American Tragedy*) and to *Crime and Punishment* (owing to the influence of the Nietzschean philosophy). But it is certainly not a novel of the first order. Levin often treats his young stand-in Silver melodramatically, romanticizing his role in the investigation. A little more of Cain's or Capote's emotional restraint would have resulted in a better book. Also, the psychology of the novel often seems amateur, especially compared to *In Cold Blood*, published only nine years later; the psychological methods used to dissect Straus and Steiner ultimately reflect its 1920s setting more than its 1950s composition (largely due to the heavy use of source material). As Tasker Witham says in *The Adolescent in the American Novel*, "*Compulsion* certainly does not rank with *Crime and Punishment* as literature, or even with *An American Tragedy* or *Native Son*; but it will probably remain as a significant landmark among literary interpretations of criminal minds" (93). Witham does call *Compulsion* "the best of the post-war novels of juvenile delinquency" (94), though one must keep in mind that this comment was written in 1963.

Ultimately, Levin's book is most valuable, as Levin himself realized, for its portrayal of a particular phase in 20th-century America. Levin wrote in the foreword that "[c]ertain crimes seem to epitomize the thinking of their era," and that, just as *Crime and Punishment* and *An American Tragedy* arose out of their particular times and places, *Compulsion* is to be taken as a period document (ix). Richard Loeb and Nathan Leopold's crime fell almost exactly in the middle of what writer F. Scott Fitzgerald called "the Jazz Age," the period between the end of World War I and the crash of the stock market in 1929. Fitzgerald also famously said that the decade of the 1920s was "one long party." Fitzgerald's Jay Gatsby is probably the best-known American literary representative of this decade, and he might seem on the surface to epitomize the American dream, with his story of having worked his way out of poverty to life in his lavish mansion with expensive cars and extravagant parties. However, Gatsby's achievements do not include Daisy Buchanan, the woman he has loved for years and whom he has staged his display of wealth to impress. Late in the novel, he is shot to death in a mix-up stemming from crass jealousy and Tom Buchanan's adulterous and deceitful behavior. Tom also reveals to the narrator, Nick Carraway, that Gatsby's money has come from bootlegging during Prohibition and other minor criminal activities. For Nick, who is trying to follow a path through wartime service, a Yale education, and bond-trading in Manhattan to his own American dream, Gatsby ultimately comes to represent the emptiness that comes from having arrived at the palace too early and without an investment of genuine hard work. James Gatz's path is not Horatio Alger's but a shortcut to a display of wealth that turns out to be hollow, and his story is a cautionary tale for young Nick Carraway, not a model to be emulated.

Meyer Levin's novel locates itself in a social sphere somewhere between the old money of Tom Buchanan's family and the new money of Jay Gatsby. The Leopold and Loeb parents might represent the American dream, particularly given that all four of them were first-generation Americans and that they appear to dedicate themselves not only to hard work but also to various philanthropic activities. At the start of World War I, Anna Loeb "publicly pledged to volunteer each of her sons for military service" for the family's adopted nation, and only Richard did not enlist. Loeb's father Albert was "the driving force behind Sears' revolutionary profit-sharing plan among employees" ("Loeb") and also built a model farm in Charlevoix, Michigan, for testing Sears' products and providing employment to local residents. Both families are regularly described as pillars in Chicago's 1920s German Jewish community. But even with regard to Richard's and Nathan's remarkable educational achievements considering their ages, their sons seem more like intellectual dilettantes than like dreamers aspiring toward any worthwhile goal. The story of their notorious crime illustrates that when two young men benefit from massive fortunes not earned incrementally through their own hard work, they may come to feel that the rules binding the community do not apply to them. During their college years, when they are not yet expected to contribute to the family business and when the work of education does not appear taxing for them, they turn—Loeb in particular—to a darker game of survival of the fittest, declaring themselves "fittest" from the outset. A crime such as theirs may illustrate another failure of the American dream: that for those who are immune to its appeal because their families have already achieved it, a perversion of values may result. For readers of the Naturalistic tales of McTeague and Clyde Griffiths, *Compulsion* offers a warning about those at the other end of the social scale, suggesting that, like poverty, prosperity also has its perils.

Taken together, *Light in August, Native Son, The Postman Always Rings Twice*, and *Compulsion* make clear that the flame of Naturalism was not extinguished after the 1925 publication of *An American Tragedy*. Rather, that flame seems to have been re-routed into several smaller blazes, each focusing on a different aspect of the Naturalistic formula. The thread of determinism has its most religious turn in Faulkner's novel and its most social in Wright's. Wright's and Levin's novels fit the prescription for accuracy more closely than Faulkner's and Cain's, although the latter most anticipates the journalistic writing style that will predominate with the onset of *The New Journalism*. Cain's and Levin's novels are colored by the darker philosophies of the later decades. And while Levin's protagonists are inhabitants of a social world far removed from that of Farrell's "bottom-dog literature," his indictment of society is perhaps the most scathing of the four. These four novels and a few others carried the Naturalistic preoccupation with social outcasts, nobodies, and misfits well past the mid-century mark. In *Native Son* and *Light in August*, Wright and Faulkner introduced into the tradition issues of racial identity and equality which would continue in *In Cold Blood*, with Perry Smith's struggle over his mixed racial ancestry, and in *The Algiers Motel Incident*, with John Hersey's examination of violence fueled by racial prejudice. Levin's dramatizing his reporter prefigures the I-centered "gonzo" journalism of *Algiers Motel* and of the New Journalism in general. And Cain's achievement in stylistic detachment and in carefully crafted, minimalist prose has much in common with *In Cold Blood*.

If the flames of Naturalism that blazed at the turn of the century continued to flicker along separate trails between the 1925 publication of *An American Tragedy* and *Compulsion*'s appearance in 1956, their convergence in a big bonfire was right around the corner.

5

The Old Naturalism Meets the New Journalism

Capote's In Cold Blood

"This could affect the type of words on pages you could be reading for a while."—Jimmy Breslin

Few critics have offered higher praise for Truman Capote's novel *In Cold Blood* than Capote himself, who upon its 1965 publication told Shana Alexander that the book was "destined to become a classic" ("A Nonfiction Visit"). The publication of the book, with its preceding *New Yorker* serialization and its paperback and movie rights deals, was what George Garrett called a "Big Package Deal" (2) and an enormous commercial success. The *New York Times Book Review* gave Capote the longest interview in its history to that date. Critics lavished superlatives on the novel, calling it "a frank bid for greatness" (Garrett 3), "brilliant" ("Capote's Dissection," "Country"), "a work of art" ("Stranger"), and "the most thorough and sensitive piece of investigative reporting that's come out in a long, long time" (Delaney). John Gregory Dunne and Conrad Knickerbocker were among many reviewers who called the novel "a masterpiece."

Time's reviewer said that the novel "drains an event of its content as few events have ever been emptied before" ("Country"). Rebecca West, reviewing for *Harper's*, called it "a formidable statement about reality" (108). John Gavin, Massachusetts Department of Corrections Commissioner, wrote in the *Boston Sunday Herald*, "[F]or the first time I have read the story of a senseless and horrible crime that takes the reader behind the scenes and reveals the true facts of the causes." Granville Hicks said the book was written with "extraordinary skill" (35). In the *Cleveland Press*, Charles Stella called Capote "a reporter without peer." F.W. Dupee (*The New York Review of Books*) declared it "the best documentary account of an American crime ever written" (3). Even Kenneth Tynan, the book's most notorious critic,[1] termed it "the most detailed and atmospheric account ever written of a contemporary crime" (442). Capote's biographer Gerald Clarke wrote later that upon the book's publication, "the modern media machine—magazines, newspapers, television, and radio—became a giant band that played only one tune: Truman Capote" (362).

He maintained to George Plimpton that *In Cold Blood* represented "a new art form," declaring, "I truly don't believe anything like it exists in the history of journalism"; he called this new art form "a nonfiction novel" (qtd. in Inge 50; "Story," 2). In April 1963, Capote told family and friends in Monroeville, Alabama, that he had written "one of the world's best books" and, trusting his reputation to it, that he "might not ever write another line" (Moates 229). Capote's claims about the literary novelty of the book's form were met with a divided response. Critical reaction to Capote's claim tends to follow two courses: those who enthusiastically defend it and those who rather mildly dismiss it in passing.

Among those who defend the claims is Irving Malin, who argued that because Capote's journalism "selects to persuade us" rather than merely to report, his claims for the book's status should be taken seriously ("Murder"). The *Miami Herald* reviewer called Capote's book "something entirely original in the novel" ("Capote's Dissection"). William Wiegand writes that "with Capote the growing obliteration of the lines that demark journalism from fiction [seems] virtually complete" (245). Reviewer John Barkham accepted Capote's claim and encouraged other writers to emulate his methods. In the *New Orleans Times-Picayune*, James Conaway called *In Cold Blood* "an original work of art." Philip French's description of the book as "the culmination of a clearly thought out and carefully executed response to the American literary situation" would seem to allow it the status Capote sought.

But an equal number of critics contemporaneous to the book's publication rejected Capote's claims. *New York Times* reviewer Dupee, despite his admiration for the book, dismissed Capote's claim of uniqueness; Dupee wrote, "to this claim the only possible retort is a disbelieving grin." Melvin Maddocks observed that Daniel Defoe's *A Journal of the Plague Year* (1722), not *In Cold Blood*, was the first nonfiction novel. Diana Trilling maintained that the book is not a novel because Capote does not shape the facts which he presents and that the book consequently lacks theme. In his *London Observer* review, which became famous for its attack on Capote's moral position with regard to the novel, Kenneth Tynan also dismissed Capote's claim for the book's status. Although generous in his praise, George Garrett said the notion of the book as a new literary form "may be blamed on the publisher and dismissed as a device. About on the level of the 'new, improved ingredients' that show up with depressing regularity in

advertisements for toothpaste, detergents, deodorants, etc." (12). Despite
Garrett's acknowledgment of numerous *In Cold Blood* cousins in fictional
"stories of crime and punishment" and in journalism, he concluded that the
"[t]he question of form … remains a challenge, unresolved and probably
unanswerable" (12). *New Republic* reviewer Stanley Kauffman dismissed
Capote's claims as "puffery" (21), maintaining that the term "Nonfiction
Novel" was as illogical as "hard-top convertible" and "fresh frozen food"
(23). The most vitriolic of those who challenged Capote's was Sol Yurick,
who wrote in a *Nation* review entitled "Sob-Sister Gothic" that "the critics are demonstrating a deplorable lack of homework in the history of literature and psychology when they respond enthusiastically to this book; we
should expect as much from fans of the *Reader's Digest*" (158).

Faced with skepticism about his assertions for the book's uniqueness,
Capote backpedaled slightly. In a lengthy *Playboy* interview, he admitted to
Eric Norden that the term "nonfiction novel" was "an awkward phrase …
technically a *non sequitur*" (qtd. in Inge 120). He also told several interviewers, including Norden and Gloria Steinem, that his claim had been misun-
derstood. "I'm not claiming to have invented anything," he told Steinem,
"but to have extended the range of this form" (qtd. in Inge 78). To Norden, he said, "I have never claimed to have *invented* narrative journalism;
I do claim to have undertaken the most comprehensive and far-reaching
experiment to date in the medium of reportage" (qtd. in Inge 120, emphasis Capote's). Essentially Capote, in true bulldog fashion, stuck to his argument, largely because he believed it, even if he never explained it to critical
satisfaction.

Certainly, in many respects, Capote had not broken new literary
ground. Despite his phenomenal achievement in the genre, Capote was not
the first to write nonfiction using the techniques and devices of fiction. His
closest predecessor among major American writers is Ernest Hemingway,
whose *Death in the Afternoon* (1932) and *The Green Hills of Africa* (1935)
had, in William Wiegand's words, "pretty well settled for this generation"
questions about "the difference between literature and journalism" (243).
Mark Twain's *Life on the Mississippi* (1883) is another well-known work in
the literary nonfiction form. And obviously, in using the novel format to
tell the story of a factual murder, Capote's ancestors go back much farther
even than the Naturalistic works of Norris and Dreiser, at least to Stendhal's
The Red and the Black (1830). A notable shorter work that uses fictional
techniques to tell the story of a famous criminal's career is Daniel Defoe's
"True and Genuine Account of the Life and Actions of the late Jonathan
Wild; not made up of Fiction and Fable, but taken from his own Mouth,
and Collected from Papers of his own Writing," a novella published in 1725.

But Capote's novel does not fit snugly into either of these traditions.

The nonfiction predecessors by writers such as Twain and Hemingway have more in common with the New Journalism as Tom Wolfe and Norman Mailer have generally practiced it than with Capote's reporting methods in *In Cold Blood*. Primarily, Twain's and Hemingway's works are first-person accounts, I-centered reportage in which a strongly committed personal voice is the primary conduit for the narrative. The writer thus dramatizes himself as a participant via this first-person point of view. A more recent twist on this self-dramatization is Norman Mailer's writing about himself in the third person in *The Armies of the Night* (1968).

In *In Cold Blood*, however, Capote uses a third-person, ostensibly highly detached narrator, a voice more like that of the newspaper feature writer. He does not dramatize his own place in the story except in veiled hints; for example, one knows that Capote is the "visitor" to whom he occasionally refers. His predecessors in this regard are far fewer and more obscure. The one he acknowledged as his immediate prototype was *New Yorker* reporter Lillian Ross's *Picture*, an account of the making of John Huston's film *The Red Badge of Courage*.

Most of Capote's predecessors in the American homicide novel tradition use real murder cases as points of departure but make no claim to journalistic accuracy. Norris, Dreiser, Faulkner, Wright, Cain, and Levin do not use murderers' real names, for example, and none conducted actual interviews with his subject(s). Of the six, Levin was the only one to have actually seen his subjects in person. Any research involved in those novels' preparation, such as Dreiser's travels through the lake region of New York or Wright's trip to Chicago, was conducted more in the interest of verisimilitude than of factual accuracy. And while Levin wrote some newspaper articles contemporary to the Leopold-Loeb case, he acknowledged that *Compulsion* is a fictionalized work.

Capote's true distinction is that he worked to splice these two traditions—combining techniques of American literary Naturalism with the factual accuracy and journalistic detachment of top-notch reporting. He believed that he had achieved a balance in what he called "the Nonfiction Novel." But while he intensified this novel's emphasis on adherence to facts, he did not fundamentally change its literary ancestry.

What Capote does *not* seem to have realized is that his treatment of Perry Smith results in a book that fulfills in every way the criteria of the Naturalistic novel. In his discussions of the book, Capote does not mention Naturalism or any of the works in the homicide novel tradition, except one: he told Lawrence Grobel that he was not, in general, "a great admirer of Faulkner," yet he "liked one novel of his very much, called *Light in August*" (131). It is interesting but probably not coincidental that Capote should single out the most Naturalistic of Faulkner's works and the novel in which homicide figures most prominently. Capote was working squarely in the Naturalistic homicide novel tradition, merely shifting the emphasis on its three defining elements. He did not create a new literary genre, but he did modify an existing one. In fact, Capote brought these three elements into a balance that they have not enjoyed in another work before or since the publication of *In Cold Blood*.

Capote's choice of protagonist, Perry Smith, follows the Naturalistic formula. Like the earlier American Naturalists, Capote followed Thomas De Quincey's advice from "On the Knocking at the Gate in 'Macbeth'" that the "poet" writing about murder

> *must throw the interest on the murderer.* Our sympathy must be with *him* (…a sympathy of comprehension, a sympathy by which we enter into his feelings, and are made to understand them—not a sympathy of pity or approbation). In the murdered person, all strife of thought, all flux and reflux of passion and of purpose, are crushed by one overwhelming panic; the fear of instant death smites him "with its petrific mace." But in the murderer, such a murderer as a poet will condescend to, there must be raging some great storm of passion—jealousy, ambition, vengeance, hatred—which will create a hell within him; and into this hell we are to look [733–34, emphasis mine].

Capote settled on Perry Smith, the murderer, for his protagonist, as Norris chose McTeague and Dreiser chose Clyde Griffiths. He chooses Smith, not a member of the Clutter family, or K.B.I. agent Dewey, or even Dick Hickock, for the same reason that he focused on the murderers rather than the victims: he must choose the character who embodied what De Quincey calls the "great storm of passion." And Capote causes the reader to develop De Quincey's "sympathy of comprehension" by manipulating the narrative in favor of Perry Smith. Thus, those who argue that Capote does not advocate a position with regard to the Clutter killings miss the novel's strong rhetorical aspect.

In Part I, "The Last to See Them Alive," Capote cuts back and forth from the Clutter family at home in middle America to the killers moving toward them, developing an atmosphere of inevitability which Donald Pizer has compared to Thomas Hardy's poem "The Convergence of the Twain" ("Documentary" 113). From his introduction at the beginning of Part II, "Persons Unknown," Perry is treated more sympathetically than any other character, and Capote begins to shape the novel around him. Capote's literary fancy was drawn toward Smith for at least three reasons: (1) Smith, not Hickock, is the confessed murderer; (2) he is by far the more dynamic of the two characters; and (3) similarities between Smith's life and Capote's life created in the writer a depth of feeling for Perry which he did not hold for Dick. Even Capote's detractor Phillip K. Tompkins admits that it is "Perry Smith—not the victims, the investigators, the lawyers, not even the pair of killers—who dominates this book" (170).

The most basic reason for Capote's choice of Perry Smith as protagonist is that he, not Hickock, was almost certainly the murderer of the Clutters. Dick maintains from the beginning that Perry shot all four Clutters, and although Perry initially accused Dick of killing the two women, he later admitted that he had implicated Dick only "to fix [him] for being such a coward. Dropping his guts all over the goddamn floor" (287). Out of consideration for Dick's family, Perry later admitted—orally and by signed confession—that he had killed all four Clutters. Obviously, Capote believed that Perry's motives in confessing were sincere, as, at the end of Part III, "Answer," he puts in Perry's mouth the grisly narrative of what happened inside the Clutter house. If De Quincey was right that the "poet" writing about murder must spotlight the murderer, then Perry would seem to be Capote's best choice.

If Perry's culpability is the most basic reason for his suitability as protagonist of a Naturalistic novel, however, it is not the most compelling. In almost any murder case, the murderer is the most intriguing of the *dramatis personae* because he (or, rarely, she) is the figure of greatest mystery, the one whose experience is farthest removed from the reader's and whom the reader will feel least capable of comprehending. It is exceedingly difficult (if possible at all) for the average person to understand Perry Smith's attitude that "[i]t's easy to kill—a lot easier than passing a bad check.... [Killing the Clutters] was like picking off targets in a shooting gallery" (327). The psyche that produces a sentiment of this magnitude is a far more suitable subject for the Naturalistic novel than the psyche of any of the victims or investigators.

It would have been a challenge for Capote to make a Naturalistic protagonist from any member of the Clutter family. Among his characterizations of the family members, only the mother, Bonnie Clutter, has dimension resembling De Quincey's "great storm of passion." This is largely because her bouts of emotional instability (perhaps depression) prevent her from being a stereotype. A bird-like, delicate woman, Mrs. Clutter has recently returned to Holcomb (at the time of her death) from a Kansas City institution where she underwent two months' treatment. In fact, because of Mrs. Clutter's widespread reputation for instability, more than one person shares local café owner Bess Hartman's response to news of the murders: "Time I heard it, ... my first thought was Bonnie ... maybe one of her spells" (86).

The other Clutter family members are flat, middle-America paper dolls who might have stepped out of a Norman Rockwell painting. Herb Clutter, the father, is an upstanding middle–American farmer whose success has led to perhaps atypical prominence. (The story of his family's murders made the *New York Times* because President Eisenhower had appointed him a representative to a regional farm board.) Capote tells the reader that Clutter was "[a]lways certain of what he wanted from the world" and "had in large measure obtained it" (16). His political and religious beliefs also seem to reflect the norm for his time and place: he is a mid-western Methodist Republican who likes his daughter's Catholic boyfriend but will not consider allowing her to marry him, reflecting the anti–Catholic bias that would rise to the fore a few years later, when John Kennedy became a presidential candidate.

Nancy Clutter is a younger and female version of her father. She has recently played Becky Thatcher in the school play, dates the quarterback of the football team, and, on the morning of her death, is teaching another local girl how to bake a cherry pie. Nancy is "the town darling" (17), an American archetype from the paintings of Norman Rockwell, so naturally helpful that she inadvertently aids those investigating her murder by hav-ing recorded in her diary the time of her boyfriend's departure (11 p.m.) on the night of her death (100). Nancy's brother Kenyon, 15, is a typical rural teenager. He learned to drive at age 11, is an amateur carpenter, harasses his sister about her boyfriend, makes teasing comments to Nancy's friends on the telephone, sneaks cigarettes behind his father's back, and "could not conceive of ever wanting to waste an hour on any girl that might be spent with guns, horses, tools, machinery, even a book" (52).

The only exception to this middle America prototype is Bonnie Clut-ter, who, after the birth of her two older children, suffered near-debili-tating post-partum depression, "seizures of grief that sent her wandering from room to room in a hand-wringing daze" (38). Despite having had four children together, the Clutter parents sleep in separate bedrooms, Capote notes with some delicacy. Otherwise, the Clutter family is depicted with a rosy aura, perhaps owing to the fact that Capote gathered information about them from respectful, admiring fellow Holcombites after the fam-ily's deaths. They appear to fulfill every characteristic of the American dream in full flower, so much so that if Capote had created them, critics would say that the characters lack dimension; they are clichés come to life. If their flatness were not a serious enough impediment, it would be diffi-cult for Capote to make a protagonist of anyone whose murder 72 pages into a 384-page book is the beginning, not the end, of the story he wants to tell. And focusing on Alvin Dewey, the 47-year-old fourth-generation Kansan assigned by the K.B.I. to the Clutter case, would result in a mur-der mystery, reducing the thematic dimensions of the story. Murder mys-teries have one theme: the murderer has disrupted order, and order must be restored. Dewey, for all his professional prowess, is by-the-book, also somewhat lacking in dimension; the most interesting aspect of his char-acterization is the relationship he and his wife developed with Capote and

Nelle Harper Lee, a friendship that continued beyond the publication of *In Cold Blood*, when Alvin and Marie Dewey attended Capote's famous 1966 Black and White Ball, a masquerade at the Plaza Hotel in New York City.

Even Dick Hickock, Smith's criminal colleague, is too typical a lower-middle-class delinquent to serve as Naturalistic protagonist. Whereas Perry comes from a broken family with an alcoholic mother and an abusive father capable of conjuring the De Quincian storm, Dick's background is exceedingly normal; he comes from a lower-middle class two-parent family living in a "modest" farmhouse where the mother makes Sunday dinner and the men hunt, discuss cars, and watch sports on television. Perry is artistic and imaginative; in his spare time, he paints and plays the guitar. Dick is realistic, crass, almost mundane; he runs over stray dogs for his own amusement. In prison, Capote brought Dick *Playboy* and Harold Robbins novels, while Perry preferred Thoreau and Freud. (It should be noted that Thoreau's anti-capitalist philosophy is almost the antithesis of the American dream trope.) When Perry describes an elaborate, romantic, fanciful recurring dream, Dick replies, "I'm a normal. I only dream about blond chicken" (111). Capote himself articulated the fundamental difference between the two men: "Dick was a small-town punk and crook, and might have remained one all his life. Perry was different, though: Perry would have killed someone eventually, if not the Clutters" (Howard 72).

Capote goes to great lengths to characterize Perry Smith as a person whose actions are entirely determined by his environment and circumstances. During the trial section of the book, Capote uses the testimony of experts to establish a psychological portrait. W. Mitchell Jones, a psychiatrist with years of experience treating the criminally insane, traces Perry's problems to his childhood. Jones classifies Smith as paranoid schizophrenic and identifies as "particularly pathological" two aspects of his personality: his paranoia and "an ever-present, poorly controlled rage" set off easily by perceived slights or insults, which Smith sometimes misinterpreted (qtd. in *ICB* 333–34). Based on prison records, Jones locates the roots of Perry's general distrust and weak self-perception in the alienation and brutality of his early years. His psychopathology seems to have rested on a series of seeming opposites: his parents were both neglectful and abusive, an unpredictable pattern of behavior that left Perry "without ever having absorbed any fixed sense of moral values" (qtd. in *ICB* 333). He both coveted and distrusted connection with other people, developing what psychologists now call "hostile attribution bias"—the notion that others behave with hostile intent toward him, even when they may not do so. Because of these complications in Perry's relationships with others, Dr. Jones concludes, "He has little feeling for others outside a very small circle of friends, and attaches little real value to human life" (qtd. in *ICB* 333–34).

Jones's evaluation is endorsed by forensic psychiatrist Joseph Satten, who says Perry typifies a kind of murderer he had recently described in the article "Murder Without Apparent Motive—A Study in Personality Disorganization," published in the July 1960 *American Journal of Psychiatry*. Satten's thesis is that murderers like Perry suffer from "severe lapses in ego-control which makes [*sic*] possible the open expression of primitive violence, born out of previous, and now unconscious, traumatic experience" (qtd. in *ICB* 335). As both doctors explained, the ego of a person like Smith becomes a sort of open wound, and when the wound is irritated, he strikes out at the person who causes the irritation—whether or not that person caused the original wound.

That salt is rubbed into the wound of Perry's ego when he is inside the Clutter house is clear even to him. In his confession to Dewey, he describes the humiliation he suffered in trying to retrieve a silver dollar which had rolled underneath a chair in Nancy Clutter's bedroom:

> I had to get down on my knees. And just then it was like I was outside myself. Watching myself in some nutty movie. It made me sick. I was just disgusted. Dick, and all his talk about a rich man's safe, and here I am crawling on my belly to steal a child's silver dollar. One dollar. And I'm crawling on my belly to get it [271–72].

At this point in his narrative, Perry rubs his knees and asks Dewey for aspirin; it is clear, though, that there is a part of Perry far more hurt than his knees, and this is demonstrated by the rage that follows. In the basement minutes later, when Perry bends again on his damaged knees with the hunting knife before Herb Clutter's throat, he relives the search for the dollar: "I knelt down beside Mr. Clutter, and the pain of kneeling—I thought of that goddamn dollar. Silver dollar. The shame. Disgust. And *they'd* [the Parole Board] told me never to come back to Kansas" (276). That Perry has some sort of break with reality in that moment seems apparent from his description of cutting Herbert Clutter's throat: "I didn't realize what I'd done till I heard the sound. Like somebody drowning. Screaming under water. I handed the knife to Dick" (276).

Perry's desire to visit his rage on the people who caused his feelings of alienation is also obvious. Dr. Jones observes that Perry's rage was generally directed at authority figures, beginning with his father but also including those who had monitored him during his repeat incarcerations (334). Perry says that the firing of the nun who put an irritating ointment on his penis in an orphanage in a cruel and misguided attempt to cure his incontinence made him feel better, although it "never changed [his] mind about her & what [he] wished [he] could have done to her & all the people who made fun of [him]" (310). Of his sister Barbara, who had treated him like a baby doll when he was an infant but cooled her affection for him when he started to run with a street gang in San Francisco, he says, "I wish she'd been in [the Clutter] house that night. What a sweet scene!" (292). And he seems to realize that the Clutters were not the true targets of his rage, but stand-ins; trying to figure out why he killed the Clutters, he says,

> I wonder why I did it…. I don't know why…I was sore at Dick. The tough brass boy. But it wasn't Dick. Or the fear of being identified. I was willing to take that gamble. And it wasn't because of anything the Clutters did. They never hurt me. Like other people. Like people have all my life. Maybe it's just that the Clutters were the ones who had to pay for it [326].

What the Clutters had to "pay for" was essentially Perry Smith's exclusion from everything the family represented. This exclusion began early in Perry's life with the failure of his own mother and father to parent him. Capote details the horror of Smith's childhood: the pain of observing his mother's alcoholism and promiscuity, watching his parents' violent fights, and, after he was separated from them, being tortured in institutions for offenses such as bedwetting over which he had no control. Most of all, the horror of his childhood was the realization of his greatest fear, abandonment and isolation, in the form of his mother's telling him when he was eight or nine "to find a new home" (148).

As an adult, Perry is even more alone than he was as a child. In fact, his decision to team up with Dick Hickock is caused by another perceived abandonment: Perry has returned to Kansas (in violation of his parole agreement) two days before the murders, on Thursday, November 12, 1959, primarily to reconnect with Willie-Jay, a prison chaplain's clerk and Perry's "real and only friend," who was to be paroled on that day (55–56). Upon his arrival, though, Perry is "dizzy with anger and disappointment" to learn that Willie-Jay already left to pursue some "fine opportunities" farther East (59). So Perry agrees to participate in Dick's "score," feeling at that point that "the choice was between Dick and nothing" (59).

When Perry and Dick finally leave Kansas a week after the murders, Capote writes that crossing the border into Oklahoma, Perry leaves behind nothing and no one (125). He has no one to miss him: his mother and two siblings are dead; he is estranged from his sister; and he has lost touch with his father. Perry has also left behind Willy-Jay, the prison chaplain's clerk who had befriended him. But Capote is quick to point out that Dick is not isolated, as his life includes "those [he] claimed to love: three sons, a mother, a father, [and] a brother" (125). While Perry would be visited in prison only by Capote and, once or twice, by an army acquaintance, Don Cullivan, Hickock continued to be visited and supported by his parents, right up to his execution.

Ironically, the murder itself isolates Perry even from Dick; on the way out of the Clutter house, Perry realizes the full implications of Dick's insistence on leaving no witnesses:

> [I]n those few seconds before we ran out to the car and drove away, that's when I decided I'd better shoot Dick. He'd said over and over, he'd drummed it into me: *No witnesses*. And I thought, *He's* a witness. I don't know what stopped me. God knows I should've done it. Shot him dead. Got in the car and kept on going till I lost myself in Mexico [277].

When upon Perry's arrest the authorities decide to isolate him for questioning, their act of separating him from Dick is merely a gesture; the first of the shotgun blasts sealed Perry's alienation from everyone.

Finally, Capote chose Smith as his protagonist because strong similarities in their lives led the writer to sympathize with the murderer. This identification with the protagonist is not uncommon in the Naturalistic homicide novel, and a similar sense of connection existed in the cases of Dreiser writing about Clyde Griffiths, Richard Wright writing about Bigger Thomas, and Meyer Levin writing about Artie Straus and Judd Steiner. Both Capote and Smith had alcoholic, somewhat promiscuous mothers and absent fathers. Despite the fact that Perry's family was far more itinerant than Capote's, both men experienced childhoods characterized by isolation. Capote was reared by elderly relatives in Alabama who were affectionate but busy with their own lives, and young Perry Smith spent several years in orphanages and juvenile facilities after his mother's alcoholism incapacitated her. The central problem of each boy's childhood was the same: his parents considered him a liability and consequently shuffled him around; this lack of stability created in both boys a deep insecurity and a constant fear of abandonment. These two families in vastly different socioeconomic circumstances isolated their sons in remarkably similar ways.

Two other similarities drew Capote to Perry Smith: Perry's latent homosexuality and his artistic inclinations. In some ways, Perry seems almost asexual. He demonstrates a strong aversion to heterosexual sex (probably due largely to his mother's promiscuity) and is disgusted by Dick's sexual braggadocio and careless habits. In Mexico and Florida, Perry is reluctant when Dick suggests that they buy sex, and he frequently makes excuses to avoid brothels (228). But Perry needs men to function as mentors and guides, and Dick largely serves this purpose for him. Capote writes that "Dick's literalness, his pragmatic approach to every subject, was the primary reason Perry had been attracted to him, for it made Dick seem, compared to himself, so authentically tough, invulnerable, 'totally masculine'" (27).

To describe the complex psychological relationship between Smith and Hickock, Capote uses the French term *folie à deux* (madness of two)

(Grobel 118). Basically, the *folie à deux* is a sort of shared psychosis resulting from two people whose combination becomes more dangerous than the sum of their parts. Thus, Dick and Perry, like Artie and Judd, together are capable of acts that neither would undertake on his own. Neither Dick nor Perry alone would have committed the Clutter murders; Perry would not have been inside the Clutter house without Dick's initiative and planning, and Dick probably could not have pulled the trigger. Dick was essentially an instigator who often lacked the wherewithal to follow through, and Perry was a follower with the potential for explosive violence. It is easy to see how each could transfer his culpability to the other and what consequences this fragmentation of responsibility might bring.

The second reason for Capote's strong identification with Perry is the artistic ability (and sensibility) both possessed. That Smith viewed Capote as an artistic mentor is well documented. In prison, the convicted murderer asked the writer to bring him classic works of literature and philosophy, as well as a dictionary and thesaurus so that he could improve his pretentious vocabulary (Clarke 344–45; *ICB* 169). Perry possessed both musical and artistic abilities. He says he could play both guitar and harmonica from the "first time [he] picked one up" (155), and Capote describes Perry's Jesus portrait in the novel as "in no way technically naïve" (56). The point is not the quality of Perry's work or the likelihood of his success, had his life been different; it is the role that art served in both men's lives. Both Smith and Capote "turned to art to compensate for what had been denied them" (Clarke 326).

Frustrated by Perry's self-pity and his insistence on blaming his background for his crime, Capote once yelled at him, "I had one of the worst childhoods in the world, and I'm a pretty decent, law-abiding citizen" (Clarke 327). Capote certainly realized, as Dreiser realized in the case of Clyde Griffiths and Levin realized in the case of Nathan Leopold and Dick Loeb, that, given the strong similarities in their childhoods, the path taken by the murderer might well have been his—as John Bradford said, "there but for the grace of God go I."[2] Nelle Harper Lee, who accompanied her lifelong friend to Kansas for the initial research, said that Truman's and Perry's relationship was "more complicated than a love affair; each looked at the other and saw, or thought he saw, the man he might have been" (qtd. in Clarke 326).

Perhaps the real irony of the relationship between the two men was that in committing the act that precipitated his own destruction, Perry Smith also became a part of the writer's masterpiece. Perry was certainly aware of this irony; he told Capote, "[A]ll [I] ever wanted to do in [my] life was to produce a work of art.... And now, what has happened?... I kill four people, and you're going to produce a work of art" (Plimpton 39). It was also clear to Capote that he owed the success of his book to Perry Smith; Capote told an interviewer that he didn't really commit himself to writing a book based on the Clutter murders until he had been conducting his research for about eight months (initially he planned only a *New Yorker* piece):

> And then something in the whole material appealed to something that has always been inside me anyway, waiting there. It was Perry that made me decide to do it really. Something about Perry turned the whole thing, because Perry was a character that was also in my imagination [qtd. in Nance 210–11].

Equally important, from a literary standpoint, to the question of why Capote chose Perry Smith as the protagonist of *In Cold Blood* is the question of how Capote arranges his material to feature Smith in that role. He employs at least three methods: first, he devotes more space to Perry than to any other character; second, he describes Perry with details intended to bend the reader's sympathy in Perry's direction; and third, he orchestrates the narrative itself in Perry's favor.

In Cold Blood is composed of four main parts: "The Last to See Them Alive," "Persons Unknown," "Answer," and "The Corner." Each part is further subdivided into short sections separated by white space; the book contains 84 such sections in all. Perry Smith is the focus of 10 sections, for a total of 72 pages (out of 384). By contrast, Dick is the primary focus of only four sections, for a total of about 13 pages. Twenty-eight additional sections involve both Perry and Dick, and at least half of these sections concern Perry more than Dick (e.g., Perry's thoughts while Dick is driving). About 10 sections involve Alvin Dewey (about 36 pages), but some of these deal with the investigation and do not focus exclusively on him. Only seven sections focus exclusively on a member of the Clutter family (Herb, three; Nancy, two; Kenyon and Bonnie, one each). In addition, 13 sections deal with Holcomb itself and the townspeople's reactions to the murder. Thus, about a fifth of the book's total pages are devoted exclusively to Perry, and 38 of 84 sections are primarily about him.

Perry Smith is also the subject of the longest section of the novel, number 35. This 27-page section (144–71) occurs nearly halfway through the book and covers Perry and Dick's last day in Mexico. It is a good example of Capote's cinematic technique of focusing on Perry in the foreground of a scene while Dick is otherwise occupied in the background. In this episode, Dick has sex with a Mexican woman (one of two he has promised to marry) on the bed in the hotel room he and Perry share while Perry sorts through his "possessions"—the maps, letters, and other memorabilia that he carries around with him. Perry is selecting the most important to take with him while he sends the rest ahead to pick up later in Las Vegas. Among the papers Perry decides to keep with him are three documents, the full texts of which are printed in the section: (1) an essay called "A History of My Boy's Life," written by Perry's father for the Kansas State Parole Board in December 1958, before Perry's release the following July; (2) a letter from Barbara Johnson, Perry's sister, dated April 28, 1958, addressing the general topic of how much people can be held responsible for their actions; and (3) Willie-Jay's "very sensitive" (in Perry's eyes) appraisal of Barbara's letter (166). From these three documents and the long reflection that his father's letter prompts in Perry, the reader develops a thorough acquaintance with Perry's life and feelings. No other character in the book is given the benefit of such lengthy treatment; the second-longest section (16 pages) contains Perry's confession to Alvin Dewey en route from Las Vegas to Garden City, while the longest section concerning Dick covers only eight pages.

In Perry Smith, Capote was fortunate to find a character with some inherently sympathetic qualities. For example, Perry's child-like attributes make it difficult for a reader not to feel some pity for him. At five feet four inches, he was a short man like Capote, who constantly reminds the reader of Perry's stature by pointing out such details as his rolled-up jeans and the fact that, when he sits, his feet often dangle above the floor. Perry chews (rather than swallowing) aspirin for his damaged knees and washes it down with root beer. He is asked to spit out his chewing gum as he mounts the scaffold. He is very protective of his possessions, carrying his guitar and his boxes of mementos everywhere he goes, like a child who wants to take his whole toy box over to grandma's. And Perry's dreams of finding buried treasure and being rescued by a giant bird are the dreams of an imaginative child, not a man.

It might be argued that Capote includes these details simply because they are what Tom Wolfe calls "status details"—facts that, by their specificity, suggest verisimilitude. But that theory does not explain why Capote includes far more of these details about Perry than about any other character, and he repeats some so often that they take on nearly symbolic value. For example, the shortness of Perry's legs and the smallness of his feet are mentioned repeatedly, probably because Capote himself was charmed by those features. Harper Lee has said that when he saw Perry seated at his arraignment, Capote exclaimed, "Look, his feet don't touch the floor!" and she thought to herself, "oh! oh! This is the beginning of a great love affair!" (Clarke 326). Scarcely two pages into the reader's first encounter with Perry, Capote points out his "stunted legs" and his "tiny feet, encased in short black boots with steel buckles, [which] would have neatly fitted into a delicate lady's dancing slippers" (26). Agent Nye notices the same detail when Perry is seated for questioning in Las Vegas (254), and Dewey notices it again when he sees Perry's feet dangling below the scaffold. Perry's small footprint outlined in blood on the mattress box where Herbert Clutter was murdered is the only physical clue in the house linking Smith to the crime. Certainly this level of emphasis would seem to go beyond status details.

Another method used by Capote to characterize Perry Smith favorably is setting up scenes in which Perry is described by a woman who feels sympathy for him (a device which Capote had used effectively in *Other Voices, Other Rooms* and which Norman Mailer uses in *The Executioner's Song* to characterize Gary Gilmore). In Perry's case, the best example of such a woman is Mrs. Josephine ("Josie") Meier, wife of Finney County Undersheriff Wendle Meier and cook for the jail prisoners. Though Mrs. Meier admits that she had little interaction or interest in Dick, she obviously developed affection for Perry (345). To separate him from Hickock, Perry was held in the ladies' cell at the Finney County jail (he is the first man in Mrs. Meier's memory to occupy it); that cell actually adjoined the Meiers' kitchen. When he has been there barely an hour, Mrs. Meier, noticing that he has not touched his food, asks if he has a favorite dish so that she can make it the next day (285). When she goes to bed the same night, Mrs. Meier tells her husband that Perry "wasn't the worst man [she] ever saw" (285). On the night of his conviction, she told Capote, she heard Perry crying and sat outside his cell holding his hand and trying to console him with offers of his favorite dish, Spanish rice. She felt bad that she and her husband had a social engagement that night and she would have to leave Perry alone. The worst part, Mrs. Meier told Capote, was bidding Perry farewell when he was transferred to death row at Leavenworth (345–46). Mrs. Meier also described a red squirrel which Perry had taught to eat from his hand and which returned looking for him after he was taken to death row. Capote describes Mrs. Meier as "a direct and practical woman who nevertheless seem[ed] illuminated by a mystical serenity"; through her eyes, the reader sees a Perry Smith surprisingly different from the one who cut Herb Clutter's throat (283).

In June 1966, four months after the book's publication, Kansas State University professor Phillip Tompkins wrote an article for *Esquire* questioning Capote's veracity. Tompkins maintained that, to him, Mrs. Meier expressed indifference toward Smith. Confronted by his biographer Clarke with Tompkins' challenge, Capote theorized that she had succumbed to pressure from her husband, and he stood by his original account. And if Capote did romanticize or exaggerate Mrs. Meier's attitudes to any extent, this would only reinforce the idea that his goal in her scenes is to win the reader's sympathy for Perry.

Capote emphasizes the differences in Perry's and Dick's behavior inside the Clutter house as another means of winning sympathy for Perry. His source for these details is Perry's confession, which, Dewey attested, was "very much" like Hickock's statement in every aspect except for who killed whom (277). Although he confessed to being the actual murderer, Perry's behavior toward the Clutters before their deaths is far more courteous and considerate than Dick's. Dick punches Kenyon Clutter when he doesn't get out of bed fast enough, threatens to rape Nancy Clutter, roars at Herb Clutter, "Didn't I tell you to shut up?" and goads Perry into committing the first murder, which leads inevitably to the rest.

Perry, on the other hand, has an extended conversation with Nancy Clutter, while Dick is looking for the fictitious safe, about music, art, her boyfriend, her love of horses, and the fact that his mother was a rodeo rider; he told Dewey that Nancy seemed "really nice. A very pretty girl, and not spoiled or anything" (274). In the basement furnace room, Perry puts down a mattress box before he asks Herb Clutter to lie down because the floor is cold (272). Throughout his confession, Perry referred to the Clutters respectfully, in his "soft" voice, as "Mr. Clutter" and "Mrs. Clutter." He placed Kenyon in the basement on a couch and cushioned his head with a pillow when the boy had a coughing episode (273). "And lest the reader object that Capote worked exclusively from Perry's own account of his behavior inside the Clutter residence, the crime scene investigators corroborated at least some of these details." Detectives Dewey and Duntz had noted early in the investigation that the brutal murders were committed with "fragmentary indications of ironic, erratic compassion," indications which had convinced them "that at least one of the killers was not altogether uncharitable" (273); Capote attributes these acts of apparent compassion to Perry Smith, even underscoring them.

Capote also softens a reader's judgment of Perry somewhat by implying that Perry did not go into the Clutter house planning to commit murder. Perry's description of his last conversation with Herb Clutter reveals a marked lack of premeditation:

> Just before I taped him, Mr. Clutter asked me—and these were his last words—wanted to know how his wife was, if she was all right, and I said she was fine, she was ready to go to sleep, and I told him it wasn't long till morning, and … somebody would find them, and then all of it, me and Dick and all, would seem like something they dreamed. *I wasn't kidding him. I didn't want to harm the man.* I thought he was a very nice gentleman. Soft-spoken. I thought so right up to the moment I cut his throat [275, emphasis mine].

The most important of the minor discrepancies documented by Phillip Tompkins between Capote's account and his sources concern Perry Smith. In addition to tangential issues like how much money Nancy Clutter's horse sold for and the degree of Bobby Rupp's athletic prowess, Tompkins challenges Capote's presentation of Smith, specifically his self-control at the time of the murders and the degree of his remorse. In a *New York Times* interview, Capote described Perry's actions in the Clutter basement as a "mental explosion" (qtd. in Tompkins 167), a psychological phenomenon akin to what Dr. Jones called "a paranoid schizophrenic reaction"

(*ICB* 334). The implication in Capote's account is that Perry had almost no self-control, as Perry's description of the murder suggests: "I didn't realize what I'd done until I heard the sound. Like somebody drowning" (276). Capote's version is based on Perry Smith's initial confession and any statements Perry may have made privately to the author.

Tompkins found a slightly different account in the version of Alvin Dewey, who was called to testify to Perry's confession because Perry never signed a statement validating it (due to the discrepancy concerning Hickock's involvement). Dewey's account differs from that described in *In Cold Blood* in two ways: first, he told the court that Smith and Hickock had discussed which of them would make the first move and that Perry had taken the initiative, and second, Dewey testified that Perry described how he hid the knife blade with his arm, pretending to tighten the cords around Herbert Clutter's wrists, so that Clutter would be taken by surprise (Tompkins 166–67). Both details indicate a degree of premeditation and calculation not present in Capote's version.

Tompkins also challenges the accuracy of Perry's final speech, maintaining that Perry did not apologize before mounting the scaffold. In Tompkins' version, Perry says that it would be "meaningless" for him to offer an apology and that he harbors no ill feelings toward authorities. (169). Capote provides considerably more detail suggesting Perry's emotional state and implying, again, his potential as an artist: he stands, staring down at his hands, which Capote describes as covered with ink and paint from the numerous portraits painted while Perry was on Death Row. He delivers a final speech that is much more emotional than in Tompkins' account:

> I think it's a helluva thing to take a life in this manner. I don't believe in capital punishment, morally or legally. Maybe I had something to contribute, something... [At this point, Capote notes, Perry's "assurance faltered; shyness blurred his voice, lowered it to a just audible level"]. It would be meaningless to apologize for what I did. Even inappropriate. But I do. I apologize [381].

Tompkins' account was corroborated, he says, by Bill Brown, editor of the *Garden City Telegram*, and by the Associated Press representatives who served as witnesses, many of whom told Tompkins that Capote was so distraught that he had to leave the gallows area and could not likely have heard Smith's last words (169). Capote's own version was that he was, in fact, "at the foot of the gallows" (Grobel 118; Alexander 22) *closer* to Smith than the media representatives, that he was, in fact, the last person to speak to both Smith and Hickock, and that it was the other journalists who didn't catch all of Perry's statement.

Smith's precise last words may never be known, but to charge Capote with inaccuracy and stop there seems beside the point. If Capote did romanticize Perry's statement and, perhaps, his own role in the execution, it only reinforces the argument that his real intention was to portray Smith as a sympathetic character. Of challenges to the accuracy of his characterization of Perry Smith, Capote told William Nance,

> All I can do is show you his letters. You read the letters of Perry Smith and you know darn well that my portrait of him is absolutely accurate, and it's not a sentimental distortion on my part, of identifying with him. I *did* identify with him to a great degree. Never did deny it. It's also quite true that my portrait of him is absolutely one hundred per cent the way he was [215].

Capote seems to admit that he was after a higher fidelity than the factual accuracy of every line; according to Nance, Capote felt he was "accurate on the deepest level [because] he [had] presented the real Perry Smith" (215).

Another device used by Capote to develop Smith as a character is his inclusion of the psychiatrists' opinions which were not a part of the official court transcript. Asked whether the defendants could distinguish right from wrong, Dr. Jones answers yes in the case of Hickock and claims no opinion about Smith; when he offers to elaborate on both answers, the prosecution's objection is upheld (330). But Capote is not content to omit the explanation; he adds information from his interviews that Dr. Jones had planned to present, had he not been thwarted by the objection. This addition includes a paragraph elaborating on his affirmative answer about Dick's sense of right and wrong and a five-and-a-half-page clarification of his indecision about Perry's (330–38). In terms of strict fidelity to the facts of the case, Capote may be out of line in including this "testimony," but he believed that its inclusion helped him get at the real truth, primarily the truth about Perry Smith. Capote believed all along that Perry understood what happened inside the Clutter house as well as anyone, telling George Plimpton that he chose to use Perry's version of events because "Perry's happens to be the one I believe is the right one" (38). There is, in fact, a startling correspondence between Perry's layman's explanation that "maybe the Clutters had to pay" for the traumas he had suffered and Drs. Jones' and Satten's professional analyses of latent hostility transferred to innocent victims. And Perry's version is vastly more literary.

But Capote's most successful strategic maneuver where Perry's characterization is concerned is his pacing the story in Perry's favor, by withholding the narrative of the murder until late in the book. Toward the end of Part I, Capote cuts from Hickock's car creeping, headlights off, up the Clutter driveway, to the discovery of the bodies the following morning. Part of his purpose, obviously, is to maintain suspense by delaying the explanation of what actually happened in the Clutter house. But the larger effect is to preserve the sympathy which the reader has begun to develop for Perry. When the gruesome details are finally revealed three-fourths of the way through the book, Smith is the narrator, leading the reader through the Clutter house, from victim to victim. By placing the reader's experience of the murder entirely within Perry's consciousness, Capote is able to mute the horror somewhat with the details of Perry's little acts of "ironic, erratic compassion"—details neither Hickock nor any other narrator would have been likely to include. As George Garrett has argued, Capote did not wish to fully dramatize "the naked brutality of the murder scene" because "[h]ad he done so, early or late, he could probably never again have engaged the reader's sympathy for Perry Smith" (9–10).

Harper Lee told *Newsweek* that her friend Truman "knows what he wants.... And if it's not the way he likes it, he'll arrange it so it is" ("*ICB*: An American Tragedy" 58). What Capote wanted in *In Cold Blood* was a narrative featuring Perry Smith in a sympathetic light, and he orchestrated his material carefully in order to achieve that version. Capote's skill in characterization and his sheer good fortune in stumbling across a person who fundamentally fit the Naturalistic bill combined to form a figure whom Norman Mailer has called "one of the great characters in American literature" (Clarke 326).

Capote's interest in writing nonfiction using the techniques of the fiction writer preceded *In Cold Blood* by several years. He had established himself as a fiction writer at the age of 24 with the publication of the short novel *Other Voices, Other Rooms* (1948) and continued to write fiction until the mid–1950s, when he published two nonfiction pieces in *The New Yorker*. The first, *The Muses Are Heard* (published as a short book in 1956), was an account of an American opera company's tour of the Soviet Union performing *Porgy and Bess*. *The Muses Are Heard* was well received, and Capote claimed he had found the writing of it surprisingly pleasurable (Clarke 294). The next year (1957), he published a profile of Marlon Brando, "The Duke in His Domain," in *The New Yorker*. The profile, based on a dinner interview during which Capote got Brando to make some startling revelations, was called "a vivisection" by reporter Dorothy Kilgallen and "a masterpiece" by legendary *New Yorker* editor William Shawn (qtd. in Clarke 303).

Although pleased with both *New Yorker* pieces, Capote's appetite for nonfiction was not sated; he wanted to try the same method "on a grand scale" (Grobel 112). During his work on *Breakfast at Tiffany's* (1958), the short novel about Holly Golightly, an eccentric young woman stirring up New York cafe society, Capote's thoughts were still on nonfiction. In fact, he had postponed the writing of *Breakfast at Tiffany's* when the opportunity to go to the Soviet Union came along (Clarke 290). He still wanted to write his nonfiction novel, which he defined as "a book that would read exactly like a novel except that every word of it would be absolutely true" (Grobel 112). Even after the warm reception of *Breakfast at Tiffany's*, he found himself unable to concentrate on writing fiction because of what he described as a greater temptation:

I couldn't sit there to write … [i]t was as though there were a box of chocolates in the next room, and I couldn't resist them. The chocolates were that I wanted to write fact instead of fiction. There were so many things that I knew I could investigate, so many things that I knew I could find out about. Suddenly the newspapers all came alive, and I realized that I was in terrible trouble as a fiction writer [Clarke 317].

It seems appropriate that Capote found his "box of chocolates" in a newspaper—*The New York Times* of Monday, November 16, 1959. In an article entitled "Wealthy Farmer, 3 of Family Slain," Capote read, "A wealthy wheat-farmer, his wife and their two young children were found shot to death today in their home. They had been killed by shotgun blasts at close range" (39). Thus, Capote turned reporter, leaving New York less than a month later with Harper Lee (whose own novel, *To Kill a Mockingbird*, was just about to be published) for the little town of Holcomb to investigate a multiple-murder case which remained unsolved for nearly six weeks after he and Lee arrived.

In his research for the book, Capote drew primarily on three kinds of sources: (1) interviews with the townspeople of Holcomb, the law enforcement officials who worked on the case, and, eventually, the murderers themselves; (2) official documents, particularly the transcript of the trial of Perry Edward Smith and Richard Eugene Hickock; and (3) his own observation of the town, the ongoing investigation, and the subsequent trial and executions. His insistence that his novel be read as journalism is obvious from the acknowledgments page, where he writes, "All the material in this book not derived from my own observation is either taken from official records or is the result of interviews with the persons directly concerned, more often than not numerous interviews conducted over a considerable period of time." The book's subtitle, "A True Account of a Multiple Murder and Its Consequences," reinforces the argument that Capote aimed for veracity.

It is worth noting that Capote is not a practitioner of what Hunter S. Thompson calls "gonzo journalism"; he does not dramatize himself as a character in his nonfiction and does not directly call attention to himself in any other way. With respect to narrative perspective, *In Cold Blood* is more strictly journalistic than any work of "gonzo journalism" (Tom Wolfe's *The Electric Kool-Aid Acid Test* or Norman Mailer's *The Armies of the Night*, both 1968, for example). Like a good reporter, he maintains a detached stance, and he is fastidious about his attributions. Early in Part I, "The Last to See Them Alive," Capote describes an encounter involving 16-year-old Nancy Clutter, 15-year-old Kenyon Clutter, and Paul Helm, the husband of the Clutter's housekeeper. Capote is careful, at the end of the chapter, to identify Helm as his source: "'And that,' [Helm] was to testify the next day, 'was the last I seen them'" (52–54).

Many of the townspeople of Holcomb became minor characters in *In Cold Blood* because of the information they were able to provide; in fact, in the novel's preface, Capote calls them his "collaborators." For example, Bobby Rupp, Nancy Clutter's boyfriend, had been at the Clutter house until around 11 p.m. on November 14 (the Clutters were killed in the early hours on the 15th). As someone who saw the family members only hours before they died, Rupp was not only a valuable source for Capote but also an early suspect for the police. Nancy Clutter's friend Nancy Ewalt and her father Clarence discovered the bodies Sunday morning when they came to the Clutter house to pick Nancy up for Sunday school. Eccentric Holcomb postmistress Myrtle Clare told Capote about seeing the ambulances heading to the Clutter farm. And Josephine "Josie" Meier, wife of the Holcomb County undersheriff, helped the author with his description of Perry and Dick's stay in the county jail.

A scene in Part IV, "The Corner," detailing Perry Smith's reaction on the evening of his conviction and sentencing clarifies Capote's willingness to hint at his fact-gathering techniques in the process of conveying the facts; the section begins with Capote's disclosure, "A week later Mrs. Meier was sitting in her parlor talking to a friend" (345). It does not seem too speculative to suggest that this "friend" is Truman Capote. The third-person generic "a friend" is his means of maintaining the journalistic stance.

Capote's method as an interviewer has been sufficiently noted and is now frequently mentioned in journalism textbook chapters about interviewing or feature writing. The *a priori* of Capote's strategy was that there would be no notetaking or recording. He bragged to anyone who would listen about his phenomenal memory, saying he had prepared for the exhaustive interviews by memorizing pages from catalogs and then having friends quiz him (Plimpton, "The Story" 38). Clarke describes Capote's rationale:

> Not once was he or [Lee] seen taking notes: ... [his] theory was that the sight of a notebook, or worse still, a tape recorder, inhibited candor. People would reveal themselves, he maintained, only in seemingly casual conversations. Unless they saw a pen or pencil flying across a page, they could not believe that their words were being recorded [322].

Later, Capote and Lee would return to their hotel, where they wrote separate accounts of the day's interviews. They apparently often conducted interviews together, and during the first few weeks of their stay in Kansas, while the diminutive, effeminate-voiced Capote had difficulty warming up the Holcombites, Lee, drawing on her experience in rural Southern towns, dominated these early interviews. Later, they would compare their versions and together, as Lee said, "get it right" (Clarke 322). Getting it right often required more interviews: according to Clarke, Capote and Lee more than once interviewed the same person three times in one day (322).

Capote was also dependent on a variety of printed sources. One of the most important was the official transcript of case number 2322, District Court of Finney County, Kansas: "The State of Kansas, Plaintiff, vs. Richard Eugene Hickock and Perry Edward Smith, Defendants," a 515-page document (Tompkins 127). Part III, "Answer," and Part IV, "The Corner," of the novel both depend heavily on the official transcript for details about the arrest and subsequent conviction of Hickock and Smith; in those sections, Capote relies particularly heavily on the testimony of the K.B.I. agents involved in the investigation. In his *Esquire* article "In Cold Fact," Phillip Tompkins alternates between Capote's description of events and the account of those same events in the official transcript. Ironically, although Tompkins does point out some of Capote's minor liberties with the facts (such as which car, the one with Dick or the one with Perry, was in front on the drive from Las Vegas to Garden City, Kansas, following the arrest), the effect of his juxtaposition of the two accounts is ultimately to convince the reader of Capote's rather strict fidelity to official records.

Other important printed sources used by Capote were (1) Perry's "confession," a document of 78 pages dictated to a court recorder and including information already given to K.B.I. agents Alvin Dewey and Clarence Duntz (*ICB* 287); (2) autobiographical essays written by Dick and Perry at the suggestion of a psychiatrist, long sections of which Capote quotes verbatim; and (3) letters written by Smith and Hickock over a period of roughly five years, between the time of their convictions and sentencing on March 29, 1960, and their executions on April 14, 1965. According to Clarke, Capote wrote both Smith and Hickock the two letters a week each was permitted on death row, and they answered regularly, their letters to Capote numbering "in the hundreds" (343). Capote also includes passages from Smith's father's essay "A History of My Boy's Life."

But perhaps Capote's most important source for the book was his own experience in Kansas. Capote and Harper Lee remained in Holcomb and Garden City more than a month, from the time of the murders in November 1959 until mid–January 1960, about two weeks after Dick and Perry's arrest. They returned for the trial and sentencing in March of the same year. A few weeks after his initial lukewarm reception, Capote began to cajole and charm the residents of Holcomb in his characteristic puckish fashion, and that manner gained him remarkable access to people and materials. Probably second in importance to the relationships he developed with the murderers themselves was his friendship with Alvin Dewey, the K.B.I. investigator assigned to the Clutter case. Dewey's wife Marie was, like Capote, a native of New Orleans, and the Deweys were apparently flattered that a writer of Capote's status would share their stories and their gumbo. In a remarkable coincidence, Capote and Harper Lee were dining at the Dewey house on December 30, 1959, when the call came that Hickock and Smith had been apprehended (Clarke 323–24).

Shortly after the trial, Capote left for Europe to piece together his narrative, believing that "[g]regariousness is the enemy of art" (Clarke 330). From his European hideaways, he corresponded regularly with Dick and Perry and returned to Kansas from time to time to conduct more interviews. In April 1965, much against his wishes but prompted by his instincts as a reporter, he was present for the executions.

Perhaps the most journalistic aspect of *In Cold Blood* is the fact that the unfolding story determined Capote's work schedule, rather than vice versa. By the beginning of 1963, he had finished the first three of the book's four parts (Clarke 339). But he could not go beyond the first section of part IV— the account of the trial—until Perry's and Dick's appeals were exhausted and their sentences either commuted or carried out. In other words, Capote could not finish the story until the story finished itself. It was a very difficult period, one which presented him with a moral dilemma: he wanted desperately to finish his book, but, as an opponent of capital punishment, he could not without considerable torment wish for the hastening of the executions.

The ordeal exhausted Capote, as Clarke describes: "His entire future awaited their walk to the Big Swing, and his comments to his friends, which indicated his real feelings, ran like a grim counterpoint to the consoling comments he was making to Perry and Dick." To his friend Cecil Beaton he wrote, "I'm finishing the last pages of my book—I *must* be rid of it regardless of what happens. I hardly give a fuck anymore *what* happens. My sanity is at stake..." (Clarke 352). He later called his work on the book "the most emotional experience of my creative life" (Grobel 117) and said that if he had realized when he initially arrived in Kansas how difficult a task lay before him, he "would have driven straight on. Like a bat out of hell" (Clarke 320).

With regard to Capote's work as a reporter, the questions raised by Phillip Tompkins are certainly relevant. Wouldn't two convicted murderers like Hickock and Smith be inclined to lie to a writer, either because they wanted to look more innocent or because, once on death row, they had nothing to lose? Are ordinary townspeople reliable sources, when they might have faulty memories or the desire to impress a famous writer from the big city? And mightn't a writer like Capote be tempted to fictionalize here and there in the interest of writing a best-seller?

Tompkins spent nine days examining the official records and inter-viewing many of the people who had provided information to Capote, but he was ultimately unable to document any glaring errors. In his article, Tompkins notes that Nancy Clutter's horse Babe was sold for $182.50, not the $75 Capote reported, that Nancy's boyfriend Bobby Rupp was a less proficient basketball player than Capote indicated, that relatively minor details about the cars' positions during the ride from Las Vegas were inac-curate, and that Perry Smith might not have apologized before his execu-tion, as Capote said he did.

These examples might support Bobby Rupp's statement to Tompkins that Capote "put things in there that to other people make good reading but the people who were actually involved know that he *exaggerated a lit-tle bit*" (125, emphasis mine), but they hardly support the charge of bla-tant inaccuracy that Tompkins' tone implies. Remarkably, Rupp's statement about Capote's "exaggerations" seems to be the only challenge to accuracy by a principal in the case, despite the book's prominence and the story's previous publication in a nationally circulated periodical, *The New Yorker*. Former postmistress Clare told a reporter that if people in Holcomb were offended in any way by Capote's account, it was largely because he had made them look so provincial. Clare said her advice to townspeople would be "if the shoe fits, wear it" (Clarke 358).

As for the trustworthiness of the murderers as sources, it is import-ant to note that there were never any inconsistencies in the stories they told either the police or Capote, even when they were questioned sep-arately, except for the question of whether Smith committed all four murders—and this question was resolved when Perry requested that his confession be changed before signing it (287–88). It should also be noted that Capote does not, at any point, attempt to adjudicate between Dick's and Perry's accounts or to ascribe motives to either man; he does not interpret. Faced with the unenviable task of describing an event to which four of the six eyewitnesses were dead, Capote did what any good journal-ist would do: he reported what he had been told by appropriate and avail-able sources.

Probably what accounts most for Capote's accuracy is the amount of time he spent in Holcomb and Garden City. He and Lee interviewed and re-interviewed, checked dates and distances, and examined documents, all with a scrupulousness impossible for most reporters, whose stories must appear in tomorrow's newspaper or next week's magazine. Capote said, "One doesn't work for almost six years on a book, the point of which is fac-tual accuracy, and then give way to minor distortions" (Clarke 358). Clarke notes that several other reporters checked on Capote's accuracy but found no "errors of substance" (358). And *The New Yorker's* own fact checker said that he had worked with many important writers and that Capote was "the most accurate" (Clarke 351).

Although Capote did not commit major factual errors in describing what happened in Kansas, it is worth noting that he did describe one scene which did *not* happen. At the conclusion of the novel, Nancy Clutter's best friend Susan Kidwell and K.B.I. agent Alvin Dewey meet at the Clutter graves on a beautiful spring day. Kidwell is a student at the University of Kansas majoring in art (Nancy Clutter's intended major), and Capote goes to great lengths to imply that her life could have been Nancy Clutter's but for the circumstances he has described. Capote created the scene, he said, because he did not want to end with the bleakness of the executions; he wanted to achieve a sense of resolution by dramatizing the idea that life goes on. Unfortunately, the scene plays like the conclusion of a made-for-television movie, and many critics expressed the sense that it was overly elegaic and thus out of tone with the rest of the narrative. Capote's biographer Clarke says that it "verges on the trite and sentimental" and that the novel "is the poorer for it" (357–58).

Interestingly, then, the one scene that Capote manufactured is probably the only scene that does not ring true for a reader. Its inclusion has perhaps been best explained by Gore Vidal's famous criticism of Capote as unable to invent his own plots. In a *Playboy* interview, Vidal charged that Capote suffered from a lack of imagination and consequently robbed the imaginations of his friends: that he was heavily indebted to Carson McCullers for his novel *Other Voices, Other Rooms* and to Christopher Isherwood, whose Sally Bowles (of *Goodbye to Berlin* and *I Am a Camera*) became Holly Golightly in *Breakfast at Tiffany's*. Vidal said that Capote was "ruthlessly unoriginal"; he maintains that *In Cold Blood* was successful because when Capote turned to nonfiction and did not have to make up his own material, he could concentrate on what he did best: the writing itself, the choosing and arranging and selecting of words and sentences and scenes. "[H]e'd found his own voice," Vidal said, "and that is what writing is all about" (Grobel 130). Thus, if the conclusion of *In Cold Blood* does not "work," it represents Capote's failure as a novelist, not as a journalist.

The most widespread misreading of *In Cold Blood* as an objective, documentary-like work stems from its journalistic texture and methods. Because Capote does not appear in the narrative except very incidentally as "a friend" in whom one of the "witnesses" confides a detail, a surprising number of critics have either praised Capote for his objectivity or criticized the novel for its lack of a central authorial vision. These perspectives amount to the same misconception about the novel—that it lacks a theme. In "The Capitulation of Literature? The Scope of the 'Nonfiction Novel,'" Ivo Vidan says that Capote has a "blind spot," which is that his "sum of facts does not become meaningful"; a reader, Vidan says, "does not see any kind of call to take up a position" (176). Vidan goes so far as to say that Capote's detached method is "diametrically opposed" to Naturalism (158). In an essay comparing *An American Tragedy* and *In Cold Blood,* John McAleer maintains that "[u]nlike Capote, Dreiser had a thesis that went deeper than a demonstration of form" and that in failing to consider "how the potentials of his materials might be utilized to express a true, universalizing experience, Capote seems to have mistaken craft for art" (570, 571). In Capote's lengthy *Playboy* interview, questioner Eric Norden reveals the same misreading in this question: "*In Cold Blood* scrupulously refrains from speculating about the motives of the two murderers. You thus avoid answering the crucial question, Why? Is it there no answer—or did you fail to find one?" (60–61). One suspects that Norden simply needs to read the book again, and more carefully this time.

Capote's response to Norden's question is succinct: "There is an answer and it's implicit in the book ... short of getting a baseball bat and clubbing you over the head with it, I don't see how I could have made the point any more clearly" (61–62). Certainly, Capote directs the reader toward the prescribed position through less obvious means than the authorial intrusion of the early Naturalists. His method falls within the realm of what Wayne Booth in *The Rhetoric of Fiction* calls "the seductive point-of-view," the employment of various subtle devices like presence—the mere devotion of space—to convince a reader to "see the human worth of a character whose actions, objectively considered, we would deplore" (378–79). As Chris Anderson points out, Capote's withholdings (the delay in the narrative of the murder itself, for example) also play a key role in clarifying the author's vision of his material: "In the space left by the withdrawal of the narrator," Anderson contends, "meaning takes place" (49). Ultimately, one would have to reply to Vidan's contention that "[t]he public does not see here any kind of call to take up a position" that the public does not read very closely.

Not only does Capote's narrative possess a clear and meaningful shape, but the critics who have read perceptively enough to see that shape are unanimous in their identification of it. Essentially, Capote presents in *In Cold Blood* an allegory of the American experience: the Clutters, in their established Midwestern paradise, represent comfort and respectability, while Perry and Dick represent restlessness and depravity. The Clutters are the "haves" and Dick and Perry the "have nots." Inevitably, when they come together, mutual destruction is the outcome. If, as David Galloway has suggested in "Why the Chickens Came Home to Roost in Holcomb, Kansas," the Clutters embody "much of what is most admirable about the American spirit," then Perry and Dick suggest what is most frightening about

America: that those who have been denied participation in "the American dream" are neither patient nor forgiving. The allegorical pattern of *In Cold Blood* fits so tightly that, had Capote not drawn his material from real life, one suspects that critics might have found the lines too neatly drawn.

Perhaps the tendency of some critics to see *In Cold Blood* as lacking in theme explains the curious absence of critical discussions of the novel as a Naturalistic work. Although a handful of reviewers (Granville Hicks, most notably) compare Capote's novel in passing with *An American Tragedy*, the word *Naturalism* itself is notably missing from scholarship, with two exceptions. In "The Novel in America Today," a 1981 overview of contemporary novels, Helen Weinberg identifies two trends in the fiction of the previous two decades, one of which is a resurgence of Naturalism. Weinberg maintains that "Naturalism has come back into the contemporary novel through the documentary impulse. Truman Capote was perhaps the trend setter with *In Cold Blood*" (62). (She also calls Mailer's *The Executioner's Song* "remarkably naturalistic" [62].) Also, toward the end of *Twentieth-Century American Literary Naturalism*, Donald Pizer contemplates the future of Naturalism beyond the 1940s, speculating that it might find an outlet in "documentary narrative (for example, *In Cold Blood*)" (152).

Despite these brief notations, however, critics have virtually ignored the Naturalistic dimensions of *In Cold Blood*, an omission that would be less surprising were those dimensions less profound. In *The Literature of Fact: Literary Nonfiction in American Writing*, Ronald Weber declares that "the challenge of documentary journalism" is "to remain faithful to the facts yet invest fact with some of the resonant implications of fiction. It is a difficult enough task, but made all the more so when the subject is murder and the facts are so stunning in themselves" (171). Certainly, Capote has met that challenge, and, in its "resonance," *In Cold Blood* has long outlived Louis Rubin's 1966 prediction that in 10 years, most readers would have forgotten it.

6

Mailer's Big "Non-Book"

The Executioner's Song *as Faux Naturalism*

"Between us, I have a big problem. Where are the sympathetic characters?"—Lawrence Schiller to Norman Mailer,
after interviewing Gary Gilmore

When Norman Mailer's *The Executioner's Song* was published in
1978, the book shocked many people—not so much due to the brutal
crimes Mailer depicts but because of the book's style. Mailer had written
so much I-centered New Journalism such as *The Armies of the Night,* dramatizing himself as a central consciousness, that long-time Mailer readers
were stunned not to see an "I" in his new narrative. The common critical
reaction, articulated with astonishment, was, as Arthur Kretchner
says, that Mailer had "changed his voice" and adopted a "flat, midwestern,
uncolored, intentionally repetitive" tone (qtd. in Manso 592–93). Judith
Scheffler points to Mailer's "unprecedented absence as a voice and controlling personality" in the work (184), and Joseph Wenke observes that *The
Executioner's Song* marks a notable departure from Mailer's earlier nonfiction in that, in the new book, Mailer is not pressing an ideology (214). Even
Lawrence Schiller, the researcher who originally involved Mailer in the
project, commented after reading the first 10 pages of manuscript, "Jesus,
you're not using your own voice," to which Mailer replied, "You've given
me so much material, so much fact, I don't have to rely on my own ego"
(581–82).

If *The Executioner's Song* marks a stylistic departure for Mailer, it represents something of a thematic one as well. The Naturalism of earlier
works such as *The Naked and the Dead* (1948) has given way to existentialism, and the author who suggested in that earlier novel that men are at
the mercy of determinism confesses that he does not know how to account
for what the poet Robert Burns called "man's inhumanity to man." Shortly
after *The Executioner's Song*'s publication, Mailer told interviewer William

143

F. Buckley, Jr., that the novel posed questions that were more important than any answers he could provide:

> what I discovered at a certain point—and I think this is really the core of it—is I thought, I can write a book that will really make people think in a way they haven't thought before. This material made me begin to look at ten or 20 serious questions in an altogether new fashion, and it made me humble in that I just didn't know the answers.... I thought it might be very nice for once just to write a book which doesn't have answers, but poses delicate questions with a great deal of evidence and a great deal of material and let people argue over it. I feel there are any number of areas in this book where there are people who have better answers to give than I have [Mailer, "Crime and Punishment" 243].

When *The Executioner's Song* won the Pulitzer Prize in 1980, no one was unhappier than Truman Capote. Still smarting from the disappointment of *In Cold Blood*'s having been dismissed by the major literary award committees, Capote charged that, if not for his book, Mailer could never have written *The Executioner's Song*. Capote felt that he had crafted the prototype for writing nonfiction like fiction, and he had commented earlier that Mailer should have subtitled *The Armies of the Night* "Variations on a Theme by Capote." Of *Armies*, Capote told his biographer Gerald Clarke, "there has never been a greater literary rip-off in the twentieth century" (399). Then, to compound Capote's frustration that Mailer had already borrowed his technique, with *The Executioner's Song* Mailer borrowed his topic as well. Nearly 20 years earlier, when Capote was working on *In Cold Blood*, Mailer had criticized him publicly for writing nonfiction, claiming that it represented "a failure of the imagination" (Grobel 113). So Mailer's literary triumph in 1980 in the same genre with the same topic was more than Capote could stand.

Despite the fact that Capote did not plow the nonfictional ground that Mailer cultivated, Capote's remark that Mailer could not have written *The Executioner's Song* if not for *In Cold Blood* is more than the self-congratulatory remark of a jealous rival. Mailer did attempt to write an accurate account of the last nine months of Gary Gilmore's life; like Capote, he uses techniques of both journalism and literature. Like Capote, he chooses the murderer himself as his protagonist. And like Capote, he avoids direct participation in the narrative.

But unlike Capote, Mailer does not approach his subject from an essentially Naturalistic standpoint. There are at least two reasons for this difference: (1) Mailer did not experience the sort of personal involvement with Gary Gilmore that Capote had with Perry Smith and Dick Hickock and (2) Mailer cannot construct a deterministic argument for Gary Gilmore's murders because, ultimately, he does not know why Gilmore committed them. As he admitted to Buckley, he has many questions but no answers. Thus, while it contains clear elements of the homicide novel as it descended from the Naturalistic tradition, *The Executioner's Song* finally resembles the New Journalism more than the Naturalistic novel. Just as it represents a departure from Mailer's earlier stylistic and thematic achievements, the book also marks a departure in the homicide novel from the Naturalistic tradition. Examining the differences in Capote's and Mailer's methods is, nevertheless, a useful exercise illuminating what the American Naturalistic homicide novel is and what it is not.

The central stay of Mailer's adherence to the Naturalistic homicide novel formula is his focus on the murderer himself, Gary Gilmore, who, when he was shot by a Utah firing squad in 1977, became the first person executed in the United States after the Supreme Court reinstated capital punishment. Like Capote in *In Cold Blood*, Mailer works to soften the reader's opinion of his protagonist by juxtaposing Gilmore with three women sympathetic to him—his cousin Brenda Nicol, his mother, Bessie Gilmore, and his girlfriend, Nicole Baker.

Mailer works to set up the reader's sympathy for Gilmore immediately, by placing chapter one, "The First Day," within the consciousness of Gary's first cousin Brenda, who has more sympathy for him than any other character does. The novel opens with Brenda's memory of helping Gary conceal a broken apple tree limb when she was six and he was seven. "The First Day" refers to April 9, 1976, when Gilmore was paroled from a Marion, Illinois, prison and flew to Provo, Utah, where Nicole met him at the airport and took him to her home. The first chapter concerns Brenda's recollections of Gary himself, his letters to her (full of self-analysis and isolation), and her hopes about his future. Thus, Mailer establishes a strong sense of the effect on Gary of over half a life spent in prison: "once in a while Gary would remark [to Brenda] that having been in prison so long he felt more like the victim than the man who did the deed" (19). This image of Gimore as a victim is reinforced at the end of chapter one, again from Brenda's point-of-view: his eyes, Brenda notices, "had the expression of rabbits she had flushed, scared rabbit was the common expression, but she had looked into those eyes of scared rabbits and they were calm and tender and kind of curious. They did not know what would happen next" (28).

Brenda's attitude toward Gary is often that of a frustrated mother figure: she loves him (in fact, "I love you" is the last thing she says to him before his arrest for murder [267]), and her desire to straighten him out by dealing firmly with him is always tempered by the fact that she can't say no to him for long. When, just a few weeks after his release, Gary calls Brenda to pick him up in Idaho where he has violated his parole by crossing the state line, gotten drunk, and initiated a barroom brawl, her advice to him is "you just get your thumb out of your rear end and put it in the air" (57).

Brenda subsequently mopes around the house all day, worrying about how Gary will get home, and finally goes after him when he calls again from Salt Lake City late in the afternoon.

Even when Gilmore is arrested for murder, Mailer depicts him through Brenda's eyes. When the police need her to keep Gary talking on the phone long enough for them to arrest him, she suffers pangs of guilt; she "felt like a traitor; Gary's trust was the weapon she was using to nail him. It was true she wanted to nail him, she told herself, but she didn't want, well, she didn't want to betray him to do it" (265). Between phone calls with Gary and the police department, Brenda bawls, and when his arrest is inevitable, she says to the police dispatcher, "he's coming out. I know he's got a gun, but for God's sake, try not to kill him. I mean it. Don't fire" (267). Emphasizing Brenda's affection for Gilmore allows Mailer to maintain the impression that there might be something redeeming—or at least human—about him, after all.

Mailer uses a second Gilmore relative, Gary's mother Bessie, similarly. Because she is more sympathetic than Gilmore himself and because *she* cares about him, a reader is encouraged to care for him, too, if only to prevent his mother's further misery. By the time of Gary's third-from-last incarceration, Bessie's world is a mere shadow of the one she shared with Frank Gilmore. Though far from a perfect husband, Frank Gilmore provided her a large Victorian-style house with marble floors and mahogany furniture, for which he had paid cash. But after Frank's death, Bessie took in only about $70 a week busing tables; her arthritis prevented her from being promoted to waitress. After the property taxes fell several years into arrears and the Mormon Church wouldn't bail her out by paying the taxes (about $1,400) and giving her a life lease in exchange for the deed, Bessie was forced to move to a $3,500 trailer. By the time of Gary's arrest on the two murder charges, Bessie's crippling arthritis cost her her job and made her feel more like 83 than 63. In Mailer's account, she sits in her trailer day after day, reading about Gary in newspapers, telling herself "I'm ugly" (487), and shouting at the teenager sent by the Mormon Church to wash her dishes, "Go away" (490).

Despite her increasing bitterness, though, Bessie Gilmore continues to offer encouragement to Gary. During his imprisonment at the Oregon State Penitentiary, she had a friend drive her the 80 miles every other Sunday (as often as the prison allowed), although she sometimes arrived to find that Gary was in solitary confinement and couldn't have visitors. When Gary's brother Gaylen died, Bessie hired two prison guards to transport Gary to and from the funeral. And when she learned of her son's desire to have his death sentence carried out, Bessie wrote to him, "I love you & I want you to live…. If you have 4 or 5 people who really love you, you are lucky. So please hold on" (491).

Bessie Brown Gilmore is, above all else, a survivor; perhaps the most moving thing about her is her simple will to endure. Bessie has endured Gary's numerous run-ins with the law. After he turned 20 in late 1960, he was in jail or prison for the rest of his life, except for a few months at a time here and there. Bessie has also survived Frank's death from cancer and her son Gaylen's stabbing and subsequent death. She reminds herself stoically that strength is in her genes: "I am the daughter of the very first people who settled in Provo. I am the granddaughter and great-granddaughter of pioneers on both sides. If they could live through it, I can live through it" (314).

Mailer also plots very deliberately the placement of the three chapters in Book One which focus on Bessie. The first, chapter 19 ("Kin to the Magician"), occurs almost exactly two-thirds of the way through Book One, immediately after Gary's arraignment on the murder charges. That chapter details Gary's family background, including the evidence that his grandfather was the magician Harry Houdini. It also includes, in a bit of foreshadowing, Bessie's childhood dread of executions (310). The next, chapters 30 ("The Slammer") and 32 ("Old Cancer, New Madness"), occur just after the death sentence is handed down. In chapter 30, Mailer describes Bessie's friendship with Grace Gilmore McGinniss (no apparent relation), who taught the Gilmore boys in high school and transported Bessie to and from the Oregon State Penitentiary. Chapter 32 records Bessie's increasing premonitions of her son's execution. Gilmore's arrest and sentencing serve as the two high points of Book One, and Mailer's juxtaposition of those crucial incidents with the consciousness and sentiment of Bessie Gilmore serves primarily to remind a reader that this murderer is still a mother's son.

Bessie describes the complexity of her feelings for Gary in a question to her youngest son, Mikal: "Can you imagine what it feels like to mother a son whom you love, when he has deprived two other mothers of *their* sons?" (492). When she hears—on *Good Morning, America*—that the execution has been carried out, she (according to Mailer) "cried into the sore flesh of her heart" and said aloud to the mountain that had become her symbol of stability and certainty, "Mountain, you can go to hell. You're not mine anymore" (975–76). Her perspective is the one least often seen in capital punishment cases—that of the murderer's survivors. Bessie's agony illustrates George Eliot's observation in *The Mill on the Floss* that it is difficult to punish the guilty without also punishing the innocent. One thinks of Clarence Darrow pleading with Judge John Caverly to spare Leopold's and Loeb's lives to alleviate their families' suffering.

Gilmore's girlfriend, Nicole Barrett Baker, also encourages the reader's sympathy for Gary Gilmore, not only because she is more inherently sympathetic than he is but also because Gilmore seems most stable when he is around her. Nicole herself is more pathetic than sympathetic. Mailer details her sexual abuse by a live-in uncle over a six-year period (from age six to about age 12) and Nicole's subsequent abandonment of the possibility of virtue; in her own words, she "became a slut" (101). By the sixth grade, she had the misfortune of having what she termed "the biggest boobs in the elementary school," a distinction which earned her the nickname "Foam Rubber" (100). At 10 or 11, she was writing shockingly pornographic letters to classmates (99). When Nicole was 12 and the abusive uncle was killed in Vietnam, she blamed herself, superstitiously believing that her "evil thoughts" had caused his death (102). Not surprisingly, at 13, Nicole was sent to a psychiatric institution for the first time.

By the time she hooks up with Gary Gilmore in 1976, Nicole has been married three times (the last time for two weeks), cohabited with several other men, prostituted herself to support her second husband's drug habit, and borne two children. When Gilmore arrives, Nicole has moved up from waiting tables to sewing in a factory. She makes $2.31 an hour and brings home $80 a week to support herself and the two children. She drives a Ford Mustang that she was able to buy for $175 because the seller liked her and she "had a nest of a hundred bucks from screwing welfare out of extra money they'd once given her in some mixup of checks" (82).

It is difficult to hold Nicole entirely responsible for her difficulties, though, at least in Mailer's characterization of her as perpetually pubescent. A tiny woman whom Gilmore called his "elf," Nicole approached the world with the logic and naiveté of a 12-year-old. For example, when she found out, at 17, that she was pregnant with her second child, she explained to a Planned Parenthood worker that she "had never known how to keep from getting pregnant" (118). Her decision to keep the baby is characteristically simple: "She thought about having an abortion. But she couldn't bring herself to kill a baby. She couldn't stand Barrett anymore, but she loved Sunny [her daughter]. So she couldn't see killing a new baby she might also love" (119).

Nicole's refusal to see Gary Gilmore anymore because he had become so demanding and dependent was the apparent catalyst of his murder spree. The day before the first of the two murders for which Gilmore would be executed, he told Brenda, "I think I'm going to kill Nicole.... I can't take it.... When she pulled the gun on me today, ... I thought about taking it. But I didn't want Nicole to start screaming. She was frantic to get away from me" (207). Later the same day, as he fired two shots at close range into the back of gas station attendant Max Jensen's head, Gilmore pronounced the first shot for himself and the second "for Nicole" (226). At least two other circumstances fueled Gilmore's violent outburst: (1) the Fiorinol, Prolixin, and alcohol he ingested to numb the pain of Nicole's departure and his chronic headaches and (2) the fact that he desperately needed money to keep his beloved new pick-up truck, which had become like an extension of his ego. Had Nicole not left him, these circumstances would probably have led him to more petty crimes, but it is doubtful that he would have killed anybody. His nominally domestic relationship with Nicole, had it continued, might have saved not only Gilmore but his victims as well.

Although Mailer's attempts at humanizing Gary Gilmore by associating him with sympathetic women is a strategy the author shares from the Naturalistic homicide novelists, Gilmore ultimately falls short as a Naturalistic protagonist. Regardless of Brenda, Bessie, and Nicole's feelings for him, it is hard for a reader to sympathize with a man who could shoot two people as coolly as Gilmore does and who says things like "Why don't we just grab a couple of bitches and rape them?" (66) and, two months after the murders, "you know, this is the first time I've ever had any feelings for either of those two guys I killed" (386). Even Lawrence Schiller, after he began interviewing Gilmore, voiced concern that the book and movie projects would be unsuccessful because his subject wasn't sufficiently sympathetic (629). Ultimately, Gilmore is much more Dick Hickock than Perry Smith. Unlike many murderers, he is of at least average intelligence. He writes insightful and interesting letters, and he is charming in a sociopathic sort of way. But on a day-to-day basis, he is an adolescent, foul-mouthed career criminal whose inability to adjust to the world outside prison is far more pathetic than tragic. Despite the fact that a reader's attention is focused on Gilmore throughout, *The Executioner's Song* is not a book in which one ever roots for the bad guy to get away. Gilmore is taken away to jail, and his cousin Brenda speaks for the reader when she says "Thank God" (273).

Truman Capote alleged that part of Norman Mailer's inability to conjure sympathy for Gilmore stemmed from the fact that Mailer never met him. Capote felt that *The Executioner's Song* suffered because Mailer did not have the level of personal involvement and intimacy with Gilmore that he himself had with Perry Smith and Dick Hickock:

> I have no respect for Norman Mailer's book *The Executioner's Song*, which, as far as I'm concerned, is a nonbook. He didn't live through it day by day, he didn't know Utah, he didn't know Gary Gilmore, he never even *met* Gary Gilmore, he didn't do an ounce of research on the book—two other people did all the research. He was just a rewrite man like you have over at the *Daily News*. I spent six *years* on *In Cold Blood* and not only knew the people I was writing about, I've known them better than I've known *anybody*. So Mailer's book just really *annoyed* me. Can you see why it annoyed me? [Grobel 113, emphasis Capote's].

Pressed by Lawrence Grobel to express some appreciation for Mailer's effort, Capote comes up empty-handed, zeroing in on his primary criticism of Mailer. "I didn't like his attitude about the characters. I didn't like his point of view.… Most of all, I didn't like the fact he hadn't done it!" (113).

Although Capote accurately recognized the absence of a sympathetic authorial viewpoint, his deep jealousy led him to understate Mailer's role in the research that formed the basis for *The Executioner's Song*. After he got involved in the project, Mailer did travel to Utah and Oregon to talk with Gilmore's survivors and other witnesses to his life and crimes. And certainly *The Executioner's Song* suggests a wealth of supporting material of the same kinds Capote used. In his afterword, Mailer writes that the book

> is directly based on interviews, documents, records of court proceedings, and other original material that came from a number of trips to Utah and Oregon. More than one hundred people were interviewed face to face, plus a good number talked to by telephone. The total, before count was lost, came to something like three hundred separate sessions, and they range in length from fifteen minutes to four hours. Perhaps ten subjects are on tape for more than ten hours each. Certainly, in the last two and a half years, Nicole Baker's interviews have added up to thirty hours, and conversations with Bessie Gilmore may come to more than that. It is safe to say that the collected transcript of every last recorded bit of talk would approach fifteen thousand pages.… In addition … [m]any trips were taken to Oregon State Prison to interview guards and prisoners who had known Gilmore during his many years in that institution [1021, 1023].

Thus, the book does reflect the journalistic methodology and effort toward factual fidelity associated with the Naturalistic homicide novel, but what Mailer hides in the passive voice of "more than one hundred people were interviewed" and "many trips were taken" is the fact that he did not do very much of this work himself. Although Mailer's lack of direct involvement with Gary Gilmore is not grounds for conviction of the literary crimes that Capote alleged, it is reasonable to suggest that his disengagement affected his critical distance and the attitude about Gilmore he conveys. Even if Capote was wrong about the cause of Mailer's detachment from Gilmore, he was right that it permeates the narrative.

The Executioner's Song consists of two sections: "Western Voices," which spans the time from Gilmore's parole to his conviction and sentencing, and "Eastern Voices," which covers the last few months of Gilmore's life and basically details the story of his marketing for posterity. That marketing was orchestrated by Lawrence Schiller, a former *Life* photographer who had syndicated the Fisher quintuplets, taken a rather famous photograph of Jack Ruby on his deathbed, covered the trials of Sirhan Sirhan and Charles Manson, and generally earned a reputation as "the journalist who dealt in death" (582). Schiller promoted the idea for a story on Gilmore first to ABC, then to Gary's uncle Vern Damico, and finally to Gilmore himself. Schiller and a team of other researchers conducted hundreds of hours of interviews with Gilmore. And, in May of 1977, nearly four months after

Gilmore's execution, Schiller brought in Norman Mailer as what Capote termed his "rewrite man" (Grobel 113).

Schiller explained that he chose Mailer because he thought the author would understand Gary Gilmore. Like Gilmore, Mailer had reportedly had a violent relationship with his father. Perhaps more importantly, the two shared "a great passion for women." Like Gilmore, Mailer could be provoked to violence if a woman threatened his masculinity; in 1960, for example, Mailer created a media stir by stabbing his second wife, Adele Morales Mailer, at a Manhattan party (Manso 579). In a *Village Voice* review of *The Executioner's Song*, James Wolcott observed that "Gilmore's life comfortably accommodated all the aspects of Mailer's evolving philosophy" (46). And Mailer himself noted that he saw in Gilmore "the perfect character" because, as he said, Gary "embodied many of the themes I've been living with all my life" (Mills 425).

Perhaps the closest similarity between Gilmore and Mailer was both men's fascination with Nicole Baker. On one of his trips to Utah, Mailer stayed overnight in the house in Spanish Fork where Nicole had lived, perhaps as a way of legitimizing his involvement in the story. Schiller has suggested that Mailer's interaction with Nicole was "figuratively ... another marriage for Norman" (Manso 579). Mailer comments in the afterword that "without the cooperation of Nicole Baker, there would not have been a way to do this factual account—this, dare I say it, *true life story*, with its real names and real lives—as if it were a novel" (1021–22).

It is difficult to imagine how Mailer could have written the first half of the book without Nicole's participation, and it seems impossible that he would have written *The Executioner's Song* at all without Lawrence Schiller. Thus, although Mailer, like Capote, got his material from journalistic techniques and had some level of identification with his protagonist, his reporting was second-hand journalism at best. And when Mailer was awarded the Pulitzer Prize, Capote felt "like a war hero who has hobbled home, expecting a parade only to discover that others, who have never even seen the enemy up close, have picked up all the medals" (Clarke 398). Mailer had, literally, never seen Gary Gilmore "up close," so his identification with Gilmore was more like that of a novelist for his fictional protagonist than that of a journalist for his flesh-and-blood subject.

In fact, at least one critic has suggested that Mailer felt a much closer attachment to Lawrence Schiller than to Gilmore, because he felt that both he and Schiller had "a problematic reputation" that was attributable to public misunderstanding (Wenke 210). But Mailer's use of Schiller as a major character in Book Two is very much a device, as Mailer himself admitted when he said to his researcher, "you have to be in the book [because] when Nicole goes into the nuthouse and Gary is in prison there's no central

character who can serve as the link between them. You're that character"
(Manso 585). Perhaps the best evidence of Mailer's error in judgment in
putting Schiller in so prominent a position is the fact that the second half
of the book is so much less interesting than the first. In the words of Arthur
Kretchmer, who edited *Playboy* when Schiller's interviews with Gilmore
were excerpted there as prelude to the novel's publication, "the story of
Schiller's negotiations … [is] nowhere near as interesting as Mailer decided
[it was]" (Manso 595). Readers of homicide novels want to read about murder, not marketing.

Besides the damage to Book II, Mailer's overdependence on Schiller
hurt *The Executioner's Song* in another way. His lack of personal involvement with Gary Gilmore left him without an explanation for Gilmore's
crimes, and he was unable to detect one from his materials. Thus, Mailer
cannot make the deterministic argument, or any other argument, for that
matter. This is the heart of Capote's claim that the novel lacks a point of
view. In this respect Mailer departs most drastically from the novel about
homicide as the Naturalists wrote it.

Like his more Naturalistic predecessors, Mailer is interested in the
"why" of Gary Gilmore's story. For this reason, he acknowledges the contributions of many "witnesses"; his list, in the book's afterword, runs to about
135 names. Mailer or his researchers talked to Bessie Gilmore about Gary's
childhood and adolescence, asked a former resident of a juvenile facility
where Gary lived for a thorough written description of his life there, visited
all the prisons where Gary was incarcerated, had Nicole go over and over
the most intimate and sordid details of her brief relationship with Gary,
and pored over six to seven hundred double-sided pages of letters.

These sources gave Mailer an abundance of insight into Gary Gilmore's
personality. Gilmore had an abusive father and relatively passive mother.
He suffered from severe migraines, for which he took Fiorinal, and depression, for which he took Prolixin; sometimes he took both drugs, washing them down with alcohol. He confessed strong pedophilic tendencies,
particularly a powerful attraction to young girls. Much of the reason he
was attracted to Nicole in the first place was her tiny physique; he repeatedly referred to her as his "elf," and he became "a hellion" after Nicole, at
his request, shaved her pubic hair (142–43). He had a similar attraction to
young boys, on which he acted in reform school. Yet Gilmore seems to have
been repulsed by his own pedophilic tendencies, and at least one psychologist suggested that Gilmore's interest in pornography involving children
disgusted him so strongly that he killed Benny Bushnell and Max Jensen in
order to commit suicide by firing squad.

From these squalid aspects of Gilmore's personality, a Naturalist would
have constructed an elaborate argument about causes, but Mailer seems to

regard them instead as Tom Wolfe's "status details," facts he included in the narrative simply because he knew them to be true. Ultimately, Mailer presents all possible explanations for Gilmore's behavior because, as he confessed, he is unable to sort them out. In the Mailer chapter of *Style as Argument: Contemporary American Nonfiction*, Chris Anderson argues convincingly that Mailer employs what Mas'ud Zavarzadeh in *The Mythopoeic Reality: The Postwar American Nonfiction Novel* calls "zero-degree interpretation" (122). Anderson says that Mailer is

> relentlessly recording all the trivia, all the meaningless details of [Gary Gilmore's] experience, reproducing the texture of his life without making it meaningful or giving it a literary shape. It's as if he has set a camera down in the middle of this event, in the tradition of Warhol and cinema vérité, and simply recorded all that passed the camera's eye [119].

This is undoubtedly the same effect Diane Johnson describes in *The New York Review of Books* when she calls Mailer's style "all tape recorder" (3). In journalism, the technique is often called "fly on the wall."

In assembling his material, then, Mailer is using the empirical method, recording what was observed, not the determinist's more selective, analytical approach. The early chapters of Book I contain many passages about Gilmore and Nicole's sex life because they apparently had sex frequently— not because Norman Mailer believed that sex was a particularly weighty factor in Gilmore's crimes. If it happened and Mailer knew about it, he put it in the book. If it happened a lot, it got more space than something that happened only once or twice. Essentially, Mailer attempts to offer a realistic description of the last nine months of Gary Gilmore's life—not to make an argument about it. Anderson correctly points out that the "Ruminator" who, in *The Armies of the Night*, reflects on and interprets the meaning and effectiveness of the anti–Vietnam rhetoric is replaced in *The Executioner's Song* by the "Recorder," who merely reports or catalogs, and that, consequently, Gilmore's story seems "undigested" (120). Perhaps there is a Naturalistic novel about Gary Gilmore still waiting to be written, but the De Quincean "great storm of passion" is not apparent in this material.

The difference between Mailer's handling of Gilmore's family background and Truman Capote's treatment of Perry Smith's family history clarifies each writer's method. In the sections of *The Executioner's Song* dealing with Gilmore's father, mother, or brothers, Mailer focuses as often on those other family members and how Gary's problems have affected them as he does on how their family life affected Gary. For example, in chapter 30, "The Slammer," the chapter immediately following Gilmore's sentencing, Mailer describes how Gary's previous incarcerations have worn down his mother and even her friend Grace McGinniss, who, after driving Bessie to and from visits with Gary for over two years, finally decides "I have only so much energy. I can't carry this. I am a devout coward.... I just have to pull out" (464). But when Capote reviews Perry Smith's family history, his intent is always to determine how that past led to Perry's present. Capote is far more selective because he is sculpting, whereas Mailer is compiling a collage. It is, again, Naturalism versus the documentary method.

Mailer's attitude about the book's editing affirms that he was not interested in carving a particular shape out of Gary Gilmore's final days. Mailer originally told Schiller that he expected the book to take six months (Manso 581), and although it took a little over twice that long, one year is still a far cry from the six that Capote spent writing *In Cold Blood*. In fact, Capote likely spent more time in Kansas doing research than Mailer spent on *The Executioner's Song* from start to finish. That getting the book to correspond to some imagined design was not among Mailer's high priorities seems clear from his response to Schiller's request for revision: "Sure ... if I had five years, I might go through it a couple of times. But I can't do that. I've gotta publish now. It would take me three months to do what needs to be done, and I'm stuck for money" (Manso 592). Although Mailer did agree to edit a little when Schiller got him an additional $100,000 (for a total project advance of $600,000), he eventually gave in to the impatience that is another likeness between him and Gilmore. Kretchmer characterized Mailer's attitude as "you hit the deadline[;] they take it away" (Manso 595).

Mailer's lackadaisical attitude about the final shape of the book resulted largely from his lack of emotional involvement with the material and, specifically, with Gary Gilmore. Capote's allegation that Mailer was no more than a "rewrite man" was certainly accurate in the sense that Mailer's emotional investment was more like an editor's than like a novelist's or even a reporter's. It is reasonable to assume that, had Norman Mailer known Gary Gilmore, he might have felt a stronger obligation to shape the book toward some theory of motive—whether or not that motive was ultimately knowable.

The emotional involvement of the novelist with the protagonist is the heart of the Naturalistic tradition, because in order to portray the character at the mercy of deterministic forces, the writer must first see him or her as a victim. This is the perspective from which Dreiser views Carrie Meeber and Clyde Griffiths; it is the way that Norris sees McTeague, Crane sees Maggie Johnson, Thomas Hardy sees Tess Durbeyfield, Richard Wright sees Bigger Thomas, and Truman Capote sees Perry Smith. But determinism is not the lens through which Mailer projects Gary Gilmore. Undeniably, he sympathizes with Gilmore (particularly where the relationship with Nicole was concerned), and he sometimes arranges the narrative for the reader to sympathize with Gilmore, too. But he does not see Gilmore as a puppet manipulated by forces outside his control. Without that perspective, Mailer never developed the rhetorical agenda of the Naturalistic writer: the need to argue that the murderer himself is a victim. As Lee Clark Mitchell argues in "Naturalism and the Languages of Determinism," "any sure evidence of effective choice, of free will or autonomous action, makes a novel something other than Naturalistic" (530). Mitchell calls this a "negative test" for Naturalism, and Mailer's book fails it.

What Mailer substitutes for a unified, deterministic theme intended to explain the protagonist's actions is a collage of different explanations, chiefly Gilmore's own and those of the psychologists appointed to examine him. Gary Gilmore himself believed in karma and reincarnation, as well as chance. In the mid-'70s, Mailer also flirted with a belief in reincarnation (Mills 425). Gilmore had dreams that he interpreted as psychic memories. For example, he believed that he had been beheaded in the 18th century (145) and that he and Nicole had been lovers in previous incarnations (329). He felt that maybe he and his cellmate Gibbs were "meant to meet" because of strong similarities in their relationships with their girlfriends (366). In his more philosophical moods, he flirted with the idea that he was a criminal because of bad karma. Asking the court to circumvent the customary appeals process and carry out his death sentence swiftly, Gilmore argued, "There is some crime from my past. I feel I have to atone for the thing I did then" (482). It was Gilmore's belief in reincarnation that finally convinced Larry Schiller that Gilmore's death wish might not be a bluff:

> For the first time it hit him that Gilmore might want to go all the way. Up to then he had assumed Gilmore would accept his execution because he was a proud con trapped in a role. Now he understood that Gary might expect to find something on the other side. Not only willing to gamble on it, but gamble everything. It must be, Schiller thought, the way he sometimes felt shooting craps when he knew he was coming up with a seven [671].

That Gilmore believed in his spiritual future as well as his past is also substantiated by his sense that he would "one day have a dream that he was a guy named GARY in 20th century America and that there was something very wrong" (359).

Despite his professed belief in spiritual debts, Gilmore ultimately felt that he was responsible for his own actions. "I believe we always have a choice," he wrote to Nicole shortly after his arrest (344). To the end, he felt that he was still making choices; indeed, the primary reason he opted not to appeal was to maintain his sense of control. His suicide pact with Nicole two months before his execution illustrates his desire to make his own choices. And the possibility that he under-drugged himself in order to survive and know whether Nicole had complied (608) demonstrates that he wanted to determine more than his own destiny. Mailer wrote that

Schiller, as he closed in on a deal with Gilmore, "began to feel how much Gilmore was in control" (641). Schiller also observed that Gary's hunger strike was motivated not by "despair" but "as a way to make Gilmore the dealer" (650–51).

Of course, Gilmore acted out his autocratic drama in an environment where he had few real moves, a paradox that Mailer skillfully exposes. In the last few weeks of his life, as the execution began to seem more and more inevitable, Gilmore increasingly gave orders to prison officials, attorneys, and media representatives; Mailer describes him as like "a graduate student going for his orals before a faculty of whom he was slightly contemptuous" (656). Faced with the growing improbability of escaping the firing squad, Gilmore exercised what few options he had within the confines of maximum security—basically, choosing whether or not to cooperate with people around him. And he was fully aware that he didn't have real freedom; in urging the Utah Board of Pardons not to commute his sentence to life imprisonment, he said, "I simply accepted the sentence that was given to me. I have accepted sentences all my life. I didn't know I had a choice in the matter" (657).

An episode late in the book illustrates the narrow limits of Gilmore's free will. On the evening before his execution, as his attorney left the visiting room, Gilmore asked him, "You wouldn't change clothes with me, would you?" and described how, with a disguise, he might escape (886). Gilmore's question does grave damage to the notion of him as a man hell-bent on his own execution and suggests his true motivation—that he chose death as a better alternative than 30 or 40 more years in prison. His choice was motivated by two factors: first, he found prison insufferable, especially the effect of the noise on his headaches, and second, his choosing execution presented more complications for the officials of the prison and legal system who had to carry it out. Scheffler says, "The final Gary Gilmore opts for free will ... though it may be purchased at others' expense" and he thus "affirm[s] the paradoxical free will that generations of prisoners have proclaimed in journals and stone wall etchings" (190). This claim is true only if making the only choice still available to you can be called an assertion of free will.

Mailer adds to the collage of explanations the theories of psychologists who examined Gary Gilmore. Gilmore's attorneys did not call on psychologists during Gilmore's trial, because they felt that he could not be found legally insane (419). In fact, the psychiatric reports' inconclusiveness is illustrated by the comments of Dr. John Woods at the mitigation hearing preceding sentencing. Dr. Woods, speaking for a group of psychologists who had examined Gilmore, testified that the combination of beer and Fiorinal could have "impair[ed] Gilmore's judgment and ... loosen[ed] the controls on a person that already ha[d] very poor control of himself," but admitted on cross-examination that he had previously written a report that declared Gilmore free of any mental illness or "altered perception of reality" and said that the alcohol and medication were "not likely" to have diminished Gilmore's sense of responsibility for his actions (433–34).

Mailer also presents the arguments of those who identify the prison system itself as the cause of Gilmore's inability to function normally in society. Gilmore spent 18 of the 22 years between ages 13 and 35 behind bars. Early in the book, the reader realizes how little prison has prepared Gilmore for the "outside" world when Brenda takes him to J.C. Penney's to buy jeans and he says pathetically, "I don't know how to go about this. Are you supposed to take the pants off the shelf, or does somebody issue them to you?" (36). Prosecutor Noall Wootton blames the prison system for much of Gilmore's trouble, calling his incarceration "a total, dismal, complete failure" (439).

In the end, a reader seeking to learn why Gary Gilmore crossed the line from shoplifting and parole violations to murder is left with many puzzle pieces but no specific directions on assembling them. Certainly Nicole's rejection, the drugs and alcohol, and Gilmore's inability to adapt to life outside prison were all factors. But Mailer leaves the reader to weigh and combine those factors; his purpose is not rhetorical. In the end, as Robert McLaughlin notes, "Gary Gilmore remains unexplained and unexplainable" (225).

Despite the critical insistence that *The Executioner's Song* represents a stylistic departure for Mailer and a movement away from his earlier Naturalism, the theme of the book is common to his literary nonfiction: the ultimate impossibility of recovering meaning from the chaos of modern life. As Anderson points out, "inexplicability" poses the same problem for Mailer in *The Executioner's Song* that it does in *Of a Fire on the Moon* and *The Armies of the Night* (129–30). McLaughlin argues that the book subverts its own attempts to make meaning, largely because, in the afterword, Mailer undercuts the authority of his own sources (226). In that afterword, Mailer admits that he can come no closer to "the truth" than "the recollections of the witnesses," that often, confronted with conflicting accounts, the author had chosen "the version that seemed most likely" and that "it would be vanity to assume he was always right" (1020). Of media accounts, Mailer suggests in the novel itself that reporters collaborated in a kind of press pool, wherein they would "put a common evaluation on the story the way an open market arrive[s] at a price" (791). McLaughlin suggests (and the book bears out) that Schiller was much more interested in resurrecting his own reputation as a journalist than in getting at "truth." Perhaps most problematic is the unreliability of Gilmore himself, who presents various "masks" to Schiller's interviewers:

Rereading the interviews and letters, Farrell began to mark the transcripts with differ-
ent-colored inks to underline each separate motif in Gilmore's replies, and before he
was done, he got twenty-seven poses. Barry had begun to spot racist Gary and Coun-
try-and-Western Gary, poetic Gary, artist manqué Gary, macho Gary, self-destructive
Gary, Karma County Gary, Texas Gary, and Gary the killer Irishman. Awfully prevalent lately was Gilmore the movie star [806].

Perhaps it was Mailer's awareness of his inability to claim accuracy that led
him to ask his publisher, Little, Brown, to classify *The Executioner's Song* as
a "truelife novel" (Mills 430). Oddly, the book won the Pulitzer Prize for
fiction, although the Pulitzer committee gives awards in categories including "General Nonfiction" and "Explanatory Journalism." Mailer's prize
clearly did not put to rest the critical questions about genre raised by *In
Cold Blood*.

Ultimately, McLaughlin maintains, *The Executioner's Song* is largely
about how difficult it is to write a work like *The Executioner's Song* (237).
Anderson says that perhaps even more than *Armies* or *Fire*, the book is
about "the dramatization of process, the story of the effort to recover the
event.... It's as if Mailer, rather than writing a book, chooses to present us
with the material he would have to work from in writing a book" (120).
This compilation resulted in another of the gargantuan manuscripts that
led Tom Wolfe, in his 1965 review of *An American Dream*, to suggest that
Mailer might improve his prose style by studying at the school of James M.
Cain (Hoopes 487–88)—or, one might add, Truman Capote.

The notion of forging meaning out of chaos points to an aspect of Mailer's work that is—and has always been—fundamentally Naturalistic: the
conviction, shared by all the Naturalistic writers, that something in American society is fundamentally askew. In *Advertisements for Myself*, Mailer
acknowledged that while he was working on *The Naked and the Dead*, he
reread three novels that had affected him profoundly when he first read them
as a college freshman: *Studs Lonigan, U.S.A.*, and *The Grapes of Wrath* (27).
In his chapter on Mailer in *Twentieth-Century American Literary Naturalism*, Donald Pizer notes that Malcolm Cowley called *The Naked and the Dead*
"The Studs Lonigan Boys in the South Pacific" (90). Pizer wrote in *Twentieth
Century American Literary Naturalism* (1982) that Mailer is a "major twentieth-century American naturalist" and that *The Naked and the Dead* is one of
the "best and most significant novels" in recent American Naturalism. Pizer
points out the definite influence of Naturalism in Mailer's use of the Army
platoon, with its struggles based on race and class conflicts, as a microcosm
of American society, and his characterization of the "fascistic" General Cum-
mings with his "willingness to view men as machines or animals" (*Twentieth*
90–91). But the preparation of this Pizer book overlapped with the appearance of *The Executioner's Song*, so Pizer does not mention it.

In addition to the Naturalists of the '30s, Mailer acknowledged the influence of Dreiser, specifically *An American Tragedy*. The actress Shelley Winters maintains that Mailer knew the novel well and explained it to her, in preparation for her role as Roberta in the film adaptation *A Place In the Sun* (1951). Mailer went scene by scene through the novel with Winters, explaining that Clyde Griffiths basically suffered the fallout from a shift in American society from morals to status. Winters said she presumed that "Norman was a protégé of Dreiser because he knew the book so well" (qtd. in Manso 141–42). In a 1963 essay, Mailer acknowledged the specific influence of Dreiser on *The Naked and the Dead*. He wrote that "the central terrain of the modern novel" was divided between the kind of novels Tolstoy wrote, about the social forces affecting men, and the sort written by Dostoevsky, more intensely psychological novels, in which individuals are observed in the "terror" of "exploring the mystery about themselves" ("Goddess" 128). Mailer says that *An American Tragedy* is a perfect example of the Tolstoyan kind and that *Moby Dick* epitomizes the Dostoevskian strain. He noted that in *The Naked and the Dead*, he sought to "straddle the categories" ("Goddess" 128). Mills' comment that Mailer's 1965 novel *An American Dream* "reenacted" to some extent both *An American Tragedy* and *Crime and Punishment* would seem to indicate that Mailer did sometimes manage that balance (277).

But Mailer's comment in 1963 that the Tolstoyan novel was getting harder to write might be read as an indication that the Naturalistic influence on him was waning. The increasing complexity of American society, he said, made it difficult to write social novels with the broad sweep of Zola and Balzac. He asks, "Who can create a vast canvas when the imagination must submit itself to a plethora of detail in each joint of society? Who can travel to many places when the complexity of each pool sucks up one's attention like a carnivorous cess-fed flower?" ("Goddess" 129). These comments represent Mailer complaining about the amount of "status details" required by the new documentary narrative or nonfiction novel form.

One is tempted to say that in *The Executioner's Song*, Mailer has given up on Tolstoy and migrated to the Dostoevskian model of exploring the terror of the self. Actually, Mailer still manages to do both, by examining social realities as they are personified in one "self"—Gary Gilmore, whom the author called "quintessentially American and yet worthy of Dostoevsky" (qtd. in Lennon). But whereas Dostoevsky and Melville look into Raskolnikov and Ahab and find motive, Mailer finds Gary Gilmore hollow. Ultimately, he says, the more he learned about the man, the less he understood (Lennon 229). Chris Anderson says that the subject of *The Executioner's Song* is ultimately "vacuum" (131), that "what [Mailer] wants us to see is the pointlessness, the dreariness of the Gilmore story.… What Gilmore's life illustrates is the fundamental mundaneness of part of America" (124–45). Commenting on the vernacular effectiveness of the book, John Garvey says that if "future readers want to know how Americans sounded in the 1970s they can come to this book" (140). By extension, if the theme of the book is that the chaos of modern life defies explanation, future generations could also get an accurate picture of the existential climate of post–'60s America from Gary Gilmore's story. In this sense, Norman Mailer fills the role that Harold Bloom has prescribed for him: "Mailer, now celebrated, doubtless will vanish into neglect, and yet always will return, as a historian of the moral consciousness of his era" (*Mailer* 6).

7

"Variations on a Theme by Capote"

The 20th Century, Part II

"Naturalism in American fiction is now about as dead as
the well-known dodo."—Randall Stewart (qtd. in Graham 1)

Truman Capote's and Norman Mailer's successes with the nonfiction novel in the 1960s and '70s constituted a "seal of approval" for the genre, as Charles H. Brown observes in "Journalism vs. Art" (33). While *In Cold Blood* may not constitute a new literary species, it and Mailer's nonfiction works in the same period were instrumental in establishing literary nonfiction as a force to be reckoned with, imitated, and analyzed. Their works also touched off a critical debate as to appropriate critical terminology for evaluation of nonfiction. Are *An American Tragedy* and *In Cold Blood* to be judged by different standards just because one was published during the zenith of first-wave Naturalism and one emerged with the New Journalism? Because literary nonfiction employs narrative as its primary strategy, critics have tended to judge it according to the criteria applicable to realistic novels rather than to reporting. Thus, many reviews of Capote's novel mention crisply paced storytelling or effective characterization, but evaluations of the book's factual fidelity are rare. In fact, Philip Tompkins' "In Cold Fact" (1966) was the only article about the book to examine the question of factual authenticity until Ralph F. Voss's book-length study *Truman Capote and the Legacy of* In Cold Blood was released in 2015. On the accuracy issue, Voss primarily defers to Tompkins' findings, but he is far more interested in the narrative artistry of Capote's novel, especially in its inclusion of gothic elements common in Capote's Southern fiction. Voss rejects as "myth" Capote's claims for having invented a new literary form, citing Capote's own description of the book as "a distillation of reality" (qtd. in Voss).[1] What Voss's study particularly reveals is that the critical questions concerning the literary pedigree of Capote's novel are ongoing.

In terms of evaluating the role of factuality in such a book, Eric Heyne provides a useful vocabulary in his essay "Literary Status for Nonfiction Narratives." Heyne argues convincingly that factual accuracy *per se* is not an appropriate standard by which to judge a nonfiction account because a reader's ability to assess a work's factuality is too variable, depending "on the epistemology and experience of the individual reader" ("Literary" 142). Heyne proposes substitution of the useful terms "factual status" and "factual adequacy." "Factual status" is the context the author gives the reader concerning the accuracy of the narrative ("Literary"). Capote, for example, notifies the reader in the preface to *In Cold Blood* that any material "not derived from [his] own observation" is derived either "from official records or ... interviews with the persons directly concerned." Statements like Capote's appear with surprising frequency in nonfiction novels; in fact, they may not have existed in nonfiction books about homicide prior to *In Cold Blood*. As Heyne maintains, such claims shape a reader's expectations with regard to the presentation of factual material ("Literary").

"Factual adequacy" is "the degree to which [the work] satisfies our standards of truthfulness" (Heyne, "Literary" 140). Once a reader determines that a writer intends a narrative to have factual status, Heyne says, then he or she can "weigh" its factual adequacy ("Literary" 140). Thus, because Dreiser makes no initial claims for factual status in *An American Tragedy*, the reader expects from it only ordinary verisimilitude (despite its being derived from fact); with *In Cold Blood* and *The Executioner's Song*, because the authors have made claims for factual status and detailed their reporting techniques (some of which, in *The Executioner's Song*, are mentioned overtly in the narrative), the reader applies a different standard. According to Heyne, factual status and factual adequacy are the primary criteria that distinguish fiction from literary nonfiction. Heyne wrote these words in 1987, and one suspects that the advent of Googling and the existence of online databases (some of which include primary documents) have significantly increased the average reader's ability to compare facts, though not necessarily the reader's competence in doing so.

The primary quality that fiction and literary nonfiction share, and that distinguishes literary nonfiction from nonfiction per se or mere reporting, is theme. Heyne says that "the first and generally most important sign of a valuable true story is its ability to convince us to see the world in a new way"; literary nonfiction, therefore, has "the capacity to alter our understanding of the world beyond the narrative" ("Literary" 142). Certainly fiction has the same capacity, so that we can distinguish *Wuthering Heights*

from a popular romance on the grocery store check-out rack by saying that the reader of *Wuthering Heights* gains a deeper understanding of (and perhaps a useful paradigm for) love and separation, while the reader of the popular romance merely has a vicarious experience of passion. The works that "alter our understandings," in other words, are the superior works. The same criterion can be used to distinguish literary nonfiction. Whereas *In Cold Blood* contributes something important to a reader's understanding of criminal behavior and how murder affects an average community, the *New York Times* article that prompted Capote to go to Kansas merely adds to its reader's store of factual information about the murders.

The Naturalistic novel—nonfiction or not—takes Heyne's contention one step further. If "literary" works can be said to "convince us to see the world in a new way," then Naturalistic literary works convince us to see the world in a *particular* way, as do Marxist works, or feminist works, or works with any specific theoretical basis, for Naturalism has an agenda. Based on the premises developed thus far about the Naturalistic homicide novel, then, what variations in its methodology and focus have evolved over the last 50 years or so, since the era of Capote's and Mailer's contributions?

By now it seems reductive to define the Naturalistic homicide novel as a factual work in which a character is driven to murder by forces outside his control and far more productive to identify patterns that persist across works. First, the protagonist is a young adult, always male, generally between the ages of 18 and 35, and the significance of age is that the protagonist has not fully matured. Thus, the reader sees him as a person not adequately prepared to deal rationally with the world. Even if he is in his late 20s or early 30s, his executive functioning may be impaired by emotional or behavioral abnormalities.

Second, his social status limits him within his culture. He is almost always poor, often a member of a cultural minority; he may be black, like Bigger Thomas; Jewish, like Judd Steiner and Artie Straus; or of mixed racial heritage, like Joe Christmas and Perry Smith. He may be a non-religious person in a predominately Mormon culture, like Gilmore. It is not coincidental that Dreiser, the early master of the Naturalistic homicide novel, was the first American Catholic writer of stature and the first to grow up speaking a foreign language (German) at home. It is worth noting that one of the most recent books by the grand master of Naturalistic literary theory, Donald Pizer, is *American Naturalism and the Jews* (2008), a study of the anti–Semitism of five major Naturalistic writers who otherwise demonstrated socially progressive attitudes in their writing.[2]

The settings of novels in this tradition exhibit one of two tendencies: to be urban, novels of crowded cities such as San Francisco (*McTeague*), Chicago (*An American Tragedy, Native Son, Compulsion*),

Kansas City, Missouri, and the fictional "Lycurgus," New York (*An American Tragedy*); or to exist "out there," in some remote, isolated locale such as the rural South (*Light in August*), the wheat fields of western Kansas (*In Cold Blood*), the highways of rural California (*The Postman Always Rings Twice*), or the foothills of central Utah (*The Executioner's Song*). Whether the protagonist is a rootless drifter in a stable rural community or an ingenuous outsider in a swarming metropolis, he contrasts with the landscape against which his story plays out.

Finally—and most importantly—the paradigmatic experience of the Naturalistic murderer is that of isolation. This begins with his parents. Joe Christmas, Bigger Thomas, and Gary Gilmore all have dead fathers (Joe's mother is dead as well). Mothers tend to be overbearing and to judge their sons based on the terms of their own lives; the mothers of Bigger Thomas, Clyde Griffiths, McTeague, and Gary Gilmore are examples. Even the sons of two-parent families experience this isolation, as their parents are distracted by religion (*An American Tragedy*), alcoholism (*McTeague, In Cold Blood*), or professional and civic obligations (*Compulsion*). Although he is writing in the confessional mode, Frank Chambers of *The Postman Always Rings Twice* makes no mention of a family. In some cases, characters' parents are also isolated or ostracized, as Gilmore's mother is outcast from her Mormon family, Perry Smith's parents are itinerant rodeo performers, and Clyde Griffiths' parents are street evangelists. Protagonists of mixed racial heritage, such as Christmas and Smith, may be double outcasts, more likely to be viewed with suspicion because their ethnicity is not easily recognizable. Noticing Christmas for the first time at the sawmill, one of Byron Bunch's co-workers utters a question illustrating the questioner's inability to categorize the newcomer: "Is he a foreigner?" (Faulkner, *Light* 29). In the beginning of the same novel, Lena Grove, who is isolated from her previous community by both her pregnancy and her parentlessness, evokes the same habit of judging based on expectations when she says she decided to walk into Doane's Mill because people who passed her would assume that a girl on foot lived nearby.

Characters are also isolated from successful relationships with potential lovers. *McTeague* is nearly as isolated married to Trina as he was when he lived alone. Women are stumbling blocks for Clyde Griffiths, Joe Christmas, and Bigger Thomas. The relationship between Frank Chambers and Cora Papadakis is seriously damaged by the lack of trust which results from Nick's murder and their subsequent legal problems. The possibility of successful relationships for other characters (Perry Smith, Joe Christmas, Artie Straus and Judd Steiner) is blunted by their latent homosexual tendencies. Gary Gilmore's relationship with Nicole Baker occasionally shows a glimmer of promise but is more often abusive or perverse (owing to Gilmore's apparent pedophiliac tendencies).

Another source of isolation for these characters is economic: with the exceptions of McTeague and Clyde Griffiths, characters are unable to hold jobs and to maintain any semblance of traditional economic security. They seldom live under their own roofs, and they are further isolated by their migratory nature, as only in *McTeague* and *Compulsion* do protagonists stay put for any length of time. They are largely uneducated, with the obvious exception of Steiner and Straus, whose education above the norm isolates them as much as Perry Smith's education below it. In most cases, this isolation is presented as largely unwilled, Steiner and Straus again being the notable exception.

The homicide-inspired books published in the same literary generation as *In Cold Blood* and *The Executioner's Song* that have been well received or prominent—those remaining in print two decades into the 21st century—vary in their degrees of conformity to the prototype for the Naturalistic homicide novel. Generally, these books can be grouped into two categories: (1) those that employ journalistic methodology and focus on the murderer but do not follow the Naturalistic formula in every detail and (2) those that follow the Naturalistic formula but focus primarily on the victim rather than the killer. Some authors also mirror Capote's interest in the response of the violated community.

Two prominent books from the 1960s and '70s illustrate those works that veer in the direction of the documentary, focusing exclusively on a murderer and his evolution, while still offering commentary on the theme of exclusion from the American dream: *Helter Skelter* (1974) by Vincent Bugliosi and Joe McGinniss's *Fatal Vision* (1983). Three others will illustrate the authors who turn the Naturalistic gaze to victims: *The Algiers Motel Incident* (1968), *The Onion Field* (1973) and *Looking for Mr. Goodbar* (1975). Finally, *The Boston Strangler* (1966) and a more recent book, Alec Wilkinson's *A Violent Act* (1992) will illustrate the community response to spontaneous, apparently senseless violence.

The title *Helter Skelter* is taken from a song on the LP *The Beatles* (better known as *The White Album*). The musical allusion is appropriate for the story of a man, Charles Manson, who fancied himself part of the counter-cultural music scene in Los Angeles in 1969, when members of his "family" killed seven people in a two-night spree in August 1969. The author, Manson prosecutor Vincent Bugliosi, would have us believe that Manson brainwashed members of his "family" of runaways and social misfits into committing the murders, victims of which included Sharon Tate, wife of film director Roman Polanski. Tate was eight and a half months pregnant. In his *New Republic* review, W.C. Woods said *Helter Skelter* "tells everything medicine and law will probably ever know" about the crimes and

life of Charles Manson. Yet for all Bugliosi's attempt at interpreting Manson's apocalyptic philosophy, the book ultimately feels like a "best guess"
approach to Manson's motives, and its authors (Bugliosi with Curt Gentry) admit their uncertainty, while still making a claim for factual status:
the book's subtitle is "The True Story of the Manson Murders." In fact, there
are books by other people who knew Manson, such as Ed Sanders, author
of *The Family* (1971) who provides a more "inside" sense of life in Manson's cult. Sanders, a member of the band The Fugs, was part of the Los
Angeles music community and "often dressed more like a Manson family
member than like Bugliosi." Because he had "countercultural bona fides,"
Sanders was occasionally invited to Spahn Ranch by Manson family "rem-
nants," devotees not involved in the criminal investigation and trials. Sanders' perspective is quite different from that of the prosecutor Bugliosi.
Nevertheless, due to its sales and its transformation in 1976 into a television
mini-series, Bugliosi's account has endured as the one that has most shaped
public perception of the murders committed by Manson's disciples.

   Like many books in this tradition (most notably *In Cold Blood*), *Helter
Skelter* opens with an establishment of the geographic and social backdrop:
"It was so quiet, one of the killers would later say, you could almost hear the
sound of ice rattling in cocktail shakers in the homes way down the canyon"
(3). Bugliosi's account is arranged chronologically into eight sections and
an epilogue. In an attempt to bolster the book's factual accuracy and to suggest its preeminence as a reference on the Manson family, *Helter Skelter* also
includes an initial seven-page "Cast of Characters," maps of the Death Valley
area, a floor plan of the Tate-Polanski residence, a "chilling 64-page photographic record of the victims, the killers, [and] the evidence" and, rare (if not
unique) among narratives of its type, an index. Bugliosi strongly suggests that
the thriving California artistic society of the 1960s was out of touch with—
even vulnerable to—the hopelessness and misguided ambition of younger
outsiders who only dreamed of joining it. Bugliosi does not sympathize with
his protagonist, which is no surprise, considering that he prosecuted the case.
His relief at seeing Manson convicted sometimes affects his tone; *New York
Times* reviewer Michael Rogers notes that "when Bugliosi raises his voice,
one still senses the calculated flavor of a closing argument to the jury."

   Helter Skelter shares something of the social awareness of the Naturalistic novel and certainly the theme of outsiders to the American dream,
aptly symbolized by a band of counter-cultural outsiders led by a musician wannabe and enacting violence on the social elite in exclusive Bene-
dict Canyon, where film stars regularly lived. Manson apparently sent his
emissaries of violence to 10050 Cielo Drive because Terry Melcher, a music
producer and songwriting partner of the Beach Boys' Brian Wilson (and
son of the actress Doris Day), had previously lived there and declined to

help Manson get a start in the music business. Manson, who had "a certain strange charm and at least a little musical talent," had auditioned for Melcher, and the Beach Boys subsequently recorded one of Manson's songs under a different title and without credit to him (La Ganga and Himmelsback-Weinstein). The month before the Tate-LaBianca murders, Manson follower Bobby Beausoleil had murdered Gary Hinman, with Manson and a few other "family" members looking on. Hinman, a music teacher, had introduced Manson to Brian Wilson. Manson had led his family to believe he was getting a recording contract, but it is reasonable to conclude that Melcher's rejection convinced him of his place as an outsider in the entertainment industry's "caste system" described by insiders such as gossip columnist Rona Barrett (La Ganga and Himmelsback-Weinstein). An artist who trusted the establishment more might have sued for appropriation, but Manson apparently chose vengeance instead.

Bugliosi's book largely established what has become the conventional explanation for the Tate and LaBianca murders: that Manson ordered the killings due to his distorted comprehension of the song "Helter Skelter" as a directive to start a race war. His "family" would murder affluent white people so that black people would likely be blamed; Manson theorized that black people would win the race war. But Sandy Gibbons, who covered the Manson family trial, says the real motivation was to "put the fear of death into Terry Melcher" (La Ganga and Himmelsback-Weinstein). Manson's perception of himself as outsider is abundantly clear in his appearance on the first day of his trial, an "X" carved into his forehead, and his associates handing out a manifesto in which he declared, "I have Xed myself from your world" (qtd. in La Ganga and Himmelsback-Weinstein).[3]

Considered in light of the mix-up about Melcher's address, the murders depicted in *Helter Skelter* share with *In Cold Blood* the possibility of the killers' motivation having its basis in a half-truth. The Clutter family was financially comfortable, but Herb Clutter died not keep excessive cash at home, as Dick Hickock had been told. Manson sent his designees to Terry Melcher's previous address, apparently not realizing that the house was occupied by different residents. These perverse facts are also consistent with the role played by chance in earlier Naturalistic novels such as the cat motif in *The Postman Always Rings Twice*. Despite the Naturalistic themes, however, Bugliosi's methods are primarily nonfictional, and his motive is establishing factual accuracy, as his copious documentation suggests. It is worth noting that *Helter Skelter* is the only book discussed in this study that has outsold *In Cold Blood*. Nearing the 50th anniversary of the Tate-LaBianca murders in late July 2019, co-prosecutor Stephen Kay declared the crimes "the case that just never goes away" (La Ganga and Himmelsback-Weinstein).

Joe McGinniss's *Fatal Vision* (1983) is the account of a crime whose perpetrator attempted to conjure Manson and his "family" in Eastern North Carolina, apparently to cover his culpability for the murder of his own family.
Former Army Captain Jeffrey MacDonald was convicted nearly nine years
after the murders of Colette, Kimberley, and Kristen MacDonald, his wife
and young daughters, at their Fort Bragg (North Carolina) home. MacDonald, a physician and member of the U.S. Marines, maintained that a group
of Manson-style hippies killed his family and wounded him in retaliation
for his refusal to continue supplying them with narcotics. The Tate-LaBianca
crimes had occurred in Los Angeles only six months before, and the Manson
"Family" was still very much in the news. Significantly, a magazine opened to
an article about Manson was found by police on a coffee table in the orderly
living room where MacDonald claimed he had been assaulted. Due largely
to inconsistencies in his stories and the persistence of his father-in-law, the
Green Beret physician was convicted and sentenced in 1979 for murders that
had occurred in February 1970.

Joe McGinniss's involvement in the MacDonald case was extremely
unusual, as he was originally recruited nine years after the crimes by Mac-
Donald's defense team, with the idea that his research and writing about
the case might help to win MacDonald's acquittal. But during the course of
his interviews and observations, McGinniss became persuaded of his subject's guilt by the evidence that Colette MacDonald's father had accumulated. *Fatal Vision* was published 13 years after the murders occurred, and
while McGinniss's method is not Naturalistic, it is definitely rhetorical. The
book has a clear thesis, which is that anyone unconvinced of MacDonald's
guilt has likely been distracted by his semi-transparent charisma and medi-
ocre acting ability.

In *The Journalist and the Murderer* (1990), Janet Malcolm tells the
story of MacDonald's libel suit against McGinniss, which was settled out of
court and has become a well-known misrepresentation case. McGinniss's
defense was that he had a higher obligation to the truth of the case than
to any promise he had made to MacDonald, a convicted murderer. Malcolm maintained that it was "morally indefensible" for a journalist, McGinniss, to continue working with his subject while being deceptive about
how he would ultimately portray that subject (3). In a subsequent lawsuit,
Colette MacDonald's parents were awarded a portion of Jeffrey MacDonald's $325,000 settlement from McGinniss (Falcon).

Needless to say, McGinniss's portrayal of his protagonist is not sympathetic. The author sees the physician as completely self-absorbed, too
threatened by the prospect of parenting a third child to continue the
marriage and too concerned with his All-American reputation to consider divorce. McGinniss is Clyde Griffiths looking for a way out of a

predicament stemming from an undesired pregnancy, but Clyde Griffiths is much more sympathetic, as his panic is more genuine in its social context, whereas McGinniss's seems calculated and almost purely narcissistic. As McGinniss presents him after the murders, Jeffrey MacDonald is preoccupied with his own status as victim and with details such as whether he should wear his khaki or green uniform for reporters' cameras. As early as page 209 (of 563), McGinniss is satirizing MacDonald as a guest on the Dick Cavett show: sympathetically introduced by Cavett as "a man living through a nightmare," the doctor is "greeted by a surge of applause"; asked to narrate the story of the murders if it isn't "too painful," MacDonald replies that he "can skim through it briefly." When Cavett inquires about the "cost" of the ordeal, MacDonald prefaces his response with, "aside from my family and what not," and goes on to discuss his legal fees. McGinniss's attitude is clear from his description of the guest's departure: "And Jeffrey MacDonald exited to music and applause" (210–13). A reader can be sure that this medical school graduate and soldier will never come near the electric chair.

Perhaps McGinniss's most revealing technique, in terms of MacDonald's character, is drawn from the New Journalism, not the Naturalistic tradition. This technique involves the way McGinniss allows MacDonald to expose himself, by interspersing throughout the book sections narrated in third person as well as sections entitled "The Voice of Jeffrey MacDonald." In the latter, MacDonald recounts his courtship with Colette and the early years of their marriage. By allowing a reader to hear his subject's broken responses to investigators' questions, McGinniss establishes MacDonald as uncomfortable at best and duplicitous at worst. Asked to explain an aspect of the fiber evidence that would help to convict him, MacDonald stammers, "Listen, I know all about that, and, ah—look, ah, all—Jesus Christ. All I can say is that it seems to me these fibers in a struggle could have gotten on everyone, and I don't know. I—I mean, obviously, I wish—I can't give you the answers specifically" (126). McGinniss's epigram for the novel is the "Is this a dagger which I see before me?" speech from *Macbeth*, and it effectively establishes McGinniss's skepticism that MacDonald's story (and his "honor") might be "A dagger of the mind, a false creation,/ Proceeding from the heat-oppressed brain" (*Macbeth*, II, 1, 33). Thus, *Fatal Vision* might be read as a documentary account of domestic violence. There is little of Naturalism about this method, although like Capote, McGinniss orchestrates his narrative to make an argument—except that, in this case, it is an argument for MacDonald's guilt.

If there is a Naturalistic aspect to Jeffrey MacDonald's story, it is suggested by a connection he shares with Richard Loeb and Nathan Leopold: like the younger killers, he may have viewed himself as sufficiently above the norm in intelligence that getting away with murder seemed feasible. If Joe McGinniss were a Naturalistic novelist, MacDonald's mindset might become an indictment of a society that fills some people (such as a narcissistic physician) so full of their own importance that they feel above the expectations imposed on ordinary people. If Leopold and Loeb's youth helps to explain their radical self-centeredness in viewing themselves as Nietzschean Supermen, that explanation might also hold for MacDonald. A popular young man and football team captain whose high school classmates voted him "Most Likely to Succeed," MacDonald had won a scholarship to Princeton University before enrolling in medical school at Northwestern. The same year he became a medical student (at 20), his high school girlfriend, Colette Stevenson, told him she was pregnant with his child; by the end of medical school, he was a father of two. He had joined the U.S. Army just over six months before his wife and daughters' murders and been assigned as surgeon to an elite special forces group, the Green Berets. He was only 26 years old when the couple learned that they were expecting a third child. In addition to inherent human decency, MacDonald's allegiance to the Hippocratic Oath should have prevented him from inflicting harm on anyone. But any reader well-versed in Naturalism will recognize an aspect of Clyde Griffith's plight in MacDonald's life story: a young man in a clear upward trajectory finds his momentum threatened by domesticity. For the Naturalistic writers, the allure of success has always had its most warping effect on ambitious young men. Joe McGinniss's departure from Naturalistic methodology is most apparent in his avoidance of these themes.

Three nonfiction homicide books of the 1960s and '70s focus primarily on victims: John Hersey's *The Algiers Motel Incident* (1968), Joseph Wambaugh's *The Onion Field* (1973), and Judith Rossner's *Looking for Mr. Goodbar* (1975). Hersey's book illustrates the continuation of the social protest tradition, and Wambaugh and Rossner apply Naturalistic methodology to victims rather than murderers. Wambaugh's and Rossner's follow the architecture of the novel, while Wambaugh's is a more a collage of witness and participant accounts.

Just after the Detroit race riots in summer 1967, John Hersey was asked to write a report for the President's Commission on Civil Disorders (*Algiers* 24). As he delved deeply into the racial situation in Detroit, he became increasingly focused on and skeptical about a confrontation between Detroit police and a group of young adults, mostly black boys and young men, but also including two young white women, at the Algiers motel. Three young men, Carl Cooper (17), Auburey Pollard (19), and Fred Temple (18), were beaten and then shot by police after what was reported as a sniper incident. Those present later said that Carl Cooper had fired a starter's pistol near a window several times in an apparent attempt to taunt police. No gun was ever found at the motel, but many seem to agree that the presence of the young white women in a group of young black men was a trigger for the responding Detroit officers and that one, David Senak, had spent so much time working the vice squad that his impression of women was generally negative ("Heart"; Schroth 109). Seven other black men and the two white women were also beaten but survived. The officers responsible were subsequently cleared of all charges, which included felonious assault, murder, and conspiracy to commit civil rights violations. More and more, Hersey came to see the dead youth as victims of institutionalized racism and the whole situation as a metaphor for racial strife in the United States. Perhaps most shocking of all, Hersey writes that "no official person ever notified any of the families of the deaths of their sons" (21). The dead men's families found out from the victims who survived.

Hersey's interest in the oppression of a cultural minority clearly has precedent in Naturalism, and his condemnation of social ills is as sincere as Dreiser's in *An American Tragedy*. But in chapter two, wherein he directly addresses his methodology, Hersey declares that writing with "conviction" means that "the events could not be described as if witnessed from above by an all-seeing eye opening on an all-knowing novelistic mind" (27). Instead, his method is almost purely collage: relying on first-person testimony tape-recorded and transcribed, he assembles a collection of eyewitness accounts. His montage of biographies and excerpts from interviews and legal documents reminds a reader of techniques used by Dos Passos in *U.S.A.* or the oral histories of Studs Terkel. The book's claims for factual status include a two-page, single-spaced list of "Persons Involved in the Incident" and a floor plan diagram of the Algiers Motel Annex where the "Incident" occurred. Reviewer Albert J. Reiss says that because of this method, the book has a "Rashomon quality," the reference being to an Akira Kurosawa film in which four witnesses to a samurai's murder in the woods tell four different, sometimes contradictory, generally self-serving stories about what happened.[4] The Kurosawa film spawned the term "the Rashomon effect," a reference to the fallibility of human perception in recalling events. The viewer, like Hersey's reader, is left to draw most of the conclusions. However, the accounts do not vary as broadly as those of the "witnesses" in *Rashomon*. Instead, a largely uniform account of events at the Algiers Motel is formed in Hersey's book.

Nevertheless, Hersey resists the use of the term "objective" to characterize his narrative. Referring to what he calls "the fraudulent tradition of American journalism," Hersey declares that "there is no such thing as objective reportage…. [T]he moment the recorder chooses nine facts out of

ten he colors the information" (27). In explaining his methodology in chapter two, Hersey also establishes a connection with the I-centered school
of the nonfiction novel practiced by Tom Wolfe and Norman Mailer, as
Hersey dramatizes his own role in the investigation: "At this point in the
narrative, enter myself," says the author (24). Despite his disdain for authorial self-dramatization, Hersey says, he felt the incident was "too urgent,
too complex, too dangerous to too many people to leave doubts strewn
along its path" and that, consequently, he could not afford "the luxury of
invisibility" (24). He abandoned a novel in progress, Hersey writes, because
he felt he "owed some sort of debt of work to this" (24). Perhaps because of
this sense of "owing," Hersey declares, "I will not take any money from any
source for the publication of this story" (28). His publisher, Knopf, printed
more than 550,000 copies and donated all the proceeds to scholarships for
African American students, according to a December 8, 1968, article in the
Detroit Free Press ("Algiers").

  Although Hersey remains mostly true to his method, he does take the
opportunity to inject commentary via some chapter headings that inevitably represent the authorial voice and may reflect irony. Some chapters
have neutral names, such as "The First Day" and "The Second Day." But
chapter one, presenting introductions to the three victims' lives, is called
"Do You Hate the Police?" The biographical chapter of just over 30 pages
about David Senak, the officer in charge during the incident, is given Senak's nickname, "Snake." A *Time* reviewer wrote, "One could scarcely find,
in journalism or in fiction, a more revealing portrait of a certain type of
policeman" than in the chapter about Senak ("Heart"). The chapter about
officer Ronald August is called "Quiet and Respectable"—including the
quotation marks. The chapter detailing the confessions of two of the officers is "Could You Get My Statement Back?" Despite Hersey's method of
reportage (or "assemblage"), most reviewers of his book agree with *Time*'s
reviewer that the author "leaves no doubt as to where his own sympathies
lie. The Negro youths, he asserts, were 'executed' not for being snipers but
for 'being considered punks, for making out with white girls, for being in
some vague way killers of a white cop,[5] for running riot—for being black
young men and part of the black rage of the time'" ("Heart").

  One reviewer contemporary to the book's publication, Ray Schroth,
has commented that Hersey seems to indict social institutions more than
individuals who were responsible for the atrocities committed in the
Algiers Motel Annex. Schroth writes that Hersey "has not tried to pass
judgment on any man. He seeks to understand men, and pass judgment on
their institutions" (119). True, Hersey includes facts flattering to the defendant police officers, including their generally positive service records, family situations, and religious affiliations (two were Roman Catholic). He

includes perspectives of those who view the police officers as underpaid and overworked, as well as those of the victims' parents and grandparents. And his habit of including the viewpoints of multiple people in their own voices largely keeps the authorial voice out of the book. Hersey therefore does not take the opportunity of a Dreiser or Norris to condemn the actions of some while lamenting the fate of others. But his narrative and the act of the Detroit police officers still speak for themselves, and the question that titles the closing section, "What Is Wrong with the Country?," is in the voice of the author, who predicts a few months before his book's publication that the trials still then in progress would be "finally brought to the weary end of the road of judgment, if not of justice" (334).

Comparisons to *In Cold Blood* are numerous in reviews of Hersey's book, and it should be noted that reviewer Ray Schroth's apparent contempt for Capote tempers the seriousness with which one can read his praise of Hersey, who, he claims, "spares" readers "another *In Cold Blood* in which absurd slaughter was served up as entertainment and a sentence on a slit throat became a matter for aesthetic consideration" (119). Schroth's use of the term "entertainment" is at best puzzling. A much better comparison is that of Alfred J. Reiss, who wrote that Capote's book is aptly titled *In Cold Blood*, and Hersey's, in capturing the atmosphere of the Detroit race riots, could have been called *In Hot Blood* (971–72). Perhaps the strongest similarity with Capote's novel is one that reviewers seem to have overlooked: the fact that the case Hersey investigated rose, as the Clutter murders did, to mythic significance. As Hersey puts it,

> The episode contained all the mythic themes of racial strife in the United States: the arm of the law taking the law into its own hands; interracial sex; the subtle poison of racist thinking by 'decent' men who deny that they are racists; the societal limbo, into which, ever since slavery, so many young black men have been driven in our country; ambiguous justice in the courts; and the devastation in both black and white human lives that follows in the wake of violence and surely as ruinous and indiscriminate flood after torrents [25].

Throughout, Hersey focuses most of his attention on the victims; in fact, several reviewers comment that the chapter about 19-year-old victim Auburey Pollard, Jr., is the most effective (Sokolov, Mitgang). Pollard is described by his father as "a good artist, a beautiful artist … just a normal American boy" (Hersey 8). Pollard's father also laments his son's lost opportunities: "It's too many nice jobs for Negro kids today for them to make the same mistakes I made. He can go to school, he can work in a bank, he can be a computer, a teacher, he can work in a scientific laboratory, it's a million things he can do—work for the government!" (Hersey 9). Auburey Pollard, Sr., tells the interviewer, Hersey, that he "learnt [life] the hard way" by lying about his age and entering military service at 16. The focus of this chapter, often praised by reviewers, is the father's lament for his son's aborted pursuit of the American dream.

Chapters about the other two young victims present them as equally typical of their time and place. Of Carl Cooper, the first to die, his mother, Omar Gill, told Hersey that her son liked school and nice clothes and wanted to be a tailor but "didn't take no stuff off of anybody, didn't like no one to mess with him" (Hersey 14). She said that starting when he was 13 or 14, Carl was picked up regularly by the police, who would keep him at the station overnight or a few days, although "there was never any charge" (15). Gill says a detective told her Carl "isn't a bad guy, he just doesn't like people to talk nasty to him, call him 'nigger,' 'punk,' all like that" (15). When Gill wanted to hire a lawyer after officers "took him in a dark street and beat him up," Carl protested that it would be his word against the officers. By Hersey's account, it sounds as though Carl Cooper was more assertive with Detroit police than officers in a predominately racist society could tolerate. This capriciousness on the part of authorities also characterizes Bigger Thomas's environment.

Fred Temple's mother described him to Hersey as "a good boy" who was "kind of slow in his books" and was in the process of learning brick-laying with his uncle, a contractor (23). Because of his low blood pressure, he had been unsuccessful in a job at Ford Motor Company working around fire. Temple's mother likely spoke for all the parents (and many readers) when she told the author, "I just feel it didn't have to come to this…. It looks like after you beat people for an hour you ought to be able to come to some kind of sense" (23).

Hersey's book was allegedly rushed to press in five weeks; it appeared in the fall of 1968 and describes events occurring as late as June 5 of the same year. Reviewers have pointed to three negative consequences of this timing: first, that Hersey did not take time to study carefully the report of the commission which he originally represented; second, that the book rambles, driven by rhetoric rather than a clear principle of organization; and third, that Hersey compromised the constitutional rights of the police defendants by publishing the book before their cases had been adjudicated. (One should note, as to this last criticism, that the book does not seem to have tainted the officers' chances of exoneration.) As Stephen Schlesinger observes in his *Atlantic* review, Hersey was motivated more by his idealism and sense of social justice than by any journalistic sense of including all the facts. The most recent affront to Hersey's social conscience had been his deep disappointment over President Lyndon B. Johnson's weak response to the report of the Commission on Civil Disorders, which the author said "did not face up to the implications of its own historic accusations" (29). *The Algiers Motel Incident* is a book written to expose "a hopelessly rotten system ... which automatically disbelieve[s] the stories of black people" (Schlesinger). Hersey, who was born in China while his parents were serving as Christian missionaries, declared that he was drawn to stories of those at the margins of American society because "I was born a foreigner. I was born in China, and I think in some ways I have been an outsider in America because of that" (Oliver). This peripheral view is a fundamentally Naturalistic sensibility, and the sense of being "an outsider in America" is consistently the Naturalist's stance.

It seems remarkable that more than half a century after the murder of Emmett Till in 1955 and the Algiers Motel Incident in 1967, the former is well known, while even many generally well-informed people have never heard of what happened in the Algiers Motel Annex. One suspects that coverage focused on the general riot atmosphere around Detroit's Twelfth Street during that week has muted any general sense of public outrage concerning the murder of three young men and the torture of nine other people by officers sworn to uphold the law. The ongoing relevance of the Algiers Motel Incident—event and book—are evident in two recent developments which may lead to their being better known. First, the 2017 film *Detroit* from Academy Award-winning director Kathryn Bigelow dramatized the confrontation in the motel annex, including a lengthy and excruciating sequence highlighting the torture of the young people held captive there. The film grossed over $16 million and brought the story to a new generation.

In September 2019, Hersey's book was published by the Johns Hopkins University Press in a new edition. The importance of this story's continuing availability in Hersey's account is clear from Danielle L. McGuire's statement that most of the physical evidence of the "Incident" has been erased; for example, the Algiers Motel's former location is now a park without a memorial, and, McGuire says, "many of those documents, particularly court and police records, have either been destroyed or are only available (redacted, of course) through a Freedom of Information Act request." In such cases, nonfiction books become the most reliable accounts, provided they are based on thorough research, because their authors have more time to place events in historical context than journalists working contemporaneously to those events.

Nearly two decades into a new millennium, in an era also marked by serious concern about confrontations between white police officers and young black men, as well as a climate of resurging white nationalism spurred by the 2016 election of Donald Trump as president ("*Detroit*"), the assaults on Auburey Pollard, Jr., Carl Cooper, and Fred Temple continue to remain instructive and socially relevant. As part of the larger history of racism in America, the 1967 murders seem to represent the sort of backlash that follows every incremental gain in any rights movement. Three years after the Civil Rights Act and two years after the Voting Rights Act were finally passed, parents like Auburey Pollard, Sr., were feeling more optimistic about their children's opportunities, as Pollard reflects in describing his son as "just a normal American boy" (Hersey 8). Auburey Pollard, Jr., Carl Cooper, and Fred Temple were all young working men who enjoyed parties and the attention of young women, who were experimenting with alcohol and cigarettes, and whose lives looked easier than those of their parents at the same age. Their early adulthood does not appear all that different from that of many young people of their era. But the assault on the young people gathered at the Algiers Motel and more particularly the acquittal of the white officers responsible for it were a reminder that the path to sharing in the American dream would be slower than they had imagined and fraught with setbacks. Fifty years after the "Incident," even after the nation had elected a black president, white supremacists staged a "Unite the Right" rally in Charlottesville, Virginia. When one Neo-Nazi drove his car into the crowd of counter-protestors, killing 32-year-old civil rights activist Heather Heyer, it was clear that the progress of the Dream is often still followed by backlash—especially when that progress is achieved by those who have historically been viewed by some as outsiders.

The Onion Field (1973) is unique among nonfiction novels in the homicide tradition as it focuses on a victim who survived a murder attempt. Wambaugh's book is the best-known account of the March 9, 1963, kidnapping of Los Angeles Police Department officers Ian Campbell and Karl Hettinger during a routine traffic stop and of Campbell's subsequent execution-style murder. In his "Note to the Reader," Wambaugh, himself a former LAPD officer, makes a claim for factual status: for example, of the trial portion, he writes, "The courtroom dialogue was not re-created. It was taken verbatim from court transcript. The names of two minor characters have been changed by request." In the same note, he also asserts factual accuracy: "The re-creation of events was at all times done as accurately as possible." Indeed, long passages in chapter eight concerning lead detective Pierce Brooks' interrogation of witnesses and suspects seem like thinly edited versions of transcripts, as does the lengthy narration in chapter 11 of courtroom proceedings from the preliminary hearing to the announcement of the death sentences.

Wambaugh takes a Naturalistic approach, but primarily with regard to Officer Karl Hettinger, Campbell's partner, who survived the shooting by escaping across an onion field. Wambaugh examines Hettinger as a victim not only of Powell's and Smith's violence but also of a rigid police department code: at gunpoint and urged by his partner, Hettinger relinquishes his service revolver (153), a decision subsequently condemned by the station captain, who orders at roll call, "*Anybody* that gives up his gun to some punk is nothing but a *coward*. And if any of you men ever think of doing such a thing you'll answer to me. By God, I'll do my best to get you fired!" (241, emphasis original). *Time* reviewer Ray Kennedy speculates that Wambaugh, a 14-year LAPD veteran, is the "young red-faced vice officer" in the squad room who realizes the absurdity of this code of honor but recognizes the imprudence of pointing it out.

Further substantiating Kennedy's speculation is Wambaugh's inclusion, as the very next narrative section, of a veteran police officer in another LAPD station confronting his captain during roll call with his conviction that his lengthy service had revolved around one core truth: "one goddamn thing we was always sure of. One thing that was sacred, you might say. And that is that you're the boss out there. You know what you shoulda done at the time you did it. Police work is that kind of business and only the guy that's there knows what he shoulda done or shouldn't a done" (243).

The Onion Field examines Hettinger's navigating between the opposing perspectives of his station captain and the veteran officer. His guilt is intensified when a memorandum circulating throughout the department implies that Campbell's murder resulted from officer error; this memo is subsequently incorporated into the LAPD manual and made part of routine training, and, according to Wambaugh, that training featured ongoing second-guessing of Hettinger's decision to give up his weapon (245). Hettinger's guilt is further exacerbated when a superior officer orders him to explain during a squad meeting how the incident resulted from the two officers' mistakes: "[L]et's hear your opinion about how you guys fouled up. The things each of you did wrong. Or what you *didn't* do and should've done" (216, emphasis original). It is little wonder that, at Campbell's funeral, Hettinger compulsively apologizes to anyone who will listen (230). His guilt literally reduces him, as he subsequently loses more than 20 pounds and actually shrinks an inch (339). One of the things Hettinger fears most is fear itself, especially its unpredictability, and his fears cause him both psychological and physiological symptoms (346). Hettinger eventually resigns, develops kleptomania, later loses a security job because of his thefts, and finally contemplates suicide.

His recovery begins only after he is rejected as a job applicant probably due to his shoplifting habit and resigns himself to letting his wife support him and their three children on a bookkeeper's salary. One afternoon while his wife works, he strikes his own youngest child in an effort to stop her crying, leaving "red finger marks on her buttocks" (Wambaugh 360–61). To complicate matters, right before hitting the baby, Karl has remembered his own literal impotence and assured himself that "at least there won't be any more of *them*" (360). The act of striking his own child (and perhaps of rejecting any future hypothetical children) takes Karl farther outside his self-image than he can bear, finally reflecting to him the extent of his own alteration. His sense of shame is compounded by his perceived inability to commit suicide, "to spare his family by ridding them of himself" (361). Having reached his lowest point, he is persuaded by a detective friend to see a psychiatrist, to find ways to make amends for his thefts, and to consider accepting a police pension (something he has denied himself out of guilt about his thefts). Reviewer C.M. Sevilla calls Wambaugh's book the story of "the near destruction of a sensitive young man." Speaking to a reporter on the 50th anniversary of the murders, Wambaugh said that Hettinger "never completely escaped from the onion field" (Mariecar).

Wambaugh also structures his narrative to reinforce Karl Hettinger's identity as protagonist and to emphasize the deterministic impact of guilt on his life. This strategy begins with a two-page italicized passage in which Hettinger, working at a gardening job, is depicted by the author as alternating between facts and fears. He is working as a gardener; there are trials ongoing (the facts); he is losing his memory and experiencing kleptomania (the fears). Wambaugh uses italics and the third-person limited omniscient point of view to reinforce the nature of these passages as essentially internal (to Karl). Wambaugh alternates this perspective using chapters in which an omniscient narrator tells the main story and fills in details from the earlier lives of the four principals: Campbell, Hettinger, and perpetrators Gregory Powell and Jimmy Smith. The passages limited in point of view to Hettinger function largely as asides do in theater; they allow the reader to experience first-hand the progress of Hettinger's post-traumatic stress disorder, a diagnosis not even recognized and included in the *Diagnostic and Statistical Manual* until 1980, seven years after publication of *The Onion Field* and 17 years after Ian Campbell's murder.

To say that Campbell's fate can be explained by determinism is both simpler and far more complex. In simple terms, his death resulted from the unlucky crossing of the officers with Powell and Smith at a Los Angeles intersection, an apt metaphor for the role of chance in the Naturalistic novel. As a police officer kidnapped and stripped of his weapon, Campbell is powerless to escape his fate. Chance intervenes again in Greg Powell's misunderstanding of the "Little Lindbergh Law," as he believes that the death penalty has been introduced by the kidnapping of the officers. In fact, the death penalty came into play only *after* the officer was shot.[6] As Wambaugh explains, "At the moment Gregory Powell made the statement [about the law], he hadn't committed a capital offense" (208). If not for Powell's error in thinking, Campbell and Hettinger would most likely have been abandoned alive in the countryside by their kidnappers. Obviously, mental health disorders can precipitate homicide, but so can poor executive functioning and, as in this case, simple ignorance.

But a range of influences far broader than a chance meeting between officers and perpetrators and a misunderstanding of the Little Lindbergh Law also come into play, and Wambaugh makes clear that these influences began early in Powell's life as a boy in Michigan with a distant father and a sometimes-invalid mother. Wambaugh describes Powell's repeated attempts to engage with his father, Rusty Powell, a former itinerant musician and Cincinnati Conservatory of Music student whose top priority seems to have been avoiding stress. When Greg's mother, Ethel, undergoes one of her frequent bouts of illness and anxiety, Rusty Powell is content to let Greg supervise and nurture his younger siblings, and when Ethel is well, Rusty is content to let her do it. Greg's every request to his father is rebuffed: the boy can't help with chores, and the father isn't interested in fishing trips to a pond in the family's own back yard. Thus, the boy turns instead to his maternal grandfather, "the Governor," who, despite assuring Greg he is "always here to help," died when his grandson was five (45). When Ethel Powell is well, Greg engages in a power struggle with her and with his siblings, and it seems understandable that a boy who had spent years serving in a parental role would resent his mother's apparent lack of gratitude and her attempts, when healthy, to disenfranchise him. Greg particularly resents the sacrifices necessitated by his family responsibilities, asking his mother, "[H]ow come you wasn't bossing [the house] when Doug needed his drawers changed, or when the girls needed help with arithmetic, or when somebody had to get up an hour early every morning so's to get them all off to school? I wanted to be a crossing guard and couldn't because I had to get the kids off to school." (47)

Rusty Powell's refusal to intervene on Greg's behalf only frustrates his son more. Concluding that his father is "a coward" and his mother "a liar ... trying to turn the kids against" him, Greg enters an academic slump, quits sports, and stops playing his saxophone. Soon, he has lost weight, and he finally leaves home at 15, returning only for brief stays and spending most of the rest of his youth in reform schools. A priest who picks Greg up hitchhiking in Kentucky soon instigates the boy's first sexual experience, explaining that it was "a gesture of love" and that "[s]hame and delight ... are man's responses, not God's" (Wambaugh 50–51). This same priest implores Greg to go back to his family, fearing that authorities will become involved, and confusing the boy with the admonition, it was "not right for you to be here" (50–51). Although he views the priest as "Judas" upon his departure, Greg's idealism appears surprisingly intact: he believes that the priest was sexually involved only with him, that "he couldn't have Father punished for it," and that "he had not been seduced. It had taken no coaxing. He had been ready" (51). But the priest's "betrayal" is the end of any idealism Greg may have preserved, and Wambaugh writes that when Greg shortly thereafter arrives in Florida, "he had learned things, and ... was a more cynical manipulative boy" (52).

Detained by police in Orlando and given a choice between home and reform school, he chooses home—but not for long. Finding that his absence has increased his mother's domineering tendencies, he steals a car with an older boy and, due to his age, gets a break from the authorities (the other boy is sent to the reformatory). His parents soon take in another boy who, Wambaugh speculates, is "a surrogate for the son they had all but lost" and to Greg, another prospective lover. When this boy, Harold, announces plans to join the Navy, Greg steals another car and this time, instead of a pass from the police, he gets a stay in a Colorado juvenile facility. From there, he is in and out of institutions—a training school in Washington, D.C., a reformatory in Ohio, and finally, at 18, the Michigan state prison. He is released at 20 (against his wishes, Wambaugh says) but promptly takes yet another stolen car across state lines and ends up in Leavenworth. When an Indian boy named Little Sheba with whom Greg has formed "an alliance" and a sexual relationship is sent home, Greg begins to exhibit self-destructive behaviors, tearing at his own wrists with his teeth, and finds himself hospitalized and restrained (54–55). The years that follow include bouts of self-harm, stints in prison, promiscuity with both men and women, contracting sexually transmitted diseases, and his mother's erratic intrusions into his life, like an indecisive guardian angel. When his family finally relocates to California, where he is an inmate at a prison hospital, Greg undergoes a brain study that reflects "mild atrophy," a development introduced as a mitigating factor in his trial for the murder of Ian Campbell (55). The news that "Greg's troubles were organic" comforts his parents, Wambaugh reports, and they view the development as "a blessing" (56). At the age of 29, Greg is released again, but by this time he has spent 10 of 13 years in custody and "admitted and surrendered at once and irrevocably to a hateful notion: he was in fact an institutional man" (54).

Wambaugh relates these facts of Greg Powell's early life without evaluation as to how the young man might have been impacted by them; it seems a good guess that he might have been suffering from an attachment disorder with regard to both parents. The elements of the Naturalistic protagonist's youth exist in abundance, but Wambaugh seems to share the opinion of Investigator Pierce Brooks, that Powell and Smith are merely "[s]mall-time losers who couldn't do anything right.... Punks. Stupid, stupid punks" (208). It stands to reason that a police officer-turned-author would have greater identification with police victims and detectives than with perpetrators in such a case, and Wambaugh's lack of sympathy with Powell and

Smith is apparent in the narrative, despite his inclusion of incidents such as Powell's being taken in as a 14-year-old runaway (two states from his Michigan home) by a Roman Catholic priest who subsequently has sex with him. At times, the author even presents Powell's own perceptions as though second-guessing him, as in this passage about Powell's sexual orientation: "though he was to maintain in later years that he was a confirmed homosexual early on, it is clear he was not" (54). Even if Powell's behavior over a period of years suggested a bisexual orientation or perhaps sexual opportunism, it would not seem to be the author's place to correct the man's own opinion about his sexuality. Wambaugh hints at Powell's potential in chapter 11, when the convicted man represents himself during the penalty phase of his trial, effectively emulating the courtroom language he has absorbed and "prompting [prosecutor] Schulman to remark that being a lawyer agrees with [Powell]" (302). And yet despite the more difficult circumstances of Powell's life and his flashes of ability (including musical ability), Wambaugh does not make him the protagonist.

It is difficult to say whether Jimmy Smith is more or less sympathetic than his accomplice, Powell. Smith comes from a more unstable background, having been taken by an aunt from his 13-year-old African American mother, who probably conceived him with "a fifteen-year-old white boy" but "couldn't take care of him" (Wambaugh 63). The "auntie," who had also raised Jimmy's mother, shot herself in the leg with her husband's revolver trying to keep it away from Jimmy when the boy was around three, ending up bedridden in a cast for a year. After the husband left, Jimmy did what a three-year-old can manage in the way of bringing her water and food. Auntie's second husband took money she intended to spend on Jimmy, once beating her when she protested. Wambaugh writes that this husband, Sylvester, was "the only man in Jimmy Lee Smith's early life," and "All he did was nag and fuss at [Jimmy]" (64). When Auntie was capable of returning to work, Sylvester tied Jimmy to the bedposts and beat him, too, drawing attention from the neighbors and a promise from Jimmy's aunt, who "came limping into the apartment, ... got Sylvester's gun, and, shoved it into his face, crying, 'You ain't never gonna lay hands on my boy again. Never!'" (65).

Jimmy grew up often hungry, hiding behind grocery counters to eat stolen food, and continually bullied about his "light skin and mulatto features," with the other boys (perhaps half-jealous that the girls found him "a fine, bright-lookin boy") calling him names such as "yella-faced ponk" and "half-blooded nigger" (Wambaugh 65). So he learned how to avoid the best-looking girls to allay other boys' envy, while developing a taste for nice clothes that he generally lacked the work ethic to acquire legally. Still a teen, he came of age in "the heart of skid row, the one street in Los Angeles which can compete with the worst of eastern slum neighborhoods" (76). He quit school early and developed ruses for avoiding truancy officers, finding that his best opportunities often involved moving stolen property for others or directing men in flashy cars to prostitutes' apartments. Until his chance meeting with Gregory Powell at the shoeshine stand that served as a neighborhood dispatch for petty crime, Jimmy Smith's crimes mostly involved theft, drug use, and parole violations; he usually got caught and—at least according to Wambaugh's account—"had never been shot at or carried a gun," his interest in firearms having been thwarted by his Auntie's accident (77). People raised in the environment around Fifth and Stanford streets in L.A.'s skid row "out of necessity have grown very tough or very cunning," Wambaugh writes, adding, "Jimmy Lee Smith" was "cunning" (68). To a newspaper reporter, Wambaugh said that Smith "started out behind the eight ball and ended up there" (Quinones).

Gregory Ulas Powell, by contrast, was controlling, stemming from his early adolescence, when his mother recovered her health and displaced him as the family manager. As an adult, he was also hot-tempered, threatening physical violence against anyone who betrayed him. During Jimmy Smith's eight days of acquaintance with Powell before the kidnapping, Powell threatens to harm someone or tells a story about his past violence almost every day. "I'd kill any one of my friends who ever ratted on me," Powell brags, and Smith, having no other response, lies that he "damn near beat a dude to death one time because he rolled over on me" (125). When Powell doesn't react to Jimmy's boast that he broke the man's arm and two ribs, Jimmy throws in a fictive broken jaw as well. After Smith joins Powell's robbery scheme as driver, Wambaugh writes that Powell, his authority bolstered by his weapons purchases in Las Vegas, "at last was the unchallenged head of his own little family" (131). After he is ordered into the Ford, Ian Campbell recognizes Powell's need for control when the officer stands at the passenger door asking, "Where do you want me?" (154).

Virtually the entire story of the Powell-Smith partnership is encapsulated in a passage in Smith's first biographical section, wherein Wambaugh describes the young man's resignation

> to a secondary role in life, a number *two* man, making small stings, someday hoping to drive a decent transportation car, taking a back seat to the big-timer. It had its advantages. The big man was always willing to do a favor for the smaller man who was no threat. If something bad went down, like a police bust … well the big timer was knocked off, but the number two man did business as usual. It was much safer not to aspire to high position here on Fifth Street [69–70].

Smith neatly fulfills his plan of becoming "a number two man" when he becomes Powell's robbery driver. Powell and Smith kidnap Officers Campbell and Hettinger on the ninth working day of both partnerships, when it already seems to both the kidnappers that they "had been partners for a long time" (77). The part of Smith's plan about "the big man [being] always willing to do a favor for the smaller man" also turns out to be true, as Powell regularly buys Smith liquor, gives him small amounts of cash, clothes him after Smith's parole, or buys him a pawn shop watch that was "the first gift since the small things [Smith] had gotten as a child" (118). Something of the *folie à deux* that characterized the relationship between Dick Hickock and Perry Smith also seems present in the pairing of Gregory Powell and Jimmy Smith. Just as Perry Smith is drawn to his partner's promise of "a big score," Jimmy Smith is lured back into partnership with Powell after vowing to "cut Greg loose after this weekend" by Greg's scheme of robbing a man who collects money from parking lots, a plan he expects to bring them "twenty-five grand" (113–14). In reality, the pair seldom take in more than a few hundred dollars from any of their four robberies together.

As in the Clutter murder case, the question of who shot Ian Campbell was the biggest mystery for investigators. Both Powell and Smith attested that Powell shot Campbell once in the mouth, an act that Powell also confessed to Investigator Pierce Brooks, with an assurance that he was sufficiently competent with guns that "the chances of it going off accidentally are nonexistent" (Wambaugh 222–23). But Campbell was also shot four times with two different weapons while lying on the ground, an action that both kidnappers disavowed. While the autopsy surgeon reported that any of these four wounds could have proven fatal, it was never definitively determined who inflicted them (202), and Officer Hettinger, fleeing and hysterical, could not see clearly, especially in the dark. Even the involvement of two guns does not implicate both perpetrators, as Powell seems to have enjoyed thinking about how to outsmart the police the way some people enjoy imagining chess moves. Although lead investigator Pierce Brooks is convinced that both Powell and Smith fired at Campbell as he lay wounded, a reader may feel skeptical, with regard to Smith. This is because of the general aversion to firearms that Wambaugh establishes early in the book and the complete absence of guns in Smith's previous criminal record. In addition, Smith's eagerness to severe ties with Powell and his inability to hit the side of a car during target practice in the Nevada desert, even while standing about eight feet away, undercut any likelihood that Smith committed murder. With investigators, Smith is adamant that he "didn't fire no gun" and when a police officer taking him into custody calls him "cop killer," Smith "thought how strange it was to hear the label … applied to him. He was only a thief, he thought…. Just a liar and a thief. Been one all my life. Just a sniveler and a crybaby and a thief. How can they say I'm that. *That.* They *gas* people for that" (204, emphasis original). On more than one occasion, Wambaugh uses the description "the young killer" for Powell, but he never uses the description for Jimmy Smith (205). However, under California's Felony Murder Rule in 1963, Smith's participation in the kidnapping of the two officers made him eligible to be prosecuted for first-degree murder, even if he did not know a murder might occur.[7]

After Ian Campbell's death, Jimmy Smith would regularly wonder what might have happened if he hadn't answered his hotel room phone on Sunday, March 3, when Greg Powell called from the lobby. Six days later, they were inextricably linked by the murder of a police officer. Wambaugh uses the theme of chance and the metaphor of card-playing so prevalent in Naturalistic homicide novels to characterize Smith's reflections: "For the rest of his life, he would wonder if he could have made another play, played his own hand, or drawn different cards. Or was the hand played around him? Does somebody stack that fuckin deck, he often wondered, and ain't nothin you can do about it? He never decided" (93–94). Smith recognizes several chances to ditch his partner, including while Powell is changing into his robbery disguise in a gas station restroom on the night of Campbell's murder. Only a slow attendant filling the car and washing the windows detains him. In the car with Powell and the two officers on the way to the onion field on Saturday, March 9, 1963, Smith craves "one more chance to cut Greg loose. If he just had one more chance" (155). And even in the early morning hours after the crime, when Smith realizes that Powell might be shot while being captured, he thinks to himself, "I got a chance, baby, a hell of a chance!" (179).

To reinforce the theme of chance or fate, cats show up in both obviously symbolic and incidental ways, just as they do in Naturalistic homicide novels by Cain, Capote, and others. Just before the fateful meeting between perpetrators and police officers, Ian Campbell shines his flashlight into the shadows of an alley but finds "just two bony cats slinking through the alleys, prowling hungrily" (149). The cat imagery used in the book—and in the Naturalistic homicide novel generally—also conveys the metaphor of predation, a metaphor used by Wambaugh in an early scene when Powell threatens a sometimes-accomplice Billy Small, whose role in the robberies is aptly conveyed by his last name. Powell holds a gun to Small's face, accusing him of stealing some missing cash, and Smith, fearing that his partner will carry through on his threat to "blow [Small's] goddamn brains out," considers that Small resembles prey: "He looked like the stunted rat Jimmy had seen in the hotel as a child. It was paralyzed when the grey cat cornered it, impotent before the great yellow eye" (96). More incidental symbolism enters the narrative when Greg and Jimmy visit a strip club "where the cocktail waitresses wore tights and cat ears and long cat tails which drunken customers could pull when they wanted a drink" (126).

New York Times reviewer, James Conaway, places *The Onion Field* squarely in the same literary tradition as *In Cold Blood*, declaring Wambaugh's book "obviously indebted to Truman Capote ... belonging to the tradition of Dreiser and Farrell—constructing, from a glut of well-observed detail, unspectacular and often squalid lives lived among the concrete freeways, the bright, tawdry strips, the transience, brutality and beleaguered decency of a society set on the edge of America." And yet despite these similarities, Wambaugh seems to practice a sort of selective Naturalism, unable to decide whether he believes in determinism or whether it applies only to "good guys." If the book is a study in the determinism of psychological trauma, demonstrating how developments in a person's life follow inevitably from a devastating event, Wambaugh seems to view that determinism as an agent acting in Karl Hettinger's physical and mental decline but much less so in the lives of the two men whose actions precipitated that ordeal. Or if he views Powell's and Smith's violence as the result of environmental determinants, he nevertheless lacks the sympathy of the Naturalistic novelist for them.

Judith Rossner's *Looking for Mr. Goodbar* is a fact-based novel following the general outlines of a 1973 murder case on New York City's Upper West Side. Roseann Quinn, a seemingly mild-mannered teacher at a Bronx school for the deaf, was brutally murdered by a drifter she had (by most accounts) picked up in a neighborhood bar on New Year's Eve. Publicity surrounding her death revealed a Roseann Quinn who, despite a typical Roman Catholic upbringing in a prominent suburban New Jersey family and colleagues who viewed the young woman as somewhat old-fashioned, appeared to regularly enjoy what later came to be called "rough sex" with almost complete strangers who seemed very different from her in education and social class. Neighbors later told reporters that Quinn's male visitors were often abusive; on at least one previous occasion, neighbors had found Quinn hurt in the hallway outside her apartment. Even more disturbing was these neighbors' perception that "Roseann had, to a degree, conspired in her own victimization" (Gelb). The term "double life" was used in many accounts of the crime.

The man who killed Quinn, John Wayne Wilson, 23, had escaped from jail in Miami the previous July and hitched to New York, making money from sporadic one-paycheck jobs. In the city, he was a bisexual street hustler who eventually moved in with a male client, a stockbroker, and was living there at the time of the murder. Out of fear that he might be implicated because he had been seen with Wilson in the bar where Wilson met Quinn (and was subsequently depicted in a police artist sketch), the former boyfriend went to police several days later to say that Wilson had described the murder to him. Four months later, Wilson hanged himself in his jail cell with his sheets.

In its approximate use of factual material, *Looking for Mr. Goodbar* more closely resembles the earlier Naturalistic homicide novels of Norris and Dreiser and seems more literary (as opposed to journalistic). Following those authors' examples, Rossner gives her characters fictional names. Quinn is Theresa Dunbar and Wilson is Gary Cooper White. Small details are changed; for example, Quinn's killer, John Wayne Wilson, was taken into custody at his brother's house in Indiana, but Rossner moves the brother to Ohio. She also changes the name of the West Seventy-Second Street bar, Tweed's, where Dunn and White meet to Goodbar's (hence the novel's title becomes vulgar sexual innuendo).

Although Rossner fictionalizes the narrative, it is, in the words of Leslie Fishbein, "similar to the facts of the original case" (174). Rossner traces the outline of the factual story without making a claim for factual status or even indicating that her source was an actual murder case. Like Roseann Quinn, Theresa Dunn grew up in the sheltered environment of suburban Irish Catholic family life and, as an adult, taught deaf children and was a devoted aunt. But in her novel, Rossner also endows Dunn with childhood polio, which has led to recurring back problems, significant shame about her physiognomy, and, as was the case with Roseann Quinn, loss of religious faith (Gelp). Quinn's physical shame and slight limp resulted from a bout with scoliosis and back surgery at age 13 that involved virtual immobilization for about a year (Gelb). And Dunn, like Quinn, also has a second self, a double who is "familiar with hard drugs, heavy drinking, and masochistic sex" (1), as Joan Bartel says in the *New York Times Book Review*.

Dunn's promiscuity and, moreover, her relatively callous regard for her one-night stands eventually do her in, as she picks up "Mr. *Dead Wrong*" in a New York bar on New Year's Eve. After having intercourse with him, she informs him bluntly that the sex was "okay" and that he is not invited to sleep at her apartment (Rossner 388). Following her refusal and threat to call the police if he doesn't leave "in one minute," White flings a telephone across the room, covers Theresa's face with a pillow (like Bigger Thomas), and subsequently picks up the lamp later determined by investigators to have smashed Dunn's head (389). The novel ends there, with Dunn in the throes of indecision, thinking frantically of her parents ("Help Mommy Daddy Dear God, help me") and her own emotional misery ("do it do it do it and get it over w–") (389–90). This is the only homicide novel discussed in this study that ends teetering on the brink of the actual crime.

Rossner sees Theresa Dunn's story as a study in victimization. As Bartel notes, the author attempts to answer the question, "[H]ow did a nice girl like you end up in a place like this?" The answer, of course, is that Theresa Dunn is not a "nice" girl—at least, not in the conventional sense of the term. She is a deeply disturbed woman, whose own feelings of low self-esteem and physiological shame began during the polio episode, during a long hospitalization, her whole torso encased in a cast for much of that time. In Roseann Quinn's case, the sense of shame was compounded by her parents' treating her differently from other siblings and the estrangement that gradually ensued. One journalist who wrote about Quinn's background speculates that her father harbored a conscious or unconscious revulsion of her mild deformity—or that the daughter simply perceived it that way (Gelp). In Rossner's account, a long and degrading relationship with a college professor (who, for example, chides her for her inability to reach orgasm) compounds Theresa Dunn's loss of self-respect. Rossner writes that the "illness was said to have altered [Theresa's] personality, and maybe that was why she couldn't remember. She'd become another person" (23). As a young "swinging single" woman in the city, she engages in a series of brief encounters, including the enactment of a rape fantasy troubling to reviewers and readers alike. Theresa's steady boyfriend, James, is so patient in the face of her alternating indecision and aloofness that some reviewers found his characterization flawed—too idealized. Ultimately, it seems, due to the strong sense of self-loathing derived from her disgust over her own body, Theresa is unable to connect her emotional and sexual lives. And in the case of Gary White, her subsequent inability to connect emotionally leads her to project her sense of rejection onto a man primed by his own hostilities to overreact. One might argue that polio was a central determinant in Theresa Dunn's life, and that she is a woman destroyed by a combination of her own biology and psychology.

Rossner's quite Naturalistic approach also extends to Dunn's murderer, Gary Cooper White. Rossner writes in her preface that "the most notable quality of his confession" was that despite his brutal crime, White "had a very clear sense of himself as the victim of the woman he had murdered" (4). To some extent, Rossner shares White's view of himself, taking several measures to mitigate his reputation with the reader. She begins the novel with her comments about his confession, followed by the confession itself, focusing Theresa's story through the lens of her killer's experience. The author presents White as a small-time hood who, in the weeks before Dunn's murder, lived with a flamboyant homosexual whom he cajoled (sometimes through sex) into supporting him while he squirreled away money for his pregnant wife in Florida. Upon his arrest, White has $6 in his pocket but over a hundred in fives in the hem of his coat, having forgotten that he hid it there (Rossner 6). Right before the murder, the reader's focus is on White's fatigue and desire to sleep, but Dunn abruptly tells him to leave. His fatigue and his shock when he is ordered out are likely the reader's strongest point of sympathy with him, as anyone can empathize with being sleepy, especially in the early morning hours, and White has behaved typically through this point.

Rossner also reduces the brutality of the original murder itself from 18 stab wounds, a beating with a blunt object, and desecration of the corpse to a single blow on the head (with a lamp) and repeated stabbing *after* Dunn is unconscious (Fishbein 174). The final image of himself which Rossner allows White via his confession is complete disorientation: he says, "I don't know why I stabbed her.... I don't know if I knew she was dead" and, concerning his Ohio arrest, "I don't know how I ended up in Cleveland. I meant to go to Miami" (19–20). Rossner begins her narrative with four pages summarizing White's life before he met Theresa Dunn, observing, "He seemed to think that almost anyone in the same situation would have committed the same murder" (3). She ends the book with his verbatim narrative of the murder. Rossner's comment that White "seems to have lived always with his back against the wall and a sense of fighting for his life, a context in which otherwise insane acts seem quite reasonable" (6) comes dangerously close to rationalizing his crime as the result of a "fight or flight" reflex. The narrative ambivalence is largely responsible for Leslie Fishbein's argument that "on every major issue Rossner treats, she exhibits her own confusion, which mirrors the confusion of her audience" (174).

Time reviewer Martha Duffy's comment that "[o]ne can even have some sympathy with [Theresa's] killer" illustrates the effect of Rossner's ambivalence concerning killer and victim, an ambivalence that drew the ire of some feminist readers. Along the same lines, in "Cautionary Tales from the Sexual Revolution," Jacqueline Foertsch claims that Rossner exhibits a "mix-mindedness on the question of women's liberated sexuality" (219). Fishbein argues that "if one accepts the view of the publisher's blurb that Theresa Dunn was trying to come to terms with a new sexual freedom and searching for liberation, then the penalty for such a search seems to be death," an implication that reinforces the notion "that women's liberation is dangerous to women." This theme of sexual appetite as problematic, perhaps even fatal, has much in common with its treatment at the hands of the early Naturalists. It is interesting to remember that Rossner's novel was published during the so-called "Sexual Revolution" that began when the birth control pill became publicly available in the 1960s and continued through the *Roe v. Wade* decision of 1973; in her novel *The Handmaid's Tale* (1985), Canadian novelist Margaret Atwood anticipates the Sexual Revolution's "backlash," depicting a patriarchal theocracy characterized by attempts to control every aspect of women's sexual experience. At the time she heard of Quinn's case, Rossner herself had recently ended a 17-year marriage and moved to New York City. The debate concerning whether Rossner endorses or betrays the cause of women's sexual independence is the subject of most literary criticism about the novel, which probably drew more scholarly attention than any other book discussed in this chapter. The problem with calling Rossner's narrative antifeminist because Theresa Dunn is murdered as a consequence of her promiscuity is that Rossner did not invent this plot.

A more strictly factual account of Roseann Quinn's murder is that of former *New York Times* reporter Lacey Fosburgh. *Closing Time: The True Story of the "Goodbar" Murder* appeared in 1977 but is somewhat obscure, compared to Rossner's novel; as with *Helter Skelter* and the Manson case, this is partly due to the success of a screen adaptation (in this case a feature film starring Diane Keaton and Richard Gere). Fosburgh had earned the respect of her editor, Arthur Gelb, by keeping the notoriously reclusive writer J.D. Salinger talking in a phone interview for half an hour after Gelb told her getting a Salinger interview was "the most difficult assignment a reporter could be given" (Gelb). In his memoir, *City Room*, Gelb writes that Fosburgh "displayed a steely desire to show her skeptical male colleagues that blond good looks did not rule out tough reportorial talent." Her coverage of Roseann Quinn's brutal murder helped establish her reputation as a hard-nosed reporter. Fosburgh calls her account of the Quinn case "an interpretive biography" and claims a sort of quasi-factual status:

> To the best of my knowledge everything here is true. After much thought, though, I have changed the names in the story and altered several identifying features. In some cases, I did this upon request and in others, at my own initiative, because I figured the amount of pain this drama caused everyone was sufficient....
>
> [A] few times I have stepped in where full and accurate accounts do not exist and created scenes or dialogue I think it reasonable and fair to assume could have taken place, perhaps even did.
>
> What I have done, then, is give myself the liberty to go beyond proven fact to probe the internal and private lives of the people involved in this story. That is why I call it an interpretive biography.

Despite the claim that "everything here is true," Fosburgh, like Rossner, gives Roseann Quinn and John Wayne Wilson pseudonyms: Katherine Cleary and Joe Willie Simpson. She acknowledges in the Prologue that she was equally interested in both; her research included extensive interviews with Wilson's family but only brief conversations with Quinn's parents, who chose not to cooperate. Fosburgh won a Mystery Writers of America Award in the category of Best Fact Crime. Her *Contemporary Authors* profile quotes from "a letter of extravagant praise" sent to Fosburgh by Truman Capote (Gelb), who called her "a skillful, selective reporter and also a literary artist" (qtd. in Pace). Her description of "Cleary" and "Simpson" drawing inevitably toward each other owes much to Capote's introduction to *In*

Cold Blood: "Yesterday they had been thousands of miles apart. Today, they were separated by just three blocks" (Fosburgh 1).

Fosburgh's greater access to relatives of the perpetrator reflects a circumstance that might be said to warp accounts of real murder cases. Homicide victims cannot be interviewed by an author, who almost always appears on the scene only after victims are dead. Victims' loved ones may avoid talking to writers for a variety of reasons, including debilitating grief, reluctance to cooperate with an effort that seems to draw attention to the killer, or fears of exploitation. But perpetrators remain alive, often in jail or prison, where they have nothing but time on their hands. And perpetrators' loved ones may be motivated by the desire to present narratives that counteract or mediate news media accounts of brutal, apparently senseless, violence. The result is quite likely a book written by an author much more familiar with the perpetrator than the victim. This is certainly true in *In Cold Blood*, where attention to the Clutter family members is largely limited to less than 30 pages (of 384), all in Part I. It is true of most of the works examined in this book, which is one reason that Hersey's, Wambaugh's, and Rossner's attention to victims sets these novels apart.

A third potential focus among homicide novels of the 1960s and '70s is found in Gerald Frank's *The Boston Strangler* (1966), which, despite its title, foregrounds a community's response to violent death. This focus on community Frank shares with Capote, whose attention to reverberations in Holcomb dominates the last 15 or 16 pages of Part I and most of Part II of *In Cold Blood*; community is emphasized in Capote's prefatory comment that after the murders, the townspeople of Holcomb "theretofore insufficiently fearful of each other to seldom trouble to lock their doors … viewed each other strangely, and as strangers" (15). This is the same community to which KBI Agent Alvin Dewey returns home one night to find that his wife has changed all the locks, asking him, "Do you think we'll ever have a normal life again?" (124).

In late 1963, Gerald Frank, a young reporter who had by his own admission "had [his] fill of crime" became interested in a series of strangling murders. Frank takes pains to establish his authority and that of his account in "A Note to the Reader," pointing out that, at the time, he was "the only writer completely involved with the case" and was "given the fullest cooperation" by legal authorities involved in the investigation (ix–x). Frank establishes what Eric Heyne would call the "factual status" ("Literary") of his narrative in his claim that "everything that is in [the] book is based on fact" and is accurate "within the limits of human error" (x). He cites as sources "hundreds of hours of personal interviews"; official records, reports, and transcripts; and personal letters and diaries (x). His account includes Capote-esque references to himself as "visitor" to principals interviewed for the book, as in a section in chapter 23 when he first visits Albert DeSalvo's mother. To reinforce the book's claim of factual accuracy, Frank also includes inside the front and back covers a map of the Boston area with crime scenes chronologically labeled and a list of the 13 known victims with the dates, based on "original police estimates" of their deaths.

Between June 1962 and January 1964, 13 women ranging in age from 19 to 85 were found dead in the Greater Boston area, having been strangled and raped or otherwise sexually assaulted. Because most victims were found with stockings around their necks, the crimes were known originally as "the silk stocking murders" ("Boston"). In late 1964, after the strangling crimes stopped, Albert DeSalvo, a handyman and factory worker, was matched by Boston police to the description given by a woman who was tied up and molested in her home by a man matching DeSalvo's description. While in police custody, DeSalvo took responsibility for the strangling murders. Initially, some investigators believed that his confession was motivated by a desire for notoriety or to acquire book and movie deals generating income for his wife and children, including a special needs daughter ("Boston").[8]

However, DeSalvo's history since the 1950s suggested to Boston police the sort of evolution typical of a sex crimes perpetrator. In 1960 DeSalvo was caught breaking into a house and, while in custody, confessed to a series of odd incidents in the late 1950s attributed by police to "the Measuring Man." In multiple instances, a man claiming to be a model scout had talked his way into women's apartments and attempted to take their measurements. No women reported being physically injured, although DeSalvo claimed that some had consensual sex with him. According to Frank, DeSalvo got "a big kick" out of fooling the women who let him in (228). College and university women who moved frequently were among his favorite targets; when he spoke with police about strangling victim number seven, Patricia Bissette, he claimed to have previously been inside the same apartment "at least four or five times" (qtd. in Frank 291). The final "Strangler" victim, Mary Sullivan, had lived at her address only three days when she was murdered (Frank 269).

Of some Harvard students who fell for his "Measuring Man" ruse, DeSalvo said, "I'm not good-looking. I'm not educated, but I was able to put something over on high-class people. They were college kids and I never had anything in my life and I outsmarted them" (228). His words reflect a sociological aspect of motive that Frank generally all but avoids. In a similar passage, Frank contrasts the suspect with Assistant Attorney General John Bottomly, highlighting the gulf between the two men:

> The two men, although separated from birth by less than ten years and the width of a city, were by nature and background worlds apart. Bottomly was the result of every-

thing our society has to offer a fortunate and gifted man; DeSalvo, the reject and misfit, the juvenile delinquent, the child molester, the housebreaker, rapist, and possible
murderer, was the result of the failure of the same society [295].

In the hands of a Naturalistic writer, this contrast would get much more
emphasis, but Frank, the journalist, prefers to focus on DeSalvo's individual psychology as it emerged from his examination by a number of mental health professionals. Frank mostly reports matter-of-factly that DeSalvo
was diagnosed as sociopathic and attributes the "Measuring Man" crimes to
a "petty sickness" (229). DeSalvo was eventually convicted of breaking and
entering on several counts but acquitted of lewdness charges and sentenced
to 18 months, serving 11 before he was released for good behavior.

Within just a few years, DeSalvo apparently began a new string of
breaking and entering and sexual assault crimes in four New England
states attributed to "the Green Man," so named for the perpetrator's habit
of wearing green slacks or uniforms, often with "huge green aviator's sun-
glasses" (Frank 229). The sheer number of women who came forward after
DeSalvo's picture appeared in Boston newspapers to tell police that he had
raped them, combined with the number of rapes he admitted and his wife's
comments, seem to substantiate Frank's claim that DeSalvo was "sexually
insatiable," a virtual prisoner of himself (231). Dr. Robert Metzer, a psychiatrist who examined De Salvo and testified during his trial concerning
the "Green Man" charges, explained that DeSalvo felt "irresistible impulses"
or "'little fires' burning inside his abdomen and would gradually be overcome by a desire—which he could not control—to obtain some sort of sexual relief" (qtd. in Bailey 222). These urges must have been pervasive, as,
according to his attorney, F. Lee Bailey,[9] Boston police "estimated that his
[sexual assault] victims numbered more than three hundred women" (231).
After an early assault, a victim heard DeSalvo murmur, "How do I leave
this place?" and directed him to her door (229). The more the reader learns
of his sexual compulsions, the more metaphoric DeSalvo's question seems:
"How do I get out of here?"

But despite DeSalvo's extensive examination by mental health professionals, Gerald Frank mostly avoids using the question of his sanity as a
source of sympathy. Like Mailer, Frank presents his perpetrator as sympathetic primarily in passages concerning the women (or girls) who are close
to him: his wife, Irmgard; his young daughter, Judy; and his mother, whose
identity Frank veils (he calls her "Mrs. Khouri," as she had remarried by the
time of the stranglings). More than once after becoming a suspect, DeSalvo
expressed concern that Irmgard be spared seeing him in handcuffs. He
wrote his wife lengthy letters during his confinement, and Frank repro-
duces the text of several. These letters mostly describe DeSalvo's frustration concerning the absence of a satisfactory sexual relationship between

himself and Irmgard, who had experienced so much pain during Judy's 1955 birth that she swore off sex, telling her husband, "I'll kill myself if I have another baby. Please, Al, no more babies" (qtd. in Frank 314). DeSalvo had promised, but the couple later had a son, Michael. Irmgard DeSalvo informed her husband that if there was to be any more sex, she would let him know, and, according to Albert, she increasingly turned her focus to their daughter after Judy's disability was diagnosed at about six months. Confused as to whether his sexual appetites were within norms, DeSalvo read "some Kinsey books"[10] and suggested that the couple see a doctor, but Irmgard rebuffed him and his suggestions (qtd. in Frank 314). To an interviewer, Albert DeSalvo was clear about the effect of her responses: "The way she was treating me would hurt anyone's ego" (qtd. in Frank 314). Whether or not one feels sympathy for DeSalvo while reading these passages, he clearly felt that his crimes might have been avoided had his marriage included a healthy sexual relationship. He told John Bottomly: "If she'd given me the proper sex I wanted, at least treated me like a person and not degraded me all these times, I wouldn't be going out to find out if I was a man or not" (qtd. in Frank 313).

Despite Irmgard DeSalvo's apparent sexual aversion and Albert DeSalvo's lack of complete self-control, he insists to investigators that he would never have hurt his wife. Asked point-blank by Bottomly why he "had ... not taken [his frustration] out on her," DeSalvo affirmed that he was afraid of losing her. "Even at this moment, I love her more than anything else in this world," he claimed. "I'm willing to do anything to see she's well taken care of" (qtd. in Frank 313–14). Even DeSalvo's mother, herself the survivor of a dysfunctional, abusive relationship, acknowledged his devotion to Irmgard: "If your father loved me like you love your wife—even though your father did what he did to your sisters and me—I still would have forgave [sic] him and loved him.... [Y]ou did everything for her" (qtd. in Frank 315). Frank reports that Albert DeSalvo was the favorite of his mother's four sons because he had practiced a similar dedication with her (315). When DeSalvo weeps during interviews, he is usually talking about his wife and daughter; by contrast, he describes his encounters with victims with detachment, sometimes in a trance-like state of recall, in Frank's account.

It is not surprising that DeSalvo's mother has difficulty believing her son had hurt anyone (Frank 315), and this gentler man who tended lovingly to his daughter was also the one his attorneys knew. Robert Sheinfeld, who had defended DeSalvo on some of the breaking and entering charges stemming from the "Measuring Man" ruse, recalled DeSalvo's sending "an intricately carved, beautifully fashioned wooden jewel case" that DeSalvo had made in prison as a gift for Sheinfeld's wife. Frustrated with DeSalvo's repeated criminal activity, Sheinfeld had told his client to call another attorney if he ever got in trouble again. DeSalvo took him at his word but wrote to Sheinfeld in 1965 to confess that the sex crimes were the real point of the "Measuring Man" encounters and that he felt something was seriously wrong with him. Of DeSalvo's claims to be the Strangler, his former attorney told Gerald Frank that he was "all but stunned" (320). Robert Clifford, the attorney who first took DeSalvo's family history as part of preparing a defense, found him to have a "Sad Sack"[11] demeanor but "when he spoke, curiously appealing" (325). Clifford attributed DeSalvo's Strangler claims as an "imposture" stemming from his low self-esteem and terrible family background. Of the notion that DeSalvo might *really* have murdered 13 women, "They'd have to convince me, thought Clifford" (Frank 327).

DeSalvo's best-known counsel, F. Lee Bailey, provides some measure of resolving the gentle son/husband who was a generally cooperative legal client with the killer of 13 women. In his memoir *The Defense Never Rests*, Bailey depicts DeSalvo's duplistic nature in a metaphor drawn from Robert Louis Stevenson's famous novel *Dr. Jekyll and Mr. Hyde* (1886):

> After knowing Albert DeSalvo for half an hour, the average person would feel perfectly comfortable about inviting him home for dinner to meet the family. That was one of the pieces that fell into place in the puzzle of the Boston Strangler. It helped explain why he had been able to evade detection despite more than two and a half years of investigation. DeSalvo was Dr. Jekyll; the police had been looking for Mr. Hyde [181].

Bailey says DeSalvo had "a courteous, even gentle manner" (181). But when he began recording DeSalvo's highly detailed accounts of the crimes, Bailey says, "I became certain that the man sitting in that dimly lit room with me was the Boston Strangler. The face was still Dr. Jekyll's, but the memories were Mr. Hyde's" (183).

Perhaps the closest the two Albert DeSalvos come to merging is during his hypnoanalysis at Bridgewater State Hospital, a Massachusetts facility for prisoners whose sanity is disputed. During his examination with Dr. William J. Bryan, Jr., a leading hypnotist, DeSalvo offered a very disturbing juxtaposition of details from his murder narratives and his family experiences. For example, some descriptions of his abuse on victims, specifically movements and positioning of their legs, were mixed with his recollections of manipulating baby Judy's legs, which caused her pain and her father significant distress. Coaxing DeSalvo through his narrative of Evelyn Corbin's murder, Dr. Bryan repeatedly asked him what he planned to do "with her thighs, with her thighs, with her thighs," whereupon DeSalvo abruptly emits "a piercing scream" (257). When Dr. Bryan asked what he was doing with Corbin's thighs, DeSalvo replied, "Judy!" (258). At this point, he began to cry. Dr. Bryan asked what he did with Judy, and DeSalvo replied, "I massaged her." Prompted by the hypnotist, he added, "She got well" (qtd. in Frank 258). Skillfully, Dr. Bryan leads DeSalvo through connecting the trauma of inflicting pain on his young daughter for the purpose of strengthening her legs to the sexual abuse of his adult female victims.

A dream that DeSalvo experienced the same night and wrote down sheds further light on the connection between his daughter's pain and his violence against women. Describing the dream, DeSalvo wrote, "I got on top of her and put my hands on her neck and pressed very firm and then I spread her legs apart and pre—" (qtd. in Frank 260). Later, Dr. Bryan helps DeSalvo to recognize that the word he could not fully articulate is "pressed," his method both of massaging Judy's legs and of strangling the 13 murder victims. Dr. Bryan read this much of DeSalvo's narrative aloud to him, then re-hypnotized him, to return him to his memory of being in Evelyn Corbin's apartment. When DeSalvo is reminded of his words "Don't scream, I won't hurt you"—words he likely said to every victim—Dr. Bryan asks, "That's what you said to Judy. She said, 'Okay, Daddy.' Isn't that what she said?" (qtd. in Frank 260). In response, DeSalvo wept. Dr. Bryan connects the pain DeSalvo inflicted on Judy in the act of her therapy, which the hypnotist articulates as "*you have to hurt her before you can help her*" with the abuse he inflicted on victims (qtd. in Frank 260, emphasis Frank's). The complex transference of attitudes from one set of experiences to the other is triggered in DeSalvo's statement, "Don't scream, I won't hurt you." Dr. Bryan asks DeSalvo what Judy said in response, and the father replied, "She can't talk. She's only a baby," leading the hypnotist to perceive a likely connection between Baby Judy's inability to talk and DeSalvo's choice of strangulation as the method of murder. And when Dr. Bryan finally confronts DeSalvo with the possibility that each murder simulated the father's desire to strangle Judy to remove the sexual impediment in his marriage, DeSalvo yells, "You're a liar!" and reaches for the hypnotist's throat (qtd. in Frank 261).

Of course, whether Dr. Bryan hit too close to DeSalvo's motives or whether the father was outraged by the insinuation that he might harm his own child (or wife, for that matter) can never be known. Nor will it ever be clear whether Albert DeSalvo's interaction with his young daughter was ever *other* than therapeutic. What is relevant to this discussion is Frank's relatively balanced presentation of DeSalvo, weighing the painful aspects of his family life with the brutality of his crimes and the terror he inflicted on Boston. Here, too, F. Lee Bailey's metaphor is apt: a reader will find Dr. Jekyll sympathetic, but not generally so with Mr. Hyde. Most Naturalistic authors would find their true subject in Mr. Hyde, but Frank does not choose. After Bailey engineered a finding of mental incompetence, DeSalvo was sentenced to life in prison and subsequently murdered at the Massachusetts Institution of Corrections at Cedar Junction in November 1973;

some sources suggest that DeSalvo's killer or killers worked with cooperation from guards, as he had been moved from his cell to the prison hospital
on the night of his death (Gaute and Odell 58). Had DeSalvo been determined incompetent to stand trial, he might have been moved instead to a
facility focusing on treatment, and he might have lived much longer and
been the subject of more intensive study.

But Albert DeSalvo is clearly not Frank's primary interest. In fact,
DeSalvo does not appear except as he is suggested by the crimes until Part
Four, 225 pages into a 364-page book, when he is finally named on page
227. In the vast majority of pages devoted to him, DeSalvo describes his
crimes in narrative that renders him quite the opposite of sympathetic.
Instead, Frank focuses primarily on the terror the stranglings inspired in
the Boston area. The author writes in his prefatory note that his interest

> was not so much in writing a book about the Boston stranglings as it was to write
> about what happens to a great city when it is besieged by terror—terror stemming
> from a horrifying explosion of the violence that seems more and more a part of con-
> temporary life. How do people behave in a climate of fear? What defenses do they put
> up? To what extremes are they driven? How does rationality cope with irrationality,
> common sense with hysteria? [ix–x]

Frank begins to focus his book as the story of a community in the very first
sentence: "This is a story about Boston" (3). He recreates the atmosphere
of a city whose citizens changed their locks, looked over their shoulders,
flinched at the sound of footsteps, clamored for each news report, and eyed
each other suspiciously, while its police probed nearly every male suspect
questioned for any crime for possible connection to the stranglings and
called in everybody from the F.B.I. to psychics. Frank even dramatizes the
red herrings, reinforcing the book's wide-angle effect. *Newsweek* reviewer
Sandra Schmidt acknowledged that Frank used methods of fact-gathering
"that Truman Capote made famous," and his interest in the crime's effect
on the community is equally Capote-esque. Clearly, a kind of determinism
operated in Boston, whose citizens are entirely at the mercy of a force not
controlled even by the man who embodies it. For several decades, Frank's
book remained the definitive account of the strangling murders in Boston, an investigation that, except for the case of Mary Sullivan (see Chapter 8), remains open ("Albert"). The terror in Boston was predicated on the
notion that stability and prosperity are no guarantees against primal forces,
a threat as old as the American Naturalistic tradition itself and one that has
much in common with Frank Norris's *McTeague*.

The influence of the back-and-forth cutting technique common in novels such as *In Cold Blood* and *The Onion Field* is also clear in Alex Wilkinson's
A Violent Act (1993), a fact-based homicide narrative whose author skillfully

alternates the perspectives of the fugitive perpetrator and of law enforcement. Wilkinson's narrative viewpoint varies among three perspectives: the background of Mike Wayne Jackson, who shot his probation officer Tom Gahl and two other people on September 22, 1986; Gahl's widow Nancy and their two sons, who are understandably devastated by his death; and the rural community where the fugitive Jackson takes cover. After an initial 32-page section narrating Jackson's crimes, Wilkinson presents a 14-page section about Nancy Gahl and her children, covering the period of Tom's funeral; then a 60-page "Case Study" of Jackson; a 50-page narrative called "A Country of Barking Dogs,"[12] detailing how the F.B.I.'s search for Jackson (who fled on foot from a wrecked car) paralyzed the community of Wright City, Missouri; a 24-page section focusing on the tracker who eventually found Jackson (based on Wilkinson's original *New Yorker* profile), and, finally, a 38-page denouement that returns to Tom Gahl's family.

Wilkinson's overriding focus in *A Violent Act* is violence itself, its causes and consequences. Mike Jackson "was incorrigibly violent and no one could really tell why" (4), according to Wilkinson, whose composite of Jackson suggests an unusually sensitive boy characterized by his sister as a natural victim: he "had no protection in him. No way of recovering from a setback, it was all just too raw. He couldn't take the shocks. He'd get knocked down and he couldn't get back up that easily" (50). Unfortunately, Jackson had a lot to recover from: an alcoholic, promiscuous father who often temporarily deserted the family (and left for good when Mike was eight) and who teased young Mike with the possibility that his father was someone else. His mother constantly reminded him that her expectations were higher than his accomplishments, that he "could have done better" (51). More and more, Jackson turned in, shutting out other people, except two—his wife Carolyn, whom he seems to have loved but treated badly, and Lee "Skip" Von Hauger, who ran a building restoration business with ex-convict labor and drug and theft rings on the side and whom Jackson considered an "idealist father figure" (75). Diagnosed with an antisocial personality disorder and low tolerance for frustration, Jackson was often incapable of controlling his anger; in fact, in the weeks before her son shot Tom Gahl, Jackson's mother had sought to have him institutionalized. Of course, mental illness, especially when not managed successfully, is isolating.

Pushed over the top by his mother's refusal to lend him $2500 for the repair and improvement of his run-down house, Jackson buys a shotgun, saws it off, and practices concealing it beneath his trench coat. Jackson's rampage is clearly the result of pent-up anger, directed at the wrong people. Ironically, his lack of self-control causes him to become a determinant in the lives of Nancy, Christopher, and Nicholas Gahl—the figure who alters the course of their ordered world. At the novel's end, Wilkinson describes the Gahls as climbing "[a] step at a time … from the hole dug for them by someone else" (226).

In the nonfiction homicide novel tradition, Wilkinson's book is probably most like Capote's and Gerald Frank's (though considerably shorter), particularly in its examination of a community held hostage by fear. After abandoning his car, Mike Jackson eludes law enforcement officers for 10 days and made the F.B.I.'s "Ten Most Wanted Fugitives" list. In the interim, residents of Wright City are escorted by police officers through roadblocks to their own houses and awakened in the middle of the night by officers tapping on their bedroom windows to check on them. Parents keep their children home from school, and mail goes undelivered. The description of the first night after Jackson's presence in the community became well known sounds very much like Capote's description of Holcomb in the days following the Clutters' murders: "Tuesday night people turned on all the lights in their houses and on their porches and in their driveways and yards. Some replaced the bulbs from their outdoor lights with more powerful ones. They sat in their houses with guns in their laps. Men walked their grounds and their downstairs rooms with rifles while their families slept" (Wilkinson 199).

Wilkinson's portrayal of a community besieged also extends to the law enforcement officials working on the case. The first few days in the woods, they jump at the sound of every squirrel or deer. They explore barns, sheds, and ravines and are sometimes so exhausted that they sleep on the grass in front of the command center. The frustration at following dead-end trails is made particularly clear when they are led by a tracking dog over miles of rural terrain into the town and to an empty house, only to suspect that the dog followed the trail backward (158).

Ultimately, A Violent Act illustrates Tony Tanner's comment about In Cold Blood that "in order to appreciate the full import of any incident you must see as much of the sequence and as many of the ramifications as possible" (345). In 32 crisply written pages, Wilkinson details Jackson's September 22 crimes. After abandoning his car, Jackson disappears from the narrative for 138 pages, then surfaces (in the present time of the novel) just long enough to commit suicide (170). Oddly, he seems most present when he is a fugitive, looming everywhere because he could be anywhere; he gives life to Chris Anderson's contention that "absence creates presence" (Class). The 51-page section "A Country of Barking Dogs" features some of the best writing for sheer style and suspense in the homicide novel tradition. With his deft manipulation of point of view, Wilkinson drops Jackson at his vanishing point and simulates the community's suspense. A reader is definitely reminded of the tension in the "Persons Unknown" section of In Cold Blood. A Violent Act is, in several respects, a Capote "copycat."

8

"The Chickens Come Home to Roost"

Naturalism Enters Its Third Century

"Never in my most creative moment could I have come up
with a story like this."—John Grisham, *The Innocent Man*

In Cold Blood and *The Executioner's Song* are the best-known homicide
novels published in the United States since 1960. But within a few decades
after Mailer's book won the Pulitzer prize, the homicide novel genre had
exploded into a phenomenon generally called "true crime," becoming a
largely journalistic and commercial endeavor. For example, the December 1996 murder of six-year-old beauty queen Jon Benet Ramsey in her
family home in Colorado spawned more than a dozen books in just a few
years; one of those accounts, *Perfect Murder, Perfect Town* (1999), was written by *Executioner's Song* researcher Lawrence Schiller. Many of these "true
crime" books appear more quickly than aesthetic logic will warrant, so that
the subgenre has acquired pejorative connotations: a commercial urgency
rushes the books to print, and they are perceived as middle-brow reading
at best.

By the 1990s, true crime was established in popular culture, a phenomenon featured in the *New York Times* on December 13, 1992, in Pat H.
Broeske's article "Serial Killers Claim Movies as Their Prey." Broeske makes
the alarming statement that "mass murderers are rapidly becoming popular culture's favorite villain for the '90s" (18). In May of that year, Amy
Fisher, a high school student on Long Island, had attempted to murder the
wife of her lover, Joey Buttafuoco, drawing reactions ranging from shock
to satire as well as several books (two by Fisher herself) and made-for-television movies. The case was satirized by the late-night television com-
edy program *Saturday Night Live* in a *Masterpiece Theatre* parody called
"The House of Buttafuoco." As if to validate Broeske's assertion about the

public's fascination with murderers, the March 14, 1993, *New York Times Book Review* featured page-one reviews of two recent homicide novels with sidebars about the circumstances of their composition and a half-page advertisement for a third true-crime book, all under the general headline "The Psychopaths Among Us" (3). By this time, some writers were making a career of true-crime writing, with Ann Rule a prime example. By the mid–2000s, Rule had resigned from the Seattle police force and published over two dozen true-crime books; she remains best known for *The Stranger Beside Me*, an account of the murders committed by Ted Bundy, whom Rule knew prior to his arrest. The popularity with works such as those by Rule suggests that some criteria are necessary for separating the true-crime best-sellers from the more literary works that still reflect the Naturalistic homicide novel subgenre.

Some homicide cases have left such a scar on the collective psyche that they have given rise to multiple book-length treatments. By the late 20th century, this was an increasingly common phenomenon, reflecting the public's voracious appetite for reading about crime, as well as the obsession with certain particularly disturbing crimes. Not surprisingly, the cases involving Charles Manson have been fertile grounds for nonfiction writers, inspiring at least a dozen books. Even before Vincent Bugliosi's *Helter Skelter* appeared in 1974, Ed Sanders, a member of the Los Angeles music culture scene in the late 1960s, published *The Family* (1971), a book updated and expanded in 1989. Several film treatments about Manson also exist, including an adaptation of *Helter Skelter* and Quentin Tarantino's *Once Upon a Time in Hollywood* (2019), released at the 50th anniversary of the Tate-LaBiana murders. Jeff Guinn, whose biography of Manson became a *New York Times* bestseller in 2013, also wrote *Go Down Together*, a 2009 account of Bonnie Parker and Clyde Barrow's criminal partnership. Although the Parker-Barrow crimes are nearly a century old, the Guinn book's subtitle, *The True, Untold Story of Bonnie and Clyde*, reflects authors' rivalry concerning factuality, as aspect that often drives the "true-crime" book market. Clearly, writers are still making Eric Heyne's claims for "factual status" and "factual accuracy" ("Literary").

The issue of factuality concerning the strangling murders in Boston in the early 1960s is one of the best examples of the factual rivalry phenomenon in American homicide writing, with multiple accounts following Gerald Frank's 1966 book *The Boston Strangler* reflecting ongoing doubt about the Strangler's identity and the question of whether all the crimes were committed by one individual. In the first two decades of the 21st century alone, more than a dozen new Strangler-inspired books appeared, and the best-known earlier books, Frank's and Susan Kelly's (whose titles differ only in Kelly's placing an "s" at the end of the word "Strangler"), have been issued in new editions (and, in the case of Kelly's, updated). More than 50 years have elapsed since these murders were committed, but very little progress has been made in answering the most basic factual questions. As the result of DNA testing in 2013, Albert DeSalvo was conclusively tied to the last Strangler victim, Mary Sullivan, murdered in 1964 ("Lab"). But that is the only murder of the 13 connected to DeSalvo by direct evidence. DeSalvo himself was never charged in connection with any of the strangling crimes, although he confessed while being investigated on another charge.

In July 2013, improved DNA technology based on a sample from a nephew connected DeSalvo by a "near certain" familial match to the murder of Mary Sullivan, the last Strangler victim (McPhee). Similar attempts at modern DNA matching involving other Strangler-suspected crimes have apparently not occurred. According to Susan Kelly, author of *The Boston Stranglers* (1995; updated 2013), "The Commonwealth of Massachusetts says that it no longer has biological evidence in any of the cases except Sullivan's, and so will not try to establish a link between DeSalvo and the murders that preceded Mary's." The authors of virtually every book about the case except Gerald Frank's either endorse the "multiple perpetrators" theory or at least express doubt about DeSalvo's having committed all 13 murders. There appears to have been more certainty about DeSalvo's responsibility at the time Gerald Frank's book was published, so the more recent books devoted to this case constitute a sort of revisionist true-crime literature.

The revisionist history of the stranglings in Boston has attracted one of the best-known contemporary nonfiction writers, Sebastian Junger, author of *A Death in Belmont* (2006). Junger's book occupies a rare (perhaps unprecedented) position in contemporary crime accounts, as it posits another *potential victim* of Albert DeSalvo not connected to the Boston Strangler corpus by law enforcement (a resident of Junger's boyhood neighborhood), as well as a woman who may have narrowly escaped being DeSalvo's victim—Junger's own mother. In fall 1962 and spring 1963, Junger's family lived in Belmont, an affluent Boston suburb where, in 2006, there had never been another murder besides the one Junger describes in this book (Grossman). In spring 1963, 62-year-old Bessie Goldberg was raped and strangled in her own home less than a mile from the Junger family's house. Roy Smith, a black man originally from Mississippi who had been sent to the Goldberg home that day by an employment agency to do cleaning work, was charged and subsequently convicted of the crimes against Goldberg. But Albert DeSalvo had been working on an art studio in the Junger family's backyard on and off for several months, and he was at the Junger home the afternoon Goldberg's murder occurred. In fact, DeSalvo was the first person Junger's mother, Ellen, told about Goldberg's death after she learned of it from a telephone call. Junger's book includes a family photograph of himself with his mother, DeSalvo, and Floyd Wiggins (who built the Junger family home and was also involved in the studio project). The photograph was taken the day after Bessie Goldberg was killed.

Junger's mother had had her own disturbing encounter with Albert DeSalvo, whom she and the other workmen called "Al," a few days after he came to work at her home in fall 1963. Early one morning after Ellen Junger's husband left for work, Al DeSalvo entered the basement from an outside door and called to her from the bottom of the stairs to come down. When she asked him why, he replied that there was something wrong with the washer—which Ellen Junger had not used that morning. Alarmed, she closed and locked the basement door and decided to tell her husband and the job supervisor about the encounter. But the next day, when DeSalvo showed up polite and solicitous, she decided she had overreacted to the "menacing look in his eyes, a strange kind of burning ... , as if he was almost trying to hypnotize [her]" (Junger 43). This account was the origin of the family story about how Ellen Junger might have escaped being the Boston Strangler's victim. Following this experience, she was wary of DeSalvo, and after he became physically affectionate with a 16-year-old art student who came to the Junger home for lessons, Ellen Junger confronted him herself. She never left him alone with her teenaged student again (Junger 47).

In chapter 19 of his book, Sebastian Junger takes the approach of Naturalistic writers to his discussion of Albert DeSalvo's family background and early life, which includes most of the typical elements that foster psychopathy in later life. Junger describes Albert's father, Frank DeSalvo, as alcoholic and abusive, a man who knocked out his wife's teeth and broke her fingers one by one in front of young Albert and who beat his six children with a strap. Junger writes that Frank "appeared before judges on criminal charges eighteen times while Albert was growing up, five of them for assault against his wife" (163–64). The seven DeSalvos lived in Chelsea, a working-class city teeming with recent immigrants who were "rough, uneducated people," in an apartment to which the elder DeSalvo and later his two sons sometimes invited prostitutes. At five, Albert learned to shoplift with his father; at seven, he demonstrated what would now be termed sexually reactive behavior with his own sister; and at 12, he was already in reform school for robbing a newspaper boy (Junger 164; "Boston," *Criminal*).

Albert's environment improved some after Charlotte DeSalvo divorced Frank and moved to a tenement building at Fourth and Broadway in a Chelsea neighborhood where the boy could more easily avoid the Irish gang activity that characterized other parts of Boston; Al's distractions there included a movie house owned by Israel Goldberg, whose wife Bessie would be murdered a few decades later in their Belmont home. At the time, Junger writes, Chelsea, Massachusetts, was "the most corrupt city in America" (164). It was so bad that the city imposed a night-time curfew for children. For recreation, Albert often swam in Boston Harbor and frequented a waterfront area where the wharves served as home to many of the city's homeless and mentally ill, and where adults sought sexual opportunities with children (168). It is clear that Albert possessed his father's sadistic tendencies by this time, as he reportedly amused himself by shooting cats with a bow and arrows. The hostility he was later suspected of directing at women was apparent by this time, according to his reflection on those years during interviews: "Sometimes when I would see [the cats] before the shot, I'd get such a feeling of anger that I think I could've torn those cats apart with my bare hands. I don't understand this. I don't usually hate cats or like them, either, for that matter" (qtd. in Junger 168).

Following another stay in reform school for stealing a car, DeSalvo was released at 15, and he and friends occupied themselves with more animal abuse: starving cats and dogs in cages before releasing them to fight to the death. He also acknowledges numerous sexual experiences during his late teens, some of them for money (Junger 169). Clearly, in his summary of DeSalvo's early life, Junger is reviewing the biological and social determinants that help to explain the psychopathology of his subsequent violence, although the accounts of animal abuse undoubtedly mitigate, in his case, the sympathy for protagonists that Naturalistic authors characteristically attempt to cultivate in their readers.

The extent of DeSalvo's apparent sexual peculiarity in adulthood seems particularly relevant to the strangling murders for which he later took responsibility. After enlisting in the army as early as possible, he was sent to Germany, where he met and married his wife, Irmgard Beck. According to Junger, the marriage "did not prevent him from getting a lot of sex on the side" (170). On base, he sometimes approached nurses as well as the wives of other servicemen, posing as a modeling scout, a preview of his later "Measuring Man" escapades. He reported that sometimes the women took off their clothes to reduce their measurements and occasionally were even willing to have sex with him. Back in the United States, he was charged with molesting a nine-year-old girl and escaped conviction only when the girl's parents did not want her to participate in a trial (Junger 171). As DeSalvo's career as the "Measuring Man" resumed on American soil, he and Irmgard welcomed a daughter, Judy, whose congenital hip deformity required time-consuming special care. By most accounts of their lives, Irmgard is said to have avoided sex with her husband after this time, feeling overwhelmed by the possibility of conceiving other special needs children. (The DeSalvos later had a healthy son, Michael.) Junger reports that Irmgard DeSalvo subsequently "told investigators that Al's sexual demands were so incessant that no woman could possibly have fulfilled them" (173). In a six-page handwritten letter from prison, Al explained to Irmgard that he felt she had rejected him after Judy's birth and caused him to feel "hopeless" (qtd. in Junger 174). He also reiterated his love for her. After claiming responsibility for the strangling murders, DeSalvo explained that he had killed the first victim, Anna Slesers, because he had been out of jail only about two months but had realized that "nothing in his marriage had changed" (Junger 174).

If the dysfunction and disappointment of DeSalvo's life before the stranglings in Boston do not render him a sympathetic figure in the sense of the typical protagonist of a Naturalistic novel, the reader must consider that Albert DeSalvo is *not* the protagonist of Sebastian Junger's book. That distinction is reserved for Roy Smith, the cleaning man unfortunate enough to be sent to the Goldberg home on the day Bessie Goldberg was murdered and who was, at least in Junger family legend, convicted of crimes likelier committed by Albert DeSalvo. Both the word count devoted to each man and the apportioning of that content in the narrative attest to Junger's focus on Smith. From the standpoint of chapters, it might initially appear that Junger has an equal interest in DeSalvo (who is the subject of 10) and Smith (11). But the chapters devoted to Smith are, for the most part, significantly longer than those devoted to DeSalvo. Three of the 10 chapters focusing on DeSalvo are his brief recollections (two pages each) of the strangling murders of Anna Slesers, Nina Nichols, and Mary Sullivan. Overall, despite the roughly equal chapter distribution, Junger devotes approximately 105 pages to Roy Smith and only 53 to Albert DeSalvo.

Of greater relevance than the total space devoted to each man is the placement of that content in the overall narrative. Nine of the 11 chapters about Smith come within the first 15 chapters. Roy Smith thus dominates the first half of the narrative; the reader comes to know him early, before learning of the circumstances of any crime except the rape and murder of Bessie Goldberg. Furthermore, Junger undermines the likelihood of Smith's culpability in the way the narrative alternates between his two prime subjects early in part one. Following the chapter about the day of Goldberg's death, Junger inserts the first chapter about Smith's youth in Oxford, Mississippi, an upbringing that, despite the obvious racial problems in Mississippi and Smith's habits of drinking and occasional fighting, has a lot more in common with wholesome community-oriented American life at mid-century than did Albert DeSalvo's. Smith's mother was a cafeteria worker, and his father, a janitor, both at the University of Mississippi. The family valued education, and although Roy quit at 14 to work at an Oxford grocery store, his four brothers all finished high school (21).[1] In

1950, Roy Smith spent six months at the notorious Parchment Farm in the Mississippi Delta, convicted of stealing cotton with two of his brothers; this charge led Smith to a brief stay in the same Oxford jail described in William Faulkner's fiction, and his attorney on the charge was a Faulkner relative (Junger 23–27). When a Massachusetts court later requested a report from Smith's Mississippi probation officer, that officer wrote (not entirely accurately), "The Smiths all have a good reputation in and around Oxford, [sic] this was attested by Sheriff Joe Ford. It seems this is the first trouble any of the Smith children have been into" (qtd. in Junger 19). On the heels of this chapter, Junger returns to his narrative of the Belmont police investigating Bessie Goldberg's murder and follows with a chapter introducing the strangling murders terrorizing Boston at the time. Nothing about these crimes would suggest the involvement of the Roy Smith that Junger has presented up to this point. Immediately after, Junger presents the chapter containing Ellen Junger's first-person account of Al DeSalvo's attempt to lure her down into her own basement, and the reader's response here can hardly be anything other than, "Now THAT is the sort of man who could have attacked Bessie Goldberg."

Of the nine chapters about Smith in sections one and two, Junger arranges eight of them consecutively; the exception is one chapter interposed between those about Smith's family life and background and those focused on his trial. The interposing chapter presents a five-page section about the psychopathy of serial killers in general, based on the insights of famed FBI profiler Robert Ressler, followed by a three-page narrative about the murder of Sophie Clark, the Strangler's pivotal seventh (of 13) victim, who broke his pattern in two ways: she was young, whereas the preceding six victims were between 55 and 85, and she was African American, whereas all the other victims were Caucasian (Thomas). The reader arrives at this chapter (number 10) after having read 25 pages or so about Roy Smith's upbringing and youth, and the characterization of the typical serial murderer and account of the crime scene involving Sophie Clark appear to describe someone alien to Smith and his entire social milieu. In fact, Junger goes to some length to demonstrate that a black man from Mississippi was significantly *less* likely than the average man to assault a white woman, even outside the Deep South. Junger devotes chapter eight to the relative lawlessness of the Parchment Farm guards and the fate awaiting black Southerners who killed white Southerners—generally, lynching. As a cautionary tale for young black men who came of age in the same generation as Roy Smith, Junger details the case of Willie McGee, arrested in 1945 for raping a white woman, Willametta Hawkins, in Laurel, Mississippi. According to Junger (and most historical sources), McGee did "the only thing worse" than forcing himself on Hawkins, in the context of "[t]he twisted white psyche of the era"—he had consensual sex with her, and not just once, but for about three years while Hawkins was his employer, all under her threat of reporting him a rapist if he *refused* sex (65). After several Supreme Court stays, Willie McGee was executed about eight months after Roy Smith was released from Parchment, and Smith was quite clear during his initial interview with Belmont police that the racial climate of his home state had left a lasting impression on him: "My home is in Mississippi," Smith said. "There's no way I'd take no white woman" (qtd. in Junger 65). Chapter eight ends with three more pages of examples of the atrocities perpetrated by some Southerners on black men accused of rape. The reader cannot miss the point here: that any black man of Roy Smith's time and place would know better than to risk becoming the victim of such atrocities.

Finally, Junger's presentation of Roy Smith as a suspect being interrogated by police detectives suggests a man with nothing to hide who makes absolutely no effort to be evasive or duplicitous. Virtually the only place in *A Death in Belmont* where there is sustained dialogue is in chapter seven, and this dialogue derives from Smith's interrogation transcript. In a room with three police officers and two detectives, Smith appears to answer questions easily and efficiently. He explains having been sent to Belmont by the Massachusetts Unemployment Service and narrates his day in the Goldberg home, including the bologna sandwich Bessie Goldberg made him for lunch and the $6.30 she paid him for working four hours (plus bus fare). By his account, Mrs. Goldberg treated him "Real nice" (Junger 56). Oddly, when he is asked what time he left the Goldberg home, he answers with a time the police know to be off by about an hour, and in the direction that would further implicate him; Smith claims that he left about 3:45 and saw a clock soon after at a pharmacy where he stopped to buy cigarettes. Yet the pharmacy clerk put Smith at his counter just after three, and that timeframe is consistent with the fact that neighborhood children remembered seeing Smith—a black man whose presence would have been a novelty in their all-white neighborhood—while on their way home from school. Israel Goldberg got home and found his wife shortly before four, so Smith's quarter-of-four estimate only allowed 10 minutes for the possibility of an alternate perpetrator (Junger 51). As his interviewers continue to pry at his memory, Smith remains calm and apparently polite, even in the face of the ridiculous questions investigators sometimes ask just to see if they can rile a suspect:

> "You are a male, aren't you, Roy?" Cahalane asked.
> "What?"
> "Are you a male—sex?"
> "I'm a male."
> "You don't use sanitary napkins, do you?"

Smith addressed the other officers. "I don't know what he's talking about now."
"Do you wear women's clothes?"
"No."
"Who [sic] do the women's clothes [in Smith's apartment] belong to?"
"Blackstone [Smith's girlfriend]. What about her clothes?" [54]

Even when the investigators begin running him through a series of irrelevant and trivial details about the day, Smith never becomes flustered. He just continues to deny his guilt and to answer questions succinctly. The investigators, writes Junger, "were playing their parts ... but Smith was not playing his" (54). Finally, Smith brings the questioning to a halt and says directly, "I'm telling you one thing: I ain't going to take no one's woman, Jesus Christ, especially a white woman, you kidding? I've got more sense that that, Jesus Christ" (55). The officers and detectives questioned him for 12 hours, and Smith never faltered. Toward the end of the interview, he even became somewhat sarcastic, challenging his inquisitors to find some technological means for him to prove that he was telling the truth or produce some evidence to support their own allegations (59). The Roy Smith that Junger depicts in this scene appears extraordinarily patient and genuine in the face of questioning.

Although the third section of *A Death in Belmont*, "Confession," is weighted toward DeSalvo, the last five chapters alternate perspectives, ending with Smith. In chapter 23, Junger narrates DeSalvo's rape trial, introduces DeSalvo's fellow prisoner George Nassar, and raises the question of whether Nassar might have committed some or all of the stranglings in Boston (and consequently been DeSalvo's source for details of the murders).[2] Then Junger returns to Roy Smith, characterizing his time at the Massachusetts Correctional Institute at Norfolk as uneventful; Smith was nearly a model prisoner, "extremely polite ... just a gentleman," according to Superintendent George Bohlinger, who was forthright with Junger about his belief in Smith's innocence (207). Junger concludes chapter 24 with the efforts of Beryl Cohen, Smith's attorney, and others to win his freedom through a governor's pardon or the commutation of his sentence to time served. Then the writer returns to DeSalvo and a brief chapter 25, which follows DeSalvo's memory of the murder of Mary Sullivan, followed by the longest chapter about him, which includes his brief escape from prison, his recapture, and his murder at Walpole on November 25, 1973 (just two days after the tenth anniversary of Roy Smith's conviction). But Junger ends the book (prior to the Epilogue) with the story of Roy Smith's eventual commutation, signed by Governor Michael Dukakis on August 19, 1976—two days before Smith died of lung cancer, too sick to leave the prison from which he had finally been freed (243–44).

Sebastian Junger's disquisition on Roy Smith's guilt or innocence did not end with his description of Smith's death, however. In April 2003, Junger went to Mississippi to find Smith's family, a search that proved fairly easy, as several of Smith's relatives were still living in Oxford. Junger met Smith's nephew Coach (not a nickname), who knew his Uncle Roy from prison phone calls and had also spent some time behind bars for robbing a woman in a parking lot, although most of his problems in and out of prison involved drugs. Finally, after a five-year prison sentence, Coach straightened up, and Sebastian Junger asked him to imagine how he might have reacted if he had found himself in his uncle's position in Boston in 1963. Coach's response was almost diametrically opposed to what Roy Smith actually did: he would have borrowed or stolen money, even if he had to kill for it ("If I'm a murderer what do I give a damn about robbin' or killin'?") and would have headed out of town, and not to Oxford, Mississippi. "If you commit a crime," Coach said, "then you got to prepare yourself for the next crime, and the next crime." To his nephew, Roy Smith's behavior after the Goldberg murder—drinking and driving around with his friends in Boston, blowing all his cash—was not the behavior of a man who had just committed a serious crime (250–51). Junger told David Gates of *Newsweek* that he wanted readers to get to the end of the book still "conflicted" about Smith's guilt, so it is curious that he concludes with an epilogue wherein he describes what might have been surmised about Bessie Goldberg's killer if Roy Smith had not been working in the Goldberg house that day, a set of inferences that Junger claims add up to "Albert DeSalvo's description of himself…. [W]ith Roy Smith out of the picture, the man who killed Bessie Goldberg becomes exactly the man that Albert DeSalvo claimed he was" (247).

Junger's book, like his first, *The Perfect Storm*, drew mixed reviews, and for some of the same reasons. The books have in common Junger's effort to explain what is fundamentally unknowable: the six crew members of the Andrea Gail who all drowned in the Nor'easter that inspired *The Perfect Storm*'s title are the only people who knew the circumstances of their final hours, and (as far as we know) only Bessie Goldberg and the person who murdered her knew her killer's identity. In both narratives, Junger is fundamentally reconstructing critical scenes from circumstantial evidence, using a methodology that one reviewer calls "a kind of informed conjecture … an intellectual experiment" (Minzesheimer). Some critics praise Junger's effort, perhaps more for the questions he raises about ambiguity than for his actual reconstruction of the events upon which his narrative is based.

 But others share Alan Dershowitz's complaint, "Nonfiction must be about the actual truth," not a possible version of the truth constructed from available facts. Dershowitz complains that Junger "tries too hard to fit the messy facts into his payoff narrative." Because some writers feel (or demonstrate, through research) that Junger "seems to have been careless with some fact-checking" in *The Perfect Storm*, perhaps they are inclined to scrutinize *A Death in Belmont* more closely (Gates).[3] Certainly the leader of Junger's critics is Leah Goldberg Scheuerman, daughter of Israel and Bessie Goldberg, who, according to the *New York Times*, launched "a campaign to discredit Mr. Junger's book" (Motoko). Scheuerman claims that Junger "starts with a false premise and then goes into a false argument" (Motoko), but it is difficult to see to what "false premise" she might be referring, as Albert DeSalvo was, in fact, working at Sebastian Junger's home on the day Bessie Goldberg was murdered, and that is the premise with which Sebastian Junger's account begins. Scheuerman does note an omission from Junger's version of events: the fact that the Massachusetts Supreme Judicial Court upheld Roy Smith's conviction, but whether this is a significant omission is debatable, as a higher court's upholding the conviction did not change Smith's fate. Scheuerman also claims that Junger put her in the courtroom when the verdict in Smith's trial was read, whereas she was actually watching television coverage of the Kennedy assassination (which had occurred the day before in Dallas) at her Connecticut home. Junger said the mistake was based on his misunderstanding.

Of perhaps even more significance than these discrepancies is Leah Scheuerman's and Sebastian Junger's differing explanations concerning places in the interrogation or trial transcripts where Roy Smith's comments do not match the crime scene (he claims not to have touched a mirror in the Goldberg living room on which his fingerprint was found, for example). Scheuerman finds Smith to have been lying in these instances, whereas Junger generally attributes differences to Smith's having been tired from hours of questioning, intoxicated to some extent, or just plain wrong (Motoko). Finally, Scheuerman claims to have been misled by Junger's original statement of intention for the book. In an email that she forwarded to the *New York Times*, Junger had stated, "I also should reassure you that I'm in no way trying to prove Roy Smith to be anything but guilty" (Motoko). Although Junger's editor told the *Times* writer that Leah Scheuerman "might not have fully absorbed everything Mr. Junger was trying to tell her" and that their disagreement might hinge on the meaning of the word "prove," it seems apparent that Junger betrayed his original statement of purpose to the Goldberg's daughter who, understandably, did not relish the prospect of revisiting her family's worst nightmare. Like Joe McGinniss researching Jeffrey MacDonald's case, Junger seems to have been led by the evidence he examined to a conclusion he may not have foreseen.

Some critics have also recognized a truth about *A Death in Belmont* that is larger than these squabbles about factual accuracy. The *New York*

Times' Rich Motoko calls Junger's book "a sort of journalistic meditation on doubt." Junger said to Motoko that he had "no fixed point" in his own mind concerning the guilt of Roy Smith or Albert DeSalvo. *Newsweek's* David Gates writes that the book is ultimately about "how we determine the things we can't know for sure." In the trial sequence in part two, Junger refers to Plato's Allegory of the Cave in explaining how human beings reach verdicts in cases based on circumstantial evidence. The prisoners bound in Plato's dark cave can see only the shadow of objects passed before the fire, and these shadows are all the prisoners know of the objects themselves. "*That* is a modern jury," Junger writes. "They are allowed to see evidence from the crime, but they can never turn their heads to see the crime itself. They must come to a conclusion based only on the evidence—the shadows— that they are allowed to see" (138). Leah Scheuerman argues that the hypo- thetical case Sebastian Junger builds in the book against Albert DeSalvo is based purely on circumstantial evidence, but it is important to bear in mind that *there was no direct evidence against Roy Smith.* With respect to this theme of uncertainty, *A Death in Belmont* seems an almost Postmod- ern commentary on the impossibility of assigning verifiable meaning even to crimes contemporary to the authors writing about them, much less those that occurred 40 or more years in the past. This notion is consistent with the philosophy of the early New Journalists, who claimed that their pur- pose was to help readers make sense of events that seemed to lack meaning or to defy comprehension.

Forty years after the publication of *In Cold Blood*, literary history nearly repeated itself when best-selling novelist John Grisham read the obituary of a Midwesterner in the *New York Times*, and his imagination fired. Ron Wil- liamson died on December 4, 2004, and his obituary ran in the *Times* on December 9. It caught Grisham's notice because Williamson was a resident of Oklahoma's Death Row who once came within five days of execution before The Innocence Project got involved in his case and eventually won his exon- eration. Within days of reading Williamson's story, Grisham called the man's sisters and bought the rights. The results of Grisham's own research, *The In- nocent Man* (2006), was promoted by the author's publisher as synonymous in texture and theme with his famous legal thrillers, but the story of Grisham's only nonfiction book to date is as Capote-esque as any other work discussed in this study. By every measure used in this analysis but one, *The Innocent Man* fits the prescription for the Naturalistic homicide novel.

Just as the Perry Smith / Truman Capote relationship was a study in strikingly similar men whose fates diverged sharply, John Grisham was drawn to Ron Williamson's life story because he saw so much of himself in it. Reviewing *The Innocent Man* for *Book Page*, Beth Williams writes,

What fascinated Grisham, he would later reveal, were the similarities between Williamson's background and his own. Both men had aimed for careers in professional baseball though Grisham eventually gave up on sports, turned to the law and became a best-selling author of legal suspense. Williamson's life trajectory was equally dramatic, but in the opposite direction. A star pitcher and catcher on his Ada, Oklahoma, high school team, Williamson was drafted by the Oakland A's in 1971 and spent six years in the minor leagues before an arm injury ended his career. Returning home to Ada, Williamson moved in with his mother and began to show signs of mental illness.

Williamson was convicted, sentenced, and nearly executed due to a combination of ineptitude and malice on the part of a small-town prosecutor and the investigators who supplied him with evidence, legal malfeasance that drew the ire of the novelist who spent 10 years practicing criminal and civil law in Mississippi before re-inventing himself as a best-selling author. Long before Grisham read Williamson's obituary, first a public defender and then the staff attorneys of The Innocence Project had saved Williamson from execution. By constructing a narrative from the details of his subject's disappointing life, Grisham restored Ron Williamson's humanity.

Five years after the rape and murder of 21-year-old cocktail waitress Debra Sue Carter in December 1982, Williamson was arrested and charged with the crimes, along with his friend Dennis Fritz. The Ada, Oklahoma, authorities' reasons for suspecting Williamson and Fritz have never been completely clear, except that after Williamson's minor-league baseball career fizzled out, he began to demonstrate symptoms of bipolar disorder, developed drug and alcohol problems (including some DUI and public drunkenness charges), and wandered around Ada playing his guitar at all times of the day and night. For all these reasons, he was an easy target for investigators, who built their case on "two 'inconclusive' polygraph exams, a bad reputation, a residence not far from that of the victim's [sic], and the delayed, half-baked eyewitness identification of Glen Gore" (Grisham, *Innocent* 75). Following Williamson's exoneration, Gore—the "eyewitness"—was convicted of the crimes on much better evidence[4]: Debbie Carter had danced with Gore on the night of her death in the bar where she was last seen alive; almost immediately, she told a girlfriend that she was afraid to spend the night alone, and later, in the parking lot, she was observed by witnesses talking heatedly with Gore and pushing him away from her car (Grisham, *Innocent* 8).

Dennis Fritz was charged for no better reasons than his friendship with Williamson, which began through their mutual interest in the guitar, and the investigators' notion that the attack on Debbie Carter would have been more easily carried out by two perpetrators than by one. Both men suffered from the lack of resources to mount a defense against charges of capital murder. Fritz was let go from his position as a ninth-grade science teacher after Ada investigators told school administrators that he had not disclosed a 1973 conviction from another locality on a charge of growing marijuana and that he was a murder suspect. In other words, Fritz was charged in the Carter case on flimsy evidence, and that charge, along with the old conviction, was then used to get him fired from his job, a development that rendered him vastly incapable of mounting an adequate defense, even with no evidence tying him to the crimes.

Although Ron Williamson had supportive and hard-working parents and siblings willing to help with the cost of his defense at the outset of his legal troubles, those troubles quickly escalated beyond the family's means, and Williamson's parents both died while their son was suspected but not yet charged. Williamson himself had no source of income and no job prospects. If not for her death, his mother might have been an alibi witness; a woman of generally unimpeachable integrity in her community, she was prepared to testify that she watched rented DVDs with her son until the early morning hours on the night the crimes occurred; she had even kept the rental receipt (Grisham, *Innocent* 104–5). But she died before she could be questioned under oath.

Possessed of an average I.Q. (114), Williamson attempted a college career, which was derailed before it got underway: he was convicted of forging the name of a university official on a financial aid check made payable to both men; while under house arrest stemming from that crime, he was subsequently convicted of escaping after he returned home 30 minutes late from a convenience store trip (Grisham, *Innocent* 74, 101). The forgery episode underscores the local law enforcement community's animosity toward Ron Williamson. After Williamson signed the check, an administrator who knew his family went to his mother's beauty salon, where Juanita Williamson wrote a check to the school and was assured that the matter was resolved. But a financial aid clerk who witnessed the forgery told her husband, an Ada police officer, and the next day Williamson was charged anyway (Grisham, *Innocent*, 74). Upon the escape charge in November 1984, Williamson declared indigency and requested court-appointed counsel; his case continued to be handled by public defenders until Dennis Fritz, who read law during his 12 years on death row, contacted The Innocence Project in May 1996.

The mental health options available to Ron Williamson were only marginally more successful than his legal resources. Diagnosed with manic-depression (now called bipolar disorder) as early as 1979, when he was 26 years old, Williamson experienced sporadic mental health treatment prior to prison and only intermittently participated willingly in his own diagnosis and treatment (Grisham, *Innocent* 54). Then, too, mental health professionals sometimes had difficulty identifying his particular combination of behaviors. For example, when Dr. M.P. Prosser examined him at St. Anthony Hospital in Oklahoma City in 1979, he wrote, "This boy has demonstrated rather bizarre and sometimes psychotic behavior[;] whether he is manic as the counselor in Ada thought or a schizoid individual with sociopathic trends, or the reverse, a sociopathic individual with schizoid trends[,] may never be determined" (qtd. in Grisham, *Innocent* 54–55). Dr. Prosser also noted that although Williamson had officially been out of minor league baseball for two years and was not involved in any sort of training, he still believed that he would be a professional baseball star. "This," Dr. Prosser wrote, "is the real schizophrenic part of his disorder" (qtd. in Grisham, *Innocent* 55). At the time, Williamson was selling household cleaning products door to door, drinking regularly, and arguing that he needed neither psychiatric medication nor the long-term treatment Prosser recommended.

At the time of Debbie Carter's death, Ron Williamson was 28 years old and had "thoroughly given up" on the possibility of a successful life (Grisham, *Innocent* 64). *Time* reviewer Lev Grossman writes that Williamson "had a knack for making the worst of his bad luck, and his luck was terrible" ("Grisham's New Pitch"). He was a loud, sometimes obnoxious, public drunk who wandered the streets of Ada playing his guitar when he could not sleep, and his successful high school baseball career had left him extremely well known. By December 1982, he was a problem of rapidly increasing severity for his family and something of a public nuisance. John Grisham writes, "It was inevitable that the Ada police would find their way to Ron Williamson; indeed, it is odd that it took them three months to question him" about Debbie Carter's murder (21). The similarities between Perry Smith and Ron Williamson are notable. Obviously, each man was convicted of murder (although Smith was convicted on four counts and Williamson, one) and each was sentenced to death. Both thus experienced being on death row, although Williamson's stay was over twice as long. Both had a history of mental health problems and petty criminal records prior to being charged with murder. Although Williamson had a permanent home and stable family to a much greater degree than Smith, both men had the reputation of being somewhat itinerant, and neither was regularly employed. As a young man, Smith had moved around the western United States and Alaska with his father. Four months before the Clutter murders, Perry had been released from Lansing Prison in Kansas and expected, as a condition of parole, to leave the state; of those four months, Capote writes that Smith was "rattling around in a fifth-hand, hundred-dollar Ford, rolling from Reno to Las Vegas, from Bellingham, Washington, to Buhl, Idaho, where he received Dick Hickock's letter about the 'score' while he was working as a truck driver" (Capote, *ICB* 58). Even in his own hometown, Ron Williamson frequently moves around, being in and out of mental health facilities, staying sometimes with family and sometimes with friends, sleeping in guest rooms and on sofas. What both men appear to have had in common might be best termed *restlessness*, being unable to stay in one place or with one idea for a fixed period of time. In Ron Williamson, it manifested itself as wandering around Ada in the middle of the night, once explaining to police officers at three a.m. that he was out looking for mowing jobs (Grisham, *Innocent* 118–19).

Of perhaps greater significance was the two men's similarity of sensibility and identity. Both Smith and Williamson were essentially dreamers, and each viewed himself as having an artistic destiny to be fulfilled. This was almost certainly a point of identification for the authors who subsequently wrote about the two subjects. Ron Williamson dreamed foremost of a career in major league baseball and continued to talk about that dream as realistic, even two years after having been cut from the minor leagues. Both were avid guitar players. Perry Smith's Gibson guitar, "sandpapered and waxed to a honey-yellow finish," was one of the cherished possessions he carried with him everywhere, and Smith dreamed of being a lounge singer in his hometown, Las Vegas, performing in "an elegant room filled with celebrities excitedly focused on the sensational new star rendering his famous, backed-by-violins version of 'I'll Be Seeing You'" (Capote, *ICB* 27). As a young professional baseball reject, Ron Williamson spent a lot of time playing his guitar on park benches, often at night, and he met Dennis Fritz when Fritz pulled up to a convenience store where Williamson was sitting on the sidewalk, strumming. Even in his late 40s after the exoneration, Ron encouraged Dennis to drive them to a nightclub, where he "thought he would somehow talk his way into a gig that night" (Grisham, *Innocent* 333). As an exoneree, Ron sometimes sang Bob Dylan songs for tips in coffeehouses, Grisham writes; he "dreamed of being on stage. He wanted to perform for thousands and sell albums and become famous" (*Innocent* 333). In addition to music, Perry Smith was also interested in literature and art; he regularly wrote poems and songs and drew or painted pictures of other inmates' family members from photographs. Although Smith's education did not continue beyond elementary school and Williamson's college plans were aborted with the forged check incident, both clearly valued learning. Williamson had an eccentric habit of reciting the chronology of U.S. presidents both backwards and forwards, and Smith routinely corrected Dick Hickock's grammar and criticized his lack of imagination.

Both protagonists possessed a rather strong religious or moralistic sensibility as well, although neither was successful in conforming his actions to it. Following his mother's death when he was 13 and his father's abandonment, Smith was sent to an orphanage run by nuns who treated him cruelly, especially over the issue of his bed-wetting. As an adult, he considered anything having to do with nuns unlucky, such as stealing from them the black stockings he and Dick needed to conceal their faces during the planned robbery (Capote, *ICB* 55). But he internalized some of the moral teaching he received among the nuns, particularly about sexuality. While Dick Hickock was eager to seek out prostitutes, Smith was more modest, and he claimed he prevented Dick from raping Nancy Clutter. Although Perry is a stronger believer in fate than in divine providence, he is moved by his prison friend Willie-Jay, the chaplain's clerk, who "persisted in courting Perry's soul until the day of its possessor's parole and departure" (Capote, *ICB* 57). Perry is moved by Willie-Jay's singing of the Lord's Prayer and flattered to be the subject of the clerk's final attempt at redeeming him via a long letter written (by Willie-Jay) just before Perry's release. Capote describes Perry's pastel drawing of Jesus as "in no way technically naïve" and looking a lot more like Willie-Jay than Jesus, leading the reader to wonder whether it was Perry's heart Willie-Jay snared, rather than his soul (Capote, *ICB* 56).

Ron Williamson grew up in the First Pentecostal Holiness Church of Ada, "an energetic, full-gospel congregation" where "[w]orship was not for the timid, with vibrant music, fiery sermons, and emotional participation from the congregation, which often included the speaking in unknown tongues, on-the-spot healing, or 'laying on of hands,' and a general openness in expressing, loudly, whatever emotion the Spirit was pulling forth." (Grisham, *Innocent* 23)

Ron's parents and sisters were well-respected members, and his sister Annette was the long-time organist until she quit after Ron's exoneration, when the minister awkwardly allowed a reception in the fellowship hall but quickly made it clear that Ron was too notorious to worship there regularly (Grisham, *Innocent* 314–15). According to Grisham, Ron was "saved" and baptized in a nearby river when he was six years old. Periodically throughout his adulthood, Ron Williamson experienced relapses of apparent faith, when he would temporarily slow his habits of drinking, smoking, and casual sex and return to the church in what appears to have been genuinely fervent attempts at redemption. When he was paroled from prison after the fraud sentence in 1986, he told a social worker at Mental Health Services in Ada that he "planned to go to a Bible college and maybe become a minister" (Grisham, *Innocent* 115). On death row in 1988, Ron learned that his newly-appointed attorney was the son of a minister in the Disciples of Christ denomination, which prompted him "into a long discussion about religion," during which Ron informed the attorney "that he was a devout Christian, had been raised in the church by God-fearing parents, and read his Bible often" (Grisham, *Innocent* 234–35).

Despite the many similarities in circumstance and personality between Perry Smith and Ron Williamson, there is one significant difference that largely accounts for why the former was put to death by the state of Kansas and the latter died a free man of cirrhosis of the liver: that, of course, is Williamson's innocence. The only fact at issue in the Clutter murders was the question of whether Perry killed two members of the family or all of them. In the case of Ron Williamson, however, an entire case was fabricated against him by inept, opportunistic, probably malicious, small-town prosecutors whom Grisham calls "the gang that couldn't shoot straight" (Grisham, *Innocent* 323).⁵ Interestingly, this difference of culpability between Smith and Williamson has little impact on their function as protagonists.

Despite these similarities, Capote and Grisham sometimes follow differing narrative strategies. A controversial practice in narratives based on actual cases has been the author's reconstruction of dialogue he (or she) could not have heard (as opposed to dialogue taken from court transcripts, investigators' notes, or actual interviews). For example, Capote recreates dialogue between Dick Hickock and Perry Smith as they are driving toward the Clutter house on the evening of the murders. Much of it is pedestrian: Are they going the right way? What landmarks did Floyd Wells tell them to look for? How do they know when they reach the Clutters' driveway? Readers understand this dialogue to be the gist of the conversation between the two men, not their exact words, and most will not view this practice as violating the criteria for nonfiction narrative. Journalism has less relaxed rules, adhering to factuality, and writers are expected to include only what people are literally known to have said.

Some reviewers of *The Innocent Man* have noted the book's apparent lack of dialogue. A *Publisher's Weekly* reviewer wrote that Grisham tells Ron Williamson and Dennis Fritz's story "as straightforward journalism, eschewing the more familiar 'nonfiction novel' approach with its reconstructed dialogue and other adjustments for dramatic purpose" ("*The Innocent Man*"). But the anonymous reviewer was listening to an abridged audiobook, so his or her perceptions of "the book's nearly total absence of conversation" may reflect a viewpoint distorted by omissions from the full book or lack of visual contact with the text. Like Capote, Grisham sometimes reconstructs dialogue that no longer exists verbatim, such as the conversation between Dennis Fritz and an Ada police officer when Fritz is being arrested, or between Ron and his brother-in-law Gary Simmons as Simmons is driving Ron to a mental health center. In these cases, Grisham writes actual dialogue in quotation marks. In other places, he writes dialogue without quotation marks. An example comes in the episode when Tommy Shaw, a young man accused in a different case, is interviewed by a polygraph examiner, wherein the dialogue suggests the actual language of the conversation but is written without quotation marks. The effect is to suggest that the dialogue is *approximate*, not exact. But this conversation could seem like summarized or approximated dialogue, especially if heard in an audiobook. Generally, Grisham uses dialogue in a manner quite similar to Capote, although he does not reproduce nearly the same amount of language directly from court documents.

The *Publisher's Weekly* reviewer also found Grisham's book less like a nonfiction novel because Grisham does not make "adjustments for dramatic purposes" ("*The Innocent Man*"). This is also an overgeneralization. Grisham, like Capote, does not narrate his story by strict chronology, but begins with an account of the central act—the murder of Debbie Carter—and then shifts to Ron Williamson's childhood, providing the reader an opportunity to come to know Ron from childhood on, as his family would have known him. Grisham also interposes in his narrative the account of another Ada case, the abduction and apparent murder of a young convenience store clerk, the case in which Tommy Shaw and his friend Karl Fontenot are suspects. As Shaw and Fontenot are also convicted and sent to death row on flimsy evidence—including something Shaw reported having *dreamt* (Grisham, *Innocent* 88–95), Grisham's aim in bringing in this adjacent case is to further indict the local justice system by demonstrating that Williamson and Fritz are not the only citizens that system failed. This is certainly an "adjustment for dramatic purposes," and it is an insertion that would be completely out of place in a purely journalistic account of the Williamson-Fritz cases.

A final aspect of Grisham's narrative craft that is extremely Capote-esque is his decision to focus on Ron Williamson, not Dennis Fritz. This decision is motivated by many of the same factors that caused Capote to focus on Perry Smith, not Dick Hickock. Fritz, like Hickock, was the product of a background relatively likely to promote success in a young man: Fritz earned a college degree in biology and got a job, married a woman who was employed at a local college, and became a father. Despite the trauma of his wife's having been murdered in their own home by a teenage neighbor, Fritz continued to raise their daughter, Elizabeth, and, after a few years focused on parenting, took a high school teaching and coaching job, moving his mother in to help care for her granddaughter. Prior to his meeting with Ron Williamson, he had experienced personal tragedy but still generally seemed on a successful trajectory. If Thomas De Quincey's prescription for writing about murder holds, Grisham would need to focus instead on Williamson, who even before the legal fiasco surrounding Debbie Carter's death was already beginning to experience what De Quincey calls a "great storm of passion": the onset of symptoms of mental illness, having already begun drinking too heavily and amassing a petty criminal record while also having been accused of a rape for which a grand jury declined to indict him (Grisham, *Innocent* 51–52). It seems unlikely that the direction of Williamson's life would have been different even if his baseball career had continued to be successful, as even while a minor leaguer, he was already drinking too much and bothering women.

It is no surprise that John Grisham told *Time* book reviewer Lev Grossman that while he was writing *The Innocent Man*, he re-read *In Cold Blood* twice ("Grisham's New Pitch"). Reviewer Edward Levine has pointed out how much the opening descriptions of both novels resemble each other:

> The village of Holcomb stands on the high wheat plains of Western Kansas, a lonesome area that other Kansans call "out there." Some seventy miles east of the Colorado border, the countryside, with its hard blue skies and desert-clear air, has an atmosphere that is rather more Far Western than Middle West [Capote, *ICB* 13].

> The rolling hills of southeast Oklahoma stretch from Norman across to Arkansas and show little evidence of the vast deposits of crude oil that were once beneath them. Some old rigs dot the countryside, the active ones churn on, pumping out a few gallons with each slow turn and prompting a passerby to ask if the effort is really worth it [Grisham, *Innocent* 3].

There is a distinct Capote-esque echo in Grisham's geographical overture, right down to Grisham's use of the word "Some" to begin the second sentence, the occurrence of the word "countryside" in that sentence, and the author's oblique, third-person reference to the "passerby" who is undoubtedly Grisham himself.

It is interesting how often reviewers of Grisham's book have drawn comparisons with *In Cold Blood*, or, like Janet Maslin of the *New York Times*, have used language that evokes Capote's. Acknowledging Grisham's invective against the criminal justice system, Maslin writes what appears to be an allusion to what is likely the most famous sentence Capote ever wrote, his description of "four shotgun blasts that, all told, ended six human lives" (15). Maslin's is also a numeric description: "'The Innocent Man' is plural, despite its title. It is about four men, four average white guys from good families, all chewed up and abused by the system and locked away for a combined total of 33 years." And Maslin's suggestion that the coming of author Grisham to Ada, Oklahoma, was "the big event" moreso than the story he came to research certainly reminds long-time readers of fact-based homicide novels that it was Capote, not the crime he went to report, that put Holcomb, Kansas, on the map.

The Innocent Man shares several qualities with *A Death in Belmont* and with *In Cold Blood*, qualities that connect all to the fact-based homicide novel tradition stretching back all the way to *McTeague*. The strongest of these is each author's inclination to indict society as well as biological circumstances for his protagonist's plight. Grisham has repeatedly acknowledged that his favorite author is John Steinbeck, whose works captivated the writer in his youth. Timothy Rutten of the *Los Angeles Times* praised Grisham's novel *The Appeal* (2010) for its "deft social realism," adding that "no other writer of his popularity is quite so keen-eyed or as fierce a social critic. He's an idealist but not an optimist; a moralist but not a moralizer." The same distinction might be used to describe Steinbeck, whose novel *The Grapes of Wrath*, which Grisham says he has read more times than any other novel, depicts the Joad family at the mercy of the Great Depression and Rose of Sharon, who is pregnant, at the mercy of her own fertility (Commencement).[6] *Grapes* is frequently cited as one of the prototypical Naturalistic texts of the 1930s. Grisham's indictment in *The Innocent Man* of a critically flawed judicial system and a mental health care network that allows people with brain disorders to slip through the social safety net is exactly the sort of novel Steinbeck himself might have written in the early 21st century.

Equally Steinbeckian is Sebastian Junger's book about a justice system that treats black and white suspects differently, based on a notion that Junger absorbed while growing up listening to the story of Bessie Goldberg's murder and his own family's experience with Albert DeSalvo. *A Death in Belmont* is not fundamentally about whether Albert DeSalvo was the Boston Strangler, although Junger does examine that question. The book is primarily the story of Junger's re-examining the family theory concerning Roy Smith and whether he was a perpetrator or a victim of sheer bad luck, a man in the wrong place on the wrong day:

> The story about Bessie Goldberg that I heard from my parents was that a nice old lady had been killed down the street and an innocent black man went to prison for the crime. Meanwhile—unknown to anyone—a violent psychopath named Al was working alone at our house all day and probably committed the murder. In our family this story eventually acquired the tidy symbolism of a folk tale. Roy Smith was a stand-in for everything that was unjust in the world, and Bessie Goldberg was a stand-in for everything that was decent but utterly defenseless. Albert DeSalvo, of course, was a stand-in for pure random evil [245].

Junger's recognition of the prototypical nature of these murders is strikingly similar to discussions of the symbolic nature of the murders in *In Cold Blood*. In "The Chickens Come Home to Roost in Holcomb, Kansas," David Galloway argued (in 1968) that violence is "idiomatic in America" and that "no single writer of the post-war era has viewed that savage potential [of violence] with so much insight or compassion as Truman Capote" (155). Calling *In Cold Blood* "a parable for our times," Galloway writes that the encounter between the Clutters and their killers has "a universal quality ... an instant symbolism" similar to the symbolism with which Melville

adapted a sea captain's journal for *Benito Cereno* or Dreiser used the Gil-
lette-Brown murder case materials in *An American Tragedy* (157–58). The
Clutters could have stepped out of a Norman Rockwell painting in their
representation of everything that is quintessentially middle American; they
are wholesome and rooted to the land, and their farm lies in almost the
exact geographic center of the United States. Except for Bonnie, they are
characterized by Capote in Part I with emphasis on their most stereotypical
qualities. "In some respects," says Galloway, "the Clutters' way of life was an
anachronism, but a genial and alluring one—the small but influential seed
of reality at the heart of the American dream" (158). Their killers, Smith
and Hickock, represent the "frantic, directionless course" of those who lack
the Clutters' stability and good fortune. When Dick and Perry are together,
they are almost always moving in a car, as in the long sequence after the
murders when the men undertake "the erratic 10,000 mile odyssey" that
takes them into Mexico and then east as far as Florida (Galloway 160). The
clash of rootedness and rootlessness in the Clutter house in the early morning hours of November 15, 1959, was significant for both its meaning, as the
prototypical clash of the haves and have-nots, and its utter meaningless-
ness—a robbery from which the perpetrators walked out with $40 and a
radio, leaving four good people dead. It is a confrontation that underscores
the truth of David Galloway's essay title: that as long as there is an ongoing
gulf between those who have achieved the American dream and those who,
for biological and environmental reasons, are unlikely ever to do so, the
chickens will indeed come home to roost.

In late 1989, Tom Wolfe issued "a literary manifesto for the new social
novel" in a *Harper's* article about the composition of his book *The Bonfire
of the Vanities* (1987). Wolfe explores what he calls "one of the most curious chapters in American literary history,"—the disappearance, beginning in
about 1960, of what he calls the realistic novel (47). It is clear from his discussion that he has in mind the novel of Social Realism, a tradition that includes
the Naturalistic novel, as Wolfe traces this tradition to Zola and Balzac and
says that Faulkner, Lewis, Hemingway, Steinbeck, and Mailer are more recent
practitioners of it (46). Citing several of the well-known obituaries for the
Naturalistic novel from the late 1940s and the 1950s, including that of Lionel
Trilling in 1948, Wolfe explains what he perceives to be the reasons for the
devaluation of Social Realism. First, he claims that the industrial age has pro-
gressed beyond the Realistic novel's usefulness, and second, as Philip Roth
observed in the early 1960s, he says that "actuality is continually outdoing
our talents, and the culture tosses up figures daily that are the envy of any
novelist" (qtd. in Wolfe 48)—essentially that, as a popular cliché paraphrases
Byron, "the truth is stranger than fiction." "By the mid–1960s," Wolfe writes,

"the conviction was not merely that the realistic novel was no longer possible but that American life itself no longer deserved the term *real*" (49, emphasis his).

As a consequence of Realism's falling out of vogue, Wolfe says, fiction writers sought "to get rid of not only realism but everything associated with it." As his example, Wolfe cites John Hawkes' comment that he "began to write fiction on the assumption that the true enemies of the novel were plot, character, setting, and theme" (49). Clearly, to Wolfe, this approach amounts to "throwing out the baby with the bath water"—he claims that the inception of realistic literature in the 18th century in the works of authors such as Richardson, Fielding, and Smollett was "like the introduction of electricity into engineering" (50) and that abandoning realistic techniques would make as much sense as an engineer attempting to improve technology "by first of all discarding the principle of electricity, on the grounds that it has been used ad nauseam for a hundred years" (51).

Wolfe maintains that the purpose of fiction is still to examine "characters' electrifying irrational acts ... the acts of a heart brought to a desperate edge by the pressure of society" (51). To accomplish this, Wolfe recommends the journalistic techniques of Zola, citing the author's experiences in the French coal mines that provided the documentation for *Germinal*. Finally, Wolfe suggests that the influence of Zola not only still applies to American life but is actually essential to the continuity of American literature, which could be re-energized by "a battalion, a brigade of Zolas to head out into this wild, bizarre, unpredictable, Hog-stomping Baroque country of ours and reclaim it as literary property." Crediting Philip Roth with the notion that "the imagination of the novelist is powerless before what he knows he's going to read in tomorrow morning's newspaper," Wolfe argues that novelists, like journalists, should "do what journalists do, or are supposed to do, which is to wrestle the beast [the material] and bring it to terms" (55).

A reader well-versed in the Naturalistic homicide novel tradition cannot help but feel that, in Wolfe's contention that fiction no longer deals with "a heart brought to a desperate edge by the pressure of society" (51), he has overlooked a number of important works, including those discussed in this chapter, by authors continuing to write Social Realism in a period that overlaps almost exactly with the one Wolfe identifies. Beginning with Capote's early work on *In Cold Blood* in late 1959, writers in the homicide tradition have increasingly incorporated the methods of journalism, so that the only real difference between *An American Tragedy* and Capote's novel is a shifting of the literature-journalism balance in the direction of the latter (and a prose style far superior to Dreiser's).

In his essay, Wolfe laments the absence of works dealing realistically with the social conflict and change of the 1960s. Writing *The Electric Kool-Aid Acid Test,* he recalls, he was constantly looking over his shoulder, sure that someone would beat him to the finish with a novel about the hippie experience. "[T]o this day," Wolfe notes, those novels "remain unwritten" (45). He notes that a similar vacuum exists where novels about "the so-called sexual revolution" and the Civil Rights movement were concerned. Although the market has not been flooded with novels about those social issues, one has to wonder what better examples Wolfe could want than *Looking for Mr. Goodbar* and *The Algiers Motel Incident.* Perhaps *Goodbar* is not sufficiently journalistic to fit Wolfe's prescription, but *Algiers Motel* seems exactly the sort of book Wolfe has in mind in formulating his prescription.

For most Americans, the most frightening social phenomenon of the 1960s was the increased threat of violence, along with the dissolution of the social fabric implied in that threat. In the aftermath of the Vietnam War, the first such conflict to be brought into the living rooms of Americans via television; of the anti-war and Civil Rights demonstrations of the 1960s; and of the assassinations of John Kennedy, Robert Kennedy, and Martin Luther King, Jr., Americans felt vulnerable in ways they previously had not. Certainly, the threat of violence and the ultimate fear—losing one's life by violent means in the course of going about everyday business—are at the heart of books such as *In Cold Blood, The Executioner's Song,* and *The Boston Strangler.* We are not all out policing the Los Angeles streets or "looking for Mr. Goodbar," but we all open the door to strangers, stop at gas stations, and sleep in our own beds. The idea that these actions can make us vulnerable—can abruptly thwart the pursuit of our own dreams—is perhaps the most disturbing fact of modern life.

There are a couple of possible explanations for Wolfe's overlooking the Naturalistic homicide novels in his assessment. First, a problem that has always tainted the genre is its commercial appeal. Starting with *The Postman Always Rings Twice,* the books in the homicide novel tradition have sold well. *Postman, In Cold Blood,* and *The Executioner's Song* spent a long time on bestseller lists, in both hardback and paperback editions. The hyping of Capote's novel certainly did nothing to dissuade critics from perceiving these books as overly commercial. Although *In Cold Blood* was published in January 1966, it had previously enjoyed a wide readership during its *New Yorker* serialization, and nearly a dozen articles about it appeared in print in late 1965. In September of that year, Glenway Wescott predicted in *Book Week* that the novel "may well be the masterpiece of next year." In the first week of its publication, the book sold 180,000 copies, and within a month of its release, it was nearing the top of *Publisher's Weekly's* all-time bestseller list ("*In Cold Blood:* Target"). Also, beginning with

McTeague, each of the novels in this tradition has inspired at least one film adaptation, with the exception of *Light in August*, which was optioned to a studio but never developed. To some extent, these novels (particularly the ones not written by major literary figures such as Norris, Dreiser, Faulkner, Wright, Capote, and Mailer), have suffered from the prejudice that commercial appeal signals compromised literary value. Wolfe notes in his *Harper's* article that

> the intelligentsia have always had contempt for the realistic novel—a form that wallows so enthusiastically in the dirt of everyday life and the dirty secrets of class envy and that, still worse, is so easily understood and obviously relished by the mob, i.e., the middle class [47].

Wolfe notes as a case in point Charles Dickens' difficulty establishing a reputation with the Victorian intelligentsia despite his popular success. The presumption is that if the average reader likes it, it must not have true aesthetic value.

In another sense, however, Wolfe's overlooking the Naturalistic homicide novels is more defensible. A few recent critics have suggested that the Naturalistic novel may not have evolved primarily from Realism, but more from the Romantic tradition. It is perhaps ironic that, while the early American Naturalists have acquired a reputation as amateur critics, Norris himself first articulated the connection between Naturalism and Romanticism. In two essays, "Zola as a Romantic Writer" (1896) and "A Plea for Romantic Fiction" (1901), Norris argues for the stature of Romanticism and for Naturalism's attachment to the Romantic tradition.

Norris's basic argument is that Realism occupies itself with "the smaller details of everyday life, things that are likely to happen between lunch and dinner, small passions, restricted emotions, dramas of the reception-room, tragedies of an afternoon call, crises involving cups of tea" ("Zola" 1106). The characters of the Romantic tale, on the other hand, "must be twisted from the ordinary, wrenched out from the quiet uneventful round of every-day life, and flung into the throes of a vast and terrible drama that works itself out in unleashed passions, in blood, and in sudden death" ("Zola" 1107). Realism, says Norris, "notes only the surface of things" ("Plea" 1166), while Romanticism considers "the unplumbed depths of the human heart, and the mystery of sex, and the problems of life, and the black, unsearched penetralia of the soul of man" ("Plea" 1168–69). Granted, these definitions are offered in highly subjective tones, but Norris's basic distinction is to say that Realism deals with the typical while Romanticism deals with the atypical, perhaps with Thomas De Quincey's "great storm of passion."

Norris applies his distinction to the novels of the *Rougon-Macquart* series, whose characters, he maintains, live in their own domain and "are not of our lives any more than are the Don Juans, the Jean Valjeans, the Ruy Blas, the Marmions, or the Ivanhoes" ("Zola" 1107). To be noted by the Romantic novelist, Norris says, one must "leave the rank and file, either run to the forefront of the marching world, or fall by the roadway ... become individual, unique" ("Zola" 1107). For Norris, then, Naturalism is a sub-species of Romanticism that deals with those who "fall by the roadway"; one supposes that tragedy deals with those who march to the forefront. The Naturalistic novel illustrates "the drama of the people, working itself out in blood and ordure ... among the lower—almost the lowest—classes; those who have been thrust or wrenched from the ranks" (1108).

Norris's argument is supported by several influential critics. In *The American Novel and Its Tradition*, Richard Chase says that the significant connection between the Naturalism of Norris and the Romanticism of writers such as Cooper, Hawthorne, and Melville "has not been understood" and that Norris's claims for that connection have been thought "merely vague and eccentric" (187). Nevertheless, says Chase, Norris "wrote books that departed from realism by becoming in a unified act of the imagination at once romances and naturalistic novels" (187). Don Graham, in "Naturalism in American Fiction: A Status Report" (1982), concurs that "the naturalistic novel seems paradoxically to share something with the pre-eminent American form, romance" (5). Graham observes that, like the "best books" of Hawthorne and Melville, the "best" by Norris, Dreiser, Dos Passos, Farrell, et al. are fundamentally romances. Ultimately, says Graham, "the American naturalistic novel is a romance in which the adventurers never achieve clarity of illumination or even the comforts of irony" (8). Even Donald Pizer's definition of Naturalism in *Realism and Naturalism in Nineteenth-Century American Literature* sounds more like a definition of Romantic than Realistic works. Pizer says that two "tensions" exist in late 19th-century Naturalistic works: (1) the identification in characters from the lower social echelons of possibilities for adventure and heroism not expected to be present in those persons, and (2) the Naturalist's attempt to find some "compensating human value" to mitigate the squalor of the protagonist's life (13). These factors of "heroism" and "compensating human value" sound more like qualities that might apply to Captain Ahab and Hester Prynne than to any of the characters of Howells or James.

Norman Mailer has said that "the war between being and nothingness is the underlying illness of the twentieth century" ("The Art" 214). Certainly, for such characters as Clyde Griffiths and Joe Christmas to struggle for "being" from the "nothingness" which is their inheritance is a more fundamentally Romantic than Realistic quest. One might argue that the protagonists of the nonfiction homicide novels are all on Romantic quests toward fulfillment of the American dream, in each character's own version: for McTeague, the goal is a giant gold tooth; for Clyde Griffiths, it is the socialite Sondra Finchley and all that she represents; Joe Christmas and Bigger Thomas seek identity in a world that tells them they are nobodies; Perry Smith's goal is acceptance and affection, as his daydream of being a lounge singer with a large, appreciative audience suggests; Ron Williamson dreams of being a major league baseball star, even after his opportunity has come and gone. In every case, because these characters inhabit a Naturalistic world, they are generally doomed not to realize these goals, and that sense of doom is the source of our sympathy for them. Whatever nobility they gain stems from their persistent attempts to achieve despite probable doom, and their striving prevents their situations from seeming merely pathetic.

Critics have noted Romantic aspects of nearly every book in the homicide novel tradition. For example, many, including Pizer, have observed vestiges of the Romantic tradition in Dreiser. Others have discussed melodramatic aspects of *McTeague* that link it with the fiction of Zola. In "The Function of Violence in Richard Wright's *Native Son*," Robert James Butler points out Bigger Thomas's Romantic and Naturalistic "selves" ("The Function" 105), and, in "How 'Bigger' Was Born," Wright speaks of Hawthorne and Poe as precursors. Because of the Naturalist's sociological and psychological approach to these characters and the acts of violence that they commit, the homicide novels have a place in the Romantic tradition which, as Norris claims, goes "straight through clothes and tissues and wrappings of flesh down deep into the red living heart of things" ("A Plea" 1165).

It remains only to adjust the New Journalism into this theory of Naturalism as derived from Romanticism. It might seem that the methods of journalism—painstaking research and meticulous documentation—seem much closer to Realism than to Romanticism. This is true of conventional journalism, reporting the news in a purely objective way. But the primary distinction between the New Journalism and the "Old" Journalism is that the New Journalists also want to comment on what they are reporting, not merely to give an account, but to give an *explanation*. This perspective is not possible in a purely realistic account, which must simply tell, and its impossibility is the primary reason for the Naturalists' rebellion against Realism and their reversion to the Romantic occupation of dissecting the human heart, seeking to explain the terror of which man is capable.

Chapter Notes

Chapter 1

1. In 1965, the Pulitzer Prize for General Nonfiction was awarded to Howard Mumford Jones for *O Strange New World*; in 1966, it was awarded to Edward Way Teale's *Wandering Through Winter*. Finalists for Pulitzer Prizes were not identified before 1980. With regard to the 1966 National Book Awards, there does not appear to have been an appropriate category for nonfiction narrative. In the category Arts and Humanities, the winner was Janet Flanner's *Paris Journal, 1944–1965*. The National Book Foundation did not present an award for General Nonfiction until 1980.

2. Lee nearly completed law school at the University of Alabama but withdrew in her final semester. But as Casey Cep puts it, "she had spent her entire life around courthouses," so she could still prove a useful advisor on legal matters (*Furious* 189).

3. At the time of Ted Bundy's execution, he had confessed to and provided information about 30 murders in the Pacific Northwest and Florida ("Ted Bundy").

4. The second surge of income inequality occurred after 1970.

Chapter 2

1. Those who study nature are called naturalists (lower case "n") while those who write literature in the tradition of American literary Naturalism are Naturalists (upper case "N").

2. Hemmings quotes the original, translated above: "Jetez-vous dans la presse à corps perdu, comme on se jette à l'eau pour apprendre à nager. C'est la seule école virile, à cette heure; c'est là qu'on se frotte aux hommes et qu'on se bronze; c'est encore là, au point de vue spécial du métier, qu'on peut forger son style sur la terrible enclume de l'article au jour le jour."

3. Caroline Meeber is the protagonist of Theodore Dreiser's novel *Sister Carrie* (1900), and Roberta Alden and Clyde Griffiths are characters in his *An American Tragedy* (1925).

Chapter 3

1. The love letters from Grace Brown to Chester Gillette were published as *Grace Brown's Love Letters* in 2006 and in a second edition including her diary in 2008, both edited by Craig Brandon, the leading expert on the Brown/Gillette case until his 2018 death. Chester Gillette's diary and letters were published as *The Prison Diary and Letters of Chester Gillette: September 18, 1907 through March 30, 1908* in 2007, edited by Jack Sherman and Craig Brandon.

2. One wonders whether Dreiser's occasional awkwardness with English syntax stems from the fact that his first language was German, a language well known for its syntactical eccentricities.

Chapter 4

1. Wright's comment concerning Hugo Black refers to the Justice's authorship of the majority U.S. Supreme Court opinion in the case *Ashcraft v. Tennessee* (1944). In a murder-for-hire case involving both a white and a black defendant, the Supreme Court invalidated the Tennessee jury's determination that the confessions of both men had been given voluntarily. In the decision,

Black wrote that contact with the police was, for any defendant, "inherently coercive" (Clapp).

2. Most of the books discussed in this volume were written closer in times to the crimes that inspired them, although Dreiser's reflects nearly the same time gap as Levin's.

3. Levin and Leopold both earned baccalaureate degrees at Chicago. Loeb had begun undergraduate study there but transferred to the University of Michigan. When he received his degree at 17 in 1923, he was Michigan's youngest ever graduate ("Richard"). Leopold graduated from the University of Chicago in 1923 ("Loeb"), Levin in 1924 (Mitgang). Leopold and Loeb both subsequently enrolled in Chicago's law school, but their crime aborted their legal careers.

Chapter 5

1. On March 13, 1966, Kenneth Tynan's review of *In Cold Blood* appeared in *The London Observer*. Tynan was generally positive and occasionally laudatory, but he also leveled at Capote a harsh criticism: that he had not done as much as he might have to save Perry Smith's and Dick Hickock's lives. Tynan wrote, "For the first time, an influential writer of the front rank has been placed in a position of privileged intimacy with criminals about to die, and—in my view—done less than he might have to save them" (445). Ultimately, Tynan argued, Capote chose his work over the lives of the two men it portrayed. Tynan concludes, "The blood in which the book is written is as cold as any in recent literature" (446). Capote's reply was published two weeks later. Clearly stung by Tynan's charge, he called the critic "a man with the morals of a baboon and the guts of a butterfly" (451) and suggesting at one point that Perry Smith and Dick Hickock were less insane than Tynan. In forceful, occasionally biting language, Capote structured his response like a judicial rebuttal; he argues that Tynan had not read his book closely, that he (Capote) had been sensitive to Smith and Hickock's plight and had postponed the book's publication until appeals were exhausted so that the frankness of his subjects' confessions would not hurt their chances, and that even if he had pressed for more psychiatric testimony in the killers'

trial, the Kansas courts' strict adherence to the McNaghten Rule would have prohibited its inclusion. In the ensuing weeks, Tynan wrote again on the subject in *The Observer*'s pages; the tone of his reply is summed up in his contention that Capote had "invented yet another new art form: after the Non-Fiction Novel, the Semi-Documentary Tantrum" (452). In his second article, Tynan argues that Capote should have urged Smith's and Hickock's attorneys to challenge the McNaghten Rule, even if they perceived it inviolable, and he produces the name of a source whose existence Capote had questioned. Two weeks later, Joseph P. Jenkins, an attorney for Smith and Hickock, entered the fray on Capote's behalf; his comments were published on April 24 under the rather misleading headline "Tynan attacked by lawyers" (454). Jenkins argues that Capote was an author, not an attorney, and that he was nevertheless helpful and sympathetic in Smith and Hickock's case. To Jenkins' defense, Tynan replied again on May 1, ending with a reiteration of his allegation that Capote was not sufficiently emotionally engaged in Smith's and Hickock's fates. The outcome of the whole interchange was a $500 check from Capote to Tynan, the result of a bet over whether one of Tynan's sources was made up, as well as each man's permanent animosity toward the other.

2. Bradford is reported by a number of sources, including the *Dictionary of National Biography* (1885) to have said "There but for the grace of God goes John Bradford" while watching a group of convicted men being led to their executions. Bradford himself was burned at the stake on Jan. 31, 1555, as a perceived anti-Catholic rabble-rouser about two years after the ascent of Queen Mary to the English throne. The well-known phrase is sometimes attributed to others but most frequently to Bradford.

Chapter 7

1. Capote's statement appeared originally in the essay "Ghosts in Sunlight" in *A Capote Reader* (623).

2. Pizer's subjects are Frank Norris, Theodore Dreiser, Hamlin Garland, Edith Wharton, and Willa Cather.

3. Despite the sociological implications of the murders at Sharon Tate and Roman

Polanski's home, the murders of Leno and Rosemary LaBianca the next night were almost completely random, except that some members of Manson's groups had recently attended a party in the LaBiancas' neighborhood.

4. Kurosawa's film is based on the 1922 short story "In the Grove" by Ryūnosuke Akutagawa. *Rashomon* was the first film by a Japanese director to receive international acclaim.

5. Detroit officer Jerome Olshove was killed on the second night of the riots, and the officers who later entered the Algiers Motel Annex learned of their colleague's death when they reported to work on the morning of the "Incident." Officer David Senak told John Hersey that Olshove's death "was the source of a great deal of anger" among his peers (111).

6. The Federal Kidnapping Act, popularly called the "Lindbergh Law" and "Little Lindbergh Law" (18 U.S.C. § 1201), was adopted in 1932, the same year that Charles and Anne Morrow Lindbergh's toddler son was kidnapped and murdered. It was intended to facilitate pursuit of kidnappers who cross state lines. Section 902 of California's Penal Code addresses the state's version of that act and makes kidnapping a capital crime if ransom or serious bodily harm is involved.

7. California's Felony Murder Rule was amended in 2018 to separate actions from intentions; thereafter, a person involved in committing a felony was subject to prosecution for murder only if it could be proven that the person directly participated in the murder (Jordan Smith). California Senate Bill 1437 was signed into law by Governor Jerry Brown.

8. At the time of the strangling murders in Boston, "Son of Sam" laws preventing perpetrators from benefitting from book and film adaptations of their stories had not yet been passed. Those laws originated in New York in the late 1980s and early 1990s.

9. F. Lee Bailey had become a media celebrity in the previous decade (1950s) when he defended Dr. Sam Sheppard in the killing of Sheppard's wife in Cleveland.

The Sheppard case became the basis for the television series and subsequent film *The Fugitive*.

10. Alfred C. Kinsey was an American biologist and pioneer of research concerning human sexuality. He founded the Institute for Sex Research at Indiana University in 1947.

11. Sad Sack, a character in a World War II-era cartoon by George Baker, was depicted as a gloomy soldier in an ill-fitting uniform who failed at most of his efforts.

12. There may be a Capote echo in this title, as he published an anthology called *The Dogs Bark* in 1973.

Chapter 8

1. Smith also had three younger sisters, whose educational attainment Junger does not include (21).

2. Note that Junger's book was published before the 2013 DNA evidence tying DeSalvo to the last Strangler victim.

3. Junger, who made a number of corrections to the paperback edition of *The Perfect Storm*, told the *New York Times'* Rich Motoko that he hired a professional fact-checker for *A Death in Belmont*.

4. Evidence against Gore was sufficient that he was convicted *twice* of the crimes against Debra Sue Carter. The first time, he was sentenced to death, but his conviction was overturned due to an error by the same judge who presided over the trial of Williamson and Fritz. A year later, Gore was convicted again, and when the jury deadlocked on punishment, a life sentence without parole was imposed (Grisham, *Innocent* 358).

5. The reference to "the gang that couldn't shoot straight" is taken from the title of a 1971 film about bumbling rival mafia gangs in New York City.

6. When *The Appeal* was issued in paperback, Grisham told an Amazon.com interviewer that one of three books currently on his bedside table was Steinbeck's *East of Eden*.

Bibliography

Abramovich, Rebekah Burgess. "Chicago's Secret Society of Death-Obsessed Journalists—and the Belly Dancer Who Exposed Them." *Chicago*, 6 May 2016, www.chicagomag.com/city-life/May-2016/Whitechapel-Club/. Accessed 18 June 2019.

Adams, James Truslow. *The Epic of America*. Ill. M.J. Gallagher. Little, Brown, 1931.

Ahlborn, Ania. "The 1950s: Death and the American Dream." *Criminal Element*, 26 October 2012, www.criminalelement.com/the-1950s-death-and-the-american-dream-ania-ahlborn-true-crime-f-b-i-spree-killer-black-dahlia-suffer-the-children/.

Ahnebrink, Lars. *The Beginnings of Naturalism in American Fiction: A Study of the Works of Hamlin Garland, Stephen Crane, and Frank Norris, with Special Reference to Some European Influences, 1891–1903.* Russell & Russell, 1961.

"Albert DeSalvo, Murderer, Criminal (1931–1973)." *Biography.com*. Updated 16 Jan. 2016. www.biography.com/people/albert-de-salvo-17169632.

Alexander, Margaret Walker. "Richard Wright." In *Richard Wright: Impressions and Perspectives* by David Ray and Robert M. Farnsworth. U of Michigan P, 1973. pp. 47–67.

Algeo, Ann M. *The Courtroom as Forum: Homicide Trials by Dreiser, Wright, Capote, and Mailer.* Modern American Literature. Gen. ed. Yoshinobu Hakutani. Peter Lang, 1996.

"Algiers Motel Incident Drags in Court." *Detroit Free Press*. 8 Dec.1968, p. 12C.

Allen, Mike. "Photographs for Social Change," *The Roanoke Times*, 6 July 2018: 2.

Anderson, Chris. Class lecture. ENG 521: Contemporary Prose Style. University of North Carolina at Greensboro. Fall 1984.

_____. *Literary Nonfiction: Theory, Criticism, Pedagogy.* Southern Illinois UP, 1989.

_____. Style *as Argument: Contemporary American Nonfiction.* Southern Illinois UP, 1987.

"Ann Rule Bio." *Author Ann Rule.* www.authorannrule.com/Ann_Rule_Bio.html.

"As American as Apple Pie, Cherry Pie—and Violence..." *ThisDayinQuotes*, 27 July 2015, www.thisdayinquotes.com/2013/07/as-american-as-apple-pie-cherry-pie-and.html.

"As You Were: After a Period on the Wane, Inequality is Waxing Again." *The Economist*, 13 Oct. 2012. www.economist.com/node/21564413.

Associated Press. "Whatever Happened to Harper Lee's True-Crime Novel Based on Alabama Murders?" *The Guardian*, 9 Sept. 2015, www.theguardian.com/books/2015/sep/09/alabama-harper-lee-true-crime-book.

Attenborough, David. *Life on Earth: A Natural History.* Little, Brown, 1979.

Baatz, Simon. *For the Thrill of It: Leopold, Loeb, and the Murder That Shocked Jazz Age Chicago.* Harper Perennial, 2009.

Bailey, F. Lee. *The Defense Never Rests.* Penguin, 1972.

Baker, Houston A., Jr., ed. *Twentieth Century Interpretations of* Native Son: *A Collection of Critical Essays.* Prentice-Hall, 1972.

Baldwin, James. "Everybody's Protest Novel." *Partisan Review,* 1949. Rpt. in Bloom, *Bigger,* pp. 5–6.
_____. "Many Thousands Gone: Richard Wright's *Native Son.*" In *Notes of a Native Son* by Baldwin. Beacon, 1955. Rpt. in Gross and Hardy, pp. 233–45.
Barkham, John. "The Bookshelf—True Murder Case Horrifies and Chills." *New York World Telegraph and Sun,* 12 January 1966: 23.
Barton, John Cyril. "An American Travesty: Capital Punishment & the Criminal Justice System in Dreiser's *An American Tragedy.*" *REAL,* vol. 18, 2002, pp. 357–84.
Bassett, John. *William Faulkner: The Critical Heritage.* Routledge, 1975.
Becker, George J., ed. *Documents of Modern Literary Realism.* Princeton UP, 1963.
Begiebing, Robert J. *Acts of Regeneration: Allegory and Archetype in the Words of Norman Mailer.* U of Missouri P, 1980.
Bendixen, Alfred, and Olivia Carr Edenfield. *The Centrality of Crime Fiction in American Popular Literature.* Routlege Interdisciplinary Perspectives on Literature. No. 77. Routledge, 2017.
Berendt, John. *Midnight in the Garden of Good and Evil.* Random House, 1994.
Berger, Douglas L. "The Murder of Moral Idealism: Kant and the Murder of Ian Campbell in *The Onion Field.*" *The Philosophy of Neo-Noir.* Ed. Mark T. Conrad. U P of Kentucky, 2007, pp. 67–82. *JSTOR,* www-jstor-org.library.acaweb.org.
Berthoff, Warner. *The Firmament of Realism: American Literature, 1884–1919.* Free Press, 1965.
Bidgood, Jess. "50 Years Later, a Break in a Boston Strangler Case." *The New York Times,* 11 July 2013, www.nytimes.com/2013/07/12/us/dna-evidence-identified-in-boston-strangler-case.html.
Birkerts, Sven. "Docu-fiction." *The Boston Phoenix,* 1986. Rpt. in *An Artificial Wilderness: Essays on Twentieth Century Literature* by Birkerts. Godine, 1987, pp. 265–70.
Blake, Caesar R. "On Richard Wright's *Native Son.*" In Friedland, pp. 187–99.
Bleikasten, Andre. "*Light in August*: The Closed Society and Its Subjects." In Millgate, pp. 81–102.
Bloom, Harold, ed. *Bigger Thomas.* Major Literary Characters Series. Chelsea, 1990.
_____. *Norman Mailer.* Modern Critical Views Series. Chelsea, 1986.
_____. *Richard Wright's* Native Son. Modern Critical Interpretations. New York: Chelsea, 1988.
_____. *Steven Crane.* Modern Critical Views. Chelsea, 1987.
Blotner, Joseph. *Faulkner: A Biography.* Two volumes. Random House, 1974.
Bone, Robert. *Richard Wright.* U of Minnesota Pamphlets on American Writers. No 74. U of Minnesota P, 1969.
"The Boston Strangler." *Crime Library.* The Crime Museum, Washington, D.C. 2017. www.crimemuseum.org/crime-library/the-boston-strangler/.
_____ *Criminal Minds.* www.criminalminds.wikia.com/wiki/The_Boston_Strangler.
Bradbury, Malcolm. *The Modern American Novel.* Oxford UP, 1984.
Bradford, John. *Oxford Dictionary of National Biography,* vol. 6, 1885.
Brandon, Craig. *Murder in the Adirondacks:* An American Tragedy *Revisited.* Fully revised and expanded edition. North Country Books, 2016.
Brantley, Ben. "Review: In 'Thérèse Raquin,' Keira Knightley as a Baleful Adulteress," *New York Times,* 29 Oct. 2015. www.nytimes.com/2015/10/30/theater/review-in-therese-raquin-keira-knightley-as-a-baleful-adulteress.html.
Braudy, Leo. "Realists, Naturalists, and Novelists of Manners." In Hoffman, pp. 84–152.
Brazil, John R. "Murder Trials, Murder, and Twenties America. *American Quarterly,* vol. 33, summer 1981, pp. 163–84.
Breen, Jon L., and Martin Greenburg. *Murder off the Rack.* Scarecrow, 1989.
Brennan, Stephen C. "Literary Naturalism as a Humanism: Donald Pizer on Definitions

of Naturalism." *Studies in American Naturalism,* vol. 5, no. 1, 2010, pp. 8–20. *JSTOR,* www.jstor.org/stable/23431184.

Brickell, Herschel. "The Literary Landscape." Review of *Light in August* by Faulkner. *North American Review,* vol. 234, Dec. 1932, pp. 571.

Broeske, Pat H. "Serial Killers Claim Movies as Their Prey." *New York Times,* 13 Dec. 1992, pp. 18–19H.

Brooks, Cleanth. "The Community and the Pariah." In *William Faulkner: The Yoknapatawpha Country* by Brooks. Yale, 1963, pp. 47–74. Rpt. in Minter, pp. 55–70.

Brown, C.H. "The Rise of the New Journalism." *Current,* vol. 141, June 1972, pp. 31–8.

Brown, DeNeen L. "'Detroit' and the Police Brutality that Left Three Black Teens Dead at the Algiers Motel." *The Washington Post,* 4 Aug. 2017. www.washingtonpost.com/news/retropolis/wp/2017/08/04/detroit-and-the-police-brutality-that-left-three-black-teens-dead-at-the-algiers-motel/?utm_term=.38faf5fa9ada

Brown, Grace. *Grace Brown's Love Letters.* Ed. Craig Brandon. Second edition. Surry Cottage Books, 2008.

Bryant, Jerry H. "The Violence of *Native Son.*" *Southern Review,* vol. 17, April 1981, pp. 303–19.

Bugliosi, Vincent, with Curt Gentry. *Helter Skelter: The True Story of the Manson Murders.* Norton, 1974.

Butler, Robert James. "The Function of Violence in Richard Wright's *Native Son.*" *Black American Literature Forum,* vol. 20, spring-summer 1986, pp. 9–25. Rpt. in Bloom, *Bigger,* pp. 103–16.

_____. "Wright's *Native Son* and Two Novels by Zola." *Black American Literature Forum,* vol. 18, fall 1984, pp. 100–5.

Cady, Edwin. *The Light of Common Day: Realism In American Fiction.* Indiana UP, 1971.

_____. *Stephen Crane.* Ed. David J. Nordloh. Rev. ed. Twayne United States Authors Series. Twayne, 1980.

Cain, James M. *The Postman Always Rings Twice.* 1934. Vintage, 1992.

_____. *60 Years of Journalism.* Edited by Roy Hoopes, Ohio State U Popular P, 1985.

Cain, William E. "Presence and Power in *McTeague.*" In *American Realism: New Essays.* Edited by Eric J. Sundquist. Johns Hopkins UP, 1982, pp. 199–214.

Campbell, Donna M. "Naturalism in American Literature." *Literary Movements.* Dept. of English, Washington State University, 8 March 2017.

Canby, Henry Seidel. "The School of Cruelty." *Saturday Review of Literature,* 21 March 1931. Rpt. in *William Faulkner: The Critical Heritage.* Routledge, 1975, pp. 107–10.

Capote, Truman. *Handcarved Coffins: A Nonfiction Account of an American Crime.* In *Music for Chameleons.* 1975. Signet-New American Library, 1980, pp. 65–147.

_____. *In Cold Blood: A True Account of a Multiple Murder and Its Consequences.* Signet-New American Library, 1965.

_____. "A Nonfiction Visit with Truman Capote." With Shana Alexander. *Life,* 18 February 1966, p. 22.

_____. "*Playboy* Interview: Truman Capote." With Eric Norden. *Playboy,* March 1968: 51–3, 56, 58–62, 160–70.

_____. "The Story Behind a Nonfiction Novel." With George Plimpton. *New York Times Book Review,* 16 Jan. 1966: pp. 2–3, 38–43.

Cep, Casey, *Furious Hours: Murder, Fraud, and the Last Trial of Harper Lee,* Knopf, 2019.

Cep, Casey N., "Harper Lee's Abandoned True-Crime Novel," *The New Yorker,* 17 April 2015. www.newyorker.com/books/page-turner/harper-lees-forgotten-true-crime-project. Retrieved 31 May 2017.

"Cesare Lombroso: Italian Criminologist." *Encyclopedia Britannica,* www.britannica.com/biography/Cesare-Lombroso. Accessed 18 June 2019.

Chase, Richard. *The American Novel and Its Traditions.* Doubleday, 1957.

Clapp, Jeffrey. "Richard Wright and the Police." *Post45.* Yale University. 12 Sept. 2011. post45.research.yale.edu/2011/09/richard-wright-and-the-police/. Accessed 6 July 2019.

Clark, Jonas. "In Search of the American Dream." *The Atlantic,* June 2007. www.theatlantic.com/magazine/archive/2007/06/in-search-of-the-american-dream/305921/.

Clarke, Gerald. *Capote: A Biography.* Simon & Schuster, 1988.

Cogny, Pierre. *Le Naturalisme.* PUF, 1976.

Collett, Alan. "Literature, Criticism, and Factual Reporting." *Philosophy and Literature,* vol. 13, Oct. 1989, pp. 282–96.

Collins, Carvel. *Introduction to* McTeague: A Story of San Francisco [by Frank Norris]. Rinehart, 1950, pp. vii–xviii.

Conder, John J. *Naturalism in American Fiction: The Classic Phase.* UP of Kentucky, 1984.

Cowan, Michael. "The Americanness of Norman Mailer." In *Norman Mailer: A Collection of Critical Essays.* Ed. Leo Braudy. Prentice-Hall, 1972, pp. 143–57.

Cowley, Malcolm. *The Flower and the Leaf: A Contemporary Record of American Writing Since 1941.* Edited by Donald W. Faulkner, Viking, 1955.

_____. "A Natural History of American Naturalism." *Kenyon Review,* vol. 9, summer 1947, pp. 414–35. Rpt. in *Documents of Modern Literary Realism.* Edited by George J. Becker. Princeton UP, 1963, pp. 429–51.

_____. Review of *Native Son. The New Republic,* vol. 102, 18 March 1940, pp. 382–83. Rpt. in Reilly, pp. 67–68.

_____. "Sister Carrie's Brother." In Kazin, Stature, pp. 153–65.

Craig, Jim. "Nathan Freudenthal Leopold, Sr." *FindaGrave.* 8 Jan. 2012. Memorial no. 83123051. www.findagrave.com/memorial/83123051/nathan-freudenthal-leopold.

_____. "The Sins of the Son Are Visited on the Father—Nathan F. Leopold, Sr." *Under Every Stone,* 17 Jan. 2012. undereverystone.blogspot.com/2012/01/sins-of-son-are-visited-on-father.html. Accessed 8 July 2019.

Crane, Stephen. *Maggie: A Girl of the Streets.* 1893. In *The Portable Stephen Crane,* pp. 3–74.

_____. "The Open Boat." 1897. In *The Portable Stephen Crane,* pp. 360–86.

_____. *The Portable Stephen Crane.* Edited by Joseph Katz, Penguin, 1969; 1979.

_____. *Stephen Crane: Letters.* Edited by Robert Stallman and Lillian Gilkes, New York UP, 1960.

Creeger, George R. *Animals in Exile: Imagery and Theme in Capote's* In Cold Blood. Monday Evening Papers: No. 12. Wesleyan U Center for Advanced Studies, 1967.

Cullen, Jim. *The American Dream: A Short History of an Idea that Shaped a Nation.* Oxford UP, 2003. *Kindle ebook.*

Cullen, John B., with Floyd C. Watkins. *Old Times in the Faulkner Country.* U of North Carolina P, 1961.

Darrow, Clarence. *The Story of My Life.* 1932. Ulwencreutz Media, 2015. *Google Books.* Accessed 31 May 2017.

Darwin, Charles. *The Descent of Man.* John Murray, 1871.

_____. "The Struggle for Existence and Natural Selection." *On the Origin of Species by Means of Natural Selection.* 1859. Rpt. in Ellmann and Feidelson, pp. 385–90.

Darwin8u. "*McTeague* by Frank Norris, Eric Solomon (Introduction)," *Goodreads,* 14 March 2014. www.goodreads.com/book/show/168655.McTeague. Accessed 11 July 2018.

Davenport, F. Garvin, Jr. *The Myth of Southern History.* Vanderbilt UP, 1970.

Davis, David Brion. *Homicide in American Fiction, 1798–1860: A Study in Social Values.* Cornell UP, 1957.

DeBellis, Jack. "Visions and Revisions: Truman Capote's *In Cold Blood.*" *Journal of Modern Literature,* vol. 7, 1979, pp. 519–36.

De Quincey, Thomas. "On the Knocking at the Gate in 'Macbeth." In *Romantic Poetry and Prose*. Edited by Harold Bloom and Lionel Trilling, Oxford UP, 1973, pp. 731–35.

Dershowitz, Alan, "The Belmont Strangler," Review of *A Death in Belmont* by Sebastian Junger, *New York Times*, 16 April 2006. www.nytimes.com/2006/04/16/books/review/the-belmont-strangler.html.

Detroit. Dir. Kathryn Bigelow. 20th Century Fox, 2017.

"*Detroit.*" *IMDB*. www.imdb.com/title/tt5390504/?ref_=fn_al_tt_1. Accessed 27 July 2019.

Didion, Joan. "I Want to Go Ahead and Do It." *New York Times Book Review*, 7 Oct. 1979, pp. 1, 26–27.

D'Imperio, Chuck. "Murder of Grace Brown: Relive Infamous Crime at Big Moose Lake in Adirondacks." *NYUp.com*, www.newyorkupstate.com/adirondacks/2016/04/grace_brown_murder_big_moose_inn_adirondacks_ny_chester_gillette.html. Accessed 18 June 2019.

Divine, Robert A., et al. "Political Realignments and the Decade of Decision: the 1890s" (Chapter 20). *America: Past and Present*. Second ed. Scott, Foresman, 1987, pp. 574–601.

Donald, Miles. *The American Novel in the Twentieth Century*. Barnes and Noble, 1978.

Downey, James [former Assistant Professor of Philosophy, Ferrum College, Ferrum, VA] Personal interview 26 May 1993.

Drabble, Margaret, ed. *The Oxford Companion to English Literature*. 5th ed. Oxford UP, 1985.

"*Drawing the Line: The Father Reimagined in Faulkner, Wright, O'Connor, and Morrison* by Doreen Fowler." *Goodreads*. www.goodreads.com/book/show/16270551-drawing-the-line. Accessed 5 July 2019.

Dreiser, Helen Richardson. *My Life With Dreiser*. World, 1951.

Dreiser, Theodore. *An American Tragedy*. 1925. Signet/New American Library, 1953.

_____. *The Financier*. 1912. World, 1940.

_____. "I Find the Real American Tragedy." *The Mystery Magazine*, vol. 11, Feb. 1935, pp. 10–11, 88–90.

_____. *Newspaper Days, or a Book About Myself*. Boni and Liveright, 1922.

_____. *Selected Magazine Articles of Theodore Dreiser*. Edited by Yoshinobu Hakutani, Farleigh Dickinson UP, 1985, 1987.

_____. *Sister Carrie*. 1900. Norton Critical Edition. Norton, 1991.

_____. *Theodore Dreiser: Journalism: Newspaper Writings 1892–1895*. Edited by T. D. Nostwich, U of Pennsylvania P, 1988.

_____. *Theodore Dreiser's "Heard in the Corridors": Articles and Related Writings*. Edited by T. D. Nostwich, Iowa State UP, 1988.

Dunbar, Sybil J. *William Faulkner and Richard Wright: Two Perspectives of the South, the Female as a Focal Point*. 1990. U Kentucky, Ph.D. Dissertation.

Dunphy, Jack. "*Dear Genius…*": *A Memoir of My Life with Truman Capote*. McGraw-Hill, 1987.

Dupee, F. W. "Truman Capote's Score." Review of *In Cold Blood*. *The New York Review of Books*, 3 Feb. 1966, pp. 3–5.

Durant, Will. *The Story of Philosophy: The Lives and Opinions of the Greater Philosophers*. 1926. Simon & Schuster, 1961.

Duvall, John. "Murder and the Communities: IdeF6logy in and Around *Light in August.*" *Novel: A Forum on Fiction*, vol. 20, winter 1987, pp. 101–22.

Dyer, Geoff, and others. "'Based on a True Story': The Fine Line Between Fact and Fiction." *The Guardian*, 6 Dec. 2015, www.theguardian.com/books/2015/dec/06/based-on-a-true-story—geoff-dyer-fine-line-between-fact-and-fiction-nonfiction.

Edmundson, Mark. "Romantic Self-Creations: Mailer and Gilmore in *The Executioner's Song.*" *Contemporary Literature*, vol. 31, 1980, pp. 434–47.

Ellison, Ralph. "The World and the Jug." 1963. *Shadow and Act*. Random House, 1964. Rpt. in Bloom, *Bigger*, pp. 9–12.

Ellmann, Richard, and Charles Feidelson, Jr., eds. *The Modern Tradition: Backgrounds of Modern Literature.* Oxford UP, 1965.

Emanuel, James A. "Fever and Feeling: Notes on the Imagery in *Native Son*." *Negro Digest,* vol. 18, Dec. 1968, pp. 16–24.

Fabre, Michel. *The Unfinished Quest of Richard Wright.* Translated by Isabel Barzun. Morrow, 1973.

"The Fabulist." *Newsweek,* 28 December 1964, p. 58.

Fadiman, Clifton. Review of *Native Son. The New Yorker,* 2 March 1940, pp. 52–53. Rpt. in Reilly, pp. 48–50.

Fadiman, Regina K. *Faulkner's* Light in August: *A Description and Interpretation of the Revisions.* U of Virginia P, 1975.

Falcon, Gabriel. "After 35 Years, 'Fatal Vision' Author, Killer Meet Again." *CNN,* 30 Sept. 2012. www.cnn.com/2012/09/29/justice/mcginniss-macdonald-appeal/.

Farrell, James T. "Dreiser's Tragedy: The Distortion of American Values." *Prospects: Annual of American Cultural Studies,* vol. 1, 1975, pp. 19–27.

_____. *Literature and Morality.* Vanguard, 1947.

Farrell, John A. *Clarence Darrow: Attorney for the Damned.* Random House, 2011. Kindle ebook.

Fass, Paula S. "Making and Remaking an Event: The Leopold and Loeb Case on American Culture." *Journal of American History,* vol. 80, no. 3, 1983, pp. 919–51. Rpt. *Children of a New World: Society, Culture, and Globalization.* By Fass. New York U P, 2007, pp. 106–40.

Faulkner, William. *Intruder in the Dust.* Modern Library College Editions. Random House, 1948.

_____. *Light in August.* 1932. Modern Library College Editions. Random House, 1959, 1968.

Feld, Rose. Review of *Compulsion. New York Herald Tribune Book Review,* 28 Oct. 1956, p. 5.

Feldman, Gayle, and Maria Simson. "11 Houses Bid, Doubleday Wins *Shot in the Heart. Publisher's Weekly,* 17 May 1991, pp. 33–34.

Felgar, Robert. *Richard Wright.* Twayne's U.S. Author's Series. Twayne, 1980.

"Fiction." [Fictional accounts of the Leopold and Loeb Case.] *The Lives and Legends of Richard Loeb and Nathan Leopold.* loebandleopold.wordpress.com/fiction/. Accessed 9 July 2019.

Fishbein, Leslie. "*Looking for Mr. Goodbar*: Murder for the Masses." *International Journal of Women's Studies,* vol. 3, 1980, pp. 173–82.

Fisher, Dorothy Canfield. Introduction. *Native Son.* By Richard Wright. New York: Harper, 1940, pp. ix–xi. Rpt. in *Twentieth Century Interpretations* of Native Son. Edited by Houston A. Baker, Jr. Prentice-Hall, 1972, pp. 109–11.

Fisher, Philip. "The Life History of Objects: The Naturalist Novel and the City." *Hard Facts: Setting and Form in the American Novel.* By Fisher. Oxford UP, 1987, pp. 128–78.

Fishkin, Shelley Fisher. "Theodore Dreiser." *From Fact to Fiction: Journalism and Imaginative Writing in America.* By Fishkin, Oxford UP, 1985, pp. 85–135.

Fitelson, David. "Stephen Crane's *Maggie* and Darwinism." *American Quarterly,* vol. 16, summer 1964, pp. 182–94.

Foertsch, Jacqueline. "Cautionary Tales from the Sexual Revolution: Freedom Gained and Lost in 1970s Novels, Films, and Memoirs." *Journal of American Culture,* vol. 40, no. 3, 2017, pp. 217–26. *EBSCOHost.* DOI: 10.1111/jacc.12737.

Foley, Barbara. *Telling the Truth: The Theory and Practice of Documentary Fiction.* Cornell UP, 1986.

Fosburgh, Lacey. *Closing Time: The True Story of the "Looking for Mr. Goodbar" Murder.* Delacorte, 1977.

Fowler, Doreen. *Drawing the Line: The Father Reimagined in Faulkner, Wright, O'Connor, and Morrison.* U of Virginia P, 2013.

France, Alan W. "Misogyny and Appropriation in *Native Son.*" *Modern Fiction Studies,* vol. 34, Autumn 1988. Rpt. in Bloom, *Bigger,* pp. 151–60.

Frank, Gerald. *The Boston Strangler.* New American Library, 1966.

Freeborn, Richard. "The Nineteenth Century: The Age of Realism, 1855–80." In Moser, pp. 248–332.

French, Warren. *Frank Norris.* Twayne, 1962.

Friedland, M. L. *Rough Justice: Essays on Crime in Literature.* U of Toronto P, 1991.

Friedman, Melvin. "Towards an Aesthetic: Truman Capote's Other Voices." In Malin, pp. 163–76.

Fritz, Dennis. *Journey toward Justice.* Seven Locks Press, 2006.

Frohock, W.M. *Frank Norris.* University of Minnesota Pamphlets on American Writers. U of Minnesota P, 1968.

_____. *The Novel of Violence in America.* Second ed. Southern Methodist UP, 1957.

Furst, Lillian R., and Peter N. Skrine. *Naturalism.* Methuen, 1971.

Galloway, David. "Why the Chickens Came Home to Roost in Holcomb, Kansas: Truman Capote's *In Cold Blood.*" In Malin, 154–63.

Gannett, Lewis. Review of *Native Son* by Richard Wright. *New York Herald Tribune,* 1 March 1940, p. 17. Rpt. in Reilly, pp. 40–42.

Gardner, Erle Stanley. "Killers for Kicks." Review of *Compulsion* by Meyer Levin. *New York Times Book Review,* 28 Oct. 1956, p. 7.

Garrett, George. "Crime and Punishment in Kansas: Truman Capote's *In Cold Blood.*" *Hollins Critic,* vol. III, pp. i, 1–12.

Garvey, John. "*The Executioner's Song.*" *Commonweal,* vol. 5, 14 March 1980, pp. 107. Rpt. in Bloom, *Norman Mailer,* pp. 139–42.

Gates, David, "A Death in the House," Review of *A Death in Belmont* by Sebastian Junger, *Newsweek,* 9 April 2006, www.newsweek.com/killer-house-107605.

Gayle, Addison. *Richard Wright: Ordeal of a* Native Son. Anchor/Doubleday, 1980.

Gelb, Arthur. *City Room.* Putnam, 2004. *GoogleBooks.* Books.google.com.

Gelfant, Blanche. *The American City Novel.* Oklahoma UP, 1954.

Gerber, Philip L. "'Society Should Ask Forgiveness': *An American Tragedy.*" In *Theodore Dreiser Revisited* by Gerber. Twayne, 1992, pp. 77–93.

_____. "Whither Naturalism?" In Papke, pp. 367–89.

Gerigk, Horst-Jurgen. "Culpabilité et liberté: Dostoevskij, Dreiser, et Richard Wright." *Revue de Litterature Comparée,* vols. 219–20, July-Dec. 1981, pp. 358–76.

Gibb, Robert. "Joe Christmas: Faulkner's Savage Innocent." *Journal of Evolutionary Psychology,* vol. 9, Aug. 1988, pp. 331–40.

Giles, James R. *Violence in the Contemporary American Novel: An End to Innocence.* U of South Carolina P, 2000.

Gillette, Chester. *The Prison Diary and Letters of Chester Gillette: September 18, 1907 through March 30, 1908.* Ed. Jack Sherman and Craig Brandon. Richard W. Couper Press, 2007.

Gilmore, Mikal. "A Death in the Family." *Rolling Stone,* 11 June 1992, pp. 111–12.

Gilroy, Harry. "A Book in a New Form Earns $2-Million for Capote." *New York Times,* 31 Dec. 1965. 15 July 1999. www.nytimes.com/books/97/12/28/home/capote-million. html.

Goncourt, Edmund de, and Jules de Goncourt. "The Fad of Naturalism." *Pages from the Goncourt Journal.* Translated by Robert Baldick, Oxford UP, 1962. Rpt. in Ellmann and Feidelson, pp. 297–99.

_____. Preface to *Germinie Lacerteux.* First Edition. Translated by John Chestershire. George Barrie, 1897, pp. 5–7.

Gordon, Andrew. *An American Dreamer: A Psychoanalytic Study of Norman Mailer.* Farleigh Dickinson UP, 1980.

Graham, Don. "Naturalism in American Fiction: A Status Report." *Studies in American Literary Fiction,* vol. 10, no. 1, spring 1982, pp. 10–16.

Green, Carol Hurd. "Stephen Crane and the Fallen Woman." *American Novelists Revisited: Essays in Feminist Criticism.* Edited by Fritz Fleischmann. G. K. Hall, 1982. Rpt. in Bloom, *Stephen Crane,* pp. 99–115.

Grisham, John. *The Appeal.* Random House, 2010.

_____. Commencement Address. University of North Carolina, 24 May 2010. In *Forbes,* 24 May 2010, www.forbes.com/2010/05/24/chapel-hill-commencement-john-grisham-leadership-education-speech.html.

_____. *The Innocent Man: Murder and Injustice in a Small Town.* Doubleday, 2006.

_____. Interview with *Amazon.com*'s Editorial Reviews. "*The Appeal*: A Novel," *Amazon.com.* www.amazon.com/Appeal-Novel-John-Grisham-ebook/dp/B003B02PFY/ref=sr_1_2?keywords=the+appeal&qid=1559611277&s=gateway&sr=8-2. Accessed 3 June 2019.

Grobel, Lawrence. *Conversations with Capote.* New American Library, 1985.

Gross, Seymour. "Introduction: Stereotype to Archetype: The Negro in American Literary Criticism." In Gross and John Edward Hardy, *Images of the Negro in American Literature.* U of Chicago P, 1966, pp. 1–26.

Grossman, Lev. "A Murderer in the Home." Review of *A Death in Belmont* by Sebastian Junger. *Time,* 10 April 2006. content.time.com/time/magazine/article/0,9171,1179347,00.html#.

Grunwald, Beverly. "The Literary Aquarium of Truman Capote." *W,* 14–21 Nov. 1975, p. 26. Rpt. in Inge, pp. 320–23.

Guest, David. *Sentenced to Death: The American Novel and Capital Punishment.* UP of Mississippi, 1997.

Guinn, Jeff. *Manson: The Life and Times of Charles Manson.* Simon & Schuster, 2013.

Gwynn, Frederick L., and Joseph L. Blotner. *Faulkner in the University.* UP of Virginia, 1959.

Hakutani, Yoshinobu. "*Native Son* and *An American Tragedy*: Two Different Interpretations of Crime and Guilt." *Centennial Review,* vol. 23, 1979, pp. 208–26.

_____. "Richard Wright and American Naturalism." *Zeitschrift fur Anglistek und Amerikanistik,* vol. 36, 1988, pp. 217–26.

_____, and Lewis Fried, eds. *American Literary Naturalism: A Reassessment.* Carl Winter Universitatsverlag, 1975.

Halttunen, Karen. *Murder Most Foul: The Killer and the American Gothic Imagination.* Harvard UP, 1998.

Hart, James D. *The Oxford Companion to American Literature.* 5th ed. Oxford UP, 1983.

Hayne, Barbara. "Dreiser's *An American Tragedy.*" In Friedland, pp. 170–86.

"The Heart of Hate." Review of *The Algiers Motel Incident* by John Hersey. *Time,* 21 June 1968, p. 58. *EBSCOHost,* 58. ebscohost.com.library.acaweb.org/.

Hellmann, John. "Death and Design in *In Cold Blood*: Capote's 'Nonfiction Novel' as Allegory." *Ball State University Forum,* vol. 21, 1980, pp. 65–78.

Hemmings, F.W.J. "Zola's Apprenticeship to Journalism (1865–70)." *PMLA,* vol. 71, no. 3, 1956, pp. 340–354. *JSTOR,* www.jstor.org/stable/460707.

Hersey, John. *The Algiers Motel Incident.* Alfred A. Knopf, 1968.

Heyne, Eric. "Literary Status for Nonfiction Narratives." In *Narrative Poetics: Innovations, Limits, Challenges.* Ed. James Phelan. Papers in Comparative Studies, vol. 5, Ohio State University, 1987, pp. 137–45.

_____. "Toward a Theory of Literary Nonfiction." In *Modern Fiction Studies,* vol. 33, no. 3, 1987, pp. 479–90. *JSTOR,* www.jstor.org/stable/26282388.

Hickock, Walter David, and Linda LeBert-Corbello. *In the Shadow of my Brother's Cold Blood.* Amazon Digital Services, 2010. Kindle ebook.

Hicks, Granville. "Dreiser to Farrell to Wright." *Saturday Review,* 30 March 1963, pp. 37–8.

Higdon, Hal. *Leopold and Loeb: The Crime of the Century.* U of Illinois P, 1999.

Hoefer, Carl. "Causal Determinism," *Stanford Encyclopedia of Philosophy,* 23 Jan. 2003, rev. 21 Jan. 2016. The Metaphysics Research Lab, Center for the Study of Society and Information, Stanford University. plato.stanford.edu/entries/determinism-causal/.

Hoffman, Daniel, ed. *Harvard Guide to Contemporary American Writing.* Harvard UP, 1979.

Hoffman, Frederick J. *The Modern Novel in America 1900–1950.* Henry Regnery, 1951.

———. "The Scene of Violence: Dostoevsky and Dreiser." *Modern Fiction Studies,* vol. 6, summer 1960, pp. 91–105.

Holloway, John. *Fact and Fiction: The New Journalism and the Nonfiction Novel.* U of North Carolina P, 1977.

Holman, Hugh C. *A Handbook to Literature.* Revised edition. U of North Carolina P, 1960.

Hoopes, Roy. *Cain: The Biography of James M. Cain.* Holt, 1982.

"Horatio Alger, Jr. Biography." *The Horatio Alger Society,* www.horatioalgersociety. net/100_biography.html. Accessed 3 June 2018.

Howard, June. *Form and History in American Literary Naturalism.* U of North Carolina P, 1985.

Howe, Irving. Afterword to *An American Tragedy.* By Dreiser, pp. 815–28.

———. From "Black Boys and Native Sons." *A World More Attractive: A View of Modern Literature and Politics.* Horizon, 1963. Rpt. in Bloom, *Bigger,* pp. 6–9.

———. *William Faulkner: A Critical Study.* 3rd ed. U of Chicago P, 1975.

Hughes, Langston. "Harlem," 1951. *Poetry Foundation,* www.poetryfoundation.org/ poems/46548/harlem. Accessed 21 May 2018.

"*In Cold Blood*: Target of Threatened Law Suit." *Publisher's Weekly* 25 April 1966, p. 81.

Inge, M. Thomas. *Truman Capote: Conversations.* U of Mississippi P, 1987.

"*The Innocent Man: Murder and Injustice in a Small Town.*" Review of *The Innocent Man* by John Grisham. *Publisher's Weekly,* 29 Nov. 2007, https://www.publishersweekly. com/978-0-7393-2419-6. Accessed 7 June 2017.

Jack, Peter Monro. "A Tragic Novel of Negro Life in America." Review of *Native Son. New York Times Book Review,* 3 March 1940, pp. 2, 20. Rpt. in Reilly, pp. 53–55.

Jackson, Blyden. "Richard Wright." In *The History of Southern Literature.* Edited by Louis D. Rubin, et al. Louisiana State UP, 1985, pp. 443–49.

Johnson, Diane. "Death for Sale." Review of *The Executioner's Song* by Norman Mailer. *The New York Review of Books,* 6 Dec. 1979, pp. 3–5.

Johnson, Michael L. *The New Journalism: The Underground Press, the Artists of Nonfiction, and Changes in the Established Media.* UP of Kansas, 1971.

Junger, Sebastian. *A Death in Belmont.* Norton, 2006.

Kaplan, Harold. "Vitalism and Redemptive Violence." *Power and Order: Henry Adams and the Naturalist Tradition in American Fiction.* U of Chicago P, 1981. Rpt. in Bloom, *Stephen Crane,* pp. 91–97.

Kauffman, Stanley. "Capote in Kansas." *New Republic,* 22 Jan. 1966, pp. 19–21, 23.

Kazin, Alfred. *Bright Book of Life: American Novelists and Storytellers from Hemingway to Mailer.* Little, Brown, 1973.

———. *On Native Grounds: An Interpretation of Modern American Prose Literature.* Harcourt, 1942.

———. *The Structure of Theodore Dreiser.* U of Indiana P, 1955.

———. "Too Honest for His Own Time." Review of two collections of works by Richard Wright. *New York Times Book Review,* 29 Dec. 1991, pp. 3, 16–17.

Keefe, Patrick Radden. "Capote's Co-Conspirators." *The New Yorker,* 22 March 2013, www. newyorker.com/books/page-turner/capotes-co-conspirators. Accessed 4 June 2019.

Keller, Bill. "John Grisham on the State of Criminal Justice." Interview with John Grisham. *The Marshall Project: Nonprofit Journalism about Criminal Justice.* 2 Jan. 2017. www. themarshallproject.org/2017/01/02/john-grisham-on-the-state-of-criminal-justice#. hFAgrpyew.

Kelley, Raina. "Why Politics Could Be Behind American Homicide." *Newsweek,* 4 Nov. 2009, www.newsweek.com/why-politics-could-be-behind-american-homicide-kelley-76731.

Kelly, Susan. "Was Albert DeSalvo Really the Boston Strangler?" *The Boston Stranglers* (product page). *Amazon.com* 2013. www.amazon.com. Accessed 29 May 2017.

Kinnamon, Keneth, ed. *New Essays on* Native Son. The American Novel. Cambridge UP, 1990.

Knickerbocker, Conrad. "One Night on a Kansas Farm." Review of *In Cold Blood* by Truman Capote. *New York Times,* 16 Jan. 1966. 14 July 1999. www.nytimes.com/ books/97/12/28/home/capote-blood2.html.

Kowalewski, Michael. *Deadly Musings: Violence and Verbal Form in American Fiction.* Princeton U P, 1993. *JSTOR,* www.jstor.org/stable/j.ctt7t583.

Krebs, Albin. "Truman Capote Is Dead at 59; Novelist of Style and Clarity." *New York Times,* 28 August 1984. 14 July 1999. www.nytimes.com/ books/97/12/28/home/capote-obit.html.

Krutch, Joseph Wood. *The Modern Temper: A Study and a Confession.* 1929. Harvest-Harcourt, Brace and World, 1956.

Kwiat, Joseph J. "The Newspaper Experience: Crane, Norris, and Dreiser." *Nineteenth-Century Fiction,* vol. 8, Sept. 1953, pp. 99–117.

"Lab: Confessed Boston Strangler's DNA on Slain Woman's Body," *CNN,* 19 July 2013. www.cnn.com/2013/07/19/justice/massachusetts-boston-strangler-dna/index.html.

LaFrance, Marston. "The Open Boat." In *A Reading of Stephen Crane.* By LaFrance. Clarendon: Oxford UP, 1971. Rpt. in Bloom, *Stephen Crane,* pp. 55–63.

La Ganga, Maria L., and Erik Himmelsbach-Weinstein. "Charles Manson's Murderous Imprint on L.A. Endures as Other Killers Have Come and Gone." *Los Angeles Times,* 28 July 2019. www.latimes.com/california/story/2019–07–27/charles-manson-family-murders-50-years-later.

Langbaum, Robert. "Capote's Nonfiction Novel." In Malin, pp. 114–20.

Leavelle, Charles. "Brick Slayer Is Likened to Jungle Beast." *Chicago Sunday Tribune* 5 June 1938, sec 1, p. 6.

Lehan, Richard. *"An American Tragedy."* In *Theodore Dreiser: His World and His Novels.* Southern Illinois UP, 1969, pp. 142–69.

Lennon, Michael J., ed. *Conversations with Norman Mailer.* Literary Conversations Series. Peggy Whitman Prenshaw, gen. ed. U P of Mississippi, 1988.

Leopold, Nathan. "In Nathan Leopold's Own Words." *Famous Trials.* Ed. Douglas O. Linder. University of Missouri at Kansas City School of Law. famous-trials.com/leopoldandloeb/1749-ownwords. Accessed 8 July 2019.

"Leopolds." *The Lives and Legends of Richard Loeb and Nathan Leopold.* loebandleopold. wordpress.com/leopolds/. *Wordpress* blog. Accessed 9 July 2019.

Levin, Meyer. *Compulsion.* Simon & Schuster, 1956.

_____. *In Search.* 1950. Pocket, 1973.

"Levin, Meyer." *Contemporary Authors.* New Revision Series. 40 Volumes. Gale, 1992. Vol. 15, pp. 281–82.

Lewis, Dorothy Otnow. *Guilty by Reason of Insanity: A Psychiatrist Explores the Minds of Killers.* Fawcett Columbine/Galantine, 1998.

Lewis, R.W.B. *The American Adam.* U of Chicago P, 1965.

Lewisohn, Ludwig. "The Naturalists." In *The Story of American Literature.* Random House, 1939, pp. 462–522.

Lind, Ilse Dusoir. "The Calvinistic Burden of *Light in August.*" *New England Quarterly,* vol. xxx, Sept. 1957, pp. 307–29.

Linder, Douglas O. "Leopold and Loeb Trial (1924)." *Famous Trials,* famous-trials.com/leopoldandloeb/1741-home. Accessed 1 June 2018.

Linedecker, Clifford L. *Thrill Killers.* 1987. PaperJacks, 1988.

Link, Eric Carl, et al. Preface. *The Vast and Terrible Drama: American Literary Naturalism in the Late Nineteenth Century,* by Link, et al, The University of Alabama Press, 2004, pp. iv.

"Loebs." *The Lives and Legends of Richard Loeb and Nathan Leopold.* loebandleopold.wordpress.com/leopolds/. *Wordpress* blog. Accessed 9 July 2019.

Loftis, John. "Domestic Prey: Richard Wright's Parody of the Hunt Tradition in 'The Man Who Was Almost a Man.'" *Studies in Short Fiction,* vol. 23, no. 4, 1986, pp. 437–42. *OneSearch, EBSCOHost.*

Long, Barbara. "In Cold Comfort." *Esquire,* June 1966, pp. 124, 126, 128, 171–80.

Longe, Laurel. "Lucas Beauchamp, Joe Christmas, and the Color of Humanity." *Center for Faulkner Studies / Teaching Faulkner.* Southeast Missouri State University. semo.edu/cfs/teaching/4879.html. Accessed 4 August 2019.

Longley, John L., Jr. Excerpt from *The Tragic Mask: A Study of Faulkner's Heroes.* U of North Carolina P, 1963. Rpt. in Minter, pp. 95–98.

Lynch, Michael Francis. *Richard Wright, Ralph Ellison, and Dostoevsky: The Choice of Individual Freedom and Dignity.* 1986. Kent State U, Ph.D. dissertation.

Madden, David. *James M. Cain.* Twayne United States Authors Series. Twayne, 1970.

Madden-Lunsford, Kerry. *Up Close: Harper Lee.* Viking, 2009.

Magill, Frank, ed. *American Literature: Realism to 1945.* Salem P, 1981.

Magistrale, Tony S. "From St. Petersburg to Chicago: Wright's *Crime and Punishment.*" *Comparative Literature Studies,* vol. 23, spring 1986, pp. 59–70.

_____. *The Quest for Identity in Modern Southern Fiction : Faulkner, Wright, O'Connor, Warren.* 1981. U Pittsburgh, Ph.D. Dissertation.

Mailer, Norman. *Advertisements for Myself.* Putnam, 1959.

_____. *The Armies of the Night.* New American Library, 1968.

_____. "The Art of Fiction: A *Paris Review* Interview." [Orig. pub. as "The Art of Fiction" and "The First Days Interview."] In *Cannibals and Christians,* pp. 209–21.

_____. *Cannibals and Christians.* Dell, 1966.

_____. "Crime and Punishment: Gary Gilmore." 1979. With William F. Buckley, Jr., and Jeff Greenfield. *Conversations with Norman Mailer.* U P Mississippi, 1988. 228–51.

_____. *The Executioner's Song.* Warner, 1979.

_____. "An Interview with Norman Mailer." With John Aldridge. *Partisan Review,* spring 1980, pp. 174–82.

_____. "The Killer: A Story." *Cannibals and Christians,* pp. 222–27.

_____. Modes and Mutations: Quick Comments on the Modern American Novel." *Commentary,* vol. 41, March 1966, pp. 37–40. Rpt. in *Cannibals and Christians,* pp. 95–103.

_____. "Some Children of the Goddess." *Esquire,* July 1963. Rpt. in *Cannibals and Christians,* pp. 104–30.

_____. "A Talk with Norman Mailer." With Harvey Breit. *The New York Times,* 3 June 1951. Rpt. in *The Writer Observed* by Breit. World, 1956, pp. 199–201.

_____. With John Leonard. "Private Lives." *New York Times,* 7 Nov. 1979, Section III, p. 14, col. 2.

Malcolm, Janet. *The Journalist and the Murderer.* Knopf, 1990.

Malin, Irving. "Murder in Kansas." Review of *In Cold Blood* by Truman Capote. *Progressive,* March 1966, p. 42.

_____, ed. *Truman Capote's* In Cold Blood: *A Critical Handbook.* Wadsworth, 1968.

Mangum, Bryant. "Crane's Red Badge and Zola's." *American Literary Realism, 1870–1910*, vol. 9, 1976, pp. 279–80.

Manso, Peter. *Mailer: His Life and Times*. Simon & Schuster, 1985.

Martin, Richard E. *American Literature and the Universe of Force*. Duke UP, 1981.

Martin, Stoddard. *California Writers: Jack London, John Steinbeck, the Tough Guys*. St. Martin's, 1983.

Maslin, Janet. "Grisham Takes on the Mystery of Reality." Review of *The Innocent Man* by John Grisham. *New York Times*, 9 Oct. 2006, www.nytimes.com/2006/10/09/books/09masl.html.

Matthiessen, F. O. "Of Crime and Punishment." *The Stature of Theodore Dreiser*. Edited by Alfred Kazin. Indiana UP, 1955, pp. 204–18.

Mayer, Robert. *The Dreams of Ada*. Broadway Books, 2006.

McAleer, John. "*An American Tragedy* and *In Cold Blood*." *Thought*, vol. 47, 1972, pp. 569–86.

_____. *Theodore Dreiser: An Introduction and Interpretation*. Barnes and Noble, 1968.

McBride, Susan. *Richard Wright's Use of His Reading of Fiction*. 1975. U of Pennsylvania, Ph.D. dissertation.

McFarland, Shannon. "Walker Investigation Shows Parts of 'In Cold Blood' Don't Add Up." *(Sarasota) Herald Tribune*, 9 Dec. 2012, www.heraldtribune.com/news/20121209/walker-investigation-shows-parts-of-in-cold-blood-dont-add-up.

McGinniss, Joe. *Fatal Vision*. Signet/New American Library, 1984.

McGuire, Danielle L. "Against Active Forgetting: On John Hersey's 'The Algiers Motel Incident.'" *LA Review of Books*, 10 Sept. 2019, lareviewofbooks.org/article/against-active-forgetting-on-john-herseys-the-algiers-motel-incident/.

McLaughlin, Robert. "History vs Fiction: The Self-Destruction of *The Executioner's Song*," Clio, Vol. 17, 1988, pp. 225–38.

McMichael, George, et. al. "The Age of Realism." In *Anthology of American Literature*. Fifth edition. Two volumes. Macmillan, 1993. Vol. II, pp. 1–7.

_____, eds. *Anthology of American Literature*. Fifth edition. Two volumes. Macmillan, 1993.

McPhee, Michelle. "Boston Strangler Case Solved 50 Years Later." *ABC News* 11 July 2013. abcnews.go.com/US/boston-strangler-case-solved-50-years/story?id=19640699.

McWilliams, John. "Innocent Criminal or Criminal Innocence: The Trial in American Fiction." In *Law and American Literature*. By McWilliams, Carl Smith, and Maxwell Bloomfield. Borzoi Books in Law and American Society. Knopf, 1983, pp. 45–123.

Mendoza, Mariecar. "The Onion Field Kidnapping and Killing—50 Years Later." *Los Angeles Daily News*, 9 March 2013, www.dailynews.com/2013/03/09/the-onion-field-kidnapping-and-killing-50-years-later/.

Meyer, Roy. "Naturalism in American Farm Fiction." *Journal of the Central Mississippi Valley American Studies Assocation*, vol. 2, no. 1, 1961, pp. 27–37. JSTOR, www.jstor.org/stable/40640230.

Michaud, Stephen G., and Hugh Aynesworth. *The Only Living Witness*. Signet/New American Library, 1983.

Miller, Laura. "Truman Capote's Greatest Lie." *Salon*, 14 Feb. 2013, www.salon.com/2013/02/14/truman_capotes_greatest_lie/.

Millgate, Michael. *American Social Fiction: James to Cozzens*. Barnes and Noble, 1964.

_____, ed. *New Essays on Light in August*. The American Novel series. Gen. ed. Emory Elliott. Cambridge UP, 1987.

_____. "'A Novel: Not an Anecdote': Faulkner's *Light in August*." In Millgate, *New Essays*, pp. 31–53.

Minter, David L., ed. *Twentieth Century Interpretations of* Light in August. Prentice-Hall, 1969.

Minzesheimer, Bob, "In Junger's World, 'Absolute Truth' Entirely Elusive," Review of *A Death in Belmont* by Sebastian Junger, *USA Today*, 12 April 2006, usatoday30.usatoday. com/life/books/news/2006-04-12-junger-main_x.htm.

Mitchell, Lee Clark. "Naturalism and the Languages of Determinism." *Columbia Literary History of the United States*. Edited by Emory Elliott, et al. Columbia UP, 1988, pp. 525–45.

Mitgang, Herbert. "Meyer Levin, Writer, 75, Dies; Books Included 'Compulsion.'" *New York Times*, 11 July 1981. *New York Times*, www.nytimes.com/1981/07/11/obituaries/ meyer-levin-writer-75-dies-books-included-compulsion.html.

Moates, Marianne M. *Truman Capote's Southern Years*. U of Alabama P, 1989.

Moers, Ellen. "The Finesse of Dreiser." *American Scholar*, vol. 33, winter 1963–64, pp. 109–14. Rpt. in *Sister Carrie*. Edited by Donald Pizer. A Norton Critical Edition. Norton, 1970, pp. 558–67.

_____. *Two Dreisers*. Viking, 1969.

Montaldo, Charles. "The Murder of Roseann Quinn: The Real Story Behind 'Looking for Mr. Goodbar.'" *ThoughtCo*, 30 May 2019, www.thoughtco.com/the-murder-of-roseann-quinn-972681.

Mueller, Matt. "'Hitchcock': Fact or Fiction?" *OnMilwaukee*, 15 Dec. 2012. www.onmil-waukee.com/movies/articles/hitchcockfactcheck.html.

"Murder and the Superman." Review of *Compulsion*. *Time*, 12 Nov. 1956, p. 130.

Nagel, James. "Stephen Crane and the Narrative Methods of Impressionism." *Studies in the Novel*, vol. 10, spring 1978. Rpt. in Bloom, *Stephen Crane*, pp. 81–89.

"Nathan Leopold." *Biography*. 1 April 2014. Updated 16 April 2019. www.biography.com/ crime-figure/nathan-leopold.

"New Novel Tells the Story of the First Mass School Shooting." *WBUR*, 31 July 2014, www.wbur.org/hereandnow/2014/07/31/school-shooting-novel-crook. Accessed 8 June 2019.

Norden, Eric. "Playboy Interview: Truman Capote." *Playboy*, March 1968, pp. 51–53, 56, 58–62, 160–62, 164–70. Rpt. in Inge, pp. 110–63.

Norris, Frank. *McTeague: A Story of San Francisco*. 1899. Edited by Donald Pizer. Norton Critical Edition. Rinehart, 1950.

_____. "A Plea for Romantic Fiction." *Boston Evening Transcript*, 18 Dec. 1901, p. 14. Rpt. *McTeague*, Ed. Donald Pizer, Norton Critical Edition, Second edition. Norton, 1996, pp. 313–16.

Nostwich, Theodore. "The Source of Dreiser's 'Nigger Jeff.'" *Resources for American Literary Study*, Autumn 1978, pp. 174–87.

Oates, Joyce Carol. "Man Under Sentence of Death: The Novels of James M. Cain." In *Tough Guy Writers of the Thirties*. Ed. David Madden. Crosscurrents/Modern Critiques. Southern Illinois UP, 1968, pp. 110–28.

O'Brien, Darcy. *Two of a Kind: The Hillside Stranglers*. 1985. Signet/New American Library, 1987.

O'Connor, Flannery. "A Good Man Is Hard to Find." 1955. Rpt. in McMichael, *Anthology*, vol. II, pp. 1948–58.

O'Cork, Shannon. "The Truth, More or Less, as Long as It Makes a Good Story." In *The Murder Mystique: Crime Writers on Their Art*. Edited by Lucy Freeman. Ungar, 1982, pp. 126–38.

Oliver, Myrna. "John Hersey; Won Pulitzer Prize for 'A Bell for Adano.'" *Los Angeles Times*, 25 March 1993, www.latimes.com/archives/la-xpm-1993-03-25-mn-14835-story.html

Ollove, Michael, "Personal Ties to Boston Strangler Case Cloud Efforts to Tie Him to Another Killing," *Baltimore Sun*, 7 May 2006, articles.baltimoresun.com/2006-05-07/ news/0605050114_1_sebastian-junger-albert-desalvo-death-in-belmont.

Orlov, Paul A. "Plot as Parody: Dreiser's Attack on the [Horatio] Alger Theme in *An American Tragedy.*" *American Literary Realism,* Autumn 1982, pp. 239–43.

Pace, Eric. "Lacey Fosburgh, Reporter and Writer of Fact and Fiction." *New York Times,* 12 January 1993, www.nytimes.com/1993/01/12/arts/lacey-fosburgh-50-reporter-and-writer-of-fact-and-fiction.html.

Papke, Mary E., ed. *Twisted from the Ordinary: Essays on American Literary Naturalism.* Tennessee Studies in Literature. Vol. 40. U of Tennessee P, 2003.

Peace, Richard. "The Nineteenth Century: The Natural School and Its Aftermath, 1840–55." In Moser, pp. 189–247.

Pember, Don, and Clay Calvert. *Mass Media Law.* 18th edition. McGraw-Hill, 2013.

"The Perfect Crime." *American Experience.* Dir. Cathleen O'Connell. *PBS,* 2016. Documentary. (*Amazon) PrimeVideo.* Accessed 8 July 2019.

Pini, Richard. "Fiction et Réalité chez Truman Capote." *Les Langues Modernes* vol. 63, 1969, pp. 176–85.

Pizer, Donald, ed. "Crime and Punishment in Dreiser's *An American Tragedy*: The Legal Debate." *Studies in the Novel,* vol. 41, no. 4, 2009, pp. 435–450. *JSTOR,* www.jstor.org/stable/29533952.

_____. *Critical Essays on Theodore Dreiser.* G. K. Hall, 1981.

_____. "Documentary Narrative as Art: Truman Capote and William Manchester." *Journal of Modern Literature,* vol. 2, 1971, pp. 105–18. *JSTOR,* www.jstor.org/stable/30053177.

_____. "Frank Norris's *McTeague*: Naturalism as Popular Myth," *ANQ,* 13:4, 2000, 21–26, *Academic Search Complete,* DOI 10.1080/08957690009598121.

_____. "Is American Literary Naturalism Dead? A Further Inquiry." In Papke, pp. 390–404.

_____. *The Novels of Frank Norris.* Indiana UP, 1966.

_____. *The Novels of Theodore Dreiser.* U of Minnesota P, 1976.

_____. *Realism and Naturalism in Nineteenth-Century American Literature.* Revised ed. Illinois UP, 1984.

_____. "Stephen Crane's Maggie and American Naturalism." *Criticism,* vol. 7, spring 1965, pp. 168–75.

_____. *Twentieth-Century American Literary Naturalism: An Interpretation.* Crosscurrents/Modern Critiques. Edited by Harry T. Moore and Matthew J. Bruccoli. Illinois UP, 1982.

Plank, Kathryn M. "Dreiser's Real American Tragedy." *Papers on Language and Literature,* vol. 27, 1991, pp. 268–87.

Plantinga, Alvin. "Naturalism vs. Evolution: A Religion/Science Conflict." *The Secular Web,* 2007, infidels.org/library/modern/alvin_plantinga/conflict.html.

Plimpton, George. "Capote's Long Ride." *The New Yorker,* 13 Oct. 1997, pp. 62–70.

_____. "The Story Behind a Nonfiction Novel." *New York Times Book Review,* 16 Jan. 1966: 2–3, 38–43. Rpt. in Inge, 47–68. Also available at www.nytimes.com/ books/97/12/28/home/capote.html.

_____. *Truman Capote: In Which Various Friends, Enemies, Acquaintances, and Detractors Recall His Turbulent Career.* Nan A. Talese/Doubleday, 1997.

Polk, Noel. "Notes of Another Native Son." *Southern Quarterly,* vol. 44, no. 2, 2007, pp. 126–137. *EBSCOHost,* eds.b.ebscohost.com.

"Post-Traumatic Stress Disorder (PTSD)." *Research Portfolio Online Reporting Tools, National Institutes of Health,* U.S. Department of Health and Human Services, report. nih.gov/nihfactsheets/ViewFactSheet.aspx?csid=58. Accessed 10 Aug. 2019.

"The Psychopaths Among Us." Reviews of *Death Benefit* and *The Misbegotten Son. New York Times Book Review,* 14 March 1993, pp. 1, 19–21.

Putnam, Robert D. *Our Kids: The American Dream in Crisis.* Simon & Schuster, 2015. *Kindle ebook.*

Quinones, Sam. "Jimmy Lee Smith, 76; [']Onion Field' Killer, Chronic Parole Violator." *Los Angeles Times,* 8 April 2007, www.latimes.com/archives/la-xpm-2007-apr-08-me-smith8-story.html.

"Race, Milieu, and Moment." *Encyclopaedia Britannica,* 20 July 1998. www.britannica.com/art/race-milieu-and-moment.

Rahv, Philip. "Notes on the Decline of Naturalism." *Partisan Review,* vol. 9, 1942, pp. 483–93. Rpt. in Becker, pp. 579–90.

Rascoe, Burton. Review of *Native Son. The American Mercury,* vol. 50, May 1940, pp. 113–16. Rpt. in Reilly, pp. 88–90.

"The Real 'Goodbar' Murder." *Naked City Stories,* www.nakedcitystories.com/goodbar-murder.php.

Reck, Tom S. "J. M. Cain's Los Angeles Novels." *Colorado Quarterly,* vol. 22, 1974, pp. 375–87.

Redden, Dorothy S. "Richard Wright and *Native Son*: Not Guilty." *Black American Literature Forum,* vol. 10, winter 1976, pp. 111–16. Rpt. in Bloom, *Bigger,* pp. 73–82.

Reed, Kenneth. "*Native Son*: An American *Crime and Punishment.*" *Studies in Black Literature,* summer 1970, pp. 33–34.

Reed, Kenneth T. *Truman Capote.* Twayne-G.K. Hall, 1981.

Reilly, John. "Giving Bigger a Voice: The Politics of Narrative in *Native Son.*" In Kinnamon, *New Essays,* pp. 35–62.

_____, ed. *Richard Wright: The Critical Reception.* The American Critical Tradition. No. 6. Gen. ed. M. Thomas Inge. Burt Franklin, 1978.

Reiss, Albert J., Jr. "The Algiers Motel Incident." Review of *The Algiers Motel Incident* by John Hersey. *American Sociological Review,* vol. 34, no. 6, 1969, pp. 971–72. *JSTOR,* DOI: 10.2307/2096008.

Review of *Compulsion. Chicago Sunday Tribune.* 28 Oct. 1956, p. 2.

"Richard Loeb." *Biography.* 1 April 2014. Updated 16 April 2019. www.biography.com/crime-figure/richard-loeb.

Richardson, Mark. "Richard Wright: Exile as Native Son" (Chapter 5). *The Wings of Atalanta: Essays Written Along the Color Line.* Camden House, 2019, pp. 204–37. *JSTOR,* www.jstor.org/stable/j.ctvb937p4.9

Riggio, Thomas. "Biography of Theodore Dreiser," *Dreiser Web Source, Penn Libraries,* 2010. www.library.upenn.edu/collections/rbm/dreiser/tdbio.html. Accessed 11 July 2018.

Rivers, William L. "The New Confession." In Weber, pp. 234–43.

Roache, Joel. "'What Had Made Him and What He Meant': The Politics of Wholeness in 'How "Bigger" Was Born.'" *Sub-Stance,* vol. 15, 1976. Rpt. in Bloom, *Richard Wright's Native Son,* pp. 39–56.

Robinson, Edwin Arlington. "The Mill." 1920. Rpt. in *Poetry Foundation* www.poetryfoundation.org/poems-and-poets/poems/detail/44977.

Rollyson, Carl E., Jr. "Biography in a New Key." Review of *The Executioner's Song* by Norman Mailer. *Chicago Review,* vol. 3, 1980, pp. 31–38.

Ross, Alex. "The Shock of the True." *The New Yorker,* 19 Aug. 1996, pp. 70–77.

Rossner, Judith. *Looking for Mr. Goodbar.* 1975. Pocket/Simon & Schuster, 1976.

Rubin, Steven. *Meyer Levin.* Twayne, 1982.

Rule, Ann. *Small Sacrifices: A True Story of Passion and Murder.* 1987. Signet/New American Library, 1988.

_____. *The Stranger Beside Me.* 1980. New York: Signet/New American Library, 1981.

Rutten, Timothy. "Deft Social Realism and Iffy Grammar." Review of *The Appeal* by John Grisham. *Los Angeles Times,* 29 Jan. 2008, articles.latimes.com/2008/ jan/29/ entertainment/et-book29.

Salzman, Jack, ed. *Studies in* An American Tragedy. Charles E. Merrill Studies. Gen. eds. Matthew J. Bruccoli and Joseph Katz. Merrill, 1971.

Samuel, Lawrence R. *The American Dream: A Cultural History.* Syracuse UP, 2012. *Kindle ebook.*

Sanders, Ed. "Why Pop Culture Still Can't Get Enough of Charles Manson." *New York Times,* 24 July 2019, www.nytimes.com/2019/07/24/movies/charles-manson-family-hollywood-tarantino.html.

Satten, Joseph. "Murder Without Apparent Motive—A Study in Personality Disorganization." *The American Journal of Psychiatry,* vol. 117, July 1960, pp. 48–53.

Scardino, Albert. "Ethics, Reporters, and the New Yorker." *New York Times,* 21 March 1989, section II, pp. 2, 6.

Schecter, Harold. "The 'American Tragedy' Murder." *Yale Review,* yalereview.yale.edu/american-tragedy-murder-1906. Accessed 18 June 2019.

Scheffler, Judith A. "The Prisoner as Creator in *The Executioner's Song.*" *The Midwest Quarterly,* vol. 4, summer 1983, p. 24. Rpt. in Bloom, *Norman Mailer,* pp. 183–92.

Schleifer, Ronald. "American Violence: Dreiser, Mailer, and the Nature of Intertextuality." *Intertextuality and Contemporary American Fiction.* Edited by Patrick O'Donnell and Robert Con Davis. Johns Hopkins UP, 1989, pp. 121–43.

Schroth, Raymond A. "The Algiers Motel Incident." Review of *The Algiers Motel Incident* by John Hersey. *America,* 17 Aug. 1968, pp. 108–9. *EBSCOHost,* 0-eds.a.ebscohost.com.library.acaweb.org.

Shaw, Patrick W. *The Modern American Novel of Violence.* Whitston, 2000.

Sherman, Stuart P. "The Naturalism of Mr. Dreiser." *The Nation,* 2 Dec. 1915, pp. 648–50.

Shipman, Evan. Review of *Light in August* by William Faulkner. *New Republic,* vol. 72, 26 Oct. 1932, pp. 300–1.

Simon, Matt. "Fantastically Wrong: The Scientist Who Seriously Believed That Criminals Were Part Ape." *Wired,* 12 Nov. 2014, www.wired.com/2014/11/fantastically-wrong-criminal-anthropology/.

Sims, Norman. "Joseph Mitchell and *The New Yorker* Nonfiction Writers." In Sims, *Literary Journalism,* pp. 82–109.

_____, ed. *Literary Journalism in the Twentieth Century.* Oxford UP, 1990.

Sinclair, Andrew. *Jack: A Biography of Jack London.* Harper and Row, 1977.

Skenazy, Paul. *James M. Cain.* Continuum, 1989.

Skerrett, Joseph T., Jr. "Composing Bigger: Wright and the Making of *Native Son.*" In Bloom, *Bigger,* pp. 125–42.

Skillin, Edward, Jr. Review of *Native Son. Commonweal,* vol. 31, 8 March 1940, p. 438. Rpt. in Reilly, pp. 62–63.

Smith, Hedrick. *Who Stole the American Dream?* Random House, 2012.

Smith, Jordan. "Landmark California Law Bars Prosecutors from Pursuing Murder Charges Against People Who Didn't Commit Murder." *The Intercept,* 23 November 2018, theintercept.com/2018/11/23/california-felony-murder-rule/.

Spencer, Herbert. *An Autobiography.* Two volumes. D. Appleton, 1904. Vol. II.

_____. *First Principles.* 1862. A. L. Burt, 1880.

Starn, Alvin. *The Influences of Stephen Crane, Theodore Dreiser, and James T. Farrell [on Richard Wright].* 1974. Kent State U, Ph.D. dissertation.

Steinem, Gloria. "'Go Right Ahead and Ask Me Anything.' (And So She Did): An Interview with Truman Capote." *McCall's,* November 1967, pp. 76–77, 148–52, 154. Rpt. in Inge, pp. 86–104.

_____. "A Visit with Truman Capote." *Glamour,* April 1966, pp. 210–11, 239–41, 255. Rpt. in Inge, pp. 73–81.

Stromberg, Roland N., ed. "Naturalism" (Part II). *Realism, Naturalism, and Symbolism: Modes of Thought and Expression in Europe, 1848–1914.* Documentary History of Western Civilization. Walker, 1968, pp. 107–187.

Strychacz, Thomas. "The Plots of Murder: Un/Original Stories in Theodore Dreiser's *An*

American Tragedy." *Modernism, Mass Culture, and Professionalism.* Cambridge UP, 1993, pp. 84–116.

Swanberg, W. A. *Dreiser.* Scribner's, 1965.

Tallmer, Jerry. "Truman Capote: Man About Town." *New York Post Weekend Magazine,* 16 Dec. 1967, p. 26. Rpt. in Inge, pp. 105–9.

Tanner, Tony. *City of Words: American Fiction 1950–1970.* Harper & Row, 1971.

Tanock, L.W. Introduction. *L'Assomoir* by Emile Zola. Translated by L. W. Tanock. Penguin, 1970.

Taylor, Troy. "The 'American Tragedy' Murder: Did Life Imitate Art in 1924?" *American Hauntings: Ghosts, Gangsters, Murder, & Mayhem in American Society,* 12 Feb. 2016, troytaylorbooks.blogspot.com/2016/02/the-american-tragedy-murder.html.

Taylor, Walter. "How to Visit the Black South Without Visiting Blacks." In *Faulkner's Search for a South.* By Taylor. U of Illinois P, 1983, pp. 65–85.

"Ted Bundy." *Crime Museum,* 2017. www.crimemuseum.org/crime-library/serial-killers/ted-bundy/. Accessed 3 June 2018.

Tennyson, Alfred, Lord. *In Memoriam A.H.H.* 1849. *All Poetry,* allpoetry.com/In-Memoriam-A.-H.-H. Accessed 20 June 2019.

Thomas, Jack. "Victims of the Boston Strangler." *Boston Globe,* 11 July 2013. www.bostonglobe.com/metro/2013/07/11/victims-boston-strangler/CwbsZlSNcfwmhSetpqNlhL/story.html.

Thompson, Frederic. "American Decadence." Review of *Light in August. Commonweal,* 30 Nov. 1932, p. 139.

Thompson, Rupert. "Rereading: Truman Capote's In Cold Blood." *The Guardian,* 5 Aug. 2011, www.theguardian.com/books/2011/aug/05/truman-capote-rupert-thomson-rereading.

"Timeline: The Case of the Boston Strangler." *CBS Boston.* 11 July 2013. www.boston.cbslocal.com/2013/07/11/timeline-the-case-of-the-boston-strangler/.

Tompkins, Phillip K. "In Cold Fact." *Esquire,* June 1966, pp. 125, 127, 166–71.

Trigg, Sally Day. "Theodore Dreiser and the Criminal Justice System in *An American Tragedy.*" *Studies in the Novel,* vol. 22, winter 1990, pp. 429–40.

Trillin, Calvin. *Killings.* 1984. Penguin, 1985.

Trillin, Calvin. [Author of *Killings.*] Personal interview. University of North Carolina at Greensboro, 9 October 1986.

Trilling, Lionel. *The Liberal Imagination.* Viking, 1950.

Turner, Rachel Keeley. "Nothing But Heart: Celebrating the Life of Herb Clutter." *High Plains / Midwest AG Journal,* 28 March 2016. www.hpj.com/ag_news/nothing-but-heart-celebrating-the-life-of-herb-clutter/article_5fe81655-1759-51cb-acla-a99eb826fd3d.html.

Tynan, Kenneth. "The Coldest of Blood." *Tynan Right and Left: Plays, Films, People, Places, and Events.* Atheneum, 1968, pp. 441–60.

"Unanswered Prayers: The Life and Times of Truman Capote." *American Masters.* PBS. 1989.

Vickery, Olga. "The Shadow and the Mirror: *Light in August.*" *The Novels of William Faulkner: A Critical Interpretation.* By Vickery. Revised ed. Louisiana State UP, 1964, pp. 66–83.

Vidan, Ivo. "The Capitulation of Literature? The Scope of the 'Nonfiction Novel.'" In *Yugoslav Perspectives on American Literature: An Anthology.* Ardis, 1979, pp. 157–80.

Vivas, Elesio. "Dreiser: An Inconsistent Mechanist." *International Journal of Ethics,* vol. 48, July 1938, pp. 498–508.

Volpe, Edward L. "*Light in August.*" In *A Reader's Guide to William Faulkner.* Farrar, Straus and Giroux, 1964, pp. 151–74.

Voss, Ralph F. *Truman Capote and the Legacy of* In Cold Blood. U of Alabama P, 2011.

Walcutt, Charles Child. *American Literary Naturalism: A Divided Stream*. U of Minnesota P, 1956.

_____. *Jack London*. University of Minnesota pamphlets on American Writers. U of Minnesota P, 1966.

_____, ed. *Seven Novelists in the American Naturalist Tradition*. Minneapolls: U of Minnesota P, 1974.

Wambaugh, Joseph. *The Onion Field*. 1973. Dell/Delacorte, 1974.

"Wealthy Farmer, 3 of Family Slain." *New York Times*, 16 November 1959, section A, p. 39.

Weber, Ronald. *The Literature of Fact: Literary Nonfiction in American Writing*. Ohio UP, 1980.

_____. *The Reporter as Artist: A Look at the New Journalism Controversy*. Hastings House, 1974.

Weimer. David R. *The City as Metaphor*. Random House, 1966.

Weinberg, Helen. "The Novel in America Today." *Gamut*, vol. 2, winter 1981, pp. 60–66.

Weinman, Sarah, *The Real Lolita: The Kidnapping of Sally Horner and the Novel That Scandalized the World*, HarperCollinsPublishers, 2018.

Welsh, Alexander. "On the Difference between Prevailing and Enduring." In Millgate, *New Essays*, pp. 123–47.

Wenke, Joseph. *Mailer's America*. UP of New England, 1987.

Wertham, Frederic. "An Unconscious Determinant in *Native Son*." *Journal of Clinical Psychology*, vol. 6, 1944–45, pp. 111–15. Rpt. in *Psychoanalysis and Literature*. Edited by Hendrik M. Ruitbeck. Dutton, 1964, pp. 321–25.

Wescott, Glenway. "Glenway Wescott," *Book Week*, 26 September 1965, p. 22.

West, Rebecca. "A Grave and Reverend Book." *Harper's*, Feb. 1966, pp. 108, 110, 112–14.

Westbrook, Perry D. *Free Will and Determinism in American Literature*. Associated University Presses, 1979.

Whitford, H. C. Review of *Compulsion. Library Journal*, vol. 18, 15 Oct. 1956, p. 2324.

Wilkinson, Alec. *A Violent Act*. Knopf, 1992.

Williams, Beth. "*The Innocent Man*: Grisham Looks at Small Town Justice." Review of *The Innocent Man* by John Grisham. *Book Page*, October 2006. www.bookpage.com/reviews/4846-john-grisham-innocent-man#.WKj1cRIrKRs.

Wilson, Charles Reagan, and William Ferris, editors. *Encyclopedia of Southern Culture*. U of North Carolina P, 1989.

Wilson, Edmund. "The Boys in the Back Room." *Classics and Commercials: A Literary Chronicle of the Forties*. Random House, 1962, pp. 19–56.

Wilson, Jennifer. "Floating in the Air: The World That Made Dostoyevsky's *Crime and Punishment*." *The Nation*, 22 March 2018, www.thenation.com/article/the-world-of-crime-and-punishment/.

Witham, W. Tasker. *The Adolescent in the American Novel: 1920–1960*. Ungar, 1964.

Wolcott, James. "Norman Mailer and the Dream of Death." Review of *The Executioner's Song. The Village Voice*, 1 Oct. 1979, pp. 46, 48.

Wolfe, Tom. *The Electric Kool-Aid Acid Test*. Farrar, Straus, & Giroux, 1968.

_____. Introduction. *Cain x 3: The Postman Always Rings Twice, Mildred Pierce, Double Indemnity*. By James M. Cain. Knopf, 1969, pp. v–viii.

_____. *The New Journalism*. Harper, 1973.

_____. "Pornoviolence." In *Mauve Gloves and Madmen, Clutter and Vine*. By Wolfe. Farrar, 1976, pp. 178–87.

_____. "Son of *Crime and Punishment*." In *Norman Mailer: The Man and His Work*. Edited by Robert F. Lucid. Little, Brown, 1971, pp. 151–61.

_____. "Stalking the Billion-Footed Beast: A Literary Manifesto for the New Social Novel." *Harper's,* November 1989, pp. 45–56.

Wordsworth, William. "Preface to *Lyrical Ballads.*" 1800. The Harvard Classics. *Bartleby. com,* www.bartleby.com/39.36.html. Accessed 1 Nov. 2019.

Wright, Richard. *Black Boy: A Record of Childhood and Youth.* 1945. Harper, 1966.

_____. "How 'Bigger' Was Born." *Native Son.* 1940. Rpt. Harper Perennial, 1993. *American Studies at the University of Virginia.* xroads.virginia.edu/~DRBR2/wright.pdf. Accessed 6 July 2019.

_____. *Native Son.* 1940. Harper Perennial, 1993.

Yagoda, Ben. "Fact Checking 'In Cold Blood.'" *Slate,* 20 March 2013, slate.com/culture/2013/03/fact-checking-in-cold-blood-what-the-new-yorkers-fact-checker-missed.html.

Young, Elizabeth. "Armchair Atrocities." *New Statesman & Society,* 9 July 1993, pp. 31–2.

Yurick, Sol. "Sob-Sister Gothic." *The Nation,* 7 Feb. 1966, pp. 158–60.

Zambrana, Maria L. "'Compulsion': The Fictionalization of the Leopold-Loeb Case and the Struggle for Creative Control of 'The Crime of the Century.'" 2015, Northern Michigan U, Master's thesis. *All NMU Masters Theses,* commons.nmu.edu/theses/41.

Zavarzadeh, Mas'ud. *The Mythopoeic Reality: The Postwar American Nonfiction Novel.* U of Illinois P, 1976.

Ziff, Larzer. *The American 1890's: Life and Times of a Lost Generation.* Viking, 1966.

Zola, Emile. *l'Assommoir.* 1876. Translated by Leonard Tancock. Penguin Classics. Edited by E. V. Rieu, et al., Penguin, 1970, 1974.

_____. *Germinal.* 1885. Translated by Leonard Tancock. Penguin Classics. Edited by E. V. Rieu. Penguin, 1954, 1981.

_____. "The Novel as Social Science." From "The Experimental Novel." *The Experimental Novel and Other Essays* by Zola. 1880. Translated by Belle M. Sherman. New York, 1893. Rpt. in Ellmann and Fiedelson, pp. 270–89.

_____. Preface. *Thérèse Raquin.* Trans. Edward Vizetelly Surbiton, Second edition, 1901. *Google Books,* www.gutenberg.org/files/6626/6626-h/6626-h.htm#link2H_PREF.

Index